Text & Thought

An Integrated Approach to College Reading & Writing

With a Special Supplement
The Correct English Handbook

Judith Resnick

Lanny Lester

Borough of Manhattan Community College
of the City University of New York

 **LONGMAN**

An imprint of Addison Wesley Longman, Inc.

New York • Reading, Massachusetts • Menlo Park, California • Harlow, England
Don Mills, Ontario • Sydney • Mexico City • Madrid • Amsterdam

Acquisitions Editor: *Steven Rigolosi*
Marketing Manager: *Melanie Goulet*
Supplements Editor: *Donna Campion*
Full Service Production Manager: *Valerie Zaborski*
Project Coordination, Text Design, and Electronic Page Makeup: *Elm Street Publishing Services, Inc.*
Cover Designer/Manager: *Nancy Danahy*
Cover Illustration: Harlequin's Carnival (Harlequinade), *Joan Miró (1893–1983), Spanish. Albright Knox Gallery, Buffalo, New York/Bridgeman Art Library, London/Superstock. © 2000 Artists Rights Society (ARS), New York/ADAGP, Paris.*
Photo Researcher: *Mira Schachne*
Senior Print Buyer: *Hugh Crawford*
Printer and Binder: *Courier/Stoughton, Inc.*
Cover Printer: *Phoenix Color Corp.*

For permission to use copyrighted material, grateful acknowledgment is made to the copyright holders on pp. 471–472, which are hereby made part of this copyright page.

Library of Congress Cataloging-in-Publication Data

Lester, Lanny Martin.
   Text & thought : an integrated approach to college reading & writing : with a special supplement, The correct English handbook / Lanny Lester, Judith Resnick.
      p. cm.
   Includes bibliographical references and index.
   ISBN 0-321-04576-9
   1. English language—Rhetoric—Problems, exercises, etc. 2. Reading (Higher education)—Problems, exercises, etc. 3. English language—Grammar—Handbooks, manuals, etc. 4. Report writing—Problems, exercises, etc. 5. College readers. I. Title: Text and thought. II. Resnick, Judith. III. Title.

PE1413 .L45 2000
808'.0427—dc21   99-043140
                                                                            CIP

Please visit our website at http://www.awlonline.com

ISBN 0-321-04576-9

1 2 3 4 5 6 7 8 9 10-CRS-02 01 00 99

Brief Contents

Detailed Contents

The Correct English Handbook 327

[1] PARTS OF SPEECH 328

[2] SENTENCE COMPONENTS 348

[3] SUBJECT AND VERB AGREEMENT 355

[4] USING PRONOUNS PROPERLY 365

[5] ACTIVE AND PASSIVE VOICE 371

[6] PHRASES 373

[7] CLAUSES 382

Preface

A Complete Reading and Writing Course in One Book

Our aim as we embarked on the writing of this book was multifaceted. We wanted to offer a comprehensive approach to reading and writing as integrated and parallel processes. Unlike other textbooks, which offer alternating chapters on reading and writing, *Text & Thought: An Integrated Approach to College Reading & Writing* combines the complementary skills of reading and writing throughout the text.

To heighten students' interest in using this text, we also decided to weave a theme throughout the book. A thematic approach provides a natural context in which to learn skills and concepts and allows students to see connections among ideas. The theme of *Text & Thought*, human needs, is one to which students can relate—and, therefore, one they are motivated to read about. Each chapter is based on one of the "steps" in Abraham Maslow's hierarchy of needs.

Text & Thought is designed for maximum flexibility. The materials are organized in such a way that the book can be used in a combined developmental reading and writing course or in either a reading or a writing course. Instructors may choose to use some or all of the skill development sections, according to their needs. The reading selections, many of which are not found in other developmental textbooks, are a rich source for both reading and writing follow-up activities. These activities are presented in a creative and stimulating manner.

Text & Thought is designed for maximum interactivity. Students read, ask questions, and complete exercises before, during, and after their reading. They prewrite, draft, revise, and proofread. A mini-handbook offers practice in grammar and mechanics, while a section of additional readings provides alternative assignments. To support the book's many reading and writing activities, *Text & Thought* also comes with two software packages on one CD-ROM. **Reading Road Trip** is a multimedia reading and study skills package designed to help students improve their reading comprehension and study skills. **The Writer's ToolKit** offers writing prompts, a mini-handbook, and additional practice on all facets of writing, from punctuation to documentation.

Text Organization

Because *Text & Thought* is geared toward students beginning (or about to begin) studies in college-level courses, each chapter includes readings similar to those from the college courses most students will be required to take. Extended readings from textbooks in psychology, health and nutrition, government, sociology, and anthropology make up some of the material for teaching specific reading and writing skills. Other genres included are newspaper articles, essays, short fiction, and poetry. All the reading materials and writing topics in any given chapter revolve around the theme of that chapter.

Chapter	Title	Theme (Maslow's Hierarchy)
1	Discovering Reading and Writing	
2	Preparing for Reading and Writing	Motivation and Emotion
3	Working with Topics and Main Ideas	Physiological Needs
4	Working with Details	Safety
5	Organizing Essays and Summarizing Passages	Love
6	Making Inferences	Belonging

Chapter 1, "Discovering Reading and Writing," begins by setting the stage, offering a process for reading (before, during, after) and a process for writing (brainstorm, draft, revise, proofread). In addition, students are asked to set their goals for the course. Chapter 2, "Preparing for Reading and Writing," offers strategies for reading textbooks, as well as strategies for discovering topics to write about. The importance of vocabulary building is also introduced in this chapter.

Chapter 3, "Working with Topics and Main Ideas," emphasizes the importance of finding the main idea while reading. From a writer's perspective, the topic sentence is equally important, so this chapter also offers instruction on writing effective topic sentences and paragraphs. Chapter 4, "Working with Details," discusses the patterns of organization, which are useful to both readers and writers. Chapter 5, "Organizing Essays and Summarizing Passages," features an in-depth discussion of the important college-level skills of summarizing reading passages as well as writing full-length essays. Chapter 6, "Making Inferences," focuses on the higher-level critical thinking issues involved in reading and writing.

The book concludes with two supplementary sections. A set of additional readings offers alternate reading selections, exercises, and writing prompts. The Correct

English Handbook is a mini-handbook offering instruction and practice in the rules of grammar, punctuation, usage, and proofreading.

Features

Text & Thought offers many features to make the text interactive, dynamic, and practical.

- **Overviews and Freewriting Activities.** Each chapter begins with a brief overview of the topics, skills, and readings covered in the chapter. Every chapter also opens with a freewriting activity designed to tap students' personal experiences and opinions as they relate to the theme of the chapter.

- **Interactive Readings, Practice, and Exercises.** Unlike most textbooks, which position all their activities *after* reading selections, *Text & Thought* asks students to actively think about their reading *while* they read. To this end, questions are interspersed among sections of the textbook excerpts, with the goal of teaching students to recognize the elements that contribute to their comprehension of the text.

- **End-of-Chapter Readings.** Additional readings at the end of each chapter ask students to apply the skills they've learned in each chapter. These readings, which are taken from a variety of textbook and nontextbook sources, include such features as vocabulary previews, multiple choice and open-ended comprehension questions, group activities, and writing topics. Each chapter concludes with a writing activity that requires students to tap into metacognitive functioning and ends with a chapter summary.

- **Integrated Coverage of Vocabulary.** The importance of building an active vocabulary is introduced in Chapter 2. Thereafter, each chapter features vocabulary exercises to help students continue to expand their vocabularies.

- **Additional Readings.** The additional readings section following Chapter 6 offers instructors maximum flexibility in designing their courses. Each reading offers the same pedagogical features—comprehension questions, critical thinking questions, vocabulary practice, and writing prompts—as the end-of-chapter readings.

- **The Correct English Handbook.** Because students are often on tight budgets, *Text & Thought* includes a brief yet comprehensive *Correct English Handbook* for students. The handbook covers the basics of grammar and usage and provides a wealth of exercises. We hope that *The Correct English Handbook* will prove to be an invaluable reference for students long after they have completed the reading/writing course.

- **Web Support.** Additional readings, exercises, and writing activities can be found on the Longman English pages at **http://longman.awl.com/englishpages**.

- **Free Software.** Because of the importance of computers in today's classroom, two free software packages are included with *Text & Thought:* Reading Road Trip and the Writer's ToolKit. For a further description of these software packages, please see "The Teaching and Learning Package" section of this preface.

Text & Thought is designed to teach basic skills while exposing students to the pleasures of reading and writing. We hope students leave your course having acquired both.

The Teaching and Learning Package

Each component of the teaching and learning package has been carefully crafted to ensure that the course is a rewarding experience for both teachers and students. To receive an examination copy of any of these supplements, please contact your Addison Wesley Longman sales representative, or send your request via e-mail to exam@awl.com.

- The **Instructor's Manual** (0-321-04578-5) offers teaching tips, answers to all text questions, and other resources for instructors whose goal is to integrate reading and writing skills in one class.

- The **Test Bank** (0-321-05526-8) offers pre-designed quizzes and tests for each chapter of the text.

Electronic and Online Offerings

- **The Writer's ToolKit.** This CD-ROM offers a wealth of tutorial, exercise, and reference material for writers. It is compatible with either a PC or Macintosh platform and is flexible enough to be used either occasionally for practice or regularly in class lab sessions. The Writer's ToolKit is included free with this text.

- **Reading Road Trip Multimedia Software.** This innovative and exciting multimedia reading software is available either in CD-ROM format (0-321-07331-2) or as a site license. The package takes students on a tour of fifteen cities and landmarks throughout the United States. Each of the fifteen modules corresponds to a reading or study skill (for example, finding the main idea, understanding patterns of organization, and thinking critically). All modules contain a tour of the location, instruction and tutorial, exercises, interactive feedback, and mastery tests. Reading Road Trip is included free with this text.

- **Daedalus Online.** Addison Wesley Longman and The Daedalus Group are proud to offer the next generation of the award-winning Daedalus Integrated Writing Environment. Daedalus Online is an Internet-based collaborative writing environment for students. The program offers prewriting strategies and prompts, computer-mediated conferencing, peer collaboration and review, comprehensive writing support, and secure, 24-hour availability.

   For educators, Daedalus Online offers a comprehensive suite of online course management tools for managing an online class, dynamically linking assignments, and facilitating a heuristic approach to writing instruction. For more information, visit **http://www.awlonline.com/daedalus**, or contact your Addison Wesley Longman sales representative.

- **The Longman English Pages Web Site.** Both students and instructors can visit our free content-rich Web site for additional reading selections and writing exercises. From the Longman English pages, visitors can conduct a simulated Web search, learn how to write a resume and cover letter, or try their hand at poetry writing. Stop by and visit us at **http://longman.awl.com/englishpages**.

- **The Longman Electronic Newsletter.** Twice a month during the spring and fall, instructors who have subscribed receive a free copy of the Longman Basic Skills Newsletter in their e-mailbox. Written by experienced classroom instructors, the newsletter offers teaching tips, classroom activities, book reviews, and more. To subscribe, visit the Longman Basic Skills Web site at **http://longman.awl.com/basicskills**, or send an e-mail to **BasicSkills@awl.com**.

- *Teaching Online: Internet Research, Conversation, and Composition,* **Second Edition.** Ideal for instructors who have never surfed the Internet, this easy-to-follow guide offers basic definitions, numerous examples, and step-by-step information about finding and using Internet sources. Free to adopters. 0-321-01957-1.

- *Researching Online,* **Third Edition.** A perfect companion for a new age, this indispensable new supplement helps students navigate the Internet. Adapted from *Teaching Online,* the instructor's Internet guide, *Researching Online* speaks directly to students, giving them detailed, step-by-step instructions for performing electronic searches. Available free when shrinkwrapped with any Longman Basic Skills text. 0-321-05802-X.

For Additional Reading and Reference

- **The Dictionary Deal.** Two dictionaries can be shrinkwrapped with any Longman Basic Skills title at a nominal fee. *The New American Webster Handy College Dictionary* (0-451-18166-2) is a paperback reference text with more than 100,000 entries. *Merriam Webster's Collegiate Dictionary*, tenth edition (0-87779-709-9), is a hardback reference with a citation file of more than 14.5 million examples of English words drawn from actual use.

- **Penguin Quality Paperback Titles.** A series of Penguin paperbacks is available at a significant discount when shrinkwrapped with any Longman Basic Skills title. Some titles available are: Toni Morrison's *Beloved* (0-452-26446-4), Julia Alvarez's *How the Garcia Girls Lost Their Accents* (0-452-26806-0), Mark Twain's *Huckleberry Finn* (0-451-52650-3), *Narrative of the Life of Frederick Douglass* (0-451-52673-2), Harriet Beecher Stowe's *Uncle Tom's Cabin* (0-451-52302-4), Dr. Martin Luther King, Jr.'s *Why We Can't Wait* (0-451-62754-7), and plays by Shakespeare, Miller, and Albee. For a complete list of titles or more information, please contact your Addison Wesley Longman sales consultant.

- *80 Readings*, **Second Edition.** This inexpensive volume contains eighty brief readings (one to three pages each) on a variety of themes: writers on writing, nature, women and men, customs and habits, politics, rights and obligations, and coming of age. Also included is an alternate rhetorical table of contents. (0-321-01648-3).

- *100 Things to Write About.* This 100-page book contains 100 individual assignments for writing on a variety of topics and in a wide range of formats, from expressive to analytical. Ask your Addison Wesley Longman sales representative for a sample copy. 0-673-98239-4

- **The Longman Textbook Reader.** This supplement, for use in developmental reading courses, offers five complete chapters from Addison Wesley Longman textbooks: computer science, biology, psychology, communications, and business. Each chapter includes additional comprehension quizzes, critical thinking questions, and group activities. Available FREE with the adoption of any Longman text. 0-321-04617-X.

- *Newsweek* **Alliance.** Instructors may choose to shrinkwrap a twelve-week subscription to *Newsweek* with any Longman text. The price of the subscription is 57 cents per issue (a total of $6.84 for the subscription). Available with the subscription is a free "Interactive Guide to Newsweek"—a workbook for students who are using the text. In addition, *Newsweek* provides a wide variety of instructor supplements free to teachers, including maps, Skills Builders, and weekly quizzes. *Newsweek* subscription card: 0-321-04759-1. Interactive Guide: 0-321-05528-4.

For Additional Reading and Writing Assessment and Practice

- **Competency Profile Test Bank, Second Edition.** This series of sixty objective tests covers ten general areas of English competency, including fragments;

comma splices and run-ons; pronouns; commas; and capitalization. Each test is available in remedial, standard, and advanced versions. Available as reproducible sheets or in computerized versions. Free to instructors. Paper version: 0-321-02224-6. Computerized IBM: 0-321-02633-0. Computerized Mac: 0-321-02632-2.

■ **Diagnostic and Editing Tests, Second Edition.** This collection of diagnostic tests helps instructors assess students' competence in Standard Written English for purpose of placement or to gauge progress. Available as reproducible sheets or in computerized versions and is free to instructors. Paper: 0-321-02222-X. Computerized IBM: 0-321-02629-2. Computerized Mac: 0-321-02628-4.

■ **ESL Worksheets, Second Edition.** These reproducible worksheets provide ESL students with extra practice in areas they find the most troublesome. A diagnostic test and post-test are provided, along with answer keys and suggested topics for writing. Free to adopters. 0-321-01955-5.

■ **80 Practices.** A collection of reproducible, ten-item exercises that provide additional practices for specific grammatical usage problems, such as comma splices, capitalization, and pronouns. Includes an answer key and is free to adopters. 0-673-53422-7.

■ **CLAST Test Package, Fourth Edition.** These two forty-item objective tests evaluate students' readiness for the CLAST exams. Strategies for teaching CLAST preparedness are included. Free with any Longman English title. Reproducible sheets: 0-321-01950-4. Computerized IBM version: 0-321-01982-2. Computerized Mac version: 0-321-01983-0.

■ **TASP Test Package, Third Edition.** These twelve practice pre-tests and post-tests assess the same reading and writing skills covered in the TASP examination. Free with any Longman English title. Reproducible sheets: 0-321-01959-8. Computerized IBM version: 0-321-02623-3. Computerized Mac version: 0-321-02622-5.

■ *Teaching Writing to the Non-Native Speaker.* This booklet examines the issues that arise when non-native speakers enter the developmental classroom. Free to instructors, it includes profiles of international and permanent ESL students, factors influencing second-language acquisition, and tips on managing a multicultural classroom. 0-673-97452-9.

■ *Learning Together: An Introduction to Collaborative Theory.* This brief guide to the fundamentals of collaborative learning teaches students how to work effectively in groups, how to revise with peer response, and how to co-author a paper or report. Shrinkwrapped free with any Longman Basic Skills text. 0-673-46848-8.

■ *A Guide for Peer Response,* **Second Edition.** This guide offers students forms for peer critiques, including general guidelines and specific forms for different stages in the writing process. Also appropriate for freshman-level course. Free to adopters. 0-321-01948-2.

Acknowledgments

We are deeply grateful to our acquisitions editor, Steven Rigolosi, for his intelligent and perceptive guidance during the writing of this book. His talents reach far beyond the printed page. We also want to thank Ann Stypuloski, Donna Campion, and Melanie Goulet at Addison Wesley Longman. Ginger Yarrow, our project editor at Elm Street Publishing Services, was particularly sensitive to the mission of the project and its audience while working with us. We appreciate her patience, availability, and direction. Thanks also to Mira Schachne for acquiring the photos for the book and to Fred Courtright for obtaining the many permissions. We also want to thank our families for all the patience and support they gave us during the writing of this book.

We'd also like to thank the following colleagues for offering their suggestions during the many drafts of this text. We greatly appreciate their perceptive comments:

Jennifer Bradner, *Virginia Commonwealth University*
Sandra Carey, *Lexington Community College*
Jessica Carroll, *Miami-Dade Community College*
Arlene Clarke, *American River College*
Denise Davis, *St. Louis Community College at Florissant Valley*
Becky Garlick, *Blinn College*
Jean Hellyer, *Raymond Walters College of the University of Cincinnati*
Barbara King, *Clayton State College*
Thomas Lackman, *Temple University*
Patricia Malinowski, *Finger Lakes Community College*
Kathy McHale, *Nassau Community College*
Theresa Rooney, *York College*
Judith Rossman, *Community College of Philadelphia*
Pamela Smith, *Pellissippi State Technical College*
Donald Stoddard, *Anne Arundel Community College*
Eleanor Vendetti, *Capital Community-Technical College*

Lanny Lester
Judith Resnick

A Word to Students about This Book

We have organized this book around a theory of human needs developed by psychologist Abraham Maslow. Maslow's theory is that there is a hierarchy of needs and, in general, people are motivated to satisfy lower needs before satisfying higher ones. The hierarchy of needs, discussed in detail in Chapter 2, is illustrated in the diagram below.

Hierarchy of Needs

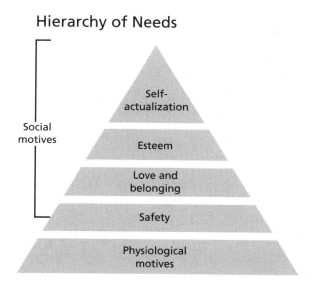

Each chapter in this book contains textbook excerpts from a different subject of college study. We have chosen each subject because it represents one of the needs depicted in the diagram above. For instance, Chapter 3 illustrates the physiological needs of diet and sleep with an excerpt from a health textbook. In considering the need for safety, you will read in Chapter 4 about the Bill of Rights and the way in which it protects your freedom and security. As you look over the Table of Contents you will see the relationship between the topic of each chapter and one of the human needs Maslow specified in his hierarchy. We organized the book in this way to help you connect various subjects you may study in college with your own personal needs and desires.

CHAPTER 1

Discovering Reading and Writing

What You Will Find in This Chapter

- Your Goals and Needs
- What Is Reading?
- Becoming a Better Reader
- What Is Writing?
- Becoming a Better Writer
- An Excerpt from *The Road Less Traveled*

This book was written with your needs in mind. Every selection in this book is related to the theme of human desires and needs. As you read each selection, you will learn more about yourself, your needs, and how to attain your goals. In a sense we might say that *you* are the theme of this book.

Although this book's main goal is to help you to read and write proficiently in college, there are many related benefits to improving these skills.

- *Learning and studying more efficiently:* The ability to distinguish between important and less important ideas helps you focus on the information you need to learn in your college courses. As a result, the time you spend studying will be devoted to the material you will be responsible for knowing in your courses. Good readers and writers find college courses less difficult and get higher grades.

- *Thinking more critically:* When you are actively involved in the reading and writing processes, your ability to think clearly and logically is sharpened.

- *Learning more about the world—its places and cultures:* Although most of us don't have the time or money to travel around the world, "armchair travelers" learn a great deal about faraway places by reading.

- *Discovering new interests and hobbies:* Just as reading might teach you about places and cultures you have never experienced firsthand, it can awaken interests that will enrich your life. And reading about those interests and hobbies you already have acquired can deepen your enjoyment of them.

- *Gaining a deeper understanding of yourself and other people:* It is not uncommon for readers to recognize behaviors similar to their own in characters they read about in books. Reading about such characters often gives people insight into their own lives and solutions to their own problems. Books can also introduce readers to behaviors completely different from their own, thus fostering an understanding and tolerance of differences among people.

- *Communicating ideas and feelings more effectively:* Just as educated adults are expected to express themselves clearly while speaking, the ability to write clearly is necessary in a variety of settings, including work and school.

- *Becoming a more interesting person:* The more you read, the more you will know. And the more you know, the more interesting you become.

Now take a few minutes to consider your goals for this course and what you believe are your strengths and weaknesses in terms of reading and writing skills.

Your Goals and Needs

What are your goals for this course?

In the space that follows, write down whatever comes to mind about what you would like to accomplish in this course.

My Goals for This Course

_____

_____

_____

What do you think you *already do well* as a reader and writer? What do you think you will need to learn in order *to improve* your reading and writing? Write your thoughts on the following lines.

What I Do Well as a Reader

_____

_____

_____

What I Do Well as a Writer

_____

_____

_____

What I Need to Improve as a Reader

_____

_____

_____

What I Need to Improve as a Writer

_____

_____

_____

Your teacher may ask you to share your lists with other members of the class. You will find that everyone has strengths and weaknesses in reading and writing. Maybe you do not read as often as you'd like. Maybe you are unsure about some aspects of your writing.

As you progress through this book, you will learn specific strategies to improve your reading and writing. By building on your strengths, you should increase your confidence and you will probably find reading and writing more enjoyable.

What Is Reading?

Most people think that by merely looking at words and sentences (the text), they will automatically understand what they are reading. But reading entails more than that. An author sends a message through text. The only way the reader can "catch" the message is by being alert and actively involved in receiving it. Although it may seem that you are getting meaning from the words you read, you are really building the meaning inside your head based on what you already know. In other words, reading is an active process because you must use your knowledge and experiences to make sense of the author's message. Reading involves your whole being—mental, emotional, physical, and even spiritual.

Becoming a Better Reader

The more you do something, the better you become at it. This is true for almost anything you do, such as typing, driving, playing sports, or playing a musical instrument. It is also true for reading. People become better and faster readers by reading a lot and by using a step-by-step approach to the reading process.

The Stages of Reading

There are specific things you can do before, during, and after reading to heighten your understanding and enjoyment of what you read. In this book you will be guided through the reading selections by engaging in activities related to each of these three stages of reading:

STAGES OF THE READING PROCESS

1. Before Reading
   - Thinking about prior knowledge of the topic
   - Freewriting
   - Surveying
   - Questioning
2. During Reading
   - Reflecting
   - Highlighting
   - Underlining
3. After Reading
   - Talking about reading
   - Journal writing
   - Note taking

Before Reading. *Motivation* is one of the most important ingredients in skilled reading. You will probably find that you are most engaged when you are reading about something that interests you. Your interests, background, thoughts, opinions, and feelings help you become interested in what you are reading. However, it is unlikely that you will be interested in everything you read in college. Therefore, you need a way to "get into" what you read. The best way is to relate what you are reading to your experiences. The more experience you have with a topic, the faster and better you can read about it. An analogy will help you to understand this important principle.

Imagine that you are about to take a long trip to another part of the world, to an exotic place you have never been before. Most people who travel make transportation arrangements, reserve rooms at a hotel, notify friends and family that they are leaving, get a map, plan an itinerary, and pack a suitcase. All of these activities are performed before they actually leave for the trip. Similarly, there are some important activities you should do before you begin to read.

Think of reading as traveling to a distant land. Your suitcase represents what you're reading about (the topic) and gets filled with information as you read. As a matter of fact, you already have many such suitcases stored inside your brain, each one containing everything you know about a particular topic. You probably have a "school" suitcase that contains everything you know about being a student, such as relating to teachers, dressing for school, choosing classes, and studying for exams.

Every time you read, your brain searches for a suitcase that might hold information you already have acquired. If you have such a suitcase, its stored contents will be available to help you understand and remember what you are reading. Therefore, the first step in reading is to think about the title and any *prior knowledge* you have about the topic at hand, before you begin to read. If you are not familiar with the topic (your suitcase is relatively empty), you will have to read more carefully as you begin to learn about that new topic.

Freewriting can help you find out what you already know about a topic. To freewrite before you read, use the title or topic of the reading passage as your focus. Then, simply begin to write whatever comes into your mind about the title. Don't pause to think about whether your ideas are good or not, and don't worry about spelling, grammar, or neatness. If you can't think of anything to write, then write, "I can't think of anything else to write." Soon something else will come to your mind. The important point is to continue writing for a few minutes or until directed to stop.

Another way to prepare yourself for reading is by **surveying** the text. You can leaf through the reading selection, noting the length, illustrations, and other graphic features. Doing so will give you some idea of what to expect from the reading.

At this point, pay particular attention to the title. Turning titles and headings into one or two questions will help you to concentrate on what you are about to read. This **questioning** technique is introduced in the next chapter.

During Reading. The purpose of reading is to understand the author's message. Thus, you need to be aware of your own comprehension as you read the text. You may respond in different ways when you have difficulties understanding. Sometimes you may **reread** parts of the text to gain a better understanding. Other times you may stop and **reflect** on what you have read. To help you reflect on the text's meaning, we have provided questions in between various sections of text throughout the book. Finally, you may want to **highlight** or **underline** to help you identify significant material while reading.

After Reading. Reading becomes most meaningful when you think about what you have read and find ways to incorporate it into your world. When you do this, you remember more of what you read, and unfamiliar material becomes easier to master in the future. After-reading activities may include collaboration, writing, and note taking.

Talking about Reading. **Collaboration** means talking with others about what you have read. This book includes many sections devoted to collaborative activities. In these activities you will get together with another student or a few students and talk about what you have read or share your thoughts about one another's writing. Sometimes you will get together with classmates to answer questions or discuss issues. You will probably better understand what you have read if you share ideas with other people. In addition, collaboration often can lead you to develop new ideas.

Writing about Reading. In the section called "Topics for Writers," which you will find throughout this book, we provide suggestions for **writing.** Your instructor may ask you to keep a notebook in which you can keep a record of what you have written. We call this notebook a **writing journal.** Sometimes no one else will read what you have written; sometimes your instructor will read your journal; sometimes you will share what you have written with other students in your class.

Just as freewriting can be used before reading, it can also be used after reading to help you put ideas together and relate better to what you have read. One way to respond to what you've read is to keep a **double-entry journal.** With this method, you fold a piece of paper down the middle, making two columns. Label the left-hand column "What I Read." In that column, write a phrase or sentence from the text you have read. Choose something that surprised you, made you feel happy or sad, confused you, reminded you of something in your own life, or in some other way impressed you. Label the right-hand column "What I Think." In that column, write your thoughts about the phrase or sentence you copied. What made you choose that particular part of the text? What thoughts went through your mind as you focused on that phrase or sentence?

Here is an example:

DOUBLE-ENTRY JOURNAL

What I Read	What I Think
"What makes life difficult is that the process of confronting and solving problems is a painful one."	This reminds me of the time my boyfriend walked out on me. It was painful but I learned a lot about myself when I realized that I had not been happy in the relationship anyway.

In a **triple-entry journal,** you fold the paper to create three columns. In addition to "What I Read" and "What I Think" columns, you will have a third column labeled "Response." In that column, another student or your instructor responds to what you wrote.

Here is an example:

TRIPLE-ENTRY JOURNAL

What I Read	What I Think	Response
"Men ran when they saw the officers."	If you are not guilty of something, why act like you are? Why give people reasons to suspect you? If these men ran it is because they had something to hide.	The question about the men running is plain and simple. If it looks like a cat, and walks like a cat, then what else could it be? Maybe they ran because they were guilty. On the other hand, maybe they were just afraid of the police.

The following practice exercise will give you a chance to apply what you have learned about the three stages of reading.

PRACTICE EXERCISE: THE STAGES OF READING

Before Reading

1. Have you ever felt like you did not belong in a group of people? Describe your experiences and why you felt like an outsider.

_____

_____

_____

_____

_____

_____

_____

_____

_____

_____

2. The title "Back, but Not Home" is from a newspaper article written by Maria L. Muniz. What does this title mean to you? Don't be afraid to guess at this point.

_____

_____

_____

During Reading

Maria Muniz was born in Cuba and came to the United States when she was five years old. This passage is from an article she wrote for the *New York Times* about her experiences. Answer the questions as you read about the experiences of Maria Muniz.

With all the talk about resuming diplomatic relations with Cuba, and with the increasing number of Cuban exiles returning to visit friends and relatives, I am constantly being asked, "Would you ever go back?" In turn, I have asked myself, "Is there any reason for me to go?" I have had to think long and hard before finding my answer. Yes.

1. Why do you think the author wants to go back to Cuba?

_____

_____

_____

I came to the United States with my parents when I was almost five years old. We left behind grandparents, aunts, uncles and several cousins. I grew up in a very middle-class neighborhood in Brooklyn. With one exception, all my friends were

American. Outside of my family, I do not know many Cubans. I often feel awkward visiting relatives in Miami because it is such a different world. The way of life in Cuban Miami seems very strange to me and I am accused of being too "Americanized." Yet, although I am now an American citizen, whenever anyone has asked me my nationality, I have always and unhesitatingly replied, "Cuban. . . ."

2. Why do you think Maria Muniz refers to herself as "Cuban"?

_____

_____

_____

_____

When I try to review my life during the past 16 years, I almost feel as if I've walked into a theater right in the middle of a movie. And I'm afraid I won't fully understand or enjoy the rest of the movie unless I can see and understand the beginning. And for me, the beginning is Cuba. I don't want to go "home" again; the life and home we all left behind are long gone. My home is here and I am happy. But I need to talk to my family still in Cuba.

3. What does the author mean by "I almost feel as if I've walked into a theater right in the middle of a movie"?

_____

_____

_____

_____

Like all immigrants, my family and I have had to build a new life from almost nothing. It was often difficult, but I believe the struggle made us strong. Most of my memories are good ones.

But I want to preserve and renew my cultural heritage. I want to keep "la Cubana" within me alive. I want to return because the journey back will also mean a journey within. Only then will I see the missing piece.

(*New York Times*, July 13, 1979, p. A25.)

4. What do you think the author means by "the missing piece"?

_____

_____

_____

_____

After Reading

1. Using the following double-entry journal form, choose something from the article you just read which either surprised you, confused you, or reminded you of something in your own life. In the first column, copy that sentence or part of the article exactly as it appears in the article. In the second column, write why you chose that part of the article.

What I Read	What I Think

2. Meet in small groups to talk about the following two questions.
    a. Share the experience of not belonging in a group that you wrote about before reading. How are your experiences similar to and different from those of others in your discussion group?
    b. Now that you are finished reading, what do you think Maria Muniz meant by the title, "Back, but Not Home"?

What Is Writing?

Just as reading involves more than looking at words, writing involves more than putting words on paper. Writing is the process of communicating through the use of words. There are many types of writing: writing a term paper or essay in a college course, writing a business report for your job, writing a letter to a friend. Because the skills required vary with the different types of writing, this book includes many types of writing.

You'll be shown how to approach writing as a step-by-step process that ends with a finished product. Also, you'll have many writing opportunities throughout the book to learn and practice your writing skills. Some of these writings will be just for yourself. Others will culminate in a finished product for you to show to others. Finally, everything you write will be based on your own knowledge or experience or in response to what you have read.

Becoming a Better Writer

Many students try to produce an effective piece of writing in one sitting, but this is rarely possible. Effective writing is a process that requires careful planning, writing, and rewriting. The best way to improve your writing is to write often and pay careful attention to the process. Use feedback from your instructor and peers to become aware of your strengths and weaknesses as a writer. Then, make changes as needed to improve what you've written. As we suggested in the section on writing after reading, keep a journal for the writings that you do in this course.

The Stages of Writing

Earlier in the chapter, you learned that there are activities you can do before, during, and after reading. Writing also develops in stages that include before, during, and after activities. The following are the main stages used by writers to construct a good piece of writing.

STAGES OF THE WRITING PROCESS

- Stage 1: Discovering Topics
- Stage 2: Discovering Ideas
- Stage 3: Organizing Information
- Stage 4: Drafting
- Stage 5: Collaborating
- Stage 6: Revising
- Stage 7: Proofreading

Before Writing. *Motivation* is an important ingredient of writing. You can write best about those things about which you have knowledge, interest, strong feelings and opinions, or personal experience. The following three stages comprise the before-writing process.

Stage 1—Discovering Topics. Discovering a topic for yourself is the first stage of writing. Responding to something you have read is a good way to discover a topic to write about. For example, agreeing or disagreeing with an author can get you started. Also, using a quotation can lead to an interesting topic. Whether you have read or heard something that interests you, you could use the quote as a springboard for your own writing.

Stage 2—Discovering Ideas. By talking and writing you discover ideas and learn new ways of thinking about a problem. In the section on writing about reading, we introduced freewriting as a way to discover ideas. Freewriting is also a method for discovering ideas to write about. Looping is an additional activity you can try when exploring ideas for writing. Other helpful methods will be introduced in Chapter 2.

Freewriting is useful for discovering what you already know about something. Simply write about a topic without stopping, putting on paper (or computer screen) whatever thoughts come into your head without censoring, judging, or evaluating them. Open your mind to whatever information and experiences you have had with the topic; allow your thoughts to pour out onto paper. To explore your ideas thoroughly, write continuously for a period of time—perhaps 5 to 10 minutes. When you are done, read what you have written. You will probably discover some ideas you will want to use in your writing. Here is an example of a student's freewriting:

MY DIETING EXPERIENCES

Counting calories—I really hate that, it's so difficult to know how many calories there are in what I'm eating. Jane told me about a protein diet; but she said it's hard to follow and gives her a stomachache. I like the carbohydrate diet better because I love pasta. I always gain the weight back as soon as I go off a diet—easy to get off, hard to keep off. Dieting makes me feel tired and hungry. I know it's important for my health but it's so difficult.

After freewriting, you can try **looping** by using a sentence from your first freewriting to begin a second one. First reread your freewriting and choose a sentence that you particularly like. Then use that sentence as the first sentence of a second freewriting activity. Once again, write nonstop for a predetermined time. From this you will probably find great ideas for your writing. Following is an example of looping from the previous freewriting. The last sentence of the previous freewriting is used as the first sentence in this example.

I know it's important for my health but it's so difficult. When my stomach is empty I really feel like I can't control myself from eating. I can't think of anything but food when I'm hungry. My friend told me I can substitute healthy food for the unhealthy food that makes me gain weight.

Stage 3—Organizing Information. Some formal writing assignments, like term papers or research projects, will require you to gather information related to your topic. When you write informally you can rely on your ideas and experiences. In either case you will need to organize your ideas in a logical manner. Here is an example of one way to group the information from the freewriting example.

My Dieting Experiences

Introduction: Why is dieting important?
My experiences
    Carbohydrate diet
    Protein diet
Similarities among diets
Differences among diets
Conclusion: Why is dieting so difficult?

Another way to organize your ideas is to ask some questions about your topic before you write. Here are questions you might ask:

Purpose

■ What is my purpose for writing?

Audience

■ Who is going to read this writing?

Interest Level

■ Why does this topic interest me?

Topic

■ What is the most important point I want to make about this topic?

Opinion

■ What do I think and feel about this topic?

In Chapters 3 and 4 we will show you how to organize ideas in a paragraph. In Chapter 5 you will learn how to organize paragraphs into an essay.

During Writing. After organizing your ideas, you are ready to create a draft, your first attempt at writing.

Stage 4—Drafting. While drafting, do not allow yourself to get stuck on any paragraph or point. Instead, just go on to the next paragraph or point. You will have opportunities to go back and make changes later in the writing process.

After Writing. Since your draft is a rough copy, it will need to be further refined. The next three stages are ways in which you can rework your draft into a piece of writing with which you will feel satisfied.

Stage 5—Collaborating. You may want to collaborate, or get the opinions of your instructor or fellow students. Feedback is useful because it tells you how clearly you are expressing your thoughts. When you are giving feedback to someone else, it is useful to let the writer know:

- what you liked about the writing.
- what you would like to know more about.
- what questions you have about the writing.
- how you think it can be improved.

Stage 6—Revising. The process of reviewing and rewriting your draft is called revising. During this stage of writing you revisit your first draft, deciding what you want to include, omit, change, or add. For instance, you may wish to reorganize ideas or change wording or sentences. You will want to use any feedback you have received to guide your revision.

Stage 7—Proofreading. The final stage of writing involves proofreading your paper for errors in grammar, punctuation, and spelling. Reading your writing aloud is an excellent technique for finding errors. Also, you may ask others to help you proofread.

A Final Note about the Writing Process

There are seven stages in the writing process. However, you will not always work through them in the order listed. For example, sometimes you may choose to change your topic, proofread and edit a paragraph before finishing the final draft, or brainstorm for more ideas at any time in the process. The important point to understand is that each stage in the process emphasizes a different aspect of writing.

As you proceed through this book, you will find many writing exercises. Often, we suggest the techniques and identify the stages in the writing process. At times we will suggest the topics and you will choose the techniques you think will help you write better. Any time you need some help you can refer to this chapter on the steps of writing. And remember: the more you write, the better and more effective your writing will become.

Practice Exercise: The Stages of Writing

Before Writing

Discover. First, freewrite for about three minutes about difficulties you have had in your life either now or in the past. Second, underline a sentence in your freewriting that you would like to write more about. Use that sentence as the beginning of a second freewrite.

Organize. List some key words or important points from your second freewriting that you want to include in your writing. Then, incorporate your key points into the answers to these questions:

- Why does this topic interest me?
- What is the most important point I want to make about this topic?
- What do I think and feel about this topic?

This will guide you through the process.

During Writing

Draft. Using your list of ideas and organizing questions as a guide, write a draft about your experience with a recent problem.

After Writing

Collaborate. Working in a small group, read aloud the draft you have written. After each draft is read, discuss the experience and give some feedback.

- What did you like about the paper?
- Was the experience described clearly?
- What one question would you want to ask the author of the paper?

Revise. Based on the feedback you have received from group members, rewrite your paper. Decide what you want to keep, add, and delete from your first draft. How can you describe your experience more clearly or vividly?

Proofread. Read your paper carefully to check for errors.

Application

Additional Reading
THE ROAD LESS TRAVELED
Dr. M. Scott Peck

Before Reading

The following excerpt is from a book that has been a best-seller for many years. The author is a practicing psychiatrist who offers some practical advice about living.

Before reading, freewrite for a few minutes about the topic: life is difficult.

During Reading

The following words are from the selection you are going to read. The numbers in parentheses are the paragraphs in which the words can be found.

VOCABULARY	
Word	**Definition**
incessantly (2)	constantly
enormity (2)	significant size
affliction (2)	hardship
engender (5)	create

1   Life is difficult. This is a great truth, one of the greatest truths. It is a great truth because once we truly see this truth, we transcend it. Once we truly know that life is difficult—once we truly understand and accept it—then life is no longer difficult. Because once it is accepted, the fact that life is difficult no longer matters.

2   Most do not fully see this truth that life is difficult. Instead they moan more or less incessantly, noisily or subtly, about the enormity of their problems, their burdens, and their difficulties as if life were generally easy, as if life *should* be easy. They voice their belief, noisily or subtly, that their difficulties represent a unique kind of affliction that should not be and that has somehow been especially visited upon them, or else upon their families, their tribe, their class, their nation, their race or even their species, and not upon others. I know about this moaning because I have done my share.

3   Life is a series of problems. Do we want to moan about them or solve them? Do we want to teach our children to solve them?

4   Discipline is the basic set of tools we require to solve life's problems. Without discipline we can solve nothing. With only some discipline we can solve only some problems. With total discipline we can solve all problems.

5   What makes life difficult is that the process of confronting and solving problems is a painful one. Problems, depending upon their nature, evoke in us frustration or grief or sadness or loneliness or guilt or regret or anger or fear or anxiety or anguish or despair. These are uncomfortable feelings, often very uncomfortable, often as painful as any kind of physical pain, sometimes equaling the very worst kind of physical pain. Indeed, it is because of the pain that events or conflicts engender in us all that we call them problems. And since life poses an endless series of problems, life is always difficult and is full of pain as well as joy.

6   Yet it is in this whole process of meeting and solving problems that life has its meaning. Problems are the cutting edge that distinguishes between success and failure. Problems call forth our courage and our wisdom; indeed, they create our courage and our wisdom. It is only because of problems that we grow mentally and spiritually. When we desire to encourage the growth of the human spirit, we challenge and encourage the human capacity to solve problems, just as in school we deliberately set problems for our children to solve. It is through the pain of confronting and resolving problems that we learn. As Benjamin Franklin said, "Those things that hurt, instruct." It is for this reason that wise people learn not to dread but actually to welcome problems and actually to welcome the pain of problems.

7   I have stated that discipline is the basic set of tools we require to solve life's problems. It will become clear that these tools are techniques of suffering, means by which we experience the pain of problems in such a way as to work them through and solve them successfully, learning and growing in the process. When we teach ourselves and our children discipline, we are teaching them and ourselves how to suffer and also how to grow.

8   What are these tools, these techniques of suffering, these means of experiencing the pain of problems constructively that I call discipline? There are four: delaying of gratification, acceptance of responsibility, dedication to truth, and balancing. As will be evident, these are not complex tools whose application demands extensive training. To the contrary, they are simple tools, and almost all children are adept in their use by the age of ten. Yet presidents and kings will often forget to use them, to their own downfall. The problem lies not in the complexity of these tools but in the will to use them. For they are tools with which pain is confronted rather than avoided, and if one seeks to avoid legitimate suffering, then one will avoid the use of these tools.

(M. Scott Peck, M.D., *The Road Less Traveled*, New York, NY: Simon & Schuster, 1978, pp. 15-16.)

After Reading

1. **Comprehension Check**

_____ 1) The main point of this passage is that
   a. without discipline we can solve nothing.
   b. problems evoke in us frustration or grief.
   c. dealing with one's problems gives life meaning.
   d. the tendency to avoid problems results in mental illness.

_____ 2) All of the following are tools of discipline *except:*
   a. dedication to truth.
   b. extensive training.
   c. delaying of gratification.
   d. balancing.

_____ 3) According to the author, people are motivated to avoid problems because
   a. they are painful.
   b. they usually cannot be solved.
   c. they cause mental illness.
   d. people desire to grow mentally and spiritually.

_____ 4) People who use a little discipline
   a. can solve all of their problems.
   b. can solve some of their problems.
   c. can solve nothing.
   d. have total discipline.

_____ 5) According to the author, what makes life difficult?
   a. physical pain
   b. frustration and guilt
   c. solving problems
   d. conflicts

_____ 6) Problems give our life meaning in all of the following ways *except* by
   a. showing us the difference between success and failure.
   b. giving us courage.
   c. challenging us to grow.
   d. teaching us to avoid problems.

_____ 7) Most people complain about their problems because
   a. they believe life should be easy.
   b. life is full of problems.
   c. problems help us distinguish between success and failure.
   d. others share their problems.

_____ 8) Choose the statement with which the author would probably agree.

    a. Successful leaders avoid their problems.

    b. The tools for solving problems are hard to learn.

    c. We need to confront emotional pain.

    d. The tools of discipline are complicated.

2. Topics for Writers

Write for a few minutes in response to one of the questions below.

1) Do you think that life is difficult? If so, how?

2) The author states, "It is only because of problems that we grow mentally and spiritually." Do you agree or disagree with the author?

3) What is your idea of an ideal society?

4) What kind of discipline do you use in your life?

Chapter Summary

Your Goals and Needs	You assessed your goals and needs as a reader and writer.
What Is Reading?	Reading is an active process. You use your knowledge and experience to make sense of what you read.
Becoming a Better Reader	The reading process consists of several stages.
The Stages of Reading	
Before Reading	Your interests, background, thoughts, opinions, and feelings help you become motivated to read. Thinking or freewriting about your prior knowledge is important.
During Reading	You need to be aware of any comprehension problems while reading and have ways of responding to those problems.
After Reading	Reading becomes more meaningful when you can incorporate what you have read into your world.
Talking about Reading	Collaboration means talking with others about what you have read.
Writing about Reading	Freewriting helps you find out what you already know about a topic.
	Double-entry and triple-entry journals are a way to respond to what you read.
What Is Writing?	Writing is the process of communicating through the use of words.
Becoming a Better Writer	The writing process consists of several stages.
The Stages of Writing	
Before Writing	The before-writing stage includes discovering topics, discovering ideas, and organizing information.
During Writing	Drafting is a first attempt at writing. You should expect to make changes to your draft later on.
After Writing	Collaborating, revising, and proofreading are the final steps in the writing process.

 **Journal**

In the space below, write about one new thing that you discovered in this chapter. Why do you think you remember that particular thing?

_____

_____

_____

_____

_____

_____

_____

_____

_____

_____

_____

_____

_____

_____

_____

_____

_____

_____

_____

_____

_____

_____

_____

Go Electronic!

For additional readings, exercises, and Internet activities, visit the Longman English pages at:

http://longman.awl.com/englishpages

If you need a user name and password, please see your instructor.

Take a Road Trip to New Orleans

Be sure to visit the Active Reading module in your Reading Road Trip CD-ROM for multimedia tutorials, exercises, and tests.

Practice Your Writing Skills

For additional practice with your writing skills, use the Writer's ToolKit CD-ROM included with this text.

CHAPTER 2

Preparing for Reading and Writing

Theme: Motivation and Emotion

What You Will Find in This Chapter

- Reading Strategies
- Writing Strategies
- Improving Your Vocabulary
- Textbook Selections on Motivation and Emotion
- A Short Story: "The Paring Knife"
- An Essay: "Unfair Game"

What do you think is happening in each of the pictures below? What emotions do you think the people in each picture are experiencing? What emotions do you feel as you look at each picture?

This chapter deals with different aspects of motivation and emotion. Included are excerpts from a psychology textbook, a short story, and an essay written by a journalist who had a disturbing experience while with a friend.

In this chapter you also will learn some strategies to prepare for effective reading and writing. These strategies involve

- increasing your familiarity with the subject,
- surveying the text's headings and subheadings,
- setting purposes by questioning before you read,
- discovering topics and ideas, and
- unlocking the meanings of new words.

Reading Strategies

Before you begin to read, it is helpful to become familiar with the material. You can do this by

- thinking about your prior knowledge of the topic, and
- surveying, which includes outlining and questioning.

An explanation of these activities follows.

Prior Knowledge

Reading is always easiest and most interesting when you recall whatever you already know about the topic. This is referred to as accessing prior knowledge of the topic before reading. You can do this in a number of ways. You might think for a few minutes about what a title or heading means to you by asking yourself questions such as:

- What do I know about the topic from my past experiences?
- What does the topic remind me of? How do I feel about it?
- Is there anything about the title or heading which is confusing?
- Am I interested in finding out more about the topic?
- What questions does the title raise in my mind?

Another way to access prior knowledge is to **freewrite** for a minute or two after reading the title, but before reading the text. As you write, you will call up from memory whatever you already know about the topic.

Surveying

Surveying is a process of looking at something as a whole to get a big picture of what it is about. It is like getting a bird's-eye view of the land by going up in a helicopter. Similarly, you can get a bird's-eye view of a large piece of text, like a textbook chapter, by looking first at the headings and subheadings.

Headings and Subheadings. Imagine trying to drive for the first time through a neighborhood with no traffic lights or street signs. You would have to drive very slowly and with extreme caution to avoid an accident. Furthermore, without street names you would have difficulty knowing your location and finding your destination.

Every textbook (and most other types of reading material) has headings and subheadings to help you keep track of the information being presented. Major **headings** are the most important road signs because they announce the topics you are about to encounter. These topics are important general categories in which information is stored.

A **subheading** is placed under a major heading. The word "subheading" contains the prefix "sub," which means "under." Each subheading introduces a section of text and gives more specific information about the major heading.

Typographical aids, such as capital letters, bold print, colors, and centering will help you identify headings and subheadings. In general, major headings tend to be in larger print and are often in capital letters. Headings and subheadings in one textbook can look different from those in another. Each publisher has its own way of designing a book. For example, one publisher might use CAPITAL LETTERS for headings but not for subheadings. Another publisher might print headings in color. The important point to remember is that headings and subheadings are set up in the same way throughout an entire textbook.

Figures 2.1 and 2.2 (pages 27 and 28) are samples of the actual headings and subheadings from two different psychology textbooks. Survey these examples and notice their arrangement of type on the page and the typographical aids used, including capital letters and print size.

Outlining. One of the best ways to become familiar with a chapter's headings and subheadings before you read is to create an outline from them. Outlining headings and subheadings helps you see how all the pieces of the chapter fit together. Because authors recognize the importance of outlines, they often provide them at the beginning of textbook chapters. If the author does not include them, you should make outlines from the headings and subheadings.

Here is an example of a general outline using the headings from the textbook excerpt on pages 44 to 49:

THE NATURE OF EMOTION

   I. The Components of Emotion

  II. What Are the Basic Emotions?

 III. Are Emotions Universal and Innate?

ATTENTIONAL PROCESSES

We'd like you to take a moment now to find ten things in your environment that had not been, so far, in your immediate awareness. Had you noticed a spot on the wall? Had you noticed the ticking of a clock? If you start to examine your surroundings very carefully, you will discover that there are literally thousands of things on which you could focus your **attention.** Generally, the more closely you attend to some object or event in the environment, the more you can perceive and learn about it. That's why attention is an important topic in the study of perception: your focus of attention determines the types of information that will be most readily available to your perceptual processes. As you will now see, researchers have tried to understand what types of environmental stimuli require your attention and how attention contributes to your experience of those stimuli. We will start by considering how attention functions to selectively highlight objects and events in your environment.

SELECTIVE ATTENTION

We began this section by asking that you try to find—to bring into attention—several things that had, up to that point, escaped your notice. This thought experiment illustrated an important function of attention: to select some part of the sensory input for further processing. Let us see how you make decisions about the subset of the world to which you will attend, and what consequences those decisions have for the information readily available to you.

Determining the Focus of Attention

What forces determine the objects that become the focus of your attention? The answer to this question has two components, which we will call goal-directed selection and stimulus-driven capture (Yantis, 1993). **Goal-directed selection** reflects the choices that you make about the objects to which you'd like to attend, as a function of your own goals. You are probably already comfortable with the idea that you can explicitly choose objects for particular scrutiny. **Stimulus-driven capture** occurs when features of the stimuli—objects in the environment—themselves automatically *capture* your attention, independent of your local goals as a perceiver. Research suggests, for example, that new objects in a perceptual display automatically capture attention.

You attend to stimuli in the environment either because you choose to—goal-directed selection—or because something about the stimulus captures your attention—stimulus-driven capture.

(Zimbardo, *Psychology and Life,* 14th ed. NY: HarperCollins, 1996, p. 27.)

FIGURE 2.1   Textbook Sample 1

Questioning before You Read. When your purpose is to study textbook material and remember what you are reading, it is a good idea to ask questions before you read. One way to do this is to turn headings and subheadings into questions before you read each section of a text. This will help you focus on the information you are studying. This activity is so valuable that sometimes authors will use questions for headings—for example, "What Are the Basic Emotions?" (page 46). However, in

T O P I C   5 A

PERCEPTION

Learning about the factors that determine what we attend to is a major concern of the psychology of perception. Imagine that you are at a party, engaged in a dreadfully boring conversation with someone you've just met. It occurs to you that wearing your new shoes was not a good idea—your feet hurt. You're munching on an assortment of tasty appetizers. Music blares from a stereo. Aromas of foods and perfume fill the air. There must be at least 50 people at this party, and you don't know any of them. Your senses are being bombarded simultaneously by all sorts of information: sights, tastes, sounds, smells, even pain. Suddenly, you hear someone mention your name. You redirect your attention toward the person who mentioned your name, disregarding the person right in front of you.

PERCEPTUAL SELECTIVITY: PAYING ATTENTION

There are many variables that influence our selection of stimuli from the environment. They can be divided into two types: stimulus factors and personal factors. By stimulus factors I mean those characteristics of stimuli that make them more compelling, or attention-grabbing, than others, no matter *who* the perceiver is. By personal factors I am referring to those characteristics of the person, the perceiver, that influence which stimuli get attended to. We'll start by considering stimulus factors.

Stimulus Factors in Selectivity

contrast
the extent to which a stimulus is in some physical way different from other surrounding stimuli

The most common and important stimulus factor in perceptual selection is **contrast**, the extent to which a stimulus is physically different from other stimuli around it. One stimulus can contrast with other stimuli in a variety of ways. For example, we are more likely to attend to a stimulus if its *intensity* is different from the intensities of other stimuli. Generally, the more intense a stimulus, the more likely we are to select it for further processing. Simply put, a shout is more compelling than a whisper; a bright light is more attention-grabbing than a dim one.

Notice that this isn't always the case, however. The context in which a stimulus occurs makes a difference. A shout may be more compelling than a whisper—unless everyone is shouting; then it may very well be the soft, quiet, reasoned tone that gets our attention. When faced with a barrage of bright lights, a dim one may be the one we process most fully.

(Gerow, *Essentials of Psychology: Concepts and Applications,*
2nd ed. NY: HarperCollins, 1996, p. 162.)

FIGURE 2.2   Textbook Sample 2

most cases you will have to ask questions for yourself. Your questions should be general and based on what the section is about.

To make sure your question will be answered, it is a good idea to use the actual heading or subheading in your question by adding a word like *who, what, why, when, where,* or *how* before the heading itself. For example, the heading "The Components of Emotion" could be changed to the question, "What are the components of emotion?" The important point is that you should ask a question before you read, and then look for the answer to that question as you read.

You might choose to write each question in your notebook or journal, then answer it in writing when you are done reading each section. You will find that questions from headings and subheadings often appear on tests, especially as essay questions. Thus, this questioning strategy can help you prepare for your exams very effectively.

Writing Strategies

Accessing your prior knowledge of a topic is as important to good writing as it is to good reading. You begin writing by discovering topics and thinking about them in an organized way. As a result, your writing will become better organized and more effective.

Stage 1: Discovering Topics

Topics can be words or phrases, such as *dating, attending college,* or *raising a child.* They are like titles or headings and describe what you are writing about in just a few words. Remember that reading and writing are always easiest and most enjoyable when you are dealing with familiar material. Therefore, if you are free to choose your own topic, think about those areas about which you already know something or have strong feelings. Following are two suggestions for finding a writing topic.

Responding to Something You Have Read. Your reaction to an author—how you feel about an idea you've read about—can give you ideas about writing topics. For example, you may read an article about someone who has a problem losing weight. You could write about attitudes in our society toward weight. Journal writing is a good way to think about your reactions to something you have read.

Using a Quotation. You could use something you have read or heard that interests you as a springboard for your own writing. For example, if someone said to you, "The government just discontinued funding the arts and humanities in the United States," you could write about the importance of art and whether or not it should be funded with public money.

PRACTICE EXERCISE 1: DISCOVERING TOPICS

List five topics you would consider writing about that you either (a) feel you know a lot about or (b) recently read about.

_____

_____

_____

_____

_____

Stage 2: Discovering Ideas

After you have decided on a topic, you can move on to stage 2—discovering ideas about your topic.

Have you ever had the experience of talking to a close friend about a problem you were trying to solve? Have you ever discovered that while talking about the problem, you hit upon a solution you hadn't thought of previously? This is not an uncommon experience, because in talking you discover ideas and actually learn new ways of thinking about an issue or problem. Consider writing a way of talking (and thinking) on paper. Sometimes you don't know what you are capable of thinking without writing.

In Chapter 1 we introduced freewriting and looping as ways of exploring ideas for writing. Here are some additional suggestions for discovering ideas for writing.

Brainstorming. Brainstorming is a method of finding solutions to a problem by thinking in as many directions as your mind and imagination can take you. It can be done by working with others in a group or sitting by yourself and writing down any ideas that come to your mind. When you brainstorm you write every idea that comes to mind when you think of a topic without rejecting any ideas or judging. There are different ways to record your ideas while brainstorming. You can make a list or a diagram (using mapping or clustering).

Listing. To list your ideas, write the topic at the top of a piece of paper, and jot down any ideas that come to you. When you are done, look over your list and cross out those items which seem less important to you and underline, circle, or number those that seem to go together or to be closely related to the topic. Here is an example of a list one student might create on the topic, "The Ideal Husband."

THE IDEAL HUSBAND

- tall
- handsome
- kind
- considerate

- wealthy
- ambitious
- likes children
- patient

Also, you may want to list information from a textbook or other source to help you get started on a writing topic. Many of the journal-writing activities in this book involve listing.

Mapping or Clustering. Mapping is a good way to discover general ideas and, at the same time, to organize these ideas. In **mapping or clustering,** you simply write the topic in a circle in the center of a page. As you think of related ideas or words, connect them to the center circle with a line. When you think of an idea or word related to a connected circle, add an additional branch. You may find yourself discovering connections you might not have thought of without mapping.

For example, if you were trying to decide on a career, you might develop the following map.

FIGURE 2.3   Mapping

PRACTICE EXERCISE 2: BRAINSTORMING

Choose two of the topics listed below. For the first topic, brainstorm what you know by making a list. For the second topic, brainstorm by mapping.

- Feeling Safe
- Love
- Friends
- Family
- My Neighborhood

Improving Your Vocabulary

What do you do when you come to a new or unknown word while you are reading? Perhaps you skip it and keep reading, or try to guess the meaning from the way it is used in the sentence. Perhaps you stop reading and look it up in a dictionary. Maybe you ask someone who happens to be nearby if she knows the meaning.

In the belief that it is necessary to know the precise meaning of every word, some people will interrupt their reading many times to look up words in the dictionary. But reading is all about extracting meaning from a text, and it is certainly possible to understand an author's message even when you do not understand a few words. Therefore, we recommend that you do not stop reading to look up words in a dictionary. Rather, you should jot down the words you don't know and look them up later.

Context Clues

The best way to figure out the meaning of an unknown word is to make an educated guess, using the *context* of the sentence or paragraph. Clues you get from the sentence and paragraph that help you guess the meaning of words are called context clues.

The most common types of context clues are synonym, contrast, example, explanation, and situation clues.

Synonym Clues. Authors sometimes provide synonyms, words that mean the same thing as words their readers may not know. Synonym clues may be set off by *commas*, *dashes*, or *parentheses*. The following sentences contain synonym context clues.

1. One of the important ways we   proximity = closeness
   organize elements in our perception
   is in terms of *proximity,* or closeness.

2. Your summary was *pithy* (short but to the point).

pithy = short but to the point

3. I felt no *compunction*—regret—about being late for class since I had a good excuse.

compunction = regret

Contrast Clues. Authors sometimes use clue words to signal when a new word means the opposite of something. This is called a contrast clue. Some words that signal contrast follow:

- although
- but
- despite
- even though
- however
- in contrast

- instead
- nevertheless
- on the other hand
- rather than
- while
- yet

Here is an example of a contrast clue for the meaning of the word *somatic.*

> Sometimes our emotions are caused by our mental state, while at other times they are controlled by *somatic* conditions.

The word *mental* in the first part of the sentence is a contrast clue for the meaning of *somatic.* The author has used the word *while* to signal the contrast. Therefore, *somatic* is the opposite of *mental.* It means *bodily.*

Use contrast clues to figure out the meaning of the italicized words in the following examples. In each sentence, underline the word(s) that help you figure out the meaning.

1. Although you appear poor, you are really from an *affluent* family.

   Affluent means _____

2. You were quite *loquacious* at the party even though you are not very talkative at home.

   Loquacious means _____

Example Clues. Authors often provide examples as part of the context. Some of the words used to indicate examples are:

- for example
- for instance

- such as
- to illustrate

In the following sentences, the meaning of the term *primary drive* is made clear by examples.

Some motives are unlearned and are common to every animal, including humans. These motives are called primary drives. Primary drives, such as hunger, thirst, and sex, are strongly influenced by stimuli from within the body.

(Morris, *Psychology: An Introduction*, Prentice-Hall, 1990, p. 410.)

The words *such as* indicate that hunger, thirst, and sex are examples of primary drives.

Use the example context clues to figure out the meanings of the italicized words in the following sentences. In each sentence, underline the words that help you figure out the meaning.

1. *Procedural memories* are memories of knowing how—for example, knowing how to comb your hair, use a pencil, or swim.

(Tavris & Wade, *Psychology in Perspective*, Addison Wesley Longman, 1995, p. 304.)

Procedural memories means _____

2. *Visceral* responses—for example, increases in heart rate and perspiration—also accompany emotion.

Visceral means _____

Explanation Clues. Most of the time the context will not give you the exact meaning of all the words you do not know. However, authors will often hint at the meaning of a word by way of explanation. If you understand the explanation, you can use it to figure out the meaning of the word. Look at the following sentence:

The man felt *despondent* because he had lost his home in a fire.

If you think about how you would feel in this situation, you can figure out that *despondent* means discouraged or depressed. The explanation is the fact that the man lost his home in a fire.

Use the explanation context clues to figure out the meanings of the italicized words in the following sentences. In each sentence, underline the words that help you figure out the meaning.

1. In the 1920s, Walter Cannon outlined the first scientific description of the way animals and humans respond to danger. He found that a sequence of activity is triggered in the nerves and glands to prepare the body either to defend itself and struggle or to run away to safety. Cannon called this dual stress response the *fight-or-flight syndrome*.

(Zimbardo & Gerrig, *Psychology and Life*, 14th ed., Longman, 1997, p. 473.)

Fxight-or-flight syndrome means _____

2. Another concept in Maslow's theory is the power of *transcendence*. The key factor in achieving joy is a striving toward something higher. This endeavor is not satisfied merely by "belonging" to a church or joining activists efforts, but must involve meaningful faith that is based on community support, purpose, and hope.

(Zimbardo & Weber, *Psychology,* 2nd ed., Longman, 1997, p. 313.)

Transcendence means _____

Situation Clues. The situation in which a word is used often provides useful clues to its meaning. Indeed, sometimes you need context to understand the meanings of even common words. For example, notice how the meaning of *run* changes in each of these sentences:

1. The man hit a home <u>run</u>.
2. The car has <u>run</u> out of gas.
3. <u>Run</u> home fast or you will be late for dinner.
4. Looks like you have a <u>run</u> in your stocking.

Next time you come across a word you don't know, try to figure out the meaning using the context before you look it up in a dictionary. You may even enjoy your reading more because you will have fewer interruptions.

PRACTICE EXERCISE 3: CONTEXT CLUES

Read the following paragraph. Use the context clues to figure out the meaning of the underlined words. Then, complete the exercise that follows.

<u>Domestic</u> violence takes place in the home between family members. Hitting anyone in your family is a <u>heinous</u> act of violence. Recently, there has been a <u>plethora</u> or large number of reported incidents. Wife beating is a common form of domestic violence. Most men are <u>reticent</u> about their acts of violence because they do not want to be discovered and arrested. Therefore, the police can only <u>speculate</u> about the exact number of cases. Wives often come to the hospital with large numbers of <u>contusions</u> like bloody noses, broken arms, and marks on the scalp. These victims of domestic violence often lie about the cause of these injuries. However, they rarely <u>abscond</u> from their husbands. Most people <u>abnegate</u> their responsibility rather than try to solve this grave problem. Even the police seem <u>skeptical</u> about solving the problem since it is so widespread. Enough <u>insouciance</u>, we need more people to become involved in the fight against domestic violence.

Word	Meaning	Context Clues from Paragraph
domestic		
heinous		
plethora		
reticent		
speculate		
contusions		
abscond		
abnegate		
skeptical		
insouciance		

Definitions

Almost every subject you study in college has its own specialized vocabulary. Because these words will be used throughout the course, it is important for you to recognize and learn these specialized words and their definitions. Often the words are printed in **boldface** or *italics* or they are underlined so that they can be easily identified.

Following is an example of some definitions found in a college textbook on psychology:

A drive is a state of tension, arousal, or activation. Drives based on one's learning experiences are called secondary drives, as opposed to primary drives, which are based on unlearned, physiological needs.

(Gerow, *Essentials of Psychology*, 2nd ed., HarperCollins, 1996, pp. 316–317.)

drive = a state of tension, arousal, or activation
secondary drives = drives based on one's learning experiences
primary drives = drives based on unlearned, physiological needs

PRACTICE EXERCISE 4: DEFINITIONS

Read the following short excerpts and underline the words being defined and their definitions.

1. In psychology, motivation refers to an inferred process within a person (or animal) that causes that organism to move toward a goal. With physiological motives, the goal is to satisfy a biological need, as in eating a sandwich to reduce hunger.

    (Tavris & Wade, *Psychology in Perspective*, HarperCollins, 1995, p. 209.)

2. Emotion is a complex pattern of bodily and mental changes including physiological arousal, feelings, cognitive processes, and behavioral response to a personally significant situation.

    (Zimbardo & Weber. *Psychology*, 2nd ed., Longman, 1997, p. 287.)

3. External stimuli serve as motivating agents or incentives for behavior. Incentives are external events that act to pull our behavior, as opposed to drives, which are internal and push our behavior.

    (Gerow, *Essentials of Psychology*, 2nd ed., HarperCollins, 1996, p. 319.)

4. A <u>locus of control orientation</u> is a belief about whether the outcomes of your actions are contingent on what you do (internal control orientation) or on environmental factors (external control orientation).

    (Zimbardo & Gerrig, *Psychology and Life*, HarperCollins, 1996, p. 451.)

Now that you have learned some prereading strategies to become familiar with a text and understand it better, it's time to practice the skills you've learned.

Application

Textbook Selection 1

MOTIVATION

Before Reading

The first reading selection is from a psychology textbook. It includes an introduction and a discussion about the nature of motivation. Before you begin to read, think about the human needs listed below. Which ones are most important to you?

Number the items from 1 to 5, with 1 being the most important to you and 5 being the least important.

Food _____

Money _____

Love _____

Respect from others _____

Reaching your full potential _____

Why did you consider the item you numbered 1 to be the most important?

_____

_____

As an adult you have developed a number of ideas about how and why people behave as they do. To prepare for reading the excerpt on the topic of motivation, consider your beliefs about each of the following statements. Later on, you can return to this exercise and find out whether your ideas are accurate according to the textbook excerpt.

Check the statements with which you agree.

a. _____ If you were stranded on a desert island, you would be more concerned with finding food than with having money.

b. _____ People are born with certain bodily needs.

c. _____ People are born with the desire to have friends.

d. _____ It's more important to feel safe walking down a street than to be in love with someone.

e. _____ Mountain climbers are more concerned with their safety than with reaching the top of the mountain.

Meet in small groups and discuss your responses to the statements listed above. Explain why you agree or disagree with each statement.

Now, look through the text selection on pages 39 to 49. Fill in this list of the typographical aids you notice.

Typographical Aids

a. headings and subheadings

b.

c.

d. italics

Anything that appears between the chapter title and first major heading can be considered an introduction. You should read the introduction first because this is where the author will try to get you interested in the topic and provide some background information. Before you begin reading, freewriting about the topic will also help you become motivated and interested in your reading. Try it now.

In this freewriting activity, write whatever comes into your mind for one or two minutes in response to the following question. You should not be concerned about grammar, spelling, or punctuation.

Have you ever donated your blood? If you have not, would you consider donating blood? Why or why not?

During Reading

Now read this introduction and think about how Diane's experience relates to yours.

Introduction

1 Diane Green had never given blood before, but the sign on the dorm bulletin board said, "We need blood to help save lives," and Diane told herself, "I should do it. I could help out." After making the initial decision, Diane felt a surge of apprehension. "Will it hurt?" she wondered. A mental image formed of a needle entering her vein and blood being drawn out, and she felt a mounting fear. Nevertheless, she headed for the Bloodmobile.

2 A few minutes later, Diane was reclining in a big padded chair, watching the technician prepare to draw her blood. Her heart raced and her pulse quickened, but

she tried to conceal her fear. After the technician had inserted the needle, Diane's fear gradually subsided. Twenty minutes later the Bloodmobile volunteers thanked her warmly, and Diane felt a glow of pride. It was all she could do to keep from laughing. Six months later—the next time the Bloodmobile came to campus—Diane gave blood again, and afterward she felt the same glow of satisfaction.

1. Why do you think Diane gave blood the first time? Why did she do it again?

   _____

   _____

   _____

   _____

2. In the following paragraph the author defines a word which is printed in **boldface**. Underline both the word and its definition.

3   To answer questions like these, we must enter the realm of **motivation**: our needs and desires to behave in a particular way—whether to eat a meal, start a business, or donate blood. As Diane's story suggests, our motives are closely related to our emotions, or feelings. Emotions, from terror to delight, often motivate our behavior.

3. What might one's motivation be for

   eating a meal? _____

   starting a business? _____

   donating blood? _____

4. Before you read each of the following textbook sections, create a question from each heading and subheading. Write each question on the line provided below the heading.

   Now, read this short textbook selection on the nature of motivation.

4   In trying to solve a crime, a detective begins with the question "What was the motive?" Was the crime committed for revenge, for money, to get someone out of the way, or for a "thrill"? Detectives are not unique in wanting to understand why people do things. We all ask questions and speculate about the underlying *whys* of human behavior—in other words, about motivation.

5   Psychologists have a central concern with unraveling the causes of human behavior. But motives are particular kinds of causes—the needs and desires that

energize and direct our actions (Gold, 1990). Our motives channel our energies into the pursuit of particular goals. When we are hungry, we devote our energy to finding food. When we are motivated to do well on an exam, we will devote hours to studying for it. In this section, we will explore the range of human motives and then look closely at three examples.

The Range of Motives

6   In one sense, the range of human motives is almost limitless. Jim needs new shoes; Terry wants to hike the Appalachian Trail; and Marie is dying to go to business school. But over and above specific needs, desires, and goals, certain general categories of motives underlie human action. Let us consider two broad categories of motives that underlie much of our behavior: physiological motives and social motives.

7   Physiological motives like hunger, thirst, and avoidance of pain are needs that must be satisfied if an organism, whether human or animal, is to survive. These motives are intimately linked to our biological functioning. As Abraham Maslow (1943) observed, when people are very hungry or thirsty, they think about little else but finding something to eat or drink. At such times, other needs—whether for security, love, or competence—become unimportant. But when a person's needs for food and water have been met, other motives—called social motives— take on greater importance. Maslow believed that our motives are organized as a hierarchy of needs, depicted in Figure 2.4. Higher-level needs cannot be addressed until those at the bottom of the hierarchy are met.

8   Social motives, such as desires to spend time with others, to have an impact on others, and to master challenges in order to confirm our personal competence, are needs that grow out of our involvement with other people. We are born with our physiological motives, but we learn our social motives from interaction with others as we grow up. Maslow divided the social and other non-physiological motives into four groups:

Safety needs—needs to feel physically and psychologically secure, including safety from physical danger and the need for economic security.

Love needs—the need to be loved and to be an accepted member of a community of friends.

Esteem needs—needs to achieve, to be competent, and to receive respect and appreciation from others.

Self-actualization needs—the need to fulfill one's own unique potential. "A musician must make music, an artist must paint, a poet must write if he [or she] is to be ultimately happy. What a man [or woman] can be, he [or she] must be" (Maslow, 1954, p. 46).

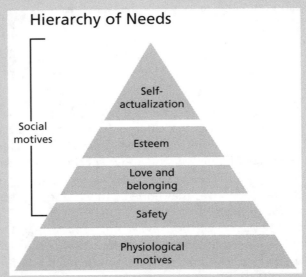

FIGURE 2.4

Physiological and social needs can be arranged in a hierarchy, according to Abraham Maslow. Needs higher in the hierarchy cannot be addressed until the needs at the lower levels of the pyramid are met.

5. Underline information in paragraphs 4 through 8 that supports the following statements:
    a. Physiological motives are innate, while social motives are learned.
    b. Physiological motives must be satisfied before a person can be concerned with social motives.
    c. Motives help us reach for goals.
    d. There are four kinds of social and nonphysiological motives.

6. Write a definition for each of the following words:
    a. physiological needs

    _____

    b. safety needs

    _____

    c. love needs

    _____

d. esteem needs

_____

e. self-actualization needs

_____

7. Can you explain Jimmy's behavior in the following situation in terms of Maslow's hierarchy of needs?

Jimmy, a six-year-old, lives with his parents in a neighborhood where drugs are often sold openly on the streets. About once a month there is a robbery or shooting incident within five blocks of his home. His father recently lost his job and has become severely depressed, often ignoring his son.

Jimmy is having problems in first grade—he fights with his classmates and is not learning to read as fast as his teacher expects him to.

After Reading

Write the question you created from the heading, "The Range of Motives."

_____

In the space below, write an answer to your question.

_____

_____

Textbook Selection 2
EMOTION

Before Reading

The reading selection that follows, "The Nature of Emotion," is from a psychology textbook. The following statements reflect ideas from this selection.

Check the statements with which you agree.

1. _____ Your emotions often make you behave the way you do.

2. _____ Emotions are always accompanied by changes in your body.

3. _____ Emotions are expressed through facial expressions.

4. _____ Your thoughts and emotions are usually consistent.

5. _____ People are born with the same basic emotions.

During Reading

As you read the following textbook excerpt, change each heading into a question and write it on the line below the heading. Look for new words being defined and underline both the words and definitions.

The Nature of Emotion

1   Virtually all of our motivated behavior is influenced by our emotions (Buck, 1988; Carlson & Hatfield, 1992). In the example at the beginning of this chapter, Diane Green's *motivation* to give blood and her *emotions* before, during, and after doing so were closely linked. Feelings of obligation or guilt contributed to her initial decision to donate. Just before the procedure, Diane felt frightened, but she went ahead despite her fear. Afterward, she felt elated and proud. Later, she gave blood again to re-create these good feelings.

2   Sometimes our actions are directly generated by emotion, such as when—all too commonly—anger stirs people to acts of violence. At other times, certain emotions are the *rewards* of motivated behavior. Examples are the pleasure we feel when we are intrinsically motivated by an activity and our pride at knowing that we have contributed to other people's welfare.

3   In this section, we will consider some basic issues concerning the nature of emotion. First we will define the components of emotion. Then we will try to zero in on the "basic" emotions. After that we will consider the extent to which human emotions are innate and universal, as opposed to being products of specific cultures.

The Components of Emotion

---

4   Suppose that, while exploring the distant reaches of the universe, we stumble on a planet occupied by beings much like ourselves, with only one major exception: they are incapable of emotion. They pursue their lives without experiencing joy or sorrow, pleasure or disgust. To us, such a life would seem to have had all the juice wrung out of it—colorless, monotonous, one-dimensional existence.

5   Relating to such beings would be like making friends with a computer or, at best, with Mr. Spock from the old *Star Trek.* The differences between us and these hypothetical extraterrestrials highlight the essential hallmarks of emotion.

6   Emotions have four defining features, all of which would be lacking among these unfeeling beings from outer space:

Subjective experience. An emotion involves a subjective experience or "feeling" of pleasure or displeasure, like or dislike, or arousal. In the last analysis, subjective experiences of this sort are probably the best single way to define emotion. In studying emotion, psychologists must rely heavily on people's subjective accounts of their feelings: "I'm thrilled!" "What a disgusting place!" "Wow!"

Physiological arousal. Emotions are accompanied by physiological changes in our bodies (Stemruler, 1989), sometimes quite dramatic ones. When we are very angry or afraid, our hearts may accelerate from about 72 beats per minute to as many as 180 beats per minute. Our breathing may become rapid and uneven, and our blood pressure may rise alarmingly. The physiological changes that accompany other emotions may be smaller and more subtle.

Expressive behavior. Emotions also involve expressive behaviors, particularly facial *expressions*—the smiles, pouts, and frowns that typically signal a person's experience of a particular emotion (Wagner, 1990). Emotions are also expressed by changes in posture and tone of voice. When we are sad, for example, we tend to slouch and to speak in a lower, less variable pitch than when we are angry or afraid (Sogon & Izard, 1987).

Changes in cognition. Emotions are also accompanied by changes in thoughts. When happy, people become more optimistic and tend to look at the bright side; when sad, people are likely to see the negative sides of situations (Mayer & Salovey, 1988). In general, our thoughts are guided by and consistent with our emotions (Isen, 1987; Schwarz, 1990).

1. Write about a time you experienced each of the following features of emotions.
   a. Subjective experience

   _____

   _____

   b. Physiological arousal

   _____

   _____

   c. Expressive behavior

   _____

   _____

   d. Changes in cognition

   _____

   _____

What Are the Basic Emotions?

7   People experience a rich spectrum of feelings. We speak of feeling ecstatic, depressed, proud, nervous, jealous, guilty, afraid, ashamed, bored, amused, amazed—you can undoubtedly add to the list. What's more, our emotional states often seem to be complex mixtures of more basic emotions. How would you feel, for example, if you received an A in your psychology course but your best friend got a D? You would no doubt be elated about your own grade and sorry for your friend. You might also be a bit embarrassed and worried that your friend will be resentful.

8   Given the complexity of human emotions, psychologists have asked whether a core of "primary emotions" might serve as building blocks of more complex emotions. In this approach, the range of human emotions resembles the range of colors. In other words, are the hundreds of shades of emotion composed of mixtures of a few primary emotions, just as hundreds of colors can be made by mixing different combinations of primary colors (red, blue, and yellow)?

9   According to some theorists, the "primary emotions" are those for which distinctive facial expressions have evolved over the course of human evolution. Proponents of this view, including Carroll Izard (1977) and Paul Ekman (Ekman, Friesen, & Ellsworth, 1982), suggest that there are from six to ten primary emotions. Nearly all theorists agree on six: joy, surprise, sadness, anger, disgust, and fear. Debate continues about a seventh emotion, contempt (Ekman & Friesen, 1988). Meanwhile, some researchers reject the concept of basic emotions altogether (Ortony & Turner, 1990).

10   Other theorists propose that human emotions are characterized by two dimensions, pleasant/unpleasant and aroused/calm (see Figure 2.5), and that every emotion falls into one or another of four possible categories: pleasant/aroused, pleasant/calm, unpleasant/aroused, and unpleasant/calm (Watson & Clark, 1991). Fear, for example, is a combination of unpleasant and aroused, and sadness is a combination of unpleasant and calm. People who are asked "How are you feeling?" seem to consider both of these dimensions—how *pleasant* they feel and how *aroused* they feel—before answering (Russell, Weiss, & Mendelsohn, 1989).

2. Divide into small groups of three to five students. To find out how well you can communicate your emotions and "read" other's emotions through facial expressions, take turns making a facial expression of each basic emotion. Write the results and conclusions and report them to the class.

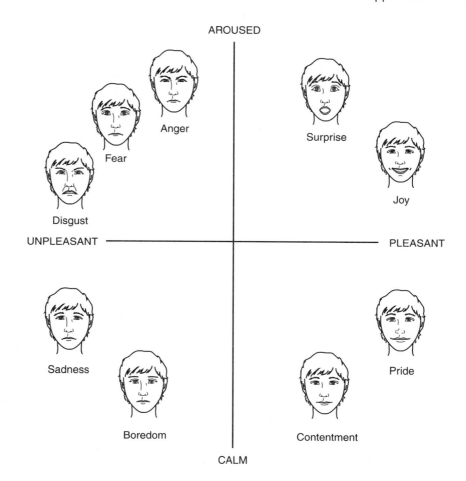

FIGURE 2.5
A two-dimensional view of emotion. According to this theory, different emotions can best be understood by considering whether each one is pleasant or unpleasant, arousing or calming.

Are Emotions Universal and Innate?

11 In what ways are emotions common to people throughout the world, and in what ways are they specific to a particular culture? Most research on this question has focused on facial expressions as indicators of emotion. For example, does a smile mean pleasure and a frown mean displeasure in all cultures, or do facial expressions depend on the conventions of a particular society? If the same facial

expressions are associated with the same feelings for all human beings, it can be argued that our basic emotions are likely innate—that they are biologically "wired in" to all human beings.

12   Charles Darwin speculated over a century ago that our expressions of emotion are a part of our evolutionary heritage and thus common to all human beings. In *The Expression of Emotions in Man and Animals*, Darwin (1872) suggested that facial expression was our ancestors' primary mode of communication before the development of language. Anger, for example, prompted our forebears to scowl and bare their teeth, warning their enemies that they were ready to bite. We still bare our teeth when we are angry, though we rarely bite our enemies. Similarly, positive emotional expressions, such as smiling, evolved as a means to promote cooperation between individuals.

3. What does "scowl" mean, as used in paragraph 12?

_____

13   The evidence supports Darwin's contention that particular modes of emotional expression are inborn characteristics of the human species. When showed posed photographs of facial expressions representing six basic emotions—joy, surprise, sadness, anger, disgust, and fear—a large majority of people worldwide identified the emotions accurately (Ekman, 1975; Ekman & Friesen, 1986). To assess the possibility that the subjects responded similarly because they had all been exposed to Western culture, Ekman and his associates (Ekman, Sorenson, & Friesen, 1969; Ekman & others, 1987) found a group of people, the Fore, in the Southeast Highlands of New Guinea, who were almost totally isolated from Western culture. The researchers showed their Fore informants photographs of white Americans expressing three different emotions. Then they described a situation, in the Fore language, and asked their informants to select the facial expression that fit the situation: for instance, "A wild pig is standing in the door of the house, and the woman is looking at the pig and is very afraid of it." The result? The isolated New Guinea tribespeople made essentially the same links between emotions and facial expressions as do Westerners. Ekman and his team also asked the Fore informants to demonstrate how *they* would look if they were in the situations described in the stories. The researchers photographed the tribespeople's expressions and asked American college students to identify them. The American students understood Fore face language almost perfectly, just as the Fore subjects had understood American face language. Ekman's research strongly suggests that the links between basic emotions and facial expressions are innate.

14   Studies of infants suggest that a range of distinctive emotional expressions—joy, surprise, disgust, and distress (a mixture of sadness, anger, and fear)—is present at birth (Fogel & Reimers, 1989). By the time infants are 8 or 9 months old,

they seem to express, distinctively and in appropriate circumstances, eight different emotions (Grunau & Craig, 1987). Even blind infants, who have never seen a human face, display these basic emotions in the same ways (Eibl-Eibesfeldt, 1970). Since blind infants cannot learn facial expressions by imitation, their expressions presumably reflect an inborn disposition.

15   The evidence from different cultures and from studies of infants converges to suggest that certain basic aspects of our emotional patterns are universal and inborn (Izard, 1978; Izard & others, 1980). Babies in Boston and in Borneo seem to come into the world equipped with the same set of emotions and the same ways of expressing them. In fact, all human beings appear to share a biological program linking specific facial muscles with specific emotions (Rinn, 1984). At the same time, it is clear that culture and environment also influence our emotions—that is, the specific things that elate, surprise, or enrage us depend to a large extent on what we learn. Although the capacity to experience fear is innate, people fear different things as a result of their personal experiences, their families, and their cultures (Mauro, Sato, & Tucker, 1992). In some societies people fear ghosts and demons; in others people fear soldiers; in still others people fear nuclear accidents. The same is true of the things that elate, depress, surprise, enrage, scare, and disgust us. In addition, the specific terms we use to express our feelings vary from culture to culture.

(Rubin, Zick, Letitia Peplau, & Peter Salovey. *Psychology.*
NJ: Houghton Mifflin, 1993, pp. 366–370.)

After Reading

1. Write for a few minutes about an experience when you showed a lot of emotion.

Identify and list the emotions which you experienced. Using the table below, categorize your list into pleasant, unpleasant, aroused, and calm emotions.

Pleasant	Unpleasant	Aroused	Calm

2. Meet in small groups. Using the categories above, make a list that includes the emotions identified by all group members.

   Do you think that each emotion on your list is universal or learned as a result of experience? Explain your answer, based on what you have read in the text on emotion.

   _____

   _____

   _____

   _____

3. Following are some statements that express important points from the preceding selection. Match each statement with the correct paragraph by writing your answer on the line next to each paragraph number. Paragraph numbers may be used more than once.

Paragraph Number	**Statements**
9 _____	a. The specific situations that provoke emotions and the words we use to express our feelings may vary a lot from culture to culture.
10 _____	b. Ekman and Izard have identified six primary emotions, based on distinctive facial expressions.
13 _____	c. Modern research has supported Darwin's contention that particular facial expressions of emotion are inborn characteristics of the human species.
14 _____	d. All infants come into the world equipped with the same basic set of emotions.
15 _____	e. One approach to classifying emotions is along two dimensions: pleasant/unpleasant and aroused/calm.
16 _____	f. All strong emotions appear to be accompanied by physiological changes.
	g. Research has shown that even people in remote cultures can recognize the emotions expressed in American photographs.

4. In this exercise you will use the triple-entry journal technique to respond to what you have read.

Write a triple-entry journal using paragraphs 11 through 15. Fold your paper into three columns. In the left column, "What I Read," write key words, phrases, or sentences from the text which surprised, confused, or interested you. In the middle column, "What I Think," write your thoughts about the text you copied on the left side. Then exchange papers with another student. In the third column, "Response," write your reaction to whatever the student wrote in his or her middle column.

5. Topics for Writers

Write for a few minutes in response to each of the questions below.

1) What are some of the ways members of your family show emotions?
2) How do you respond physically when you experience emotions of joy and sadness?

Additional Reading 1

THE PARING KNIFE

Michael Oppenheimer

Before Reading

1. Following are several quotations. After discussing the meaning of each with classmates, check the ones with which you agree.

Quotation   **I Agree**

"Better by far you should forget and smile
Than that you should remember and be sad."
(Christina Georgina Rossetti, in *Remember*, 1862)

"Perhaps someday it will be pleasant to remember even this."
(Virgil, 70–19 B.C., in *Aenid*, bk. I, line 203)

"If you remember'st not the slightest folly
That ever love did make thee run into,
Thou hast not loved."
(William Shakespeare, *As You Like It*, act II, scene iv)

2. Working with several other students, discuss your reasons for agreeing or disagreeing with each quote.

During Reading

A paring knife is a small knife used to peel fruits and vegetables. Read the following story, "The Paring Knife," to find out what part a paring knife played in the lives of two people.

1   I found a knife under the refrigerator while the woman I love and I were cleaning our house. It was a small paring knife that we lost many years before and had since forgotten about. I showed the knife to the woman I love and she said, "Oh. Where did you find it?" After I told her, she put the knife on the table and then went into the next room and continued to clean. While I cleaned the kitchen floor, I remembered something that happened four years before that explained how the knife had gotten under the refrigerator.

2   We had eaten a large dinner and had drunk many glasses of wine. We turned all the lights out, took our clothing off, and went to bed. We thought we would make love, but something happened and we had an argument while making love. We had never experienced such a thing. We both became extremely angry. I said some very hurtful things to the woman I love. She kicked at me in bed and I got out and went into the kitchen. I fumbled for a chair and sat down. I wanted to rest my arms on the table and then rest my head in my arms, but I felt the dirty dishes on the table and they were in the way. I became incensed. I swept everything that was on the table onto the floor. The noise was tremendous, but then the room was very quiet and I suddenly felt sad. I thought I had destroyed everything. I began to cry. The woman I love came into the kitchen and asked if I was all right. I said, "Yes." She turned the light on and we looked at the kitchen floor. Nothing much was broken, but the floor was very messy. We both laughed and then went back to bed and made love. The next morning we cleaned up the mess, but obviously overlooked the knife.

3   I was about to ask the woman I love if she remembered that incident when she came in from the next room and without saying a word, picked up the knife from the table and slid it back under the refrigerator.

(From James Thomas & D. Thomas (eds.), *Flash Fiction*, New York, NY: W.W. Norton, 1992. *Sundog*, vol. 4, no. 1, 1982.)

After Reading

1. **Comprehension Check**

—— 1) The man and woman in the story have lived together at least
   a. many years.
   b. four years.
   c. a few months.
   d. not enough information given.

_____ 2) The man and woman had a fight about
     a. making love.
     b. drinking too many glasses of wine.
     c. the woman kicking the man in bed.
     d. not enough information given.

_____ 3) The man pushed the dishes onto the floor because
     a. they had not been washed.
     b. they were in the way.
     c. he was drunk.
     d. he didn't see them there.

4) Reread the story and underline all the words that indicate the characters are experiencing emotion. Compare your choices with that of another student.

5) In your opinion, what was the woman's motivation for sliding the knife back under the refrigerator?

_____

_____

_____

_____

6) What does "incensed" mean as used in the second paragraph?

_____

7) What does the paring knife represent in this story?

_____

_____

_____

_____

2. Discuss your answers to the following questions with other students in a small group or with the entire class.

1) Look back at the quotations at the beginning of this section. Which of the two characters would agree with each statement? Why?

2) What is your opinion of the way the characters in this story reacted to the argument they had four years earlier? In what other ways could the characters have responded to the argument?

3) What do you think the couple's argument of four years ago was about?

4) Pretend you are one of the characters in the story. How might you have handled the situation differently?

3. Memories are often accompanied by emotions.

    1) In your journal, create a map by brainstorming about specific events you remember from your past.

    2) Choose one of the memories you put in your map that you would like to think more about. Freewrite about this memory and the emotions you feel when you think about that memory.

Additional Reading 2

UNFAIR GAME

Susan Jacoby

Before Reading

Meet in small groups to discuss the following questions:

1. Do you think you have been treated unfairly by the opposite sex in certain circumstances because of your gender? Describe your experiences.
2. What are some of the different ways in which men and women are treated differently in our society?

During Reading

In the following article, Susan Jacoby, a newspaper reporter who writes about the rights of women, describes how she handled two situations in which she felt she was mistreated by the opposite sex.

VOCABULARY	
Word	**Definition**
engrossed (1)	very interested
explicit (3)	clearly expressed
flaw (7)	defect or fault
terse (9)	brief, concise
ostentatious (9)	excessive display
crucial (15)	very important, critical
demure (17)	shy and modest
modicum (18)	small quantity
whiling (19)	passing time pleasantly

1   My friend and I, two women obviously engrossed in conversation, are sitting at a corner table in the crowded Oak Room of the Plaza at ten o'clock on a Tuesday night. A man materializes and interrupts us with the snappy opening line, "A good woman is hard to find."

2   We say nothing, hoping he will disappear back into his bottle. But he fancies himself as our genie and asks, "Are you visiting?" Still we say nothing. Finally my friend looks up and says, "We live here." She and I look at each other, the thread of our conversation mapped, our thoughts focused on how to get rid of this intruder. In a minute, if something isn't done, he will scrunch down next to me on the banquette and start offering to buy us drinks.

3   "Would you leave us alone, please," I say in a loud but reasonably polite voice. He looks slightly offended but goes on with his bright social patter. I become more explicit. "We don't want to talk to you, we didn't ask you over here, and we want to be alone. Go away." This time he directs his full attention to me—and he is mad. "All right, all right, *excuse me.*" He pushes up the corners of his mouth in a Howdy Doody smile. "You ought to try smiling. You might even be pretty if you smiled once in a while."

4   At last the man leaves. He goes back to his buddy at the bar. I watch them out of the corner of my eye, and he gestures angrily at me for at least fifteen minutes. When he passes our table on the way out of the room, this well-dressed, obviously affluent man mutters, "Good-bye, bitch," under his breath.

5   Why is this man calling me names? Because I have asserted my right to sit at a table in a public place without being drawn into a sexual flirtation. Because he has been told, in no uncertain terms, that two attractive women prefer each other's company to his.

6   This sort of experience is an old story to any woman who travels, eats, or drinks—for business or pleasure—without a male escort. In Holiday Inns and at the Plaza, on buses and airplanes, in tourist and first class, a woman is always thought to be looking for a man in addition to whatever else she may be doing. The man who barged in on us at the bar would never have broken into the conversation of two men, and it goes without saying that he wouldn't have imposed himself on a man and a woman who were having a drink. But two women at a table are an entirely different matter. Fair game.

7   This might be viewed as a relatively small flaw in the order of the universe—something in a class with an airline losing luggage or a computer fouling up a bank statement. Except a computer doesn't foul up your bank account every month and an airline doesn't lose your suitcase every time you fly. But if you are an independent woman, you have to spend a certain amount of energy, day in and day out, in order to go about your business without being bothered by strange men.

8   On airplanes, I am a close-mouthed traveler. As soon as the "No Smoking" sign is turned off, I usually pull some papers out of my briefcase and start working. Work helps me forget that I am scared of flying. When I am sitting next to a woman, she quickly realizes from my monosyllabic replies that I don't want to chat during the flight. Most men, though, are not content to be ignored.

9   Once I was flying from New York to San Antonio on a plane that was scheduled to stop in Dallas. My seatmate was an advertising executive who kept questioning me about what I was doing and who remained undiscouraged by my terse replies until I ostentatiously covered myself with a blanket and shut my eyes. When the plane started its descent into Dallas, he made his move.

10   "You don't really have to get to San Antonio today, do you?"

11   "Yes."

12   "Come on, change your ticket. Spend the evening with me here. I'm staying at a wonderful hotel, with a pool, we could go dancing . . ."

13   "No."

14   "Well, you can't blame a man for trying."

15   I do blame a man for trying in this situation—for suggesting that a woman change her work and travel plans to spend a night with a perfect stranger in whom she had displayed no personal interest. The "no personal interest" is crucial; I wouldn't have blamed the man for trying if I had been stroking his cheek and complaining about my dull social life.

16   There is a nice postscript to this story. Several months later, I was walking my dog in Carl Schurz Park when I ran into my erstwhile seatmate, who was taking a stroll with his wife and children. He recognized me, all right, and was trying to avoid me when I went over and courteously reintroduced myself. I reminded him that we had been on the same flight to Dallas. "Oh yes," he said. "As I recall you were going on to somewhere else." "San Antonio," I said. "I was in a hurry that day."

17   The code of feminine politeness, instilled in girlhood, is no help in dealing with the unwanted approaches of strange men. Our mothers didn't teach us to tell a man to get lost; they told us to smile and hint that we'd be just delighted to spend time with the gentleman if we didn't have other commitments. The man in the Oak Room bar would not be put off by a demure lowering of eyelids; he had to be told, roughly and loudly, that his presence was a nuisance.

18   Not that I am necessarily against men and women picking each other up in public places. In most instances, a modicum of sensitivity will tell a woman or a man whether someone is open to approaches.

19   Mistakes can easily be corrected by the kind of courtesy so many people have abandoned since the "sexual revolution." One summer evening, I was whiling away a half hour in the outdoor bar of the Stanhope Hotel. I was alone, dressed up, having a drink before going on to meet someone in a restaurant. A man at the next

table asked, "If you're not busy, would you like to have a drink with me?" I told him I was sorry but I would be leaving shortly. "Excuse me for disturbing you," he said, turning back to his own drink. Simple courtesy. No insults and no hurt feelings.

20   One friend suggested that I might have avoided the incident in the Oak Room by going to the Palm Court instead. It's true that the Palm Court is a traditional meeting place for unescorted ladies. But I don't like violins when I want to talk. And I wanted to sit in a large, comfortable leather chair. Why should I have to hide among the potted palms to avoid men who think I'm looking for something else?

(*New York Times*, January 26, 1978.)

After Reading

1.   Comprehension Check

_____ 1) In the first two paragraphs, what is the author suggesting about the man's motive for interrupting the conversation of the two women?
   a. He wanted to bother the women.
   b. Since he thought they were visiting, he wanted to show them around the town.
   c. He wanted to pay for their drinks.
   d. He thought the women wished for his company.

2) What is the writer implying by putting the words, "excuse me," into italics in paragraph 3?

_____

_____

3) What does "affluent" mean as used in paragraph 4? How does the author know that this man is affluent?

_____

_____

4) What does the author mean by "fair game" in paragraph 6?

_____

_____

_____ 5) According to the author in paragraph 8, the difference between men and women is
   a. women are scared of flying and men are not.
   b. women like to work and men do not.
   c. women don't like to chat during a flight and men do.
   d. women understand when someone does not want to talk and men do not.

_____ 6) What was the author's motive for reintroducing herself to the man from the airplane in paragraph 16?
   a. She wanted to get revenge.
   b. She forgot to get his name.
   c. She was happy to see someone she had met on an airplane.
   d. She wanted to meet his wife and children.

7) True _____ or False _____ The author's opinion of the "sexual revolution" is negative. Support your answer.

_____

_____

8) According to the author, what is the solution to the problem of men trying to pick up women?

_____

_____

_____ 9) From this article you can conclude that the author is trying to
   a. get back at men.
   b. be assertive.
   c. solve the problems between the sexes.
   d. travel alone.

2. **Topics for Writers**
    In your journal, write about one of the following topics:

    1) Write about a time you found it difficult but rewarding to assert yourself. What were the circumstances? What were the consequences of your actions?

    2) Write about a time you did not assert yourself but wished you had. Describe the circumstances and the consequences of your actions.

    3) What is your definition of independence? Do you feel independent in your life now? What factors contribute to the way you feel?

    4) Write about a time someone intruded upon you. What did you do? What were your feelings at the time? What would you do differently today?

Chapter Summary

Reading Strategies	In this chapter you learned some important strategies to prepare for reading.
Prior Knowledge	Prior knowledge is what you already know about a topic. Recalling prior knowledge makes reading easier.
Surveying	You can survey headings and subheadings to become familiar with the material before you begin reading.
Outlining	Outlining helps you see the text as a whole. It shows you how all of the pieces of text fit together.
Questioning before You Read	Questioning helps you focus and understand better.
Writing Strategies	In this chapter you learned important strategies to help you write more effectively.
Discovering Topics	You can discover topics to write about by responding to something you have read or by using quotations.
Discovering Ideas	To discover ideas on your chosen topic, you can freewrite or brainstorm by listing or mapping.
Improving Your Vocabulary	Various types of context clues were introduced to help you unlock the meaning of new words. Also, you learned to recognize important definitions found in textbooks.

 **Journal**

In the space below, write about one new thing that you found interesting in this chapter. Why do you think you remember that particular thing?

_____

_____

_____

_____

_____

_____

_____

_____

_____

_____

_____

_____

_____

_____

_____

_____

_____

_____

_____

_____

_____

_____

_____

Go Electronic!

For additional readings, exercises, and Internet activities, visit the Longman English pages at:

http://longman.awl.com/englishpages

If you need a user name and password, please see your instructor.

Take a Road Trip to the Grand Canyon and the Library of Congress

Be sure to visit the Reading Textbooks and Vocabulary modules in your Reading Road Trip CD-ROM for multimedia tutorials, exercises, and tests.

Practice Your Writing Skills

For additional practice with your writing skills, use the Writer's ToolKit CD-ROM included with this text.

CHAPTER 3

Working with Topics and Main Ideas

Theme: Physiological Needs

What You Will Find in This Chapter

- Topics and Main Ideas for Readers
- Writing Paragraphs
- Textbook Selection 1: The Psychology of Eating
- Textbook Selection 2: Weight Management
- Textbook Selection 3: Eating Disorders
- Textbook Selection 4: Sleep and Dreaming
- Additional Reading: "To Sleep, Perchance to Stay Awake in Class"

Here is an excerpt from a conversation between Gloria Cahill, a writer for *Radiance*, a magazine for large women, and Rosie O'Donnell, a talk show host who has starred in major films. In this conversation Rosie O'Donnell reveals her feelings about her weight.

GLORIA: Did you have any problems with your own self-image when you were growing up?

ROSIE: No, I wasn't really heavy until I was older. I was the homecoming queen. I was on every sports team. I was the senior class president. I was very popular in high school. It wasn't until I became an adult and wasn't doing as many sports that my weight became more of an issue. As I grew up emotionally, all of the issues surrounding weight that deal with emotions came to the forefront for me. As I became a grown-up, I had to deal with these issues, and with them came weight, because the way that people deal with problems is often with food, which is a symptom of another thing.

(www.radiancemagazine.com\rosie.html.)

What do you think Rosie meant by ". . . the way that people deal with problems is often with food, which is a symptom of another thing"?

_____

_____

_____

_____

_____

_____

_____

_____

In this chapter you will read about nutrition, weight management, eating disorders, sleep, and dreaming from a health science textbook and a psychology textbook. Also, you will learn some strategies to help you better understand and remember what you read. You will also find ways to organize what you write. These strategies involve

- recognizing topics and main ideas as a reader
- recognizing paragraph patterns
- generating topics and main ideas as a writer

An additional reading is a newspaper article about students' sleep needs.

Topics and Main Ideas for Readers

When you read, it is essential to know the topic of the selection—what the selection is about. The topic can usually be stated in just one or a few words and is usually repeated or referred to frequently throughout the selection. The selection may be as short as a paragraph or as long as an essay or novel.

If you understand what the author wants you to know, in general, about the topic, you understand the author's main idea. Whether or not the author states the main idea directly in a sentence, the author is always trying to make a point about the topic. A goal of reading is to get the author's message, the main idea.

Identifying Topics

As we explained in Chapter 2, you can usually identify the topic of what you will be reading from the title or headings. Topics are general; they are broad enough to include specific ideas. For example, a reading on the general topic of emotion may include additional information on specific emotions, such as joy, surprise, sadness, and anger.

PRACTICE EXERCISE 1: IDENTIFYING TOPICS

In each group below, check the topic. This will be the most general term and will include the other items in the group.

1. _____ food

   _____ dessert

   _____ ice cream

   _____ soup

2. _____ vitamins

   _____ nutrition

   _____ carbohydrates

   _____ protein

3. _____ causes of obesity

   _____ heredity

   _____ external factors

   _____ poor health

4. _____ height

   _____ weight

   _____ physical appearance

   _____ eye color

5. _____ emotions

   _____ sadness

   _____ anger

   _____ crying

6. _____ forced vomiting

   _____ eating too much

   _____ eating too little

   _____ eating disorders

7. _____ survival

_____ eating

_____ sleeping

_____ drinking

8. _____ nightmares

_____ sleep disturbances

_____ insomnia

_____ snoring

9. _____ hunger

_____ thirst

_____ human drives

_____ sleep

10. _____ lunch

_____ breakfast

_____ bacon and eggs

_____ meals

PRACTICE EXERCISE 2: PROVIDING TOPICS

For each group below, write a word or phrase that describes the topic of the list.

1. Topic _____

carbohydrates

sugar

protein

fat

2. Topic _____

chemistry

psychology

biology

history

3. Topic _____

going to a party

studying for an exam

playing basketball

watching television

4. Topic _____

fork

plate

tablecloth

spoon

5. Topic _____

comedy

tragedy

musical

drama

6. Topic _____

east

west

south

up

7. Topic _____

novel

bible

dictionary

encyclopedia

8. Topic _____

hospital

college dormitory

library

supermarket

9. Topic _____   10. Topic _____

computer operator   soccer

nurse   baseball

musician   football

travel agent   swimming

The following paragraph comes from a nutrition chapter in a health textbook. Read it and determine the topic by asking yourself the question, **"What is this mainly about?"**

Food is part of everyday life, whether we are socializing with friends over meals, gathering with family for the holidays, or discussing a business proposition over lunch. Certain foods may even trigger memories, good or bad, of certain events from our childhood. You can even improve the quality of your life by eating healthy food. Food is essential to life.

What is the topic of this paragraph? You know that it is about food because the word *food* is repeated many times and is the issue being discussed throughout the paragraph.

PRACTICE EXERCISE 3: IDENTIFYING TOPICS IN PARAGRAPHS

Choose the topic of each paragraph from the list below it.

1   Responsiveness is the ability to detect and respond to changes in the external environment (the environment outside the body) or internal environment (the environment inside the body). Different cells detect different changes and respond in characteristic ways. For example, neurons (nerve cells) respond by generating electrical signals, known as nerve impulses, sometimes carrying them over long distances, such as between your big toe and your brain.

(Tortora, *Introduction to the Human Body,* HarperCollins, 1994, p. 5.)

   a. cells
   b. responsiveness
   c. nerve impulses
   d. the environment

2   Homeostasis may be disturbed by stress, which is any stimulus that creates an imbalance in the internal environment. The stress may come from the external environment in the form of stimuli such as heat, cold, or lack of oxygen. Or the stress may originate within the body in the form of stimuli such as high blood pressure, tumors, or unpleasant thoughts. Most stresses are mild and routine. Extreme

stress might be caused by poisoning, overexposure to temperature extremes, and surgical operations.

(Tortora, *Introduction to the Human Body,* HarperCollins, 1994, p. 5.)

   a. stimuli
   b. homeostasis
   c. imbalance
   d. stress

3   Nutrients are chemical substances in food that provide energy, form new body components, or assist in the functioning of various body processes. The six principal classes of nutrients are carbohydrates, lipids, proteins, minerals, vitamins, and water. Carbohydrates, proteins, and lipids are digested by enzymes in the gastrointestinal tract. Some of the end products of digestion are used to synthesize new structural molecules in cells or new regulatory molecules, such as hormones and enzymes. Most are used to produce energy to sustain life processes.

(Tortora, *Introduction to the Human Body,*
HarperCollins, 1994, p. 440.)

   a. life processes
   b. nutrients
   c. carbohydrates
   d. digestion

4   Most vitamins cannot be synthesized by the body; they must be ingested in foods or pills. (Vitamin D is an example of a vitamin made by the skin.) Other vitamins, such as vitamin K, are produced by bacteria in the gastrointestinal tract. The body can assemble some vitamins if the raw materials called provitamins are provided. Vitamin A is produced by the body from the provitamin carotene, a chemical present in spinach, carrots, liver, and milk. No single food contains all the required vitamins—one of the best reasons for eating a balanced diet.

(Tortora, *Introduction to the Human Body,*
HarperCollins, 1994, p. 448.)

   a. provitamins
   b. a balanced diet
   c. carotene
   d. vitamins

5   Exercise is any muscular activity that maintains fitness. Exercise, especially running, tends to increase muscle mass and bone density. When you ask people who exercise regularly how they have benefitted, they usually say that it makes them feel better. Whether exercise is moderate or vigorous, feeling better and having an improved sense of satisfaction provides more drive and zest for life. Exercise has both psychological and physical benefits.

(Byer & Schainberg, *Living Well,* HarperCollins,
1995, p. 333, adapted.)

a. fitness
b. exercise
c. running
d. psychological and physical benefits

6   A person's body composition is affected by aerobic exercise, those continuous exercises involving major muscle groups and requiring oxygen, such as swimming, fast walking, jogging, and fast bicycling. Exercise alters a person's metabolism, causing increases in daily energy expenditures, even while resting. In fact, vigorous exercise speeds up the rate of metabolism by about 5 percent for as long as two days after the exercise has taken place. An aerobic exercise program results in an increase in lean body mass and a decrease in body fat.
(Byer & Shainberg, *Living Well*, HarperCollins, 1995, p. 333, adapted.)

a. body composition
b. metabolism
c. aerobic exercise
d. major muscle groups

7   People are increasingly concerned about food safety, and matters such as food-borne illnesses, environmental contaminants, natural toxicants in foods, pesticides, and food additives. Moving the food from the field to processors, stores, and onto your table requires a vast network. Public agencies monitor this huge network.
(Byer & Shainberg, *Living Well*, HarperCollins, 1995, p. 289.)

a. food safety
b. public agencies
c. food-borne illnesses
d. pesticides

8   Health is a cultural concept that is defined differently in different cultures. The prevailing definition of health has evolved from the "absence of illness" to the broader term, wellness, with its definition as "a life-style that emphasizes such health-promoting behaviors as eating a healthful diet, avoiding harmful substances, enjoying regular exercise, and cultivating self-esteem."
(Byer & Shainberg, *Living Well*, HarperCollins, 1995, p. 23.)

a. cultural concepts
b. definition of health
c. cultivating self-esteem
d. eating a healthful diet

9   Stress management begins with adopting the philosophy that you, as an individual, are basically responsible for your own emotional and physical well-being. You can no longer allow other people to determine whether or not you are happy.

> You have little control over the behavior of anyone but yourself. Your goal should be to develop such positive emotional wellness that nobody can ruin your day.
>
> (Byer & Shainberg, *Living Well*, HarperCollins, 1995, p. 87.)

a. emotional wellness
b. goals
c. being responsible
d. behavior

10 Suppose we asked you to keep track of all the emotions you experience in the course of a day. You might report that for brief periods you felt happiness, sadness, anger, relief, and so on. There is one emotion, however, that people often report as a kind of background noise for much of their day-to-day experience, and that is stress. Modern industrialized society sets a rapid, hectic pace for living. People often have too many demands placed on their time, are worried about uncertain futures, and have little time for family and fun. But would you be better off without stress? A stress-free life would offer no challenge—no difficulties to surmount, no new fields to conquer, and no reasons to sharpen your wits or improve your abilities.

(Zimbardo & Gerrig, *Psychology and Life*, 14th ed., HarperCollins, 1996, p. 472, adapted.)

a. emotions
b. modern society
c. stress
d. challenges

Identifying Main Ideas

The main idea expresses the most important point about the topic. It is a general idea supported by all the sentences in the paragraph. You can recognize the main idea of any paragraph by asking yourself the question:

What is the author saying, in general, about the topic?

The main idea about the topic is often expressed in a main idea sentence somewhere in the paragraph.

Earlier in the chapter you found the topic of the paragraph below. Now, reread it and underline the sentence you think best expresses the main idea.

Food is part of everyday life, whether we are socializing with friends over meals, gathering with family for the holidays, or discussing a business proposition over lunch. Certain foods may even trigger memories, good or bad, of certain events from our childhood. You can even improve the quality of your life by eating healthy food. Food is essential to life.

(Byer & Shainberg, *Living Well*, HarperCollins, 1995, p.256, adapted.)

Do all of the other sentences in the paragraph support the sentence you underlined? The last sentence in the paragraph is the main idea sentence—it expresses the main idea of the paragraph.

The main idea sentence may appear anywhere in the paragraph, although it is often the first or last sentence. Sometimes the main idea is given in more than one sentence, and sometimes it is only part of a sentence. In the previous example, the main idea is also stated in the beginning of the first sentence, "Food is part of everyday life. . . ." In some paragraphs, the main idea may not be stated at all, in which case you must express it in your own words.

Main Idea Sentence at the Beginning. In some paragraphs, the author states the main idea at the beginning of the paragraph and then supports it with details. Thus the paragraph starts out with a general idea and gets more specific as the author provides more information about the main idea. Here is an example:

Water is one of the most essential nutrients in the body. It is a major component of all body fluids, as well as a solvent that distributes nutrients throughout the body and eliminates waste products. Water also plays a major role in regulating body temperature, maintaining the body's acid-base balance, and taking part in every chemical reaction that occurs in the body.

(Byer & Shainberg, *Living Well*, HarperCollins, 1995, p. 274, adapted.)

Notice that the first sentence contains the topic and main idea. It contains the topic, *water*, and the message that *water is one of the most essential nutrients in the body.* The other sentences in the paragraph tell you more specific information about water. They are supporting details that show the essential functions of water in the body.

Main Idea Sentence at the End. Sometimes an author states the main idea at the end of a paragraph. Here the author starts out with specific information and ends with a general idea. This pattern is useful when the author wants to support or emphasize an idea before it is stated. An example:

When you think about your diet you probably do so in terms of the foods you like to eat—a turkey sandwich and a glass of milk or a steak and a baked potato. What's important for your health, though, is the nutrients contained in those foods. Your body requires carbohydrates, proteins, fats, vitamins, minerals, and water—about 45 essential nutrients. Your body obtains these nutrients when the foods you eat are broken down (digested) into compounds that your gastrointestinal tract can absorb and your body can use. *A diet containing adequate amounts of all essential nutrients is vital because nutrients provide energy, help build and maintain body tissues, and help regulate body functions.*

(Insel & Roth. *Core Concepts in Health.* California: Mayfield, 1994, p. 305.)

The topic is *essential nutrients,* and the main idea is that *a diet containing adequate amounts of all essential nutrients is vital.* Notice that the author supports the main idea before it is stated, thereby emphasizing the importance of a good diet.

Main Idea Sentence in the Middle. In some paragraphs the main idea is stated in the middle. Authors often use this pattern when they want to tell you something about the topic before giving the main point and supporting it.

The most important basis for an acceptable weight is the condition of your health. *The ideal is to have enough fat to meet your body's basic needs without developing health risks.* Health problems have been found to develop when body fat exceeds 22 percent in younger men, 25 percent in older men, 32 percent in younger women, and 35 percent in older women. In terms of a health definition, these values also help define obesity.

(Byer & Shainberg, *Living Well: Health in Your Hands,* 2nd ed. HarperCollins, 1995, p. 303, adapted.)

Although it may be tempting to choose the first sentence as the main idea sentence, notice that it does not answer our two questions adequately. First, what is the paragraph *mainly* about? (What is repeated or referred to most often?) It is *body fat.* *Second,* what does the author want us to know in general about body fat? The main idea is that *body fat should not exceed the level at which health problems may develop,* as stated in the second sentence.

In the example above, the first sentence is an *introductory sentence* that introduces the concepts of acceptable weight and health. Introductory sentences can be easily confused with main idea sentences because they are generalizations. However, such sentences tend to be somewhat vague and do not get to the point of the paragraph. Thus, you should carefully evaluate the first sentence of a paragraph before assuming that it is the main idea sentence.

Unstated Main Idea. From time to time the main idea of a paragraph is not stated directly. Authors sometimes avoid main idea sentences when they want readers to put the details together and reach a generalization for themselves. Remember to ask yourself the two questions—What is the paragraph mainly about? What is the author saying, in general, about the topic?—and you will be able to figure out the main idea.

Purging can upset the body's balance of electrolytes (mineral tissue fluids) and lead to abnormal heart rhythms and injury to the kidneys. Kidney and bladder infections can lead to kidney failure. Repeated vomiting may damage the esophagus and stomach and induce bleeding; it may cause receding gums and damage to tooth enamel from the wash of gastric acid.

(Byer & Shainberg, *Living Well: Health in Your Hands,* 2nd ed., HarperCollins, 1995, p. 316, adapted.)

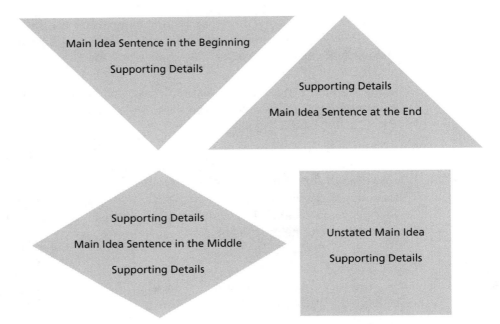

FIGURE 3.1   Paragraph Patterns

What is the paragraph mainly about? *Bulimic purging* (or vomiting) is referred to frequently. What does the author want us to know about purging that is supported by all of the paragraph's details? *Bulimic purging may cause severe harm to the body.* This main idea is supported by the entire paragraph, even though it is not stated directly by the author.

As you can see in Figure 3.1, there are four possible paragraph patterns that depend on the position of the main idea.

TO FIND THE MAIN IDEA ASK YOURSELF THESE QUESTIONS

1. What is the paragraph mainly about?
   (It will be repeated or referred to throughout the paragraph.)
2. What is the author saying, in general, about the topic?
   (It will be supported by the details.)

PRACTICE EXERCISE 4: STATED MAIN IDEAS

Read each of the following paragraphs and underline the main idea sentence.

1   DeAnna Mori, Shelley Chaiken, and Patricia Pliner (1987) discovered that college women—but not men—adjusted their eating depending on their companions.

Men and women in contemporary American society appear to differ in their responses to social signals regarding eating. Women ate less when their eating partners were men than when they were with other women. When the women were seated with attractive, unattached men, they ate especially lightly. The researchers hypothesized that the women may have eaten lightly as a way of demonstrating their femininity to desirable men.

(Rubin, Peplau, & Salovey, *Psychology*, Houghton Mifflin, 1993, p. 360, adapted.)

2   Fat serves as an integral part of cell membranes, nerve tissue, and bone; it helps protect and pad internal organs, such as the kidneys and liver; and makes it more comfortable for sitting, lying down, and keeping warm. A certain amount of body fat is essential.

(Byer & Shainberg, *Living Well*, HarperCollins, 1995, p. 302, adapted.)

3   Research has suggested that people who include fish in their diet have a lower risk of heart disease. Cold water fish such as salmon, mackerel, trout, bluefish, and herring contain omega-3 fatty acids. These fatty acids may prevent heart disease by decreasing the tendency of platelets to clump and perhaps by lowering total serum cholesterol as well.

(Tortora, *Introduction to the Human Body*, HarperCollins, 1994, p. 339.)

4   The biological perspective also teaches us that our bodies and brains need proper care and maintenance to function well. Lack of exercise, irregular sleep habits, or work shifts that interfere with normal biological rhythms can all affect how we function mentally and emotionally in our everyday lives. Even ordinary foods affect our psychological well-being and alertness, because certain nutrients are the precursors, or building blocks, for neurotransmitters (Wurtman, 1982). Because mental functioning and mood involve many different neurotransmitters, restrictive fad diets (the ones that eliminate all protein, or all carbohydrates, or all whatever) are probably a bad idea both in physiological and psychological terms. The best "brain food" and probably the best "mood food," too, is a well-balanced diet.

(Tavris, *Psychology in Perspective*, HarperCollins, 1995, p. 147.)

5   Your body, which was meant to function for a long, vigorous lifetime on healthy foods becomes more and more sensitive to the actions of unhealthy ones. Your metabolism begins to creak and groan. Not only the pounds get added on but also the pains. Crushing fatigue, headaches, lassitude, irritability, depression—these are not really part of the process of reaching middle age, even though in our society they seem to be, largely because of the way we eat.

(Atkins, *Dr. Atkins' New Diet Revolution*, Avon Books, 1992, p. 14.)

6   There is increasing evidence of the importance of the role of aerobic exercise in managing high blood pressure (hypertension). Generally, people who are cardio-vascularly fit have lower blood pressures than people who are unfit. In an 18-year study of exercising and nonexercising people, the exercising group had an average resting blood pressure of 120/79, compared to an average of 150/90 for the nonexercising group.

(Byer & Shainberg, Living Well,
HarperCollins, 1995, p. 335.)

7   Motivating other people to behave in healthful ways is a difficult, if not impos-sible, task. One can inspire motivation, but cannot motivate another person. Thus, it is difficult for physicians to motivate their patients, for drug abuse counselors to motivate their clients, and for health educators to motivate their students. Knowing how to behave healthfully is one thing; doing it is quite another.

(Byer & Shainberg, Living Well,
HarperCollins, 1995, p. 21.)

8   Emotionally healthy people develop effective and appropriate ways of dealing with the frustration of their needs. Like need-fulfillment, this is a learned ability that develops with maturity. Mature people understand that no one can have all of their needs met at all times. They maintain a positive outlook on life, knowing that their frustration is just temporary. They focus on the positive aspects of each life situation, instead of the negative ones. They have learned to talk about their frustrations, rather than bottle them up inside and let them fester. Mature people "work off" their frustrations by being active, rather than by sitting and brooding or by attempting to escape from their frustrations with alcohol or other drugs or, even more commonly, overeating.

(Byer & Shainberg, Living Well,
HarperCollins, 1995, p. 66.)

9   Noise, perhaps the most neglected form of environmental pollution, is one of the most troublesome stressors for many people. Trying to sleep, work, study, or relax in a noisy place mobilizes the body's stress response, with measurable increases in blood pressure, heart rate, and muscle tension. Even though we seem to "get used to" a certain noise, it can still be causing physical changes.

(Byer & Shainberg, Living Well,
HarperCollins, 1995, p. 79.)

10   You may agree that the end of a relationship, an earthquake, or prejudice might cause stress, but what about the smaller stressors you experience on a day-to-day basis? What happened to you yesterday? You probably didn't get a divorce or survive a plane crash. You're more likely to have lost your notes or textbook. Perhaps you were late for an important appointment, or got a parking ticket, or a noisy neighbor ruined your sleep. These are the types of recurring day-to-day stressors that confront most people, most of the time. One analysis suggests that

an accumulation of small frustrations leads to more stress than infrequent big jolts of change do.

(Zimbardo & Gerrig, *Psychology and Life*, 14th ed., HarperCollins, 1996, p. 484.)

PRACTICE EXERCISE 5: UNSTATED MAIN IDEAS

In the following paragraphs, the main ideas are not stated directly. After you read each one, ask yourself the two questions: "What is the paragraph mainly about?" and "What is the author saying, in general, about the topic?" For each paragraph write a main idea sentence.

1   Calcium intake has been the most publicized factor for promoting healthy bones and the one with which Americans are probably most familiar. Several scientific and government groups have recommended increasing calcium intake to prevent osteoporosis, and the calcium supplement industry has not been slow to jump on the bandwagon. A great deal of controversy surrounds the calcium supplementation issue, since studies of whether calcium supplements help prevent or treat osteoporosis have yielded mixed results. Nevertheless, nutritionists still agree that an adequate intake of dietary calcium is important for good health, which includes the growth and maintenance of bone tissue.

(Tortura, *Introduction to the Human Body*, 3rd ed., HarperCollins, 1994, p.109.)

_____

_____

2   The nervous system regulates homeostasis by detecting when the body deviates from its balanced state and then sending messages (nerve impulses) to the proper organs to counteract the stress. The endocrine system is a group of glands that secrete chemical messengers, called hormones, into the blood. Whereas nerve impulses coordinate homeostasis rapidly, hormones work more slowly.

(Tortura, *Introduction to the Human Body*, 3rd ed., HarperCollins, 1994, p.5.)

_____

3   At one time most people thought that being fat was a sign of emotional disturbance; if you were heavy, it was because you hated your mother, or feared intimacy, or were trying to fill an emotional hole in your psyche by loading up on rich desserts. The assumption, of course, was that weight gain was caused by eating too much, an assumption so "obvious" that hardly anyone bothered to test it. But when researchers did put these ideas to the test, they found that fat people were no more and no less emotionally disturbed than average-weight people (Stunkard, 1980). Even more surprising, studies showed that heaviness is not caused by overeating (Bouchard et al., 1990). Some heavy people do eat enormous quantities of food, but so do some very thin people. Some thin people eat

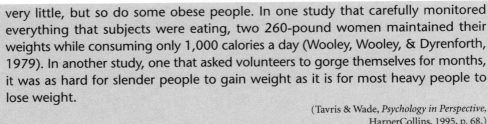

very little, but so do some obese people. In one study that carefully monitored everything that subjects were eating, two 260-pound women maintained their weights while consuming only 1,000 calories a day (Wooley, Wooley, & Dyrenforth, 1979). In another study, one that asked volunteers to gorge themselves for months, it was as hard for slender people to gain weight as it is for most heavy people to lose weight.

(Tavris & Wade, *Psychology in Perspective*,
HarperCollins, 1995, p. 68.)

4   In a recent study, young men who showed evidence of chronic sleepiness (they apparently needed more sleep than they were getting) performed more poorly than other subjects on tasks that required vigilance or divided attention (Roehrs et al., 1990). Laboratory studies and observations of people participating in "wake-athons" have shown that after several days of sleep loss, people become irritable and begin to have hallucinations and delusions (Dement, 1978; Luce & Segal, 1996).

(Tavris & Wade, *Psychology in Perspective*,
HarperCollins, 1995, p. 139.)

5   Reviewing dozens of studies of opportunity and ambition, Rosabeth Kantner (1977/1993) found that men and women who work in dead-end jobs with no prospect of promotion behave the same way. They play down the importance of achievement, fantasize about quitting, or emphasize the social benefits of their jobs instead of the intellectual and financial benefits. Yet if opportunities are created for such people, if the structure of work changes, their motivation often changes too.

(Tavris & Wade, *Psychology in Perspective*,
HarperCollins, 1995, p. 365.)

Writing Paragraphs

A reader *recognizes* topics and main ideas of paragraphs while reading. In contrast, a writer

- chooses a topic to write about
- discovers main ideas

■ writes main idea sentences

■ develops main ideas into paragraphs

We introduced techniques to discover topics and main ideas in Chapters 1 and 2. In this section we introduce the paragraph.

A paragraph consists of a series of sentences that are related to the same topic. Although most writing is made up of many paragraphs, a completed piece of writing may consist of a single paragraph. In any case, a paragraph consists of three types of sentences. They are

■ main idea sentence

■ supporting details

■ concluding sentence

First of all, a paragraph must have a topic and a main idea. The main idea may be stated anywhere in the paragraph or not stated at all. However, it is a common pattern to state your main idea clearly in the first sentence. This helps your reader get the point before reading the supporting details. Second, most of the paragraph is made up of supporting details that describe, explain, or clarify the main idea. Finally, a paragraph usually ends with a final statement that tells the reader the paragraph is finished. If you are writing a single paragraph, it should not just end abruptly.

Here is an example of a paragraph. Notice each of the elements labeled in the margin:

Main Idea Sentence (1)

Supporting Details (2 through 5)

Concluding Sentence (6)

¹Exercising every day is very important. ²First, exercise helps us burn more calories during the day. ³Without exercise most of us will gain weight from even normal eating. ⁴Second, exercise keeps the heart and lungs healthy. ⁵Third, exercise can be fun and entertaining, especially if we play sports. ⁶In short, daily exercise is a key ingredient for a happy and healthy life.

Writing Main Idea Sentences

A main idea sentence is a statement of the main idea, usually found at the beginning of a paragraph. It consists of the topic (what it is about) and the message (a point or opinion concerning the topic). To write a good main idea, ask yourself the following questions:

■ What is my paragraph about? (Topic)

■ What do I want my readers to know about the topic in general? (Message)

A good main idea sentence should be general or broad enough to include all the other sentences in the paragraph. However, it should not be too general or too specific. If it is too general, it will be difficult to support in just one paragraph. If it is too specific, there won't be much more to say about it.

To find a topic, you may use any of the discovery techniques described in Chapters 1 and 2, or your instructor may assign a topic. Let's say your topic is eating disorders. To write a good main idea sentence, ask yourself, "What do I want my readers to know about eating disorders in general?"

One possible main idea sentence about eating disorders is, "People who have an eating disorder should seek professional medical treatment right away." If your main idea sentence was, "Eating disorders are a problem," it would be too general. You would have a difficult time supporting this broad idea in just one paragraph. On the other hand, a main idea sentence such as, "Mary refused to eat because she thought she was too fat," would be too specific. You'd have difficulty supporting it.

Which of the following sentences do you think makes the best main idea sentence?

1. Life is very complicated.
2. I drink four glasses of water each day.
3. Water has several important functions in the human body.

The first sentence is too general. It would be very difficult to support it in a single paragraph. There are too many aspects of life to adequately discuss in one paragraph. The second sentence is too specific. It is a fact that could be used to support a more general idea about water. The third sentence makes a good main idea sentence for a paragraph. It introduces the topic of water and the idea of water's important functions. It is broad enough to be supported by several examples of the important functions of water.

PRACTICE EXERCISE 6: IDENTIFYING MAIN IDEA SENTENCES

For each group below write MI *next to the sentence you think makes the best main idea. Put a* G *next to the sentence that is too general and an* SP *next to the two sentences that are too specific.*

1. _____ a. Walking for twenty minutes a day three times a week strengthens the heart.
   _____ b. Swimming utilizes all the muscles of the body and improves lung capacity.
   _____ c. Exercise is important.
   _____ d. Exercise can contribute to a healthier heart and stronger lungs.

2. _____ a. As a college student there are many appealing courses of study from which to choose.
   _____ b. Computer science programs are increasingly popular.
   _____ c. Child care and teaching appeal to a large number of students.
   _____ d. Many high school students attend college.

3. _____ a. Carbohydrates are a good source of the energy the body needs.
   _____ b. Nutrients are found in the foods we eat and are needed by the body to maintain life.

_____ c. Food is an essential element of life.

_____ d. Proteins are used by the body in more ways than any other nutrient.

4. _____ a. To feel your best, aerobic exercise is necessary at least a few times a week.

_____ b. With proper diet and moderate exercise you can feel your best almost every day.

_____ c. Fitness requires a number of healthful activities.

_____ d. A well-balanced diet includes a combination of healthy foods in the proper amounts.

5. _____ a. Some of us suffer great stress over our relationships.

_____ b. Much of our adult lives is spent trying to come to terms with one of our parents.

_____ c. Many people seek therapy to cope with parental relationships.

_____ d. For many of us, our relationship with our parents is unquestionably our greatest cause of stress.

PRACTICE EXERCISE 7: WRITING MAIN IDEA SENTENCES

Write a main idea sentence for each of these topics.

1. School

_____

_____

2. Homework

_____

_____

3. Work

_____

_____

Writing Supporting Details

When you write a paragraph you want all the sentences to "hang together" so the reader can follow your ideas and understand your message. That means every sentence in a paragraph must be related to a single topic and main idea. These sentences are the details that provide specific information about the main idea.

In the following paragraph, notice that every sentence adds information about the topic, aerobic exercise. Can you identify the one sentence that does not relate directly to the topic?

Aerobic activity is an important addition to an individual's exercise program. Aerobic activities help make your heart stronger and more efficient. Your heart beats approximately 70 times a minute. They also use more calories than other activities. Some examples of aerobic activities include brisk walking, jogging, swimming, and bicycling.

(www.mc.vanderbilt.edu/health/nutrit/pubs/physact.htm, adapted.)

The sentence that does not help you understand more about aerobic activity is "Your heart beats approximately 70 times a minute."

PRACTICE EXERCISE 8: EDITING PARAGRAPHS FOR UNRELATED DETAILS

In each of the following paragraphs, underline the main idea sentence and cross out the one sentence you think does not belong with the other sentences in supporting the main idea.

1   The same life situation can be perceived very differently by different people. Those with a positive outlook know that there are few situations with which they can't deal. They expect that everything will turn out all right and it usually does. A death in the family is difficult to deal with. Those with a negative outlook focus on the possible adverse outcomes of any situation and develop stress over problems that are not very likely to occur.

(Byer & Shainberg, *Living Well*, HarperCollins,
1995, p. 77, adapted.)

2   People who have difficulty making decisions are often immature and insecure. They are afraid to face the consequences of the decisions they make, so they make as few decisions as possible. Some decisions are easy to make. Growth involves making mistakes as well as achieving success. Our mistakes are best viewed as learning experiences. We must take some risks in order to live our lives most fully.

(Byer & Shainberg, *Living Well*, HarperCollins,
1995, p. 77, adapted.)

3   The type of fat eaten, as well as the amount, is important to one's health. Monounsaturated fatty acids, which are found especially in olive and canola oil, appear to reduce the risk of heart disease. Olive oil has a particularly long shelf life. Polyunsaturated fats, found primarily in sunflower, safflower, corn, soybean, cottonseed, and fish oils, do the same. Saturated fats, on the other hand, increase heart disease risk. Butter and milk fat, animal fat, and coconut and palm oils ("tropical oils") are important sources of saturated fats.

(www.mc.vanderbilt.edu/health/wellness/nutrition_moore.htm).

4   Are you sleepy sometimes in the afternoon? Do you seem to handle physical tasks more easily late in the day? If so, you already know about circadian rhythms. Your body has more than 100 circadian rhythms. Each unique 24-hour cycle influences an aspect of your body's function, including body temperature, hormone

levels, heart rate, blood pressure—even pain threshold. Some people can withstand more pain than others. Understanding how these cycles interplay is fascinating. And, in some cases, you may be able to plan your day to take advantage of your body's natural rhythms .

(www.mayohealth.org/mayo/9503/htm/circadia.htm).

A good way to generate specific details is to ask yourself questions about your main idea sentence. As an example, let's look again at this paragraph about exercising.

¹Exercising every day is very important. ²First, exercise helps us burn more calories during the day. ³Without exercise most of us will gain weight from even normal eating. ⁴Second, exercise keeps the heart and lungs healthy. ⁵Third, exercise can be fun and entertaining especially if we play sports. ⁶In short, daily exercise is a key ingredient for a happy and healthy life.

The main idea sentence is, "Exercising every day is very important." You can turn this statement into questions by asking *why* and *how*.

- *Why* is exercising every day very important?
- *How* can people exercise every day?

Read the model paragraph again. Which of the above questions was answered by the supporting details?

You probably decided that the details answer the question *Why is exercising every day very important?* The supporting details in the paragraph give three reasons why exercising is important.

PRACTICE EXERCISE 9: WRITING SUPPORTING DETAILS

Write a question about each main idea sentence. Then write three supporting details that answer your question. For example:

Main Idea:	You can remember more of what you read.
Question:	How can you remember more of what you read?
Supporting Details:	a. Concentrating on the topic and main idea of each paragraph will help you remember more details.
	b. When you read, try visualizing the important details, including the main characters and events.
	c. Underlining topics and main ideas and writing important ideas and reactions in the margins will help you remember more.

Now you try it.

1.

Main Idea:	College registration can be a frustrating experience.
Question:	_____

Supporting Details: a.

b.

c.

2.

Main Idea: Many college students have difficulty getting enough sleep.

Question: _____

Supporting Details: a.

b.

c.

3.

Main Idea: There are many types of exercise for good health.

Question: _____

Supporting Details: a.

b.

c.

4.

Main Idea: Many people need to lose weight.

Question: _____

Supporting Details: a.

b.

c.

PRACTICE EXERCISE 10: WRITING PARAGRAPHS

1. Choose one of the main idea sentences below. Write a paragraph by supporting your main idea sentence with four to five detail sentences.

1) Getting a good night's sleep is very important to me.

2) There are several reasons that I do well in school.

3) My family is very important to me.

2. Freewrite for a few minutes about your eating habits. Then find a key idea that you can use for a main idea of a paragraph. Turn this idea into a main idea sentence. Write a paragraph by supporting this main idea sentence with four to five detail sentences.

Writing Concluding Sentences

When you want to end a conversation, you usually say good-bye or something that indicates you are finished and want to leave. Similarly, a paragraph needs a final sentence that gives readers a sense of completeness. This is the purpose of the concluding sentence, which usually is the last sentence of the paragraph.

You can conclude a paragraph in many different ways, but two types of concluding statements are commonly used. One way is to restate the main idea or sum up your paragraph with a general statement. For example:

In brief, children of divorced parents have a difficult time adjusting to life.

The following words may be used with this type of concluding sentence:

- in sum
- in summary
- all in all

- in brief
- in other words
- in short

Another way to conclude a paragraph is to make a judgment, recommendation, or prediction. You may begin this type of concluding sentence with words such as

- therefore
- in any event
- in conclusion

- indeed
- all in all

Here are some examples of concluding statements that express judgments, recommendations, or predictions.

Main Idea Statement: The sun's ultraviolet rays are becoming more and more intense and are dangerous to our health.

Concluding Sentences:
1. Indeed, as long as we continue destroying the ozone layer, the problems caused by the sun's intensity will not go away. (Judgment)
2. If you think that the sun is not a serious problem to your health, visit your doctor right away. (Recommendation)
3. Therefore, don't forget to use sunscreen to counteract the dangerous effects of the sun. (Recommendation)
4. As the sun's rays continue to become more and more powerful, in the future we may have to stay indoors during the daytime hours. (Prediction)

PRACTICE EXERCISE 11: WRITING CONCLUDING SENTENCES

Write a concluding sentence for each of these thesis statements. For example:

Main Idea Sentence: Too many Americans are overweight.

Concluding Sentence: Indeed, most Americans should consider that diet and exercise are an important part of their life.

1.
Main Idea: Dieting can be dangerous.

Concluding Sentence: _____

2.
Main Idea: Watching violence on television causes violent
                          behavior in society.

Concluding Sentence: _____

3.
Main Idea: Juvenile delinquency is on the rise in the United
                          States.

Concluding Sentence: _____

4.
Main Idea: It is difficult to function effectively without an
                          adequate amount of sleep.

Concluding Sentence: _____

5.
Main Idea: Good nutrition plays an important role in disease
                          prevention.

Concluding Sentence: _____

PRACTICE EXERCISE 12: WRITING CONCLUDING SENTENCES FOR PARAGRAPHS

Write a concluding sentence for each of the paragraphs you wrote in Exercise 10.

PRACTICE EXERCISE 13: PUTTING IT ALL TOGETHER

Work with several other students on this task. Together, choose one of the following topics and write it in the center of your group's diagram (see Figure 3.2):

- choosing a career
- marriage
- leisure activities
- advantages of being a college graduate

As a group, think of four main idea sentences related to the topic you put in the diagram. Write each main idea sentence on a line in the diagram.

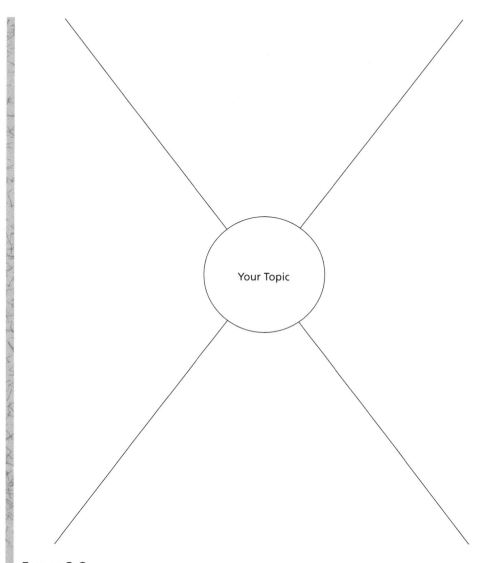

FIGURE 3.2

Working alone, choose one of the four main idea sentences from the diagram. Do not tell the other students in your group which sentence you chose. Write a paragraph supporting your main idea sentence with several details.

Finally, read your paragraph to the other students in your group, but do not read aloud the main idea sentence you used. Ask the students in your group to figure out which main idea sentence you included in your paragraph.

Application

Textbook Selection 1
THE PSYCHOLOGY OF EATING

Before Reading

Before reading the next section, think about your own eating habits.

1. How would you define the word *meal?*

   _____

2. How many meals a day do you eat? _____

3. What kind of foods do you eat between meals?

   _____

   _____

4. Do you read the labels on food packages? Why or why not?

   _____

   _____

   _____

5. Are you satisfied with your current weight? If not, would you like to gain or lose pounds? If you are satisfied, how do you maintain your weight?

   _____

   _____

6. Have you ever dieted? What kind of diet did you follow? Were you successful in losing weight? In keeping the weight off?

   _____

   _____

7. Do you think emotions affect your eating habits? Check the following statements as they apply to you:

   When I am under stress, I eat more _____ eat less _____.

   When I am happy, I eat more _____ eat less _____.

When I am sad, I eat more _____ eat less _____.

When I am angry, I eat more _____ eat less _____.

8. Below are some of the headings from the textbook excerpts included in this chapter. Try to predict under which heading each of the following sentences will be found. Write the letter of the sentence on the line before that heading.

Headings

_____   I. The Psychology of Eating

_____   II. Causes of Obesity

_____ III. Fat Cells and the Onset of Obesity

_____   IV. External Factors

_____   V. Eating Disorders

Sentences

a. Obesity that occurs in adults is mainly the result of an increase in the size of fat cells.

b. This means that rather than relying on internal physical hunger cues, we respond to the sight, color, and availability of food or to the time of day when we are programmed to eat.

c. What is almost certainly clear to you is that the way you think about eating, and its consequences for your body shape or size, also influences the amount of food you eat.

d. Genetics is the most important factor in determining a person's weight.

e. We are extremely image conscious and are pressured to match an "ideal" of thinness as portrayed by models in magazines and on television.

Now, you are ready to read from a textbook selection on eating and food. *Before you begin reading each text section, write a question using the heading.*

During Reading

The Psychology of Eating

Question: _____

_____

1   We have seen so far that your body is equipped with a variety of mechanisms that regulate the amount of food you eat. But do you eat only in response to hunger? You are likely to respond, "Of course not!" What is almost certainly clear to you is that the way you think about eating, and its consequences for your body shape or size, also influences the amount of food you eat. To discuss the psychology of eating, we will focus largely on circumstances in which people try to exercise control over the consequences—to try to reshape their bodies in response to their perceptions of some personal or societal ideal.

2   Peter Herman and Janet Polivy have proposed that the critical dimension that underlies the psychology of eating behaviors is *restrained* versus *unrestrained* eating (Herman & Polivy, 1975). *Restrained eaters* put constant limits on the amount of food they will let themselves eat: they are chronically on diets; they constantly worry about food. Although obese people may be more likely to report these kinds of thoughts and behaviors, individuals can be restrained eaters whatever their body size. How do people gain weight if they are constantly on a diet? Research suggests that when restrained eaters become *disinhibited*—when life circumstances cause them to let down their restraints—they tend to indulge in high-calorie binges. Disinhibition appears to arise most often when the restrained eaters are made to feel stress about their capabilities and self-esteem (Greeno & Wing, 1994; Heatherton et al., 1991).

3   The theory of restrained eating suggests why it might be difficult for people to lose weight once they have become overweight. Many overweight people report themselves as constantly on diets—they are often restrained eaters. If stressful life events occur that cause these eaters to become disinhibited, binge eating can easily lead to weight gain. Thus the psychological consequences of being constantly on a diet can create circumstances that are more likely to lead to weight gain than to weight loss. In the next section, we will see how these same psychological forces can lead to health- and life-threatening eating disorders.

(Zimbardo & Gerrig, *Psychology and Life*, HarperCollins, 1996, pp. 436-437, 439.)

1. The main idea of paragraph 1 includes reasons for eating other than hunger. Underline the main idea sentence in paragraph 1.
2. Paragraph 2 contains several words printed in *italics*, an indication that these words are important and attention should be paid to them. Underline the italicized words and any information about them which you think is important.
3. Using the following chart, list the characteristics of restrained eaters as stated in paragraph 2. Then complete the chart by listing what you think are the characteristics of unrestrained eaters.

Restrained Eaters	Unrestrained Eaters

After Reading

1. In a freewriting, answer the question you raised from the heading of this section.

2. **Words in Context**

    Try to figure out the meaning of each word in the chart below from the context of the selection. Write what you think (or guess) the words mean in the third column. Then, using a dictionary, write a short definition in the fourth column. Finally, if you know any other words that are similar in spelling or meaning to the word, write them in the fifth column.

Word	Par.	Meaning from Context	Dictionary Meaning	Similar Words
mechanisms	1			
perceptions	1			
societal	1			
ideal	1			
critical	2			
dimension	2			
restrained	2			
chronically	2			
disinhibited	2			
indulge	2			
binges	2			
theory	3			

3. **Topics for Writers**

During the next three days, keep a journal of what and when you eat. Also include a few words to describe your emotional state each time you eat.

At the end of three days, review your journal entries. Then write a paragraph that answers each of the following questions. Remember to state your main idea sentence and support it with information you discovered in your writing journal.

1) What kinds of foods did you eat during these three days? What different kinds of feelings did you have at different times you ate? What is the relationship between what you ate and how you felt? Support your answer with examples from your journal.

2) Do you think you are a restrained or an unrestrained eater? Use the record of your eating behavior as it relates to your emotional states to support your opinion.

Textbook Selection 2
WEIGHT MANAGEMENT

Before Reading

Have you ever been on a diet to lose weight? Maybe you have been on a diet to gain weight. If not, you probably know at least one person who has tried to change his or her weight. In your journal, freewrite for a few minutes about your feelings about and experiences with dieting.

During Reading

Weight Management

Question: _____

_____

1   Many of us have a degree of preoccupation with our weight. The results of a recent survey show that almost 90 percent of us perceive of ourselves as weighing too much, and more than one third want to lose at least 15 pounds. At any one time it's estimated that one-third to one-half of U.S. women, and up to one-fourth of U.S. men, are dieting. Polls indicate that almost one-third of U.S. women, ages 19–39, diet at least once a month, and 16 percent consider themselves as perpetual dieters.

2   With such acute awareness of our tendency to overeat, we should be a country of thin, fit people, yet obesity has become the number one nutrition problem in the United States. Approximately 34 million people in the United States are considered by the National Institutes of Health to be obese. Close to one-fifth of American youth are overweight by the time they graduate from high school. While the proportion of overweight adults increases with age, overweight people are found at all age levels.

1. The topic of paragraph 1 is _____.
2. Underline the main idea sentence in paragraph 1.
3. The topic of paragraph 2 is _____.
4. Underline the main idea sentence of paragraph 2.
5. Why do you think so many people have an obsession with losing weight?

_____

_____

_____

Causes of Obesity

Question: _____

_____

3   Researchers have tried to identify factors that will explain why people become obese, yet many questions remain unanswered. Why can some people seem to eat and never gain weight, while others perpetually diet and retain their fat? Factors considered when explaining these differences can be broken down into two categories: the physiological reaction to food, which is controlled by metabolism and genetic makeup; and environmental pressure, which includes psychological, social, and cultural factors.

6. In paragraph 3, underline the two factors that explain why some people get fat.

Genetic Factors

Question: _____

_____

4   A genetic predisposition is now believed to play the most important part in determining a person's body weight and body composition. It is observed, for example, that adopted children's distribution of fat and the size of their fat cells is more similar to that of their biological parents than to that of their adoptive parents. It is also found that if both of your parents are obese your risk of becoming obese is about 80 percent. If both parents are lean, the risk of becoming obese is less than 10 percent.

5   To separate the effects of genetic and environmental factors on body weight and body composition, researchers have studied identical twins. In one study, 600 pairs of identical and fraternal twins were studied (identical twins are alike genetically; fraternal twins are alike genetically only in the same way as brothers and sisters). Whether reared together or apart, identical twins were twice as likely to have similar weights than were fraternal twins, supporting the conclusion that genetics is the most important factor in determining a person's weight.

7. The topic of paragraph 4 is _____.
8. Underline the main idea sentence of paragraph 4.
9. The main idea of paragraph 5 is the same as that in paragraph 4. Can you find the main idea in paragraph 5? (*Hint:* It is found in only part of a sentence.)

Set-Point Theory

Question: _____

_____

6   Within the body are a number of internal physiological variables, such as blood glucose, blood pH, and body temperature, which are maintained within certain limits. It is proposed that these factors have an effect on body weight. According to the set-point theory, the body has a certain amount of fat that it is "biologically set," or programmed, to carry. This is the weight the body *wants* to weigh. This set-point may be a weight different from some "ideal" weight. If so, the person who seeks to *lose* or *gain* more or less weight than the body *wants* may not succeed in his or her effort.

7   The body may *defend* its set-point by increasing or decreasing appetite by speeding up or slowing down its metabolic rate. This way the body expends more or fewer calories, depending on how much energy from food it receives.

8   Initially, the level of the set-point may be determined largely by genes. Exercise may lower the set-point, which makes it possible for the body to settle on a lower level of fatness. Dieting seems to have little effect on adjusting the set-point. When dieting displaces someone from a set-point, a whole series of physical forces fight

that displacement, which makes it possible to regain (or lose) that weight more efficiently.

9   The concept of a set-point is theoretical. No one has yet been able to determine the biological mechanisms that may make it work; yet there is a belief among researchers that fatness may be regulated by the body in this way.

10. The topic of paragraph 6 is _____.

11. Underline the main idea sentence of paragraph 6.

12. The main idea of paragraph 8 is not stated directly. Write it in your own words.

_____

13. According to what you have read, what is one explanation of why some people can eat and never gain weight, while others perpetually diet and still get fat?

_____

_____

External Factors

Question: _____

_____

10   The external cue theory holds that environmental cues prompt us to eat. This means that rather than relying on internal physical hunger cues, we respond to the sight, color, and availability of food or to the time of day when we are programmed to eat. This is further complicated by the fact that food is available around the clock—at home, at work, in restaurants and grocery stores (some restaurants even offer home delivery!).

11   Other factors that may contribute to people's attitudes toward food are the way in which individual families perceive food. Some families are "food-centered," which means they tend to overeat at mealtime, eat rapidly, snack excessively, eat for reasons other than hunger, or eat until all their dishes are empty. Unwittingly, family members may become involved as *codependents* in the exercise of overeating, and serve as *enablers* for a person whose eating habits are out of control. Overeating by children may be an imitation of overeating by parents. Obese children, over a given time interval, tend to take more bites of food and chew their food less thoroughly than nonobese children. Some parents preach the "clean plate ethic" by which they praise their children for eating all the food on their plates as a token of thanks for having enough food to eat.

12   Some people eat in response to stress, boredom, insecurity, anxiety, loneliness, or as reward for being good. Parents who console a child with food may be initiating a life-long behavior pattern. Some people use food as an inappropriate response to psychological stimuli. As you experience pain, anxiety, insecurity, stress, arousal, or excitement, the brain responds by producing substances that soothe pain and lessen arousal. Another effect of these substances is that they enhance appetite for food and reduce activity. If, in addition, you are unusually sensitive to stress, you are likely to eat to compensate for stress, whether negative or positive. Eating may be an appropriate response to all of these stimuli on occasion, but the person who uses them to overeat creates a whole new set of emotional problems relating to his or her overeating. They may get caught in a vicious cycle—depression causing overeating and vice versa.

13   Exacerbating the effect of external factors on eating habits is the tendency of many people to underexercise. In this age of automation, everything can be done with the press of a button—opening the garage door, turning the television on and off, and riding elevators. With such conveniences available, the temptation to remain sedentary may be overpowering, leading to underactivity. With reduced physical activity and with sustained or increased amounts of food intake, weight gain is bound to occur.

14. The topic of paragraph 10 is _____.

15. Underline the main idea sentence of paragraph 10.

16. What are the four examples given of environmental cues that stimulate us to eat?

_____

_____

17. The topic of paragraph 11 is _____.

18. Underline the main idea sentence of paragraph 11.

19. The topic of paragraph 12 is _____.

20. Underline the main idea sentence of paragraph 12.

21. The topic of paragraph 13 is _____.

22. Underline the main idea sentence of paragraph 13.

Fat Cells and the Onset of Obesity

Question: _____

_____

14   The body is composed of many kinds of cells, such as muscle, bone, nerve, and fat. Most of the space inside a fat or adipose cell is filled with triglycerides; its nucleus and other cell components are squeezed into a small area. Active in storing unused fat in the body, fat cells are able to expand considerably as they store triglycerides. The fat cells in an obese person may be 100 times as large as those in a thin person.

15   The total amount of fat in the body depends on two factors: the *number* and the *size* of fat cells. The degree of a person's fatness depends on how many of these cells a person has and how full the cells are. When we eat more energy foods than we use, we accumulate fat, which fills and expands the individual cells. When we use up more energy than we take in, these cells shrink, although their number remains the same. Every calorie eaten must be either burned or stored.

23. Underline the main idea sentence in paragraph 15.

After Reading

1.   Words in Context

Listed below are words from the preceding section on weight management and the number of the paragraphs in which they can be found. Find each word in the text and, in the margin next to the paragraph, write the meaning of each word based on the context or a definition from the dictionary.

Word	Paragraph Number
perpetual	1
acute	2
predisposition	4
perceive	11
unwittingly	11
console	12
exacerbating	13
sedentary	13

2.   Topics for Writers

Write a paragraph about one of the following topics.

1) In your opinion, why are so many people overweight today? Support your opinion with relevant information from the text selection.

2) What do you think is your set-point weight? Write about experiences that helped you determine this.

3) Describe one eating habit with which you are satisfied and one eating habit you would like to change. What do you think influenced you in forming these habits?

Textbook Selection 3
EATING DISORDERS

Before Reading

Have you ever known someone who had an eating disorder? Discuss it in your class.

During Reading

Eating Disorders

Question: _____

_____

1   Our society has a preoccupation with food; eating is one of our most popular activities. At the same time, we are extremely image conscious and are pressured to match an "ideal" of thinness as portrayed by models in magazines and on television. This is further perpetuated by adult authority figures such as team coaches, cheerleader advisors, and dance instructors. Yet, the perception of thinness may become an obsession and therefore lead to eating disorders. Two such disorders common in today's society are *bulimia* and *anorexia nervosa*.

Bulimia

Question: _____

_____

2   Patricia is a single woman in her early twenties. Intelligent and well-trained, she was a high achiever in school. Of normal body weight, she has experienced more than her share of social anxiety and finds it difficult to develop personal relationships. This leaves her depressed and she has compensated by displaying impulsive behavior. Trying not to let it interfere with her work, she periodically goes through eating binges, usually after having deprived herself of food. At night, when no one else is around, she badly overeats and then induces vomiting. Patricia knows she shouldn't do it, is ashamed of what she does and feels guilty after it's all over.

3   Binge eating followed by purging is a serious psychological and medical problem known as bulimia or bulimarexia. Both mean to "eat like an ox." A related term, bulimia nervosa, applies to recurring cycles of binge eating followed by vomiting.

4   People who have bulimia, or bulimics, are typically overcome with a powerful urge to eat, especially "forbidden" sweets or starches, most often in secret. This is a compulsive behavior; the food is not consumed for its nutritional value.

5   Bulimia usually begins in conjunction with a diet that gets out of control and may follow a period of rigid dieting. A binge may be set off by the taste or even the perception of food and may be accelerated by hunger. The first bite triggers the loss of control and the person goes into a compulsive eating frenzy. During the binge the person consumes massive quantities of food—ice cream, cakes, pastries, croissants—stopping only when the stomach pain is unbearable. In the case of bulimia nervosa, the bulimic then vomits everything that has just been eaten. Using the well-trained reflex, he or she may then return and begin the binge process all over again. Some victims binge as often as ten times a day, others only a few times a week. The binge may be ended by self-induced vomiting through gagging or use of a chemical to induce vomiting, or by taking laxatives, diuretics, or enemas. Some end their binges only when the pain is too intense, when interrupted, or by falling asleep. Repeated use of emetics can cause poisoning and lead to heart failure. The binge eater often goes through stages: "anticipation and planning, anxiety, urgency to begin, rapid and uncontrolled consumption of food, relief and relaxation, disappointment, and finally shame or disgust."

6   Overall, bulimics tend to maintain a near normal weight. Yet the female menstrual cycle often becomes irregular, sexual interest is reduced, and the bulimic may evidence impulsive behavior such as alcohol, cigarette, or drug abuse and shoplifting.

7   Purging can upset the body's balance of electrolytes (mineral tissue fluids) and lead to abnormal heart rhythms and injury to the kidneys. Kidney and bladder infections can lead to kidney failure. Repeated vomiting may damage the esophagus and stomach and induce bleeding; it may cause receding gums and damage to tooth enamel from the wash of gastric acid.

8   Bulimia often begins when individuals are between 17 and 25 years of age, and may follow a long series of failures with weight-reduction programs. Bulimics commonly intersperse restrictive dieting with bulimic behaviors and may experience weight fluctuations of 10 pounds up and down over short periods of time. Most often females, victims are typically of higher than average intelligence and are close to their recommended weight. They may appear healthy, successful, and competent. In the January 1985 issue of *Cosmopolitan,* Jane Fonda told her story of having been a secret bulimic from age 12 to 35, binging and purging up to 20 times a day. For individuals obsessed with food, binges are often associated with great distress and marked by feelings of loss of self-control, self-disgust, anger, and

depression. The vomiting may be a catharsis, or release from guilt feelings as well as from the food itself.

1. Paragraphs 3–8 deal with several topics. In the margins of the reading selection, write each of the following topics next to the appropriate paragraph or groups of paragraphs.
   - Definition of bulimia
   - Description of the disorder
   - Other characteristics of bulimics
   - Effects of purging
2. The main idea of paragraph 6 is not stated directly. Write it in your own words.

   _____

   _____

Anorexia Nervosa

Question: _____

_____

9 Marie is in her first year of college and a fine dancer. Living at home, she eats very carefully and works out daily at the fitness center. Although slender, she still feels her weight is too high. Unaware that she is actually undernourished, she says she feels fine, although she stopped menstruating some months ago. The concern of her family bothers her. Marie has worked hard to please her parents, who she feels have set her goals for her. Unable to gain control of her life from her parents the way she wants, she insists on severely controlling her weight, even though she is usually hungry. Even though she looks physically exhausted, she still contends that she is fat. Her friends and family are becoming concerned. Marie has anorexia nervosa.

10 Anorexia nervosa, meaning "nervous lack of appetite," is a condition in which a person, usually a female teenager, takes dieting to the point of self-starvation and loses 25 percent or more of his or her body weight. The condition is estimated to occur in 1 of every 200 females, usually aged 12–18; about 5–10 percent of anorexics are males. The victim of this disorder is most commonly an adolescent or young adult who has an intense fear of fat and is plagued with a distorted body image. The victim of anorexia nervosa is so obsessed with losing weight that he or she sees even normal body contours as fat. Refusing to maintain a minimal normal weight, the anorectic individual maintains a body weight below the weight expected for his or her age and height.

11 Anorexia, like bulimia, may begin as a diet that has gotten out of control. It may occur suddenly and for a limited time, or it may develop gradually and over

many years. The behavior and body changes of an anorexic are typical of a starving person. An anorexic's behavior toward food may be atypical; for instance, he or she may crumble food, minutely dissecting it before eating it, or may not eat when others eat. As weight is lost, the absence of fat tissue padding the body makes sitting or lying down uncomfortable. The body tries to protect its two main organs—the brain and the heart—by slowing down or stopping other less vital functions. Menstruation stops, blood pressure and body temperature both drop, and respiratory rate slows down. Constipation, intolerance of the cold, and light-headedness follow. Due to severe electrolyte imbalance, irregular heartbeat, heart failure, and bone loss may occur. The anorexic may not sleep well and may withdraw from friends. *Lanugo,* or soft hair, forms over the skin.

12   In addition to starvation, some anorexics purge the little bit of food they do eat, further risking their health. Recording artist Karen Carpenter was an anorexic who died when the effects of induced vomiting irreversibly damaged her heart.

13   Anorexics are often from educated, successful, middle-class families, and are usually competitive perfectionists who have lost control, or fear losing control, of their lives. The anorexia may be induced by a life situation with which the person is unable to cope—puberty, death of a loved one, first sexual contact, ridicule over weight, or over-controlling parents. The anorexic may feel the media/culture imposed "body concept" of being thin is the "ideal." Victims of this disorder become skilled in manipulating their appetites, which gives them a sense of control (even though self-destructive) over their emotions, family, and friends.

3. This section deals with several aspects of anorexia nervosa. Draw a line between paragraphs where you think the topic changes. Write the topic of each section in the margin.

Treatment

Question: _____

_____

14   Early treatment of eating disorders is imperative; however, there is no quick cure for either anorexia or bulimia. Due to their denial of being too thin and not eating enough, it may be hard to convince anorexics to gain weight. Bulimics tend to cooperate with treatment more easily and may actually seek treatment. The longer bulimia and anorexia persist, the more the damage to the body becomes irreversible. A realistic body image is necessary for recovery, especially with anorexia. Since family dynamics are a common cause of eating disorders, treatment programs need to involve the family. Medical care by a physician is necessary, as is psychotherapy, so that victims can deal with their low self-esteem, depression, and

> helplessness. Behavior modification may be used as another method of treatment for eating disorders. Some people with eating disorders find effective help by joining self-help groups such as Bulimic and Anorexic Self-Help (BASH).
>
> (Byer & Shainberg, *Living Well.* HarperCollins, 1995, pp. 298, 304–307, 315–318.)

4. How many types of treatments are mentioned in paragraph 14? _____

After Reading

1. **Matching Definitions and Words**
   Below is a list of words from the section on eating disorders, each followed by the number of the paragraph in which it is found. Reread the relevant sentences to figure out the meaning of the words, then match each word with the correct definition.

Words	Definitions
1) perpetuated (1)	a. in an extremely small way
2) compensated (2)	b. continued, preserved
3) purging (3)	c. necessary, essential
4) atypical (11)	d. clearing or emptying
5) minutely (11)	e. irregular, abnormal
6) vital (11)	f. counterbalanced, offset

2. **Topics for Writers**
   1) Why do you think so many people become obsessed with their weight?
   2) Have you ever felt like you were out of control in some way? Describe your experience.
   3) What is your idea of the perfect body for a man? For a woman? Where do you think your ideas came from?

Textbook Selection 4
SLEEP AND DREAMING

Before Reading

1. Before reading the next section, think about your own sleeping and dreaming habits.

   1) How many hours of sleep do you need each night to feel rested the next day? _____

2) How many hours do you usually sleep at night? _____

3) How do you feel when you do not get enough sleep?

_____

_____

4) What do you think would happen if you did not sleep for a long period

of time? _____

5) Approximately how often do you dream? _____

6) How often do you remember your dreams? _____

7) Do you believe dreams have any meaning? Explain.

_____

_____

_____

2. In as much detail as possible, describe the last dream you remember having.

_____

_____

_____

_____

During Reading

Sleep and Dreaming

1   We spend about one-third of our lives in the state of consciousness called sleep. Sleep appears to be an automatic behavior necessary for survival. Rats that are kept awake for more than a week or two, for example, suffer severe physical breakdown and ultimately die, and sleep-deprived humans have been known to suffer hallucinations and other distortions of reality (Dement, 1992; Everson, Bergmann, & Rechtschaffen, 1989). The amount people sleep varies with age. A 3-day-old infant sleeps an average of 16 hours out of 24, spread over five or six periods during the day and night. As the infant matures, daytime sleep slowly decreases while nighttime sleep remains stable at about 10 hours. Adults average 7 to 8 hours of sleep out of 24, but what constitutes a "normal" night's sleep varies widely among individuals. Middle-aged and older people tend to sleep less than younger adults and to wake up more frequently at night. Although there does not

appear to be an identifiable quota of sleep that a person requires, most people in industrialized societies get less sleep than they feel they need (Dotto, 1990). Sleep patterns also vary from day to day. Physical exercise in the afternoon tends to result in longer sleep that night. People also sleep less soundly at first in unfamiliar places (Webb & Bonnet, 1979).

(Rubin, Peplau & Salovey, *Psychology*, Houghton Mifflin, 1993, p. 330.)

1. In Group A below are statements highlighting the main points in paragraph 1. In Group B are statements illustrating each main point. Match each supporting detail in Group B with a main point from Group A.

Group A:

1) Sleep appears to be an automatic behavior necessary for survival.

2) The amount people sleep varies with age.

3) A "normal" night's sleep varies among individuals.

4) Many people get less sleep than they feel they need.

Group B:

a. Maria feels best if she gets 10 hours of sleep a night but her husband only needs to sleep 5 hours to feel rested.

b. People don't have to be taught how to sleep.

c. When John was a young boy he usually slept 9 hours a night. Now he is 70 years old and he sleeps about 5 hours a night.

d. More work-related injuries occur during the night hours than during daytime hours.

2. The topic of paragraph 1 is:
    a. what happens to rats who do not sleep.
    b. how much older people sleep.
    c. the amount people sleep.

3. State three factors mentioned in paragraph 1 that influence the amount you sleep.

_____

_____

_____

4. Why do you think that most people in industrialized societies get less sleep than they need?

_____

5. What does "quota" mean as used in paragraph 1?

_____

_____

The next few paragraphs describe the stages of sleep. As you read, underline information you consider important.

2   How do we know when someone is asleep? Self-reports of sleeping are notoriously unreliable. A person who claims that he or she "didn't sleep a wink last night," may have slept soundly for several hours (Dement, 1974).

3   Our best indicators of sleep are measurements of brain activity and muscle tone. The **electroencephalograph (EEG)** is an instrument that records electrical activity in the brain. It does so through small electrodes that are placed onto the scalp. The process is slightly messy, but is not painful. An **electromyograph (EMG)** produces a record of a muscle's activity or relaxation.

4   When you are in a calm, relaxed state, with your eyes closed but not yet asleep, your EEG pattern shows a rhythmic cycle of brain waves called alpha activity. In this presleep stage, we find relatively smooth EEG waves cycling 8 to 12 times per second. If, as you sit or lie there, you start worrying about events of the day, or try to solve a problem, smooth alpha waves become disrupted and are replaced by an apparently random pattern of heightened electrical activity typical of what we find in wakefulness.

5   As you drift from relaxation into sleep, brain waves change, as alpha waves give way to the stages of sleep. The EEG tracings of sleeping subjects can be divided into four different stages (Borbely, 1986). As I review these four stages, you can refer to Figure 3.3 on page 104, which shows the EEGs of a person in each stage. These tracings were chosen because they best illustrate each of the four stages. Actual EEG tracings are not always this clear.

Stage 1. This is a very light sleep from which you can be easily aroused. The smooth, cyclical alpha pattern disappears, replaced by the slower _theta waves_ (3–7 cycles per second). The amplitude, or magnitude, of the electrical activity also lessens considerably. At the same time, your breathing is becoming more regular, and your heart rate is slowing and blood pressure is decreasing. This stage does not last very long—generally less than 10 minutes. Then, you start to slide into Stage 2 sleep.

Stage 2. In this stage, the EEG pattern is similar to Stage 1—low amplitude with no noticeable wavelike pattern. The difference is that we now see _sleep spindles_ in the EEG record. These are brief, high amplitude bursts of electrical activity that occur with regularity (about every 15 seconds or so). You're really getting off to sleep now, but still can be easily awakened.

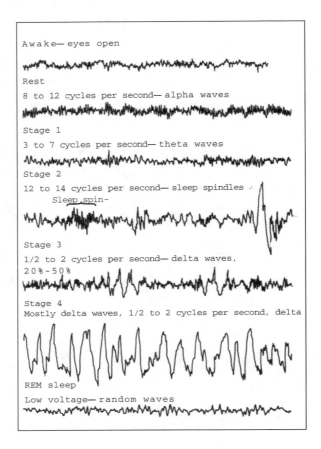

Awake— eyes open

Rest

8 to 12 cycles per second— alpha waves

Stage 1

3 to 7 cycles per second— theta waves

Stage 2

12 to 14 cycles per second— sleep spindles

Sleep spin-

Stage 3

1/2 to 2 cycles per second— delta waves,
20%-50%

Stage 4

Mostly delta waves, 1/2 to 2 cycles per second, delta

REM sleep

Low voltage— random waves

FIGURE 3.3

EEG records showing the general electrical activity of the brain for a person at various levels of wakefulness and sleep.

Stage 3. Now you're getting into deep sleep. There is a reduction in the brain's electrical activity. We can clearly make out *delta wave* activity in your EEG. Delta waves are high, slow waves (from 0.5 to 3 cycles every second). In Stage 3, delta waves constitute between 20 and 50 percent of your EEG pattern. Your internal functions (temperature, heart rate, breathing) are lowering and slowing. It is difficult to wake you now.

Stage 4. You are in deep sleep. Your EEG record is virtually filled with slow delta waves, recurring over and over again (as opposed to Stage 3, where delta waves comprise only a portion of your brain wave activity). Readings from an electromyogram indicate that your muscles have become totally relaxed. About 15 percent of your night's sleep will be spent in this stage of deep sleep.

6   It usually takes about an hour to go from Stage 1 to Stage 4, depending on such things as how tired you are and the physical conditions surrounding you. After an hour's passage through these four stages, the sequence reverses itself. You go back through Stage 3, then to Stage 2, but before going through the cycle again, something remarkable happens. Your eyes start to move rapidly under closed eyelids.

REM and NREM Sleep

7   In the early 1950s, Nathaniel Kleitman and Eugene Aserinsky made quite a discovery. They noticed that as sleeping subjects began their second cycle into deeper levels of sleep, their eyes began to dart back and forth under their closed eyelids (Aserinsky & Kleitman, 1953). This period of rapid eye movement is called REM sleep. When subjects are awakened during REM sleep, they usually (about 85% of the time) report that they are having a vivid, storylike dream. When awakened during sleep periods that are not accompanied by rapid eye movements—NREM sleep—people report fewer and much more fragmented dreams (Kleitman, 1963a; NCSDR, 1993). At first it was believed that eye movements during REM sleep were a result of the dreamer literally viewing, or scanning, images produced by the dream. It turns out that a dreamer's eye movements are unrelated to the content of his or her dream. Instead, eye movements are produced by a cluster of cells in the brain stem (Hobson, 1977; Kiester, 1980).

8   Periods of REM sleep occur throughout the night, normally lasting from a few minutes to half an hour. About 90 to 120 minutes each night is spent in REM sleep. As one goes through a night's sleep, REM periods tend to become longer and dreams more vivid (NCSDR, 1993).

9   Everyone REMs. Everyone dreams. Some of us have difficulty remembering what we have dreamed when we awake in the morning, but we can be sure that in the course of a normal night's sleep, we have dreamed several times. There is no great mystery why we don't remember our dreams any better than we do. Most dreams are quite ordinary, boring, and forgettable. Unless we make an effort to do so, we seldom try to store dream content in our memories so that they can be recalled later. That is, we are seldom motivated to remember our dreams.

(Gerow, Essentials of Psychology, 2nd ed.,
HarperCollins, 1996, p. 181–185.)

6. The topic of paragraph 4 is:
    a. alpha waves.
    b. worrying about events.
    c. a calm, relaxed state.
    d. heightened electrical activity.

7. Now fill in the chart below. Most of the information needed to complete the chart should be information you have underlined.

Stage	Brain Waves	Physical Signs	Other Characteristics
1			
2			
3			
4			

8. What is REM sleep?

_____

9. True _____ or False _____ You dream only in REM sleep.

10. True _____ or False _____ As the night progresses, dreams become longer.

11. True _____ or False _____ When you don't remember any dreams in the morning it is because you did not have any dreams the night before.

Dreaming

10   Throughout most of human history, dreams have been regarded as magical states, as ways of taking on new selves and new capacities, and as divine prophecies. Today we are still fascinated by dreams and their meanings. The interpretation of dreams and their symbols was given new impetus early in this century by Sigmund Freud, who saw dreams as "the royal road to the unconscious." More recently, systematic studies have explored the physiological bases of dreaming and its contributions to our well-being.

12. Dreams used to be thought of as _____ but now they are considered _____.

The Interpretation of Dreams

11   In *The Interpretation of Dreams,* Freud (1900/1953) argues that dreams represent the fulfillment of unconscious impulses, both sexual and aggressive, that are unacceptable on a conscious level. While we sleep, Freud believed, our repressed

wishes—especially our sexual desires—express themselves and are fulfilled. If we were to experience these wishes in an undisguised form, we would be filled with anxiety and guilt. To enable us to sleep peacefully, therefore, our impulses are camouflaged in our dreams. Freud thus distinguished between two types of content in dreams: the latent content and the manifest content. **Latent dream content** is the underlying meaning of the dream. **Manifest dream content** is the disguised form that we remember when we wake up. For example, a woman dreams that she is at a carnival, where she tosses a ring onto a bottle and wins a giant teddy bear. That is the manifest content of the dream. The latent content may be that she wants to conceive and bear a baby.

12   Freud identified three processes by which our dreams conceal our wishes and impulses: symbolism, condensation, and displacement. By *symbolism,* Freud meant the translation of unacceptable wishes into a more acceptable, or symbolic, form in dreams. He concentrated on sexual symbols, suggesting that sharp, elongated objects (umbrellas, swords, sticks) represent the penis and that containers (cups, boxes, houses) are symbols of the vagina. By *condensation,* Freud meant the representation of several elements in a person's life by a single image in a dream. A dream about scoring a touchdown, for instance, might encompass a man's feelings about competition, fame, and sexual accomplishment. *Displacement* is Freud's term for disguising unacceptable wishes by addressing them to a substitute object other than their real object. For instance, a dream about hitting a tiger with a baseball bat might represent a wish to harm one's boss.

13. Underline the basic premise of Freud's theory concerning dreams.
14. What does "camouflaged" mean as used in paragraph 11?

_____

15. Circle the terms and underline the definitions given in paragraph 12.
16. The main idea sentence in paragraph 12 is a general statement about the terms and definitions you underlined. Underline the main idea sentence.

13   Sexual impulses are central to Freud's theory of personality, and Freud often found sexual desires in the latent content of dreams. Other dream theorists have given sex less prominence in their interpretations. Today, most dream analysts attribute a much wider range of meanings and functions to dreams than did Freud. The manifest content of dreams is often closely tied to waking thoughts, feelings, and worries (Hobson, 1989).

14   Extensive sets of dream reports collected from college students reveal that men and women tend to dream differently, presumably because of differences in their interests and concerns (Hall, 1984). Men report more dreams characterized by outdoor settings and acts of aggression. Women usually dream about people they know or recognize; men are more likely to dream about strangers.

15   To explore your own dreams, you may want to compile a dream diary for a month or two. Keep a pad and pen at your bedside, and ask your roommates not to disturb you first thing in the morning. When you wake up, lie still for a couple of minutes and recall your most recent dream in as much detail as possible. Tell yourself the story a couple of times, trying to recreate the mental images. Then write a detailed account of the dream. Do leftover worries from the day appear in your dreams?

(Rubin, Peplau & Salovey, *Psychology,* Houghton Mifflin, 1993, pp. 335–336.)

17. Underline the main idea sentence in paragraph 13.
18. Underline the main idea sentence in paragraph 14.
19. Using the boldface type as an aid, count the number of sleep disorders discussed in paragraphs 16 to 22. How many did you find? _____

Sleep Disorders

16   Some people who suffer from insomnia toss and turn until they fall asleep but then sleep soundly the rest of the night. Others wake up repeatedly throughout the night. One study conducted in a large metropolitan area found that over 40 percent of adults report a current or past problem with insomnia (Bixler & others, 1979). Some cities even have insomniac clubs—the meetings are typically held late at night.

17   Insomnia has many causes. Some people take their daytime worries to bed with them. Others are afraid of falling asleep for fear of nightmares or emergencies that might arise. Insomnia is also a common symptom of depression. In addition, people with irregular schedules often have difficulty sleeping.

18   Paradoxically, sleeping pills can produce insomnia by disrupting the natural sequence of sleep stages. Studies of brain-wave patterns following the intake of sleeping pills show that they reduce the duration of deep (Stage 4) sleep (Borbely, 1986). Several nondrug methods of combating sleeplessness have proved effective. Some involve progressive muscle relaxation, starting with the toes and moving up toward the shoulders and neck; others emphasize concentrating on pleasant mental images.

19   Insomnia is the most common sleep disorder, but there are others. Most of us had the embarrassing experience of falling asleep at an inappropriate moment, such as in class or at a movie with friends. Fatigue and boredom are the usual culprits. But a small number of people have a disorder called **narcolepsy**, which causes them to drop suddenly into a deep sleep, at any time of day, for up to 30 minutes. Such "sleep attacks" may occur at very inopportune moments, such as while driving a car (Aldrich, 1989). In attacks of narcolepsy, the person plunges directly into REM sleep. The precise causes of narcolepsy are unknown, but it appears to be a disorder in the brain mechanisms that control REM sleep (Browman & others, 1982; Douglass, Harris, & Pazderka, 1989).

20 Another sleep disorder, **sleep apnea**, is characterized by periodic interruptions in breathing. These stoppages of airflow may last only a moment or as long as two minutes. They can occur dozens or even hundreds of times during the night. The person may periodically gasp for air, with or without waking. The disorder occurs because the throat loses its muscle tension, resulting in a blocked airway. Unsurprisingly, people with sleep apnea feel drowsy and lethargic during the day (Borbely, 1986).

21 **Sleepwalking** is most common among children. Sleepwalkers are not acting out their dreams; in fact, they typically sleepwalk during Stage 4, during which there is little dreaming. Sometimes sleepwalking is accompanied by complex semipurposeful unconscious acts, like fixing a snack (Restak, 1979). Sleepwalking usually disappears after adolescence (Lochel, 1989) but persists in some adults (Kavey & others, 1990).

22 **Night terrors** are different from nightmares, which occur during REM sleep (Pagel, 1989). The person awakens in a panic from Stage 4 sleep, screaming or cowering in fear, with an elevated heart rate. Night terrors are most common in children between the ages of 3 and 5 but occasionally occur in adults.

(Rubin, Peplau & Salovey, *Psychology,* Houghton Mifflin,
1993. pp. 333–334.)

After Reading

1. Fill in the chart below using the information from paragraphs 16 to 22.

Sleep Disorder	Description of Symptoms	Causes

2. **Words in Context**

Try to figure out the meaning of each word in the chart below from the context of the selection. Write what you think (or guess) the words mean in the third column. Then, using a dictionary, write a short definition in the fourth column. Finally, if you know any other words that are similar in spelling or meaning to the word, write them in the fifth column.

Word	Par.	Meaning from Context	Dictionary Meaning	Similar Words
distortions	1			
quota	1			
notoriously	2			
disrupted	4			
random	4			
amplitude	5			
magnitude	5			
constitute	5			
recurring	5			
comprise	5			
fragmented	7			
cluster	7			
vivid	8			
prophecies	10			
impetus	10			
repressed	11			

Word	Par.	Meaning from Context	Dictionary Meaning	Similar Words
manifest	11			
presumably	14			
culprits	19			
lethargic	20			
cowering	22			

3. **Topics for Writers**

1) Have you ever had any difficulty getting to sleep? Write about a time you had a sleep problem. Describe your experience and what you think caused it.

2) Write about a recent dream you remember. Describe what happened and the feelings you have about the dream.

Additional Reading

To Sleep, Perchance to Stay Awake in Class
Lynda Richardson
New York Times, December 27, 1995

Before Reading

1. What time did you wake up in the morning to get to class in high school? _____

2. What time did you usually go to sleep on school nights when you were in high school? _____

3. How did you feel during your morning classes in high school? Completely alert and awake? Somewhat alert and awake? Sleepy? _____

4. At what time of the day do you feel most alert? _____

The following article is about the sleep needs of teenagers and the effect of school schedules on their lives. Read the article to find out what researchers have discovered about sleep.

During Reading

VOCABULARY	
Word	**Definition**
slouches (1)	droops, bends downward
grueling (3)	exhausting
defies (4)	opposes
vulnerable (11)	open to
amenable (13)	agreeable
flurry (20)	commotion
trek (21)	excursion, trip

1   At 8 o'clock on school mornings, Jillian Lastra stares intently at the chalkboard during her math class at the New York City Museum School in Chelsea. She appears to be learning geometry formulas about line segments, but she can barely keep her eyes open. She slouches in her chair. She sneaks a catnap when her teacher is not looking, head propped between her palms.

2   Jillian, 13, is in what sleep researchers call a twilight zone, caused by sleep deprivation.

3   As every teen-ager and every teacher knows, the first hour of the school day can be a grueling exercise. When children reach puberty, many want to stay up later and sleep in, not rise and shine for school. Teachers, parents and even experts in sleep disorders long blamed the morning sleepiness on television or the telephone, peer pressure, rebelliousness, more homework or laziness.

4   But now, the nation's leading researchers in sleep disorders agree that biology, as well as social pressure, plays a large role. They have observed teen-agers in sleep laboratories, measuring their levels of melatonin, a hormone that helps regulate the body's cycles of sleepiness and wakefulness. And they seem to agree that it defies nature to expect teen-agers to get up early for class and perform at their peak.

5   "We have these kids so sleep-deprived, it's almost as if they are drugged," said James B. Maas, a psychology professor at Cornell University who is an expert in sleep disorders. "Educators like myself are teaching walking zombies."

6   Instead of wanting to sleep from 11 P.M. to 7 A.M., students like Jillian are more naturally inclined to go to sleep as late as 2 A.M. and stay in bed until noon, researchers say.

7   To be sure, researchers caution, there are teen-agers who, like adults, are naturally early risers and tend to perform better in morning classes. But for Jillian, every morning is a struggle. Having fallen asleep about midnight, she gets up at 6 A.M., and her body acts as if she has jet lag.

8   "What is happening to their biology may be preventing them and working against them going to bed earlier," said Mary A. Carskadon, a professor of psychiatry and human behavior at Brown University's School of Medicine who is another of the nation's sleep-disorder experts.

9   Sleep researchers are still investigating how biology affects teen-agers' sleep patterns, but Dr. Carskadon said that during puberty, children appear to adjust less flexibly than adults do to schedule changes—say later hours on weekends.

10   "It really does seem to be the body driving these preferences," she said. "We think it's more difficult for adolescents to make enforced adjustments."

11   Dr. Carskadon said that teen-agers also appear to be more vulnerable to what is known as "delayed phase preference," in which people "feel better and perform activities later in the day and into the night, and feel worse doing things early in the morning."

12   Teen-agers who start the day a little later may also get better grades, according to preliminary research at Johns Hopkins University. Dr. Richard Allen, who founded the Sleep Disorder Center at the university, studied two groups of adolescents with

different starting times, 7:30 and 9:30. He found that the later risers performed better academically.

13 "Kids in early-starting schools have accumulated a sleep loss," he said. "Kids get increasingly sleepy during the day, and since you are sleepy, the mind is less amenable to learning."

14 Sleep researchers dream of a world where high school starts at 9:30 or 10, instead of the more typical 7:30 or 8. They say the sleep patterns of teen-agers shift when they are moving through high school, a biological change that is compounded by school days that begin earlier than when the students were in middle and elementary school.

15 When Dr. Carskadon and a colleague conducted a survey recently of more than 3,000 high school students in the Providence, R.I., area who began the school day between 7:10 and 7:30, about 85 percent reported an amount of sleep that the researchers called inadequate. The remaining 15 percent slept eight and a half hours or more on school nights.

16 And as students got older, they were sleeping less. The students, who were 17 to 19, were sleeping 40 minutes less on school nights than 14-year-olds were.

17 As a result, some students, like Jillian, nod off in 10-second "micro-sleeps." They lose their concentration and miss important facts during lectures.

18 "I'll be thinking about my boyfriend, Carlos, or thinking about playing basketball," Jillian said. An eighth grader, she has fond memories of her elementary school days at Public School 3 in Greenwich Village, when the school bell rang at a more reasonable 9 o'clock in the morning. "I felt more comfortable. I didn't find myself dozing off in class."

19 Now, she and her classmates are so sluggish in the morning that they have informally worked out pacts to poke each other when their teacher, Ron Chaluisan, glares in their direction. "They're not like up yet," he said. "They are still sleeping."

20 Mr. Chaluisan said he tries to adjust his teaching style to the time of day. During first period, he does not anticipate a flurry of eagerly raised hands.

21 "I know a lot of the motivation and a lot of the energy is going to have to come from me," said Mr. Chaluisan, who is also a co-director of the small alternative school that makes treks to museums several times a week. "I end up with a lot of back and forth between me and the class, a lot of direct calling on students."

22 Despite the research, many school officials say that a change in high school starting time is not the most pressing matter they face.

23 "It's not something we're going to consider right now," said David Begel, a spokesman for the New York City Board of Education. "We're all post-puberty. We all ought to be able to wake up when it's time to pay attention."

24 According to John A. Lammel, the director of high school services for the National Association of Secondary School Principals, the issue probably merits a closer look.

25 A few districts are already discussing a change. In Minneapolis, the school board has said that the issue of the teen-age biological clock needs to be addressed and the researchers should be heeded, Ginny Craig, a spokeswoman, said.

26 "We're constantly considering it," Ms. Craig said. "We know they're right, but we're stuck just as many school districts are."

27 In Minneapolis, as in many districts, a move to change school starting times is proving difficult, mostly because of bus schedules. High schools, particularly those in less-populated areas, stagger schedules so that buses can be used more than once each morning. The buses transport high school students first, then complete runs for elementary and middle schools; that way, younger students do not have to wait in the dark for their school buses.

28 In larger districts, many overcrowded schools also have extended schedules to allow students to attend class at different times. A change in the school day would also interfere with after-school work or extra-curricular activities of many high school students, like Lauren Kotick, 15.

29 "I'd rather get up early and leave early than get up later and leave later," said Lauren, who attends Edward R. Murrow High School, an academically rigorous school in the Midwood section of Brooklyn. "By the time you got home, you'd be so wiped out you wouldn't be able to do anything."

30 Many of Edward R. Murrow High's nearly 4,000 students are preoccupied after school with jobs, science projects, band practice and drama productions, like their recent "Bye Bye Birdie."

31 Lauren said she dreads waking up at 6:45 for class an hour and a half later, but added that it evens out in the end. The teen-ager, who works backstage on drama productions, said that after-school rehearsals usually last until 6 in the evening and the current schedule allows students more free time.

32 "If school began later, it would mean getting out of rehearsal after 9 P.M., and that's not fair to us," she said. "We have other commitments like homework, work and tests."

33 But Hillary Miller, 15, is inclined to believe her class performance would improve if the school day began later. She often has to wake up in the dark to be at Murrow High at 7:30 A.M. She has debate club sessions and an advanced-placement class in Western civilization. She also goes to drama rehearsal after school, which often lasts four hours.

34 On weekends, she said, she routinely sleeps until noon.

35 Hillary said she would "freak out" if administrators were to shift to a later schedule. "I've been getting to school early for too long," she said.

36 Sleep experts know that persuading people of the importance of sleep is not easy. The subject is not included in many high school health textbooks. And to their annoyance, the issue did not come up in an announcement from the National Institutes of Health a few years ago heralding the decade of the brain.

37 But researchers are moving to raise awareness. They envision the day when sleep will be as high a priority as exercise and nutrition in maintaining good health. As students become adults and move into positions of power, the researchers also would like them to forget about grabbing a cup of coffee to stay alert. How about a power nap instead?

38 "It's hard to get people to take sleep seriously," said Amy R. Wolfson, an assistant professor of psychology at the College of the Holy Cross in Worcester, Mass. "We're trying."

(Lynda Richardson, "To Sleep, Perchance to Stay Awake in Class," *New York Times*, December 27, 1995, Sec. A., p. 1, col. 4.)

After Reading

1. Column A lists the number of several paragraphs from the article. Column B lists the main ideas from the paragraphs. Match the correct main idea statement to each of the paragraph numbers.

Column A: Paragraph Number

a. 12
b. 27
c. 28
d. 38
e. 28

Column B: Main Idea

1) Staggered class schedules to accommodate overcrowded schools make it difficult to start the high school day late.

2) Teenagers who start the school day later may be more successful academically.

3) Most people do not appreciate the importance of sleep to their health.

4) One difficulty in changing the starting time in high school to a later hour is the way school buses are scheduled.

5) Extra-curricular activities would be curtailed if the high school day began later.

2. **Comprehension Check**

_____ 1) According to paragraph 1, which of the following statements about Jillian Lastra is *not* true?

a. She is looking at math formulas on the blackboard.

b. She is learning geometry formulas about line segments.

      c. She is having difficulty concentrating.

      d. She is suffering from sleep deprivation.

2) What is melatonin? (paragraph 4) _____

3) True _____ or False _____ : A person who is vulnerable to delayed phase preference would probably prefer working an early morning shift.

4) True _____ or False _____ : Social pressure is no longer considered a cause of sleep deprivation.

_____ 5) Which of the following is true?

      a. All teenagers feel more comfortable going to bed at 2 A.M. and sleeping until noon.

      b. An adult returning to school has more difficulty than a teenager does adjusting to an early morning schedule.

      c. Sleep researchers support the idea that high school should start later in the morning.

      d. Sleep disorders do not affect grades in school.

_____ 6) Which of the following are mentioned as difficulties in changing a school's starting time?

      a. bus schedules, after-school activities, overcrowded schools

      b. bus schedules, overcrowded schools, National Institutes of Health

      c. after-school activities, homework, band practice

3. **Topics for Writers**

1) What occupation do you think would be most compatible with your preferred sleeping schedule? What is it about this job that makes it compatible with your sleep schedule?

2) Do you agree or disagree with the author that high school should start later in the morning? Support your opinion with your experiences from high school and facts from the article.

Chapter Summary

Topics and Main Ideas for Readers

Identifying Topics	The topic is what you are reading about in general. It is repeated or referred to throughout a paragraph.
Identifying Main Ideas	A main idea expresses the most important point about the topic. It may or may not be stated in a paragraph.

Writing Paragraphs

	A paragraph consists of a series of sentences that are related to the same topic.
Writing Main Idea Sentences	To write a good main idea sentence, ask yourself two questions: (1) What is my paragraph about? (2) What do I want my readers to know about the topic in general?
Writing Supporting Details	To achieve paragraph unity, all the sentences should be related to the topic of the paragraph.
Writing Concluding Sentences	A concluding sentence gives a paragraph a sense of completeness.

Journal

In the space below, write about the one thing you found most interesting in this chapter. Why is it interesting to you?

_____

_____

_____

_____

_____

_____

_____

_____

_____

_____

_____

_____

_____

_____

_____

_____

_____

_____

_____

_____

_____

_____

Go Electronic!

For additional readings, exercises, and Internet activities, visit the Longman English pages at:

http://longman.awl.com/englishpages

If you need a user name and password, please see your instructor.

Take a Road Trip to the Maine Woods

Be sure to visit the Main Idea module in your Reading Road Trip CD-ROM for multimedia tutorials, exercises, and tests.

Practice Your Writing Skills

For additional practice with your writing skills, use the Writer's ToolKit CD-ROM included with this text.

CHAPTER 4

Working with Details

Theme: Safety

What You Will Find in This Chapter

- The Relationship between Readers and Writers
- Patterns of Organization and Signal Words
- Major and Minor Details
- Writing Coherent Paragraphs
- Textbook Selections on the Bill of Rights
- Newspaper Articles Dealing with a Civil Rights Case

What is your opinion of the following statement? Freewrite for a few minutes about what you think it means, and whether or not you agree with it.

The people's safety is the highest law.

_____

_____

_____

_____

_____

The theme of this chapter is *safety*. We are all motivated by the need to feel physically and psychologically secure. We get some of our feelings of security by knowing that there are laws that protect us in many ways. In this chapter you will read about the Bill of Rights and how it protects United States citizens. These readings are from a text, *Government in America: People, Politics, and Policy,* used in some college history courses. Also, you will read some newspaper articles about a criminal justice case that involved constitutional rights.

In this chapter we introduce the following reading and writing skills:

- understanding the relationship between the reader and the writer
- recognizing and using signal words
- recognizing major and minor details
- writing coherent paragraphs

Also, you will have the opportunity to develop your vocabulary and practice your main idea skills, which you learned in earlier chapters.

The Relationship between Readers and Writers

When you read, you are getting a message from an author. You use the details to understand the author's main ideas. Details serve to clarify, explain, or illustrate the main idea. When you write, you are sending a message to your readers. Readers are your audience. As a writer, you think of the main ideas and often state them in the form of main idea sentences. Then you develop the details that support your main ideas.

Essentially, reading and writing are part of a communication process. The message begins in the mind of the writer and ends in the mind of the reader. Details are the vehicle to ensure that the message is understood clearly.

The diagram in Figure 4.1 shows this intimate connection between readers and writers.

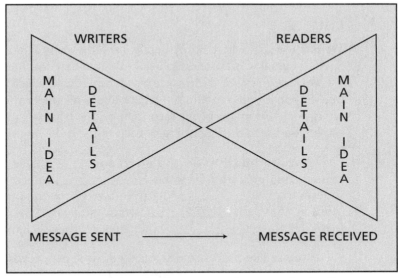

Relationship between Readers and Writers
The Communication Process

Writers *produce* details
to *support* main ideas.

Readers *recognize* details
to *understand* main ideas.

FIGURE 4.1

Patterns of Organization and Signal Words

To write a well-organized paragraph, writers have to create details that have a clear relationship to the main idea. And, to comprehend a paragraph, readers must learn to recognize the way in which details relate to the main idea.

Writers often use the following patterns to establish a relationship between the main idea of a paragraph and its supporting details:

- lists
- examples
- comparison or contrast
- definitions
- cause and effect

Many times you can tell which pattern is used by special *signal words*. These special words tell you about the relationship between the main idea and the details in a paragraph.

Let's look more closely at some patterns of organization and the signal words that help you recognize them.

Lists

Writers use lists when all the details have the same relationship to the main idea. Specific signal words are often used to signal that another item is being added to a list. You use many of these same words when you have a conversation with someone. Suppose you are telling a friend about all the errands you plan to do in an afternoon. You might begin each item on the list with a signal word. What words might you use at the beginning of each of the following sentences?

I have so much to do this afternoon. _____, I have to stop at the cleaners and pick up my clothes. _____, I need to buy some food at the supermarket. _____, my friend asked me to go with him to the doctor's office at 4:00 p.m. _____, I must stop in at the library to return a book that's due today._____, I'd better get the oil changed in my car.

If you're like most people, you used the signal words "first," "second," "third," and so on. You can probably think of other words you could have used in the sentences above. Many words signal the addition of an item to a list:

WORDS THAT SIGNAL A LIST

■ first of all	■ another
■ second	■ in addition
■ one	■ moreover
■ also	■ furthermore
■ finally	■ next
■ then	■ last

These words are frequently used in textbooks and help you follow important details that support main ideas. Underlining significant items on a list in a textbook will help you remember them for more effective study.

PRACTICE EXERCISE 1: RECOGNIZING LISTS

Here is a paragraph that includes a list. What is the topic of the list? How many items are included on the list?

The Bill of Rights entitles suspects or defendants to be represented by a lawyer; to be informed of their legal rights and of the charges against them; to have a speedy and public trial by jury; to summon witnesses to testify in their behalf; to cross-examine prosecution witnesses; and to refuse to testify against themselves.

(Cummings & Wise, *Democracy Under Pressure*, 8th ed., Harcourt Brace, 1997, p. 128.)

The topic of the list is _____.

There are _____ items included in the list.

PRACTICE EXERCISE 2: WRITING PARAGRAPHS WITH LISTS

Choose one of the following topics and write a paragraph using at least four of the words that signal a list.

- your daily routine on a day you attend classes
- the things you like most about one of your close friends
- the reasons you have chosen your major at college
- the challenges you have faced as a college student

Examples

Examples are details that illustrate the main idea. Examples are extremely helpful in making a main idea more understandable and, for this reason, textbooks contain many examples. Sometimes entire paragraphs are examples of a main idea presented in a previous paragraph.

Here is a paragraph with an example that clarifies the main idea.

There are laws in some states that control certain kinds of weapons. New York, for instance, has tight restrictions on the ownership of concealable hand guns. No one, with certain exceptions, can own a pistol or revolver unless he has first obtained a license.

In the paragraph above, the main idea is the first sentence. New York is an *example* of a state that has laws to control a certain kind of weapon, a gun.

The signal words to introduce an example include the following:

WORDS THAT SIGNAL EXAMPLES

- for example
- for instance
- to illustrate
- such as
- like
- including
- to demonstrate
- specifically

PRACTICE EXERCISE 3: RECOGNIZING EXAMPLES

Here are two paragraphs that include examples. Underline the main idea sentence and circle the signal words that introduce the examples in each paragraph.

Political scientists have discovered that people are devotees of rights in theory, but their support waivers when it comes time to put those rights into practice. For example, Americans in general believe in freedom of speech, but many citizens would not let the Ku Klux Klan speak in their neighborhood or allow their public schools to teach about atheism or homosexuality.

(Edwards, Wattenberg, & Lineberry. *Government in America*, 7th. ed., HarperCollins, 1996, p. 83 ed.)

When asked in opinion polls, Americans express more confidence in the Supreme Court than they do in the presidency, Congress, or the federal bureaucracy. Federal judges and justices also rank ahead of members of Congress and bureaucrats in public esteem. In fact, members of the federal bench typically rank higher in opinion polls than nearly any other job category. Moreover, public opinion is more consistently favorable toward the judiciary than toward other institutions.

(Patterson, *We The People: A Concise Introduction to American Politics*, McGraw-Hill, 1995, p. 480.)

PRACTICE EXERCISE 4: WRITING PARAGRAPHS WITH EXAMPLES

Choose one of the main idea sentences below and list three examples to support it. Then write a paragraph using your examples. Be sure to include signal words to introduce each of your examples.

- One of my parents has been a help to me many times in my life.
- It is difficult to find time to do everything I need to do in a day.
- College is a challenging experience.

Comparisons

A comparison indicates a similarity or difference between two things or ideas. A comparison that shows a difference is sometimes called a contrast. Paragraph 1 in Practice Exercise 3 contains a contrast between two ideas. The contrast is as follows: People say they believe in human rights, but do not support what they claim to believe in. The word that signals this relationship is "but." It is used twice—once in the topic sentence (the first sentence) and also in the example (the second sentence).

Signal words that show differences include the following:

WORDS THAT SIGNAL DIFFERENCES

■ but	■ in contrast
■ however	■ instead
■ yet	■ despite
■ in spite of	■ although
■ on the contrary	■ even though
■ on the other hand	■ while

Signal words that show similarities include the following:

Words That Signal Similarities

- like, likewise
- similarly
- in the same way
- just as
- as well
- equally

In the paragraph that follows, underline the main idea sentence (it is actually in two places) and circle the signal word indicating a comparison.

> Today Americans still believe in the Bill of Rights and its commitment to freedom—up to a point. Mark Twain wrote that God gave the American people "the three precious gifts of freedom of speech, freedom of religion, and the prudence never to exercise either of them." Likewise, you have probably heard remarks like "Freedom of the press demands responsibility of the press," "You shouldn't criticize something unless you suggest an alternative," or "Criminals are not entitled to human dignity." These statements reflect the belief that civil liberties sometimes have to yield to other individual or societal values.
>
> (Edwards, Wattenberg, & Lineberry. *Government in America: People, Politics, and Policy,* 7th ed., HarperCollins, 1996, p. 83.)

The main idea is stated in both the first and last sentences. Either one can be considered the main idea sentence. The word *likewise* signals a comparison—that the second example is similar to the first one.

Practice Exercise 5: Recognizing Comparison

In the following paragraph, circle the two things being compared in sentence 1 and underline the signal word in sentence 2 that refers to the comparison.

> [1]What voters actually see and hear of a candidate is primarily determined by the paid media (such as television advertising) accompanying the campaign and the free media (newspaper and television coverage). [2]The two kinds of media are fundamentally different: paid advertising is completely under the control of the campaign, whereas the press is totally independent.
>
> (O'Connor & Sabato, *The Essentials of American Government: Continuity and Change,* 3rd ed., Allyn & Bacon, 1998, p. 351, adapted.)

Practice Exercise 6: Writing Paragraphs with Comparisons

Choose one of the following topics and write a main idea sentence about it. Then write a paragraph in which you explain the similarities or differences of your topic. Use some of the signal words to introduce each point you make.

- living in the United States and another country you have lived in
- living with your parents and living on your own
- the differences between talking and writing

Definitions

Definitions are probably the most common details found in textbooks. That is because every subject you study in college is full of specialized vocabulary you need to learn. Authors often use typographical aids to help you recognize important definitions. For example, the following paragraph contains two definitions. Notice the typographical aids that are used.

> Another type of expression not protected by the First Amendment is **libel**: the publication of false statements that are malicious and damage a person's reputation. *Slander* refers to spoken defamation, while libel refers to written defamation.
>
> (Edwards, Wattenberg, & Lineberry. *Government in America: People, Politics, and Policy,* 7th ed., HarperCollins, 1996, p. 92.)

The use of boldface helps identify the first definition. Another word defined in this paragraph is "slander," but this time the author uses italics rather than boldface. Authors may choose from a variety of typographical aids. In the example above, both terms and definitions are equally important despite the use of different aids. Did you notice that the signal word "while" (in the last sentence) shows that the two terms are being contrasted?

Sometimes definitions follow immediately after a term, sometimes the definition appears in the next sentence, and sometimes the definition is in a sentence before the term. Signal words guide you in pairing the term with its definition. When you read textbooks, be certain to underline all terms and their definitions because this information is crucial to a course's content.

PRACTICE EXERCISE 7: RECOGNIZING DEFINITIONS

In the following paragraph, underline the terms and definitions. Circle the words that signal the definitions.

Eighteenth-century republicans saw the struggle between liberty and power as the core of political life. Power meant dominion or control. Although necessary for the maintenance of order, power's natural tendency was to exceed legitimate boundaries and to invade the sphere of liberty. By liberty, republicans meant both private liberty—such as property rights—and public liberty—the right of the people to have a collective say in government. This view of politics made the actions of the British government especially frightening to the American colonists.

(Miroff, Seidelman, & Swanstrom, *The Democratic Debate: An Introduction to American Politics,* 2nd ed., Houghton Mifflin, 1998, p. 18.)

Cause and Effect

Cause and effect is one of the most important patterns used by writers. You can think of a *cause* as a reason and an *effect* as the result. In the sentence, "It rained so the picnic was canceled," the *cause* is the rain, and the *effect* is the cancellation of the picnic. Sometimes the effect is written first even though it doesn't occur first. For instance, in the sentence, "The picnic was canceled because of the rain," the order has been reversed, but the cause is still the rain and the effect is still the cancellation.

Words that signal a cause–effect relationship include the following:

WORDS THAT SIGNAL CAUSE AND EFFECT

- thus
- because
- as a result
- since

- therefore
- if/then
- reason
- effect

PRACTICE EXERCISE 8: RECOGNIZING CAUSE AND EFFECT

In the paragraph below, decide what cause is given for the effect that "the first ten amendments enjoyed great popular support."

The Bill of Rights was passed when British abuses of the colonists' civil liberties were still a fresh and bitter memory. Newspaper editors had been jailed; citizens had been arrested without cause, detained, and forced to confess at gunpoint or worse. Thus, the first ten amendments enjoyed great popular support.

(Edwards, Wattenberg & Lineberry, *Government in America*, 7th ed., HarperCollins, 1996, p. 83.)

Effect: *The first ten amendments enjoyed great popular support.*

Cause: _____

PRACTICE EXERCISE 9: WRITING PARAGRAPHS
WITH CAUSE AND EFFECT

Choose a topic from the list below and write a paragraph to indicate a cause–effect relationship. Be sure to use signal words to make the relationship clear.

- the attitudes of someone toward you and how those attitudes make you feel
- what would happen if you won a million-dollar lottery
- what would happen if you changed one thing about yourself

PRACTICE EXERCISE 10: DETAILS AND SIGNAL WORDS

Each of the following paragraphs contains different combinations of details. Read each paragraph and answer the questions that follow.

1   ¹In establishing a system of government, the United States Constitution did three things. ²First, it *established the structure* of government. ³In setting up three branches of government within a federal system, it gave the country a political framework that has existed down to the present. ⁴Second, the Constitution *distributed certain powers* to this government. Article I gave legislative powers, such as the power to raise and spend money, to Congress. ⁵Article II gave executive powers to the president, including command over the armed forces and wide authority over foreign policy. . . . ⁶Third, the Constitution *restrained the government* in exercising these powers.

(Wasserman, *The Basics of American Politics*, 7th ed., HarperCollins, 1994, p. 28.)

The main idea sentence is number _____.

This paragraph contains signal words that signal
  a. examples.   d. a cause–effect.
  b. a list.   e. a definition.
  c. a comparison.

2   ¹Civil liberties are a set of protections against government agencies that restrict freedom of expression, such as freedom of speech and religion. ²Civil liberties are those First Amendment rights of freedom of speech, petition, assembly, and press which protect people against governmental actions that would interfere with their participation in a democratic political system. . . . ³Civil rights are a set of protections for some groups, defined in terms of race, religion, ethnicity, or gender, against discrimination by others. ⁴Civil rights involve the protections granted in the Fourteenth Amendment to the Constitution recognizing that all citizens are entitled to be treated equally under the law.

(Wasserman, *The Basics of American Politics*, 7th ed., HarperCollins, 1994, pp. 159–160.)

Sentence 1
  a. defines a term and gives an example.
  b. explains a cause–effect relationship.
  c. compares the similarities between two things.

Sentence 3
  a. gives an example.
  b. defines a term.
  c. presents a list.

The paragraph mostly
   a. defines and contrasts.
   b. contrasts and gives examples.
   c. defines and lists.

3   ¹(The Supreme Court) . . . has ruled that widows and widowers should get equal social security benefits, that men have an equal right to sue for alimony, that the drinking age must be the same for both sexes, that men may not be given preference in administering a relative's estate, and that unwed fathers have rights in deciding whether or not a baby is put up for adoption.
   ²On the other hand, the Court has allowed state laws granting certain tax benefits to widows but not widowers. ³It upheld a state law permitting men but not women to serve as guards in a maximum security prison. ⁴It let stand a lower court decision permitting single-sex schools to continue to receive federal funds. ⁵No challenges to single-sex bathroom facilities have succeeded.

(Wasserman, *The Basics of American Politics*, 7th ed.,
HarperCollins, 1994, p. 179.)

How many details are in sentence 1? _____

The topic of the list in sentence 1 is _____

How many details are listed in sentences 2 through 5? _____

The topic of the list in sentences 2 through 5 is _____

Circle the signal word(s) that show a comparison is being made.

4   ¹The First Amendment provides no protection to speech that directly leads to illegal conduct, or that might be considered conduct in and of itself. ²Shouting "fire" in a crowded theater (where there is no fire) is not considered speech, but rather a reckless action which the state may punish. ³Writing or speaking falsehoods about a person which is damaging (libel and slander) is not protected, and you can be sued for doing so. ⁴Making or selling child pornography is not protected speech and does not involve freedom of expression, and you go to jail for doing so.

(Wasserman, *The Basics of American Politics*, 7th ed., 1994,
HarperCollins, p. 167.)

Underline the main idea sentence.

How many examples are given to illustrate the main idea? _____

In sentence 3, underline the cause and circle the effect.

In sentence 4, underline the cause and circle the effect.

5   ¹The Constitution provided that there would be no religious test for office, and the First Amendment provided for "free exercise of religion" and prohibited the establishment of an official religion by Congress. ²Yet there has never been a complete "wall of separation" between church and state in America. ³The armed forces have chaplains paid for by Congress; the Supreme Court chambers have a mural of Moses giving the Ten Commandments; the dollar bill proclaims "In God We Trust."

(Wasserman, *The Basics of American Politics*, 7th ed., HarperCollins, 1994, p. 168.)

The relationship between sentence 1 and sentence 2 is
   a. cause–effect.
   b. comparison.
   c. example.
   d. definition.

How many examples are in sentence 3? _____

6   ¹In many parts of the country African-Americans find it difficult to rent apartments or purchase homes of their choice because landlords and sellers discriminate against them. ²To combat discriminatory practices many states and the national government have passed fair housing laws, which make such discrimination illegal.

(Wasserman, *The Basics of American Politics*, 7th ed., HarperCollins, 1994, p. 172.)

The signal word in sentence 1 is _____
Sentence 1
   a. explains a cause–effect relationship.
   b. compares the similarities between two things
   c. gives an example.

Using the information in sentence 2, complete the following diagram.

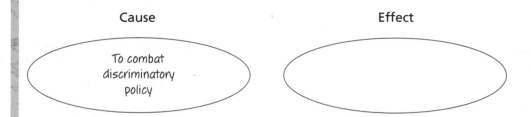

Cause

Effect

To combat discriminatory policy

7   [1]At one time, courts asked private attorneys to donate their services in order to defend the poor. [2]But donating time to help suspected crooks was not popular among the members of the legal profession. [3]As a result, most states have created the office of public defender, an attorney whose full-time responsibility is to provide for legal defense of indigent criminal suspects.

(Fiorina & Peterson, *The New American Democracy,*
Allyn & Bacon, 1998, p. 539.)

Circle the signal word in sentence 2.
The signal word in sentence 2 indicates a
 a. comparison.
 b. example.
 c. definition.
Circle the signal word(s) in sentence 3.
Sentence 3 contains a(n)
 a. example.
 b. definition.
 c. list.
 d. effect.

8   [1]. . . In 1995 the Supreme Court held, 6-3, that public schools could require student athletes to submit to random drug testing. [2]The case arose when James Acton, a seventh-grade student in Vernonia, Oregon, refused to take a urine test required by the school before he could play football.

(Cummings & Wise, *Democracy Under Pressure,*
Harcourt Brace, 1997, p. 121.)

What is the relationship between the two sentences in the paragraph?
 a. The first sentence is the cause and the second sentence is the effect.
 b. The first sentence is the effect and the second sentence is the cause.
 c. The second sentence is an example of the first sentence.
 d. The second sentence is a contrast to the first sentence.

9   [1]Capital punishment remains one of the most debated aspects of our criminal justice system. [2]Those in favor of it maintain that it serves as a deterrent to serious crime and satisfies society's need for justice and fair play. [3]Those opposed to the death penalty do not believe it has any deterrent value and hold that it constitutes a barbaric act in an otherwise civilized society.

(Schmidt, Shelley & Bardes, *American Government and Politics
Today,* West/Wadsworth, 1997, p. 131.)

Underline the main idea sentence.

Complete the diagram below by writing the main idea in the box at the top and writing the details in the larger boxes at the bottom.

```
┌─────────────────────────────────┐
│                                 │
│                                 │
└─────────────────────────────────┘

┌─────────────────┐      ┌─────────────────────┐
│                 │      │                     │
│                 │      │                     │
│                 │      │                     │
└─────────────────┘      └─────────────────────┘
```

10   [1]Several types of expression do not enjoy constitutional immunity from government regulation. [2]These include fraudulent advertising, obscenity, child pornography, libel, and, in some cases, street oratory.

(Cummings & Wise, *Democracy Under Pressure*, 8th ed., Harcourt Brace, 1997, p. 103.)

Underline the main idea sentence.

How many examples are listed in the second sentence? _____

What is the relationship between the second and third sentence?
   a. comparison/contrast
   b. cause–effect
   c. examples

Major and Minor Details

As we've seen, details support a main idea by clarifying or explaining it. However, some details are more important than others. The most important details are called major details because they are directly related to the main idea. In every college course, you are expected to identify, understand, and remember major details in textbooks. Details that support the major details are minor details. They are indirectly related to the main idea.

Paragraphs usually contain a main idea, major details, and minor details. The following chart illustrates these three levels of development:

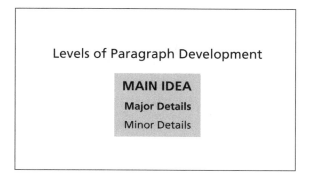

The following paragraph contains a topic sentence, two major details, and two minor details. Try to identify these three levels of development.

¹The Supreme Court ruled that the sponsorship or encouragement of prayer in public schools is unconstitutional and, therefore, forbidden. ²School authorities were no longer allowed to post the Ten Commandments on the walls of public classrooms. ³However, students may carry the Ten Commandments, display it on their clothing, or wear it as jewelry. ⁴Furthermore, the Court rejected the Alabama law which authorized schools to hold one-minute periods of silence for "meditation or voluntary prayer." ⁵Still, students may pray silently as much as they wish.

The first sentence is the topic sentence, because it expresses the main idea that school-supported prayer is unconstitutional and is therefore forbidden. The second sentence is a major detail because it relates directly to the main idea by providing an example of a form of prayer that is prohibited in public schools (posting the Ten Commandments). The third sentence is a minor detail. It relates to the major detail in the second sentence by clarifying when the Ten Commandments may be viewed. However, it does not *directly* support the main idea. The fourth sentence is another major detail because it also gives an example of prayer that is forbidden (periods of silence for meditation). Finally, the last sentence is a minor detail that clarifies the major detail about silent prayer.

The following diagram shows the levels of development in the paragraph.

MAIN IDEA

Supreme Court prohibits prayer in public schools.

First Major Detail	**Second Major Detail**
Ten Commandments may not be posted in public schools.	Public school silence for prayers prohibited.

Minor Detail	**Minor Detail**
Carrying Ten Commandments by individuals allowed.	Private prayer allowed.

PRACTICE EXERCISE 11: RECOGNIZING LEVELS OF DETAILS

Read the following paragraphs and answer the questions that follow each.

1   ¹People of different social and especially educational backgrounds not only have different political opinions but also participate in politics in different ways. ²Ordinarily we think of such participation in terms of voting. ³However, there are many other—and probably more important—ways to participate. ⁴For example, a citizen can join political organizations, contribute money to candidates, write to members of Congress, or simply talk politics with friends and neighbors.

(Wilson, *American Government*, 4th ed., New York: Houghton Mifflin, 1997, p. 140, adapted.)

The main idea is stated in sentence number _____.

The major details are in sentence number _____.

How many examples are mentioned? _____

Circle the signal word that shows a contrast is being made.

2   ¹Social movements tend to beget new social movements; thus, the African-American civil rights movements of the 1960s affected other minorities. ²American Indians and Hispanics began organizing and became newly active. ³American Indian activists like Dennis Means of the American Indian Movement (AIM), Vine Deloria, and Dee Brown drew attention to the plight of the American Indian tribes. ⁴Twenty years later, this movement continues to struggle against the poverty, low

education, and poor health of many American Indians. [5]Led by Cesar Chavez, the United Farm Workers publicized the plight of migrant workers—a large proportion of whom are Hispanic.

(Edwards, Wattenberg, & Lineberry, *Government in America: People, Politics, and Policy,* 7th ed., HarperCollins, 1996, p. 126.)

Complete the following.

Main Idea: The African-American civil rights movements of the 1960s affected other minorities.

Major Detail: _____

Minor Detail: Several American Indian activists drew attention to the plight of the American Indian tribes.

Minor Detail: _____

3   [1]Civil rights laws tell individuals and institutions that there are things they must do and things they cannot do. [2]Restaurant owners must serve all patrons regardless of race. [3]Professional schools must admit women. [4]Employers must accommodate people with disabilities and make an effort to find minority workers, whether they want to or not.

(Edwards, Wattenberg, & Lineberry, *Government in America: People, Politics, and Policy,* 7th ed., HarperCollins, 1996, p. 139, adapted.)

The main idea sentence is sentence number _____.

There are _____ major details that support the main idea.

The major details are
   a. examples.
   b. comparisons.
   c. definitions.
   d. cause–effect.

4   [1]Throughout most of American history, public and private buildings have been hostile to the blind, deaf, and mobility-impaired. [2]Stairs, buses, telephones, and other necessities of modern life have been designed in ways that keep these individuals out of offices, stores, and restaurants. [3]Many people with disabilities have been excluded from the workforce and isolated without overt discrimination. [4]As one slogan said: "Once, blacks had to ride at the back of the bus. [5]We can't even get on the bus."

(Edwards, Wattenberg, & Lineberry, *Government in America: People, Politics, and Policy,* 7th ed., HarperCollins, 1996, p. 134.)

Complete the following.

Main Idea: Throughout most of American history, public and private buildings have been hostile to the blind, deaf, and mobility-impaired.

Major Detail: _____

Major Detail: Many people with disabilities have been excluded from the workforce and isolated without overt discrimination.

Writing Coherent Paragraphs

When you write a paragraph, you want it to make sense to the reader. When you present your ideas and facts logically, readers will understand your message more easily, more accurately, and with more enjoyment. The orderly progression of facts and ideas arranged in a logical sequence is called paragraph coherence. You may organize the ideas in a coherent paragraph by time, place, or importance.

Time Order

Time order (also called *chronological order*) is a way of organizing events in the order in which they occur. It is a good way to arrange paragraphs when you write about your own experiences or are telling a story.

The following paragraph is about the writer's experience of voting in a political election. Underline the main idea sentence and notice how the detail sentences are organized.

The pamphlet said voting was easy—just go and pull the lever of your choice. However, the first time I voted I became very frustrated. *First,* I had to stand in a long line to sign in. *Then,* the woman at the sign-in desk had some trouble finding my name. I guess that's because I changed it since the time I registered to vote. *Next,* I was told to go and stand in another long line by this big machine with a gray curtain. I guess I should have done some homework on what to expect when I got into this contraption, but I didn't. *At this point* I was feeling nervous. *Finally,* I was at the front of the line. I was told to go in to the voting booth and pull the lever behind me. *After* stepping into the booth, I turned around and pulled the lever, closing the curtain. *Now,* I was really nervous. Imagine, I could become the first person in the United States to fail at voting. Since I really wanted to exercise my right as a citizen, I pulled a few levers. *After* I was finished, I ran all the way home having decided that next time, I would be better prepared before going to vote.

In the above example the main idea is in the second sentence, *the first time I voted I became very frustrated.* The details are arranged in the order in which they occurred. Notice that signal words (*first, then, next, after, at this point, now*) are used to help guide you through the sequence of events. As you may have noticed, signal words for time order are similar to those used for listing. In fact, time order is a way of listing events.

PRACTICE EXERCISE 12: RECOGNIZING TIME ORDER IN PARAGRAPHS

In each group below, the first sentence is the main idea sentence. Number the sentences listed below the main idea to indicate correct time order. Circle any signal words you can find.

1. A criminal trial goes through several stages.

_____ Second, the prosecuting attorney calls the first witness.

_____ When the prosecutor is finished with his examination, the defense attorney may question the same witness.

_____ First, the jury is selected by both attorneys.

_____ Next, the defense attorney begins calling his witnesses to the stand.

_____ After all witnesses have been questioned, the jury begins deliberation to reach a verdict.

2. Over the years, the Supreme Court has shown a definite interest in protecting the civil liberties of individuals.

_____ Three years later the Court established the Miranda rights, doing away with the possibility of police obtaining confessions under coercion.

_____ In 1963 the Court held that if a person is accused of a felony and cannot afford an attorney, one must be made available to the accused person at the government's expense.

_____ In 1984 the Court held that when "public safety" required action, police could interrogate the suspect before advising him of his right to remain silent.

_____ In 1968 the Omnibus Crime Control and Safe Streets Act provided that in federal cases, a voluntary confession could be used as evidence even if the accused person was not informed of his or her rights.

(Schmidt, Shelley II, & Bardes, *American Government and Politics Today,* West/Wadsworth, 1998, p. 130, adapted.)

3. The Supreme Court has frequently placed limits on speech.

_____ Supreme Court Justice Oliver Wendell Holmes, Jr., in 1919, established the classic "clear and present danger" test to define the point at which speech loses First Amendment protection.

_____ The Court's free-speech yardstick shifted again in the 1930s to 1940s, during the New Deal and the Second World War.

_____ Finally, the Court appeared to swing back to the "clear and present danger" test in the 1950s.

_____ In 1925 the Court ruled that some speech could be prohibited if it threatened the overthrow of the government or in other ways injured the public welfare.

(Cummings & Wise, *Democracy Under Pressure*, Harcourt Brace, 1997. pp. 103–104, adapted.)

4. In interpreting the establishment clause, the Supreme Court has sometimes been less restrictive in permitting religious-oriented extracurricular activities.

_____ Mergens took her case to court.

_____ The Supreme Court ruled that Mergen's Bible club should have been allowed to meet in her public high school on the same basis as other extracurricular clubs.

_____ Bridget Mergens, a high school senior at a school in Omaha, Nebraska, asked permission to organize a Christian Bible study group at the school.

_____ The principal and the school board refused to allow a Bible club.

(Cummings & Wise, *Democracy Under Pressure*, Harcourt Brace, 1997, pp. 117–118, adapted.)

5. Sometimes a change in venue to avoid publicity can have a dramatic effect on the outcome of a trial.

_____ In 1992, black motorist Rodney King was videotaped by an amateur cameraman as he was beaten by Los Angeles police after he tried to get away when asked to stop by a police officer.

_____ The jury found three of the four officers innocent of all charges, and it could not agree on charges against the fourth.

_____ Since many residents of Simi Valley were former police officers and army personnel, the jury ended up consisting of several people associated with law enforcement.

_____ The trial court judge picked Simi Valley as the new venue because its docket was short and extra space was available for the expected avalanche of reporters.

_____ When the officers were brought to trial, a state appeals court ordered a change of venue to escape the racial passions that had been aroused in Los Angeles.

(Fiorina & Peterson, *The New American Democracy,* Allyn & Bacon, 1998, p. 538, adapted.)

PRACTICE EXERCISE 13: WRITING PARAGRAPHS IN TIME ORDER

Write a paragraph about one of the following topics. Arrange your details in time order.

■ Describe what you have done since you woke up this morning.
■ Tell about an experience you had while traveling.
■ Describe an experience you had looking for a job.

Place Order

Place order is a way of organizing details according to where they are located. Writers often use place order when describing places. Using place order makes it easier for readers to understand where objects and people are in relation to one another. This way of organizing details helps paint a picture in the reader's mind.

The following paragraph describes a jail facility in Indiana. Notice that the details are arranged in such a way as to let you visualize the scene.

The Gibson County Jail is a modern 32,000-square-foot facility, constructed in 1988 and opened in July 1989. The all steel and concrete facility houses a maximum of 68 prisoners in cell blocks on two floors, as well as having a padded cell, two isolation cells and a detoxification cell. Work release inmates are housed in a separate area above the Sheriff's Department.

The booking room is located adjacent to the parking garage in the basement. All inmates are processed through here by Corrections Officers prior to being assigned a cell. A holding cell and clothing storage room are also located near the booking room. The jail also has its own kitchen, interrogation room, medical examination room, Corrections Division offices and indoor and outdoor recreation yards for inmates.

(www.comsource.net/~gcsd/corrections/corrections.html)

PRACTICE EXERCISE 14: RECOGNIZING PLACE ORDER IN PARAGRAPHS

As you read the following paragraph, visualize the scene described.

There is no right or wrong way to demonstrate—the demo should be conducted in a way to best highlight the political issues involved. However, in New York City the police appear to be increasingly permitting less variety and spontaneity in demonstrations. If the demonstration is on a city sidewalk the police will usually construct a pen with barricades within which they will confine stationary demonstrators. Often these pens are a block or more from the actual site being protested. Demonstrators that march will be required to stay on the sidewalk and not completely block the sidewalk.

(www.actupny.org/documents/demomanual/atthedemo.html)

In the space below, sketch the scene you imagined as you read the paragraph.

PRACTICE EXERCISE 15: WRITING PARAGRAPHS USING PLACE ORDER

Write a paragraph about one of the following topics. Arrange your details in place order.

- Describe the street on which you live.
- Describe the room in which you sleep.
- Describe the route you take to get from home to school.

Order of Importance

As a writer you have a choice in how you order details in terms of importance. One way often used is to start with less important or dramatic details and work toward the more important or more dramatic ones. Leaving more dramatic or remarkable details until the end creates a climax for your readers. Another option is to start your paragraph with the most important details in order to emphasize them.

Here is a paragraph with details in order of importance.

Having a good routine is an important part of studying. First of all, avoid studying when you're hungry or tired. You may also want to find a comfortable place to study that is quiet and free of distractions. But most importantly, schedule enough time so you can concentrate without feeling pressured. Now you will be able to do the important task of comprehending and remembering what you are studying.

The writer has listed the ingredients for an effective study routine by first mentioning what he considers to be the least important point. He has used signal words to help the reader understand the order of importance.

PRACTICE EXERCISE 16: RECOGNIZING ORDER OF IMPORTANCE IN PARAGRAPHS

Read the paragraph below. Then complete the story by numbering the sentences in order of importance, with 1 being the most important, and 4 being the least important.

The worst night of my life was the night my best friend, Joe, and I decided to take a drive. It was a cold night in February, and after we had gone about 30 miles it began to snow heavily. The road quickly became slippery; I could only see a few yards ahead of me as I carefully steered the car toward home. Suddenly another car came around the curve and swerved, hitting my car head on.

_____ It would cost a lot of money to repair the car.

_____ Later I learned that Joe lost his leg in the accident.

_____ The car was not as badly damaged as it might have been.

_____ The radio was broken, the cigarette lighter didn't work, the headlights were smashed, and the bumper was torn off.

PRACTICE EXERCISE 17: WRITING PARAGRAPHS USING ORDER OF IMPORTANCE

Write a paragraph about one of the following topics. Use order of importance in writing your details.

■ going out on a date
■ putting a child to sleep
■ reasons for not taking illegal drugs or smoking

In the next section of this chapter you will read a textbook selection dealing with civil liberties. The word *civil* is related to the word *citizens*. Think about the liberties you enjoy as a citizen.

Application

Textbook Selections
Civil Liberties

Before Reading

The second level of Maslow's hierarchy of needs is *safety*. To consider this need you will read a section of a chapter from an American Government textbook that deals with the Bill of Rights.

1. Quickly write down everything you thought of when you read the words "Bill of Rights."

   _____

   _____

   _____

   _____

2. Most people who live in the United States would agree that, as residents of this country, they are entitled to certain rights. What rights do you believe you are entitled to because you live in the United States?

   _____

   _____

   _____

   _____

3. Which of the rights you listed above gives you a sense of safety? In other words, without which rights would you feel less safe than you do now? Explain the effect that right has on your personal sense of safety as a citizen of the United States.

   _____

   _____

   _____

   _____

4. As mentioned earlier, every textbook has a different way of presenting headings and subheadings. It is very important to accustom yourself to these typographical features of your textbooks. Once you are able to determine the difference between the headings and subheadings, you can develop an outline of the chapter before you begin to read. Such an outline serves as a kind of road map for traveling through the chapter. You can also use the headings and subheadings to decide how many sections of a chapter you want to read in one study session.

The headings in this chapter from *Government in America: People, Politics, and Policy* are different from the headings in the previous chapter on physiological needs taken from a health textbook. The main headings in this chapter are The Bill of Rights—Then and Now, Defendants' Rights, and Freedom of Expression. Look through pages 147 to 155 and, in the space below, write what you notice about the appearance of these headings.

---

5. Now complete the outline by writing the correct subheadings under the headings.

The Bill of Rights—Then and Now

Defendants' Rights

Freedom of Expression

During Reading

Now read the introductory section of the chapter, "Civil Liberties and Public Policy," from *Government in America*.

1   Civil liberties are individual legal and constitutional protections against the government. Americans' civil liberties are set down in the Bill of Rights, but disputes

about civil liberties often end up in court. The courts are the arbiters of these liberties because they determine what the Constitution means in the cases that they decide. The Supreme Court of the United States is the final interpreter of the content and scope of our liberties; this ultimate power to interpret the Constitution accounts for much of the ferocious debate over presidential appointments to the Supreme Court.

1. Paragraph 1 contains a definition of civil liberties. Underline the definition.
2. There are two important details in this paragraph: where our civil liberties are written down, and which government agency has final say over the interpretation of these liberties. Underline these details.

As you continue to read, underline information you think is important. The questions at the end of this section can be used as a self-check. If you have underlined the answers to the questions, you have identified the important details.

The Bill of Rights—Then and Now

2   By the time of the 1787 Convention, all of the state constitutions had bills of rights, some of which survive, intact, to this day. Although the new U.S. Constitution had no bill of rights, the states made it clear that a condition of ratification was the addition of a Bill of Rights. The first ten amendments to the Constitution comprise the Bill of Rights. They were passed as a group by the First Congress in 1789 and sent to the states for ratification. In 1791, these amendments became part of the Constitution.

3   The Bill of Rights ensures Americans basic liberties: freedom of speech and religion, protection against arbitrary searches and being held for long periods without trial, and so forth. Since the rest of this chapter will discuss the Bill of Rights, this is a good time for you to read it carefully. Pay particular attention to the First Amendment, the source of Americans' freedom of religion, speech, press, and assembly. The Bill of Rights was passed when British abuses of the colonists' civil liberties were still a fresh and bitter memory. Newspaper editors had been jailed; citizens had been arrested without cause, detained, and forced to confess at gunpoint or worse. Thus, the first ten amendments enjoyed great popular support.

4   Today Americans still believe in the Bill of Rights and its commitment to freedom—up to a point. Mark Twain wrote that God gave the American people "the three precious gifts of freedom of speech, freedom of religion, and the prudence never to exercise either of them." Likewise, you have probably heard remarks like "Freedom of the press demands responsibility of the press," "You shouldn't criticize something unless you suggest an alternative," or "Criminals are not entitled to human dignity." These statements reflect the belief that civil liberties sometimes have to yield to other individual or societal values.

5   Political scientists have discovered that people are devotees of rights in theory, but their support waivers when it comes time to put those rights into practice. For example, Americans in general believe in freedom of speech, but many citizens would not let the Ku Klux Klan speak in their neighborhood or allow their public schools to teach about atheism or homosexuality.

(Edwards, Wattenberg, & Lineberry, Government in America:
People, Politics, and Policy, HarperCollins, 1996, p. 83.)

3. What is the Bill of Rights?
4. When was the Bill of Rights passed?
5. When did the Bill of Rights become part of the Constitution?
6. What rights does the First Amendment include?
7. Why did the Bill of Rights enjoy popular support from the colonists when it was passed?
8. Underline the topic sentence of paragraph 5. (Remember, examples are never topic sentences.)

After Reading

Vocabulary in Context

Listed below are words from the textbook selection you have read. After rereading the sentences in which these words are located, write the meaning you think each word has. Finally, for each word, write the definition you find in a dictionary.

Word and Paragraph	My Guess at Meaning	Dictionary Definition
ferocious (1)		
intact (2)		
ensure (3)		
waiver (5)		

During Reading

Defendants' Rights

1   The Bill of Rights contains only forty-four words that guarantee the freedoms of religion, speech, press, and assembly. Most of the remaining words concern the rights of people accused of crimes. These rights were originally intended to protect the accused in *political* arrests and trials; British abuse of colonial political leaders was still fresh in the memory of American citizens. Today the protections in the Fourth, Fifth, Sixth, Seventh, and Eighth Amendments are mostly applied in criminal justice cases.

2   It is useful to think of the stages of the criminal justice system as a series of funnels decreasing in size. Generally speaking, a *crime* is (sometimes) followed by an *arrest*, which is (sometimes) followed by a *prosecution*, which is (sometimes) followed by a *trial*, which (usually) results in a verdict of innocence or guilt. The funnels get smaller and smaller, each dripping into the next. Many more crimes occur than are reported; many more crimes are reported than arrests are made (the ratio is about five to one); many more arrests are made than prosecutors prosecute; and many more prosecutions occur than jury trials.

Interpreting Defendants' Rights

3   The Bill of Rights sets out a number of civil liberties that American citizens have if they are arrested or brought to court. The Bill of Rights covers every stage of the criminal justice system; at every step, police, prosecutors, and judges must behave in accordance with the Bill of Rights. Any misstep may invalidate a conviction.

4   The language of the Bill of Rights comes, of course, from the late 1700s. It is often vague. For example, just how speedy is a "speedy trial"? How "cruel and unusual" does a punishment have to be in order to violate the Eighth Amendment? The courts continually must rule on the constitutionality of actions by police, prosecutors, judges, and legislatures—actions that a citizen or group could claim violate certain rights. Defendants' rights, just as those rights protected by the First Amendment, are not well defined in the Bill of Rights.

Searches and Seizures

5   Police cannot arrest a citizen without reason. They need evidence to arrest, and courts need evidence to convict. Before making an arrest, police need what the courts call probable cause to believe that someone is guilty of a crime. Often police need to get physical evidence—a car thief's fingerprints, a snatched purse—to use in court. The Fourth Amendment is quite specific in forbidding unreasonable searches and seizures. To prevent abuse of police power, the Constitution requires that no court may issue a search warrant unless probable cause exists to believe that a crime has occurred or is about to occur. Warrants must specify the area to be searched and what police believe is likely to be found in the search.

6   There is no constitutional requirement that a warrant is necessary for a reasonable police search, however. Most searches in this country take place without warrants. Such searches are valid if probable cause exists, if the search is necessary to protect an officer's safety, or if the search is limited to material relevant to the suspected crime or within the suspect's immediate control.

7   Normally, if police find anything in a search, they find what they have probable cause to believe is there. In two cases involving Fourth Amendment issues, authorities used aerial searches to secure the evidence they needed. The first case involved a marijuana grower named Ciraolo. When police, responding to a tip, went to look at his place, it was surrounded by ten-foot fences. The police then rented a private plane, took pictures of the crop, and secured a conviction. Environmental Protection Agency officials took a similar aerial photo of Dow Chemical's Midland, Michigan, plant and located environmental violations. Both Ciraolo and Dow sued, claiming they were the victims of unconstitutional search and seizure. Both, however, lost when their cases came before the Supreme Court. Since then, the Court has also upheld roadside checkpoints in which police randomly examine drivers for signs of intoxication (*Michigan v. Sitz,* 1990).

8   Ever since 1914, the courts have used an exclusionary rule to prevent illegally seized evidence from being introduced in the courtroom. The logic of the exclusionary rule is as follows: if police officers are forced to gather evidence properly, their competence will be rewarded in a conviction; if they are slapdash or ignore the rights of a suspect, they will not win a conviction. Critics of the exclusionary rule, some of whom sit on the Supreme Court, argue that its strict application may permit guilty persons to go free because of police carelessness or innocent errors. The guilty, they say, should not go free because of a "technicality." Defenders of the exclusionary rule respond that the Constitution is not a technicality. Defendants' rights protect the accused (everyone is supposed to be presumed innocent until proven guilty), not the guilty.

(Edwards, Wattenberg, & Lineberry, *Government in America: People, Politics, and Policy,* HarperCollins, 1996, p. 99–102.)

1. According to paragraph 1, which Amendments of the Bill of Rights are concerned with a defendant's rights?

   _____

2. Complete the table below using the information from paragraph 5.

Cause	Effect
probable cause	
search warrant	

3. Paragraph 6 lists criteria for a valid police search without a warrant. How many criteria are listed? _____
4. Underline the main idea sentence of paragraph 7.
5. Paragraph 8 discusses the exclusionary rule. Check all of the following aspects of the exclusionary rule mentioned in the paragraph:

   ■ exceptions to the rule _____

   ■ arguments defending the rule _____

   ■ an explanation of what the rule means _____

   ■ arguments against the rule _____

   ■ who wrote the rule _____

Self-Incrimination

9   Suppose that evidence has been gathered and suspicion directed toward a particular person, and the police are ready to make an arrest. In the American system, the burden of proof rests on the police and the prosecutors. Suspects cannot be forced to help with their own conviction by, say, blurting out a confession in the stationhouse. The **Fifth Amendment** forbids forced self-incrimination, stating that no person "shall be compelled to be a witness against himself." Whether in a congressional hearing, a courtroom, or a police station, suspects need not provide evidence that can later be used against them. Under law, though, the government may guarantee suspects *immunity*—exemption from prosecution. In return, suspects must testify regarding their own and others' misdeeds.

10   You have probably seen television shows in which an arrest is made and the arresting officers recite, often from memory, a set of rights to the arrestee. These rights are authentic and originated from a famous court decision—perhaps the most important modern decision in criminal law—involving an Arizona man named Ernesto Miranda.

11   Miranda was picked up as a prime suspect in the rape and kidnapping of an 18-year-old girl. Selected by the girl from a police lineup, Miranda was questioned for two hours. During this time, he was told of neither his constitutional right against self-incrimination nor his right to counsel. In fact, it seems highly unlikely that Miranda had even heard of the Fifth Amendment. He said enough to eventually lead to a conviction. The Supreme Court reversed his conviction on appeal, however (*Miranda v. Arizona,* 1966) and also set the following guidelines for police questioning of suspects:

- Suspects must be told that they have a constitutional right to remain silent and may stop answering questions at any time.
- They must be warned that what they say can be used against them in a court of law.
- They must be told that they have a right to have a lawyer present during questioning and that a public defender is available.

12   Police departments throughout the country were originally disgruntled by *Miranda.* Officers felt that interrogation was crucial to any investigation. Warning suspects of their rights and letting them call a lawyer were almost certain to silence them. Most departments today, however, seem to take *Miranda* seriously. They usually read a *Miranda* card advising suspects of their rights. Ironically, when Ernesto Miranda himself was murdered, the suspect was read his rights from a *Miranda* card.

The Right to Counsel

13   One of the most important of the *Miranda* rights is the right to secure counsel. Even lawyers taken to court hire another lawyer to represent them. There is an old

saying in the legal profession that a lawyer who defends himself has a fool for a client. Although the **Sixth Amendment** has always ensured the right to counsel in federal courts, this right was not extended to people tried in state courts until recently. Winning this right for poor defendants was a long fight. Until the 1930s, individuals were tried and sometimes convicted for capital offenses (those in which the death penalty could be imposed) without a lawyer. In 1932, the Supreme Court ordered the states to provide an attorney for indigent (poor) defendants accused of a capital crime (*Powell v. Alabama*).

Trial by Jury

14   If you ever visit a typical American criminal courtroom, you will rarely see a trial complete with judge and jury. In American courts, 90 percent of all cases begin and end with a guilty plea. Most cases are settled through a process called **plea bargaining.** A plea bargain results from an actual bargain struck between a defendant's lawyer and a prosecutor to the effect that a defendant will plead guilty to a lesser crime (or fewer crimes) in exchange for a state's not prosecuting that defendant for a more serious (or additional) crime.

15   Critics of the plea-bargaining system believe that it permits many criminals to avoid "facing the music"—or as much music as they could face if tried for a more serious offense. The process, however, works to the advantage of both sides; it saves the state the time and money that would otherwise be spent on a trial, and it permits defendants who think they might be convicted of a serious charge to plead guilty to a lesser one.

16   For those 300,000 cases per year that actually go to trial, there are many rights available to defendants. The Sixth Amendment ensures the right to a speedy trial by an impartial jury. These days, defendants—those who can afford it, at least—do not leave jury selection to chance. A sophisticated technology of jury selection has developed. Jury consultants—often psychologists or other social scientists putting some of their statistical training to use—develop profiles of jurors likely to be sympathetic or hostile to a defendant. Lawyers for both sides spend hours questioning prospective jurors in a major case.

(Edwards, Wattenberg, & Lineberry, *Government in America: People, Politics, and Policy,* HarperCollins, 1996, p. 102–105.)

6. Underline the main idea sentence in paragraph 9.
7. Underline the definition of *immunity* in paragraph 9.
8. The *Miranda* ruling functions to protect individuals against

_____ .

9. True _____ or False _____ : According to the Sixth Amendment, courts are required to appoint a lawyer only for those who are accused of a capital crime and do not have the money to hire one.
10. Underline the explanation of plea bargaining in paragraph 14.
11. List the disadvantage and advantages of plea bargaining mentioned in paragraph 15.

Disadvantage   **Advantages**

1)   1)

                                              2)

12. List the two rights to which defendants are entitled as mentioned in paragraph 16.

_____

_____

After Reading

1. Vocabulary in Context

Listed below are words from the textbook selection you have read on defendants' rights. After rereading the sentences in which these words are located, write the meaning you think each word has. Finally, for each word, write the definition you find in a dictionary.

Word and Paragraph	My Guess at Meaning	Dictionary Definition
funnel (2)		
misstep (3)		
invalidate (3)		
aerial (7)		
slapdash (8)		
blurt (9)		
disgruntled (12)		
interrogation (12)		
crucial (12)		
ironically (12)		
counsel (13)		

2. **Topics for Writers—Defendants' Rights**

   1) Have you ever served on a jury? Have you ever witnessed an actual courtroom proceeding? What is your opinion of our jury system?

   2) Do you believe police should have the right to carry out a search without a warrant? Explain your reasons for your opinion.

   3) Do you think everyone in this country receives equal and fair treatment from our court system? Explain your reasons for your opinion.

During Reading

Freedom of Expression

1   A democracy depends on the free expression of ideas. Thoughts that are muffled, speech that is forbidden, and meetings that cannot be held are the enemies of the democratic process. Totalitarian governments know this, which is the reason that they go to enormous trouble to limit expression.

2   Americans pride themselves on their free and open society. Freedom of conscience is absolute; Americans can *believe* whatever they want to believe. The First Amendment plainly forbids the national government from limiting freedom of *expression,* that is, the right to say or publish what one believes. Is freedom of expression, then, like freedom of conscience, also *absolute*? Supreme Court Justice Hugo Black thought so; he was fond of pointing out that the First Amendment said Congress shall make *no* law. "I read no law abridging to mean *no* law abridging." In fact, in 1992, the Supreme Court ruled in *R.A.V. v. St. Paul* that legislatures or universities may not single out racial, religious, or sexual insults or threats for prosecution as "hate speech" or "bias crimes."

3   Yet courts have often ruled that there are instances when speech needs to be controlled, especially when the First Amendment conflicts with other rights. A classic example of impermissible speech was offered in 1919 by Justice Oliver Wendell Holmes: "The most stringent protection of free speech would not protect a man in falsely shouting 'fire' in a theater and causing a panic." The courts have been called upon to decide where to draw the line separating permissible from impermissible speech. In doing so, judges have had to balance freedom of expression against competing values like public order, national security, and the right to a fair trial.

4   The courts have also had to decide what kinds of activities do and do not constitute *speech* (or press) within the meaning of the First Amendment. Holding a political rally to attack an opposing candidate's stand on important issues gets First Amendment protection. Obscenity and libel, which are also expressions, do not. To make things still more complicated, certain forms of nonverbal speech, like picketing, are considered symbolic speech and receive First Amendment protection. Other forms of expression, such as fraud and incitement to violence, are considered *action* rather than speech. Government can limit action more easily than it can limit expression.

(Edwards, Wattenberg, & Lineberry, *Government in America:
People, Politics, and Policy,* HarperCollins, 1996, p. 90.)

1. Paragraph 2 contrasts freedom of _____
   with freedom of _____.

2. Paragraph 3 discusses controlling speech. The example given of speech that
   needs to be controlled is about _____.

3. Complete the table below using the information from paragraph 4.

Protected	Not Protected
1) _____	1) _____
2) _____	2) _____
	3) _____
	4) _____

After Reading

1. Words in Context

In the left column below are a list of words and the paragraphs in which they can be found. In the right column are definitions of the words. Reread the sentences that contain these words and then match each word with its definition.

Word and Paragraph	Definition
1) muffle (1)	a. anything that damagingly misrepresents
2) stringent (3)	b. deceit to gain some dishonest advantage
3) libel (4)	c. urging on, prompting to action
4) fraud (4)	d. to deaden sound
5) incitement (4)	e. strict, severe

2. Topics for Writers

1) Have you ever been stopped from expressing your thoughts, ideas, or feelings? What were the circumstances? How did it make you feel? What did you do?

2) Would you be strongly opposed to having any of the following speakers give a lecture at your college campus? Why?

- a Nazi supporter
- a member of the Ku Klux Klan
- a supporter of the right of a woman to have an abortion
- a supporter of the "Right to Life" movement
- a member of the Communist party

Additional Readings

THE CASE OF CAROL BAYLESS

Article One

Not Suspicious To Flee Police, Judge Declares

New York Times, January 25, 1996, sec. B, p. 1

Before Reading

Freewrite for a few minutes in response to one of the following questions:

1. Have you ever been stopped by the police? Describe the circumstances. What was the reason for being stopped? How did you feel? Write about your memories of the event.
2. When police make an illegal search, what do you think should happen to any evidence that is obtained?

This article describes an incident that took place in Washington Heights, a neighborhood of New York City.

1   A Federal judge ruled yesterday that 80 pounds of cocaine and heroin seized from a woman's car in Washington Heights could not be used as evidence, saying that it was understandable—and not suspicious—for four men who had just delivered the packages to run away when they recognized a police officer.

2   In a sharply worded ruling yesterday, Judge Harold Baer Jr. said the act of running away from the police—which an officer said he had found suspicious enough to pull over the woman's car and search it—is considered reasonable behavior in Washington Heights, a neighborhood racked by police brutality and corruption scandals.

3   "Even before this prosecution and the public hearing and final report of the Mollen Commission, residents in this neighborhood tended to regard police officers as corrupt, abusive and violent," wrote Judge Baer, who once served on the Mollen Commission, which investigated police corruption during the Dinkins (mayoral) administration. "After the attendant publicity surrounding the above events, had the men not run when the cops began to stare at them, it would have been unusual."

4   The judge's order in Federal District Court in Manhattan knocked out Federal prosecutors' best evidence against Carol Bayless, a 41-year-old Detroit woman charged with possessing 75 pounds of cocaine and more than 4 pounds of heroin. The police found the drugs stuffed inside two black duffel bags in the trunk of her rental car, which they had stopped at the corner of Amsterdam Avenue and 176th Street just before dawn on April 21, 1995.

5   Besides the seized drugs, Judge Baer also threw out Ms. Bayless's 40-minute videotaped confession, in which she told detectives that she had made at least 20 trips from Michigan to New York City to buy cocaine for her son and others starting in 1991. She told the police she was to be paid $20,000 to trade $1 million in cash for cocaine and heroin with a street value of at least $4 million.

6   In an unmarked patrol car parked behind Ms. Bayless's car, a New York City police officer had watched four men walk single file up to the trunk, place the bags inside and—after seeing the plainclothes officer—run away in different directions.

For that reason, and others, the officer said he decided to stop Ms. Bayless's car and search it. After finding the drugs in the trunk of her 1995 red Chevrolet Caprice rental car, Officer Richard Carroll arrested her.

7   Judge Baer, however, said that the officer did not have a reasonable suspicion that she had committed a crime before he opened her trunk. He viewed Ms. Bayless's behavior before being pulled over as "innocuous" and "consistent with a person leaving early in the morning on a long drive to return home to Michigan after visiting relatives in New York City."

8   If Federal prosecutors do not appeal the decision, the three felony charges against Ms. Bayless will be dropped and she will be released from Metropolitan Correctional Center, where she has been jailed for nine months, since the arrest. Ms. Bayless reacted with glee yesterday over the ruling, her lawyer, Ramon W. Pagan, said. If convicted, Ms. Bayless faced a maximum sentence of life in prison and a minimum of 10 years in prison.

9   "What's happening in upper Manhattan is a lot of police officers are being cowboys and they are doing whatever they want," Mr. Pagan said. "There are very few judges willing to say, 'We do not believe your stories.' But this judge had the courage to say that."

10   Mr. Pagan contended that race was a motive for suspecting Ms. Bayless. "Because my client is black," he said, "the police decided they had an unfettered right to stop her and look in the trunk of her car."

11   The judge, who is white, and who served as the first executive director of the Police Department's Civilian Complaint Review Board, appeared to agree. In an aside in his ruling, he wrote, "What I find shattering is that in this day and age blacks in black neighborhoods and blacks in white neighborhoods can count on little security for their person."

12   Marvin Smilon, a spokesman for the United States Attorney's Office, said prosecutors were reviewing the judge's order and would decide in a few weeks whether to appeal. He declined to discuss the order.

13   Officer Carroll could not be reached for comment yesterday; calls to the Police Department for him were not returned. But when told about Judge Baer's ruling late yesterday, Patrick J. Harnett, the commander of the Police Department's narcotics division, said simply: "Incredible. The citizenry would expect the police to make those kinds of inquiries."

14   Besides seeing the men flee, Officer Carroll said at a hearing in Federal District Court in Manhattan earlier this month that he had other reasons for suspecting Ms. Bayless: the Washington Heights neighborhood, which he called "a hub of drug activity," the car's Michigan tag, the slow manner in which Ms. Bayless drove through the neighborhood, and her double-parking.

15   But Judge Baer, who was appointed to the Federal bench by President Clinton in 1994, rejected the officer's argument that those factors met the Federal court

standard of a "reasonable, articulable suspicion" that Ms. Bayless had committed a crime.

16   Judge Baer ruled that Ms. Bayless's videotaped confession was not admissible because the initial stopping of her car was not justified.

17   "It follows," the judge wrote, "that the subsequent search of her car, the seizure of the drugs from the trunk and the defendant's post-arrest statements being the fruits of a tainted search must and will be suppressed."

After Reading

1.   Comprehension Check

_____ 1) What is the main idea of this article?
   a. Carol Bayless's car was searched illegally by the police when they seized drugs.
   b. Four men ran away from the police.
   c. A criminal involved in transporting drugs may go free.
   d. The judge ruled to exclude drug evidence, saying it is reasonable to run from the police.

_____ 2) The police stopped and searched Ms. Bayless's car because
   a. she was a black woman.
   b. she had Michigan license plates.
   c. she had drugs in her car.
   d. seeing the men run made the police suspicious.

_____ 3) The judge believes that the reason the men ran away was
   a. they were afraid of the police.
   b. they were guilty of criminal behavior.
   c. the cops stared at them.
   d. they were in a rush.

_____ 4) How was the work of the Mollen Commission related to Judge Baer's decision in this case?
   a. The Mollen Commission found Ms. Bayless guilty.
   b. The Commission helped get rid of police corruption.
   c. It may have contributed to his belief that people have good reason to run from the police.
   d. It was not related.

5) Put this list of the events, which led to the arrest of Carol Bayless, into the correct time order.
   a. An unmarked patrol car was parked behind Ms. Bayless.
   b. Four men ran away in different directions.
   c. Officer Carroll searched the trunk of the car.

    d. Police watched four men walk single file up to the car.

    e. Four men saw the plainclothes officer.

    f. Ms. Bayless was arrested.

    g. Bags were placed inside the trunk of the car.

    h. Officers stopped Ms. Bayless's car.

2. Mapping

Mapping is a good way to recognize cause and effect relationships. Fill in the blanks in this map with reasons (causes) that the police thought were suspicious enough to warrant a search and seizure.

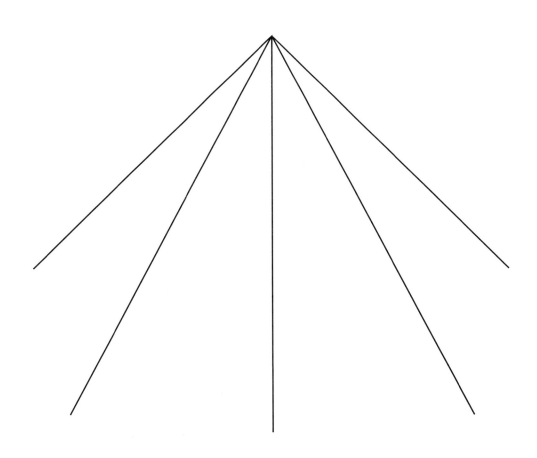

Search and Seizure

Reasonable Suspicion

3. **Vocabulary in Context**

Find each of the following words in the article and guess its meaning from the context. Then match each of the words with the definition with which you think it belongs.

Word and Paragraph	Definition
1) glee (8)	a. harmless
2) unfettered (10)	b. to contaminate or corrupt
3) racked (2)	c. joy
4) innocuous (7)	d. able to express clearly
5) hub (14)	e. tormented, distressed
6) articulable (15)	f. not confined or restrained
7) tainted (17)	g. the center of activity

4. **A Topic for Writers**

How would you have decided this case if you were the judge?

Article Two

Handcuffing the Police

New York Times, February 1, 1996, sec. A, p. 21, col. 2

Before Reading

If you lived in Washington Heights, would you feel more protected or less protected as a result of Judge Baer's decision in the Carol Bayless case? Why?

The following editorial was written by the former Police Commissioner of New York City, Raymond W. Kelly. Read it and find out if it changes your opinion of this case.

VOCABULARY	
Word	**Definition**
impugn (6)	malign, challenge as false
naive (8)	unsuspecting, unsophisticated
hunch (8)	a suspicion
cited (8)	referred to as an example
undermine (8)	to weaken or cause to collapse

1   In the vast drug bazaar that Washington Heights has become, homicide is the leading cause of death for young men. A Federal judge's decision to dismiss charges against a woman caught with a carload of cocaine there is bound to make things even worse.

2   Around 5 A.M. on April 21, 1995, Officer Richard Carroll saw four young men loading duffel bags into the trunk of a car with Michigan license plates. When Officer Carroll and his partner approached, the men fled. The officers found 75 pounds of cocaine and four pounds of heroin in the bags. The driver, Carol Bayless of Detroit, later confessed that she had made 20 such trips before.

3   While the size of this transaction was unusual, the things that made Officer Carroll suspicious—the location, the early hour, the out-of-state plates and the men running away—surprised no one familiar with the Washington Heights drug trade. No one, that is, except Harold Baer Jr., the Federal judge who found Officer Carroll's explanation "incredible." Judge Baer declared the search illegal and threw out the confession, saying that Mrs. Bayless could just as easily have been an innocent visitor getting help with her luggage.

4   As for the reason the men fled, Judge Baer had a simple explanation: The police in the neighborhood have a reputation for being corrupt and brutal. "Had the men not run when the cops began to stare at them, it would have been unusual," said the judge, who served on the Mollen Commission, which investigated police corruption.

5   This was not so obvious to the many residents who, when asked about the judge's decision, told reporters that the only people who run from the police in Washington Heights are drug dealers and other criminals.

6   In basing his decision on allegations of police corruption, Judge Baer impugned an honest officer who had confiscated drugs worth $4 million. Such judgments will only encourage the few dishonest cops to keep looking the other way while the drug trade flourishes.

7   Judge Baer also said there was nothing unusual about out-of-state plates in New York City. He's right that Washington Heights is a draw: The most recent drug-crime study of the area found that 61 percent of those arrested for drug possession there in 1992 were from out of town, as against only 8 percent of those arrested for drugs in Manhattan as a whole. Real tourists go to Radio City Music Hall. Drug dealers go to Washington Heights. Officer Carroll was aware of the problem, but apparently Judge Baer was not.

8   Judge Baer's naive decision will inflict long-term damage on the police. Officer Carroll was not acting on a hunch; he cited real factors that pointed to a drug deal. If the police cannot act in such situations, they will be forced into dangerous, time-consuming undercover operations, resulting in fewer arrests and undermining the community policing strategy. The public, seeing fewer uniformed officers, will assume that the police have turned the streets back to the dealers.

9   Officers will be forced to stand by helplessly as drug deals take place under their noses. Some might even be tempted to fight crime with perjury, tailoring their testimony to meet the unrealistic expectations of the courts.

10   How the police will react is uncertain. What we do know is that Judge Baer's decision will allow the drug dealers to strengthen their grip on Washington Heights.

After Reading

1.   Comprehension Check

_____ 1) According to the information in paragraph 1, the judge's decision may cause the following result:
   a. dropping of the charges against the woman
   b. increasing the homicide rate in Washington Heights
   c. making Washington Heights a drug bazaar

2) In paragraph 3, how many things that made the officer suspicious are listed? _____

_____ 3) Judge Baer gave all of the following reasons for declaring the search illegal *except*
   a. Ms. Bayless could have been an innocent tourist.
   b. the police in that neighborhood have a bad reputation.
   c. it is unusual to see out-of-state plates in Washington Heights.
   d. the police in Washington Heights are corrupt and brutal.

_____ 4) According to the article, many people who live in Washington Heights believe that people who run from police in their neighborhood
   a. are afraid of the police.
   b. are criminals.
   c. are carrying illegal guns.
   d. are not really running from them.

5) True _____ or False _____ : According to the author, Judge Baer's decision will cause cops to ignore dealers selling drugs on the street.

2.   A Topic for Writers

After reading Raymond Kelly's editorial, has your opinion about this case changed? What are the main reasons you have for changing or not changing your beliefs?

Article Three
Presumed to Be Guilty

New York Times, February 2, 1996, sec. A, p. 13

Before Reading

Did you ever believe that your civil rights were violated? Describe the situation and how you felt.

This editorial was written by Bob Herbert, who expresses an opposing point of view from Mr. Kelly.

VOCABULARY	
Word	**Definition**
consternation (3)	dismay, alarm, fear, panic
gratuitous (5)	being without apparent reason or cause
bizarre (5)	strange or odd
contention (5)	disagreement
hyperbole (6)	obvious and intentional exaggeration
contraband (11)	illegal trade, smuggling
vile (12)	evil, despicable

Presumed to Be Guilty

1   Ira Glasser of the American Civil Liberties Union tells the story of a black couple who, some years ago, went to a movie in Times Square. When they came out of the theater around 11 P.M. it was raining, so the husband went alone to get their car, which was parked in a garage a few blocks away. When he returned to pick up his wife, she was gone.

2   The man later learned, to his rage and sorrow, that his wife, who was five months pregnant, had been picked up by the police, taken to jail, strip-searched and charged with loitering for the purpose of prostitution. No one could have convinced the arresting officers, least of all the woman herself, that she was not a prostitute. She was a woman, she was black, she was alone, she was in Times Square at 11 o'clock at night. The totality of the circumstances, from the perspective of the police, practically screamed that she was a hooker.

3   Now comes a ruling by a Federal judge in Manhattan named Harold Baer Jr. that has caused widespread consternation and driven some folks to the edge of hysteria. The uniformity of opinion is remarkable. Just about everyone thinks the judge is a bozo.

4   On Jan. 22 Judge Baer threw out as evidence 75 pounds of cocaine, 4 pounds of heroin and a videotaped confession by Carol Bayless, a middle-aged black woman who said she regularly traveled from Michigan to New York to purchase cocaine for her son and others: The drugs were seized from the trunk of a rented car driven by Ms. Bayless, who was stopped by plainclothes police officers in Washington Heights last April. Judge Baer ruled that the police did not have sufficient reason for stopping Ms. Bayless, and thus her Fourth Amendment rights had been violated.

5   Where the judge went wrong in this ruling—and where he guaranteed himself headlines—was in his gratuitous attack on the police in general and his bizarre contention that in Washington Heights, where police corruption and brutality have been pervasive, it would not be unusual for men (presumably even innocent men) to flee whenever a police officer looked at them.

6   Those kinds of wild declarations are better left to columnists, who are professionally licensed and far better equipped to handle dangerous assault weapons like hyperbole.

7   But there was nothing at all unreasonable about Judge Baer's finding that the cops should never have stopped Ms. Bayless. The facts that are not in dispute are as follows: Four men loaded two duffle bags containing the drugs into the trunk of Ms. Bayless's car, which was double-parked on 176th Street. It was about 5 A.M. The men took off on foot and Ms. Bayless drove away.

8   According to the police, at least one of the men eventually started running after noticing a plainclothesman looking at him. That's it. The cops and the U.S. Attorney's office argue that the totality of the circumstances was suspicious enough to warrant the stop.

9   The judge disagreed. "It is far from suspicious," he wrote, "to see people placing duffle bags into the trunk of an out-of-state car in the early morning."

10   What is most significant about this case is that, as with the woman arrested in Times Square, the circumstances leading to the arrest of Carol Bayless were considered suspicious primarily because of the reputation of the neighborhood and the ethnic background of the alleged violators. A middle-aged white woman in a similar situation in Riverdale or Forest Hills would not have been intruded upon by the police.

11   The fact that the cops hit the jackpot in the Bayless case does not matter. The legitimacy of a search is not determined by the value of the contraband. We seldom hear about the many instances in which the police stop, harass and illegally search the persons and belongings of law-abiding people in neighborhoods like Washington Heights. One of the reasons we have judges is to keep such behavior to a minimum.

12   I have no sympathy for the vile habits of Carol Bayless. But not everyone in Washington Heights is a drug criminal, and the people there do not surrender their Fourth Amendment or any other rights when they enter the neighborhood. Constitutional protections should not hinge on a geographical crapshoot or the color of one's skin.

After Reading

1.   In order to be persuasive, the author states many cause and effect relationships. Look through the article and circle the clue words that signal a cause and effect. Complete these cause–effect relationships by filling in the blanks using appropriate details from the article.

Cause   **Effect**

1) _____   thus her Fourth Amendment rights
                                                           had been violated (paragraph 4)

2) because of the reputation of   _____
   the neighborhood and the ethnic   _____
   background of the alleged violators _____
   (paragraph 10)

3) One of the reasons we have   _____
   judges (paragraph 11)   _____

2.   Comprehension Check

_____ 1) Which of the following are mistakes the author thinks the judge made in this case? Check all of those you think apply.

    _____ The judge found that the cops should not have stopped Ms. Bayless.

    _____ The judge thought it was not suspicious to see people putting bags in an out-of-state car.

    _____ The judge claimed that people in Washington Heights run from the police.

    _____ The judge accused the police of corruption and brutality.

_____ 2) The author believes that
    a. people are entitled to Fourth Amendment rights regardless of the color of their skin.
    b. the search of Ms. Bayless's car was legitimate.
    c. a middle-aged white woman in Riverdale should also be searched.
    d. Carol Bayless deserves his sympathy.

_____ 3) The author states that the similarities between this case and the Times Square case are:

    a. the reputation of the neighborhood and the race of the suspects.

    b. the race of the suspects and the out-of-state license plates.

    c. the time of night and the reputation of the neighborhood.

    d. both suspects were female and alone.

4) True _____ or False _____ : According to the author, the judge was unreasonable in finding that the cops should never have stopped Ms. Bayless.

3. Topics for Writers

1) Now that you have read two sides of the issue concerning Judge Baer's decision in the case of Ms. Bayless, with whom do you agree more? Explain your reasons.

2) A few months later, the following appeared in the *New York Times*.

> 1   After enduring an avalanche of criticism and calls for his ouster, a Federal judge yesterday reversed his decision suppressing evidence and a videotaped confession in a Washington Heights drug case.
>
> 2   The judge, Harold Baer Jr. of Federal District Court in Manhattan, made no direct reference to the political storm his ruling had whipped up from City Hall to the White House. But he expressed regret for the remarks in his original decision that prompted the greatest outrage, in which he had questioned the credibility of police officers and suggested that it was not necessarily suspicious even for innocent people in Washington Heights to run from the police.
>
> (*New York Times*, April 2, 1966, sec. B, p. 2.)

    ■ Why do you think Judge Baer changed his decision in this case? Do you think he was right to do this? Why?

    ■ If you were to rewrite the Bill of Rights, under what conditions would you allow police to carry out searches? What limits would you impose?

Chapter Summary

The Relationship between Readers and Writers	Reading and writing are part of a communication process; a message begins in the mind of the writer and ends in the mind of the reader.
Patterns of Organization and Signal Words	Writers often use patterns to establish a relationship between the main idea of a paragraph and its supporting details. Signal words are special words that let you know about the relationship between the details and the main idea.
Lists	Lists consist of details, all of which have the same relationship to the main idea.
Examples	Examples are details that illustrate the main idea.
Comparisons	Comparisons indicate a similarity or difference between two things or ideas. A comparison that shows a difference may be called a contrast.
Definitions	Definitions are one of the most common types of details found in textbooks.
Cause and Effect	A cause is a reason and an effect is a result.
Major and Minor Details	Major details are important because they directly support the main idea. Minor details support major details.
Writing Coherent Paragraphs	The orderly progression of facts and ideas arranged in a logical sequence is called paragraph coherence. Ideas can be organized by time, place, or importance.
Time Order	Also called chronological order, time order is a way of organizing events in the order in which they occur.
Place Order	Place order is a way of organizing details according to where they are located and is often used to describe places.
Order of Importance	Order of importance is a way of organizing details according to their importance.

Journal

In the space below, write your reaction to the readings and activities in this chapter. What did you like most? What did you like least? Why?

_____

_____

_____

_____

_____

_____

_____

_____

_____

_____

_____

_____

_____

_____

_____

_____

_____

_____

_____

_____

_____

_____

_____

_____

_____

Go Electronic!

For additional readings, exercises, and Internet activities, visit the Longman English pages at:

http://longman.awl.com/englishpages

If you need a user name and password, please see your instructor.

Take a Road Trip to the St. Louis Arch and Ellis Island

Be sure to visit the Supporting Details and Patterns of Organization modules in your Reading Road Trip CD-ROM for multimedia tutorials, exercises, and tests.

Practice Your Writing Skills

For additional practice with your writing skills, use the Writer's ToolKit CD-ROM included with this text.

CHAPTER 5

Organizing Essays and Summarizing Passages

Theme: Love

What You Will Find in This Chapter

- Elements of an Essay
- Revising an Essay
- Summarizing Passages
- Types of Essays and Passages
- Textbook Selection: Relationships
- Poem: "Poem for a Divorced Daughter"

What does the following quote mean to you?
"If there is anything better than to be loved it is loving."

(Anonymous)

_____

_____

_____

_____

The themes of this chapter are family life and relationships between men and women. Our desire to be part of a group, to be part of a family, or to have friends motivates us to form relationships.

In this chapter we explain how to write essays and how to read long passages. We show you the parts of an essay, how they can be put together effectively, and the different types of essays. As a reader you will also learn how to summarize what you have read.

In addition, you'll further develop the skills you learned in the preceding chapters—using context for vocabulary development, identifying main ideas, understanding significant details, and using signal words. You will have an opportunity to apply your skills by reading an excerpt from an anthropology textbook, as well as a poem about a family relationship.

Elements of an Essay

An essay is an organized piece of writing that centers around a single topic. Although the length will vary, essays are usually a few pages in length. There are a few reasons why you might choose to write an essay. First, essays help you express your ideas more clearly and effectively. For example, you can use essays to persuade others to adopt your point of view on important issues. Second, essays help you convey a lot of information in a small amount of space. Third, essays are a vehicle for entertaining others by conveying interesting stories about ourselves and others. Finally, essay writing is a required part of almost all college courses. Every college student needs to learn how to write effective essays.

In the last chapter we showed you how to write a coherent paragraph. In this section we show you how to write an effective essay. Actually, the organizational structure of a paragraph and the organizational structure of an essay are very similar. An essay is a group of related paragraphs. Therefore, everything you have learned about paragraphs will help you write an essay.

While a paragraph is organized around a main idea, an essay is organized around a more general idea called a **thesis**. The thesis of an essay develops from all the main ideas in the supporting paragraphs. Paragraphs that help develop the thesis are called the **body** of the essay.

A paragraph may begin with an introductory sentence. An essay usually begins with an **introduction**, which may be the entire first paragraph. A paragraph may end with a concluding sentence. An essay usually ends with a **concluding paragraph**.

The following chart compares the elements of paragraphs and essays:

Paragraph	Essay
Organized around a main idea	Organized around a thesis
Introductory sentence	Introductory paragraph
Developed by supporting details	Developed by supporting body paragraphs
Concluding sentence	Concluding paragraph

The elements of the following paragraph are labeled in the margin.

Introductory sentence

Main idea (underlined)

Supporting details

Concluding sentence

The number of older Americans is increasing each year. <u>Therefore, we must start planning now for the care of the elderly.</u> Medical programs that take into account the special needs of the elderly must be created and funded. Construction of new homes for the elderly should begin. If we do not continue to support programs like Medicare and Social Security, we will have to pay the price later. In conclusion, care of our elderly should become a national priority.

An essay is usually developed in three sections: (1) introduction, (2) body, and (3) conclusion. All the sections are organized around a thesis. These organizational aspects are demonstrated in the following student essay about children of separated or divorced parents.

CONFLICTING PARENTING STYLES

by Nancy Rocks

INTRODUCTORY PARAGRAPH

Entire essay organized around thesis (how divorce or separation affects a child's behavior and development)

SUPPORTING BODY PARAGRAPH 1

The first sentence is the main idea statement.

Imagine how you would feel if you had to live in two separate households every week. Now, imagine it from a child's perspective, with different daily routines and different interpersonal relationships. Clearly, children of separated or divorced parents sometimes have to adjust to very different parenting styles and living arrangements. To understand how a child has to balance his changed environment, let's examine some of these contrasts to see how they affect behavior and development.

Often, the most conflicting parenting style is illustrated in after-school and bedtime routines. In our home, my 11-year-old son, Andrew, has a bedtime of 8:30 on school nights. He generally does his homework at 6:30, showers at 8:15, and then

Signal word for contrast (conversely)

gets ready for bed. He usually reads for 15 or 20 minutes before falling asleep. Conversely, on the days he is with his father, Andrew goes to his grandmother's after school and does his homework there. After his dad picks him up, they have dinner at approximately 7:30, and Andrew stays up until 10:00. He has a television in his room at his dad's; so, instead of reading at bedtime, he most often plays video games.

SUPPORTING BODY PARAGRAPH 2

First sentence is main idea statement.

Signal words are used to make transitions between sentences (for example, instead, in contrast).

Another conflicting living arrangement is the introduction of new relationships. Just as children need time to adjust to their parents' separation, so, too, do they need to prepare for their parents' new partners. For example, I chose not to introduce anyone into my children's lives until I am divorced from their father. Instead, I am allowing them to become accustomed to the changes already taking place. In contrast, our children share their father's home with his new woman. That arrangement has provided them very little opportunity to adapt to the new intimacy through a steady, natural process.

SUPPORTING BODY PARAGRAPH 3

First sentence is main idea statement.

On the other hand and consequently *are used to signal contrast.*

A very important transition for the child is in maintaining friendships at both homes. Here, Andrew has many friends on our block and has grown up with most of them. They play basketball at our house, baseball at Joey's, and jailbreak at Eric's. Andrew knows everyone's mom, and we parents are attuned to looking out for each other's children. On the other hand, Andrew has a new friendship with a boy who lives near his dad's apartment. Living in an apartment complex, there is less freedom and peace of mind to let the children play outside. Consequently, Andrew and his friend Steve are more likely to play indoors, with less chance for Andrew to experience the nurturing sense of community.

SUPPORTING BODY PARAGRAPH 4

Main idea is stated in first sentence.

Conversely *signals contrast.*

A further disparity in recreational activities involves toys and gifts. Andrew earns an allowance from me by doing his weekly chores, and I deposit a portion of it into his savings account. He lets the balance accumulate for several weeks until he can't wait any longer to spend it. Since the first time I took him to Border's Bookstores, he enjoys going there to buy books. Of course, there are times when only a new toy will do, but, about half the time, I suggest we go to Border's, and he carefully chooses the best books for his money. Conversely, on those occasions that his dad rewards Andrew for a great report card, for example, Andrew most often chooses to buy a toy or a video game. Because Andrew's dad does not read for leisure, Andrew follows the pattern of that household.

CONCLUDING PARAGRAPH

First sentence summarizes all of the examples discussed in each body paragraph.

As a conclusion, the author offers an opinion to help children of divorced or separated parents.

All of these examples illustrate the difficult transitions children face in just one aspect of a divorce—that of two households. It is particularly difficult when the parents have such contrasting parenting styles. As a mother, I look for ways to ease their passage and soften the effects, but I oversee my own household, and only my own. Therefore, I believe it is critical to the emotional health of the children that parents find a way to cooperate and maintain open communication with each other. The well-being of the children is, and should always be, the first priority.

Let's now consider each of the components of an essay and how you can develop them when you write an essay.

Thesis and Thesis Statement

The thesis of your essay is what you are writing about and supporting throughout the essay. Like the main idea of a paragraph, the thesis is a generalization that includes all of the paragraphs in the essay. The thesis statement is a sentence in the essay that states the thesis. It is usually expressed in the first paragraph of the essay as part of the introduction.

The thesis statement should not be too general, or it will not provide adequate direction for the rest of the essay. It should not be too specific, either, or it will be difficult to develop into a series of related paragraphs.

Following is an example of thesis statements that are too general and too specific.

Topic:	Controlling Our Children
Too General Thesis:	We must discipline our children.
Too Specific Thesis:	Teachers have a role in the discipline of children.
Precise Thesis:	By using disciplinary techniques, parents, teachers, and police are the main agents responsible for controlling our children.

Although the thesis that is too general gives an idea about the topic, it does not provide any direction and would be difficult to develop into specific main ideas for the body of the essay. The specific thesis would force us to write only about teachers. The precise thesis statement lets the reader know that three groups of people are to be discussed in the context of controlling children. It is general enough to allow for the development of several main ideas, but specific enough to give the essay structure and organization.

The following box contains three main ideas that follow naturally from the thesis statement. Each main idea forms the basis of a paragraph that will be included in the essay.

THESIS STATEMENT:	By using disciplinary techniques, parents, teachers, and police are the main agents responsible for controlling our children.
Main Idea 1:	There are a variety of techniques available to parents who are willing to take the responsibility of disciplining their children.
Main Idea 2:	Teachers are also important agents of discipline for children in our society.
Main Idea 3:	If criminal behavior is involved, police will take the responsibility to control our children through the legal system.

Writing a good thesis statement is an important step in developing an essay, because it gives a purpose and direction to the entire essay.

PRACTICE EXERCISE 1: IDENTIFYING PRECISE THESIS STATEMENTS

In each group, decide which thesis statement is most precise. On the line before each statement put a G if the statement is too general, an S if it is too specific, and a P if it is most precise.

1. _____ My family is the most important part of my life.

    _____ My mother, father, brother, and sister all make me feel that my family is the most important part of my life.

    _____ My sister knows how to make me feel important.

2. _____ Classes in this school are too crowded.

    _____ There are many reasons that students fail.

    _____ In the United States, students fail because there are not enough teachers who care.

3. _____ The Yankees lost the game.

    _____ The Yankees need better pitching and more consistent hitting.

    _____ The Yankees need to improve.

4. _____ There are many reasons why traveling to a new place can be an interesting experience.

    _____ My trip to Spain was interesting.

    _____ Traveling is interesting.

5. _____ I prefer living in New York.

    _____ There are lots of cultural activities in most large cities.

    _____ Living in a large city has several advantages over living in a small town.

PRACTICE EXERCISE 2: WRITING PRECISE THESIS STATEMENTS

Write a precise thesis statement for each of these topics. Remember that you'll need to use your thesis statement as the basis for the paragraphs that you'll write for an essay.

1. Passing a college course

_____

2. Television watching and violence

_____

3. Single parents and children

_____

4. Women in the police force

_____

5. Getting married

_____

PRACTICE EXERCISE 3: DEVELOPING MAIN IDEAS FROM A THESIS STATEMENT

The following topics are from Practice Exercise 2. First, write the precise thesis statement that you created in that exercise. Then, write three main ideas that you could develop from your thesis.

1. *Topic:*   Television watching and violence
   Thesis Statement: _____
   Main Idea 1: _____
   Main Idea 2: _____
   Main Idea 3: _____

2. *Topic:*   Getting married
   Thesis Statement: _____
   Main Idea 1: _____
   Main Idea 2: _____
   Main Idea 3: _____

3. *Topic:*   Passing a college course
   Thesis Statement: _____
   Main Idea 1: _____
   Main Idea 2: _____
   Main Idea 3: _____

Introduction to an Essay

The first part of an essay contains the introduction. The introduction is the reader's first contact with the topic and is usually written in the form of a paragraph called the introductory paragraph. As you think about a topic and thesis for an essay, ideas for writing an introductory paragraph will take shape.

Introductory paragraphs often begin with an *attention-getter* to attract the reader's interest. Next, the writer tells the reader what the essay is about by stating the *thesis*. These two parts are connected by a *bridge*.

Here are some ways to get the reader's attention in the first sentence of your introductory paragraphs. All examples are based on the topic, "controlling our children."

ATTENTION-GETTERS FOR INTRODUCTORY PARAGRAPHS

Strategy	Example
1. Provide some interesting background about the topic in the form of a general statement.	Today's children become tomorrow's leaders.
2. Use a thought-provoking quotation.	"Adolescence is not a stage of life, it is a disease!"—Dr. S. Rosner
3. Ask a question about your topic.	Why don't children want to be controlled by adults?
4. State a surprising fact or a puzzling statement.	Teenagers join gangs because they need the support of a family.
5. State a common misconception.	Children don't learn bad habits from adults.
6. Describe a problem.	Everyone knows what a problem juvenile delinquency has become in our society.
7. Give an analogy.	Children are just like animals.
8. Show how the topic is related to the reader's experience.	We all know how difficult it is to raise children.

Next, use a bridge to connect the attention-getting sentence(s) to your thesis statement. A bridge helps readers make a transition from the introduction to the thesis statement. Depending on the complexity of your topic, you might need more than one sentence to create an effective bridge. A common way to make a bridge to the thesis statement is to explain why the topic is important—for example, "Controlling the behavior of our children is one of the most important tasks in our society." Explaining to readers the importance of controlling children should motivate them to want to read more about that topic in your essay.

Finally, conclude the introductory paragraph with the most important idea of the essay, the thesis statement. Here is an example of an introductory paragraph to an essay about controlling children.

CONTROLLING OUR CHILDREN

[1]Everyone knows what a problem juvenile delinquency has become in our society. [2]Without proper control our children will run wild and create a danger to themselves and everyone around them. [3]Controlling the behavior of our children is one of the most important tasks in our society. [4]By using discipline techniques, parents, teachers, and police are the main agents responsible for controlling our children.

In this paragraph, the introductory sentence states a popular belief about adolescents. The second sentence is an attention-getter because it creates some strong emotion about the topic—controlling children. This sentence gives readers a reason to continue reading. The third sentence is a bridge, or *transition*, sentence. It leads readers directly into the thesis statement by stating the importance of the topic. The last sentence in the paragraph is the thesis statement because it explains generally what the rest of the essay will be about.

PRACTICE EXERCISE 4: WRITING INTRODUCTORY PARAGRAPHS

Write an introductory paragraph for each of these thesis statements.

1. There are three reasons why I believe _____ is the career for which I am best suited.
2. Women should (or should not) be allowed to compete with men in professional sports.
3. Day care is a serious problem for many working parents in the United States.

Body of an Essay

The body of an essay is usually a series of paragraphs that develop the idea expressed in the thesis statement. Each body paragraph provides information about the thesis statement, and usually includes a main idea sentence and supporting details.

A good first step in developing the body of an essay is to make a list of main ideas that support the thesis statement, an activity you practiced in Practice Exercise 3. Each main idea can then become the main idea sentence for a body paragraph. Next, arrange the main ideas in a logical order (time, place, or importance). Plan out each body paragraph by listing major details to support each main idea. Next, order the details within each paragraph in a logical way. Body paragraphs may end with a concluding sentence.

Here is a plan for the body paragraphs of an essay, using the thesis statement about controlling children.

THESIS STATEMENT

By using discipline techniques, parents, teachers, and police are the main agents responsible for controlling our children.

BODY PARAGRAPH 1

Main Idea Sentence 1:   There are a variety of techniques available to parents who are willing to take the responsibility of disciplining their children.

Major Details:
1. Give rewards
2. Punish bad behavior
3. Be consistent and reasonable

BODY PARAGRAPH 2

Main Idea Sentence 2:   Teachers are also important agents of discipline for children in our society.

Major Details:
1. Direct communication
2. Nonverbal communication
3. Grades

BODY PARAGRAPH 3

Main Idea Sentence 3:   If criminal behavior is involved, police will take the responsibility to control our children through the legal system.

Major Details:
1. Various forms of punishment
2. Advising parents of the children's behavior
3. Setting curfews

After planning and arranging your main ideas and major details, you can begin writing your body paragraphs. Don't forget that signal words (see Chapter 4, p. 123) can be used to make smooth transitions between sentences and paragraphs. The number of body paragraphs depends on the nature of the topic in terms of complexity, inclusiveness, and your purpose for writing. Usually, a short essay contains three to five body paragraphs.

Here is an example of a body paragraph. Notice that each of the major details from the earlier outline has been included in the paragraph.

¹There are a variety of techniques available to parents who are willing to take the responsibility of disciplining their children. ²Most of these involve a combination of rewards and punishments. ³Rewarded behaviors will be repeated by children; therefore, rewards should be given for behaviors that are acceptable. ⁴Unacceptable behavior should be punished in some way. ⁵Try to make the punishment fit the seriousness of the behavior. ⁶Be reasonable; but be consistent, too. ⁷Consistency and fairness are the key elements when it comes to rewarding and punishing your children.

The first sentence in this body paragraph is the main idea sentence. The second sentence is a major detail because it classifies discipline into two major categories—*reward* and *punishment*. The third, fourth, and fifth sentences are minor details because they tell us more about the two major categories of discipline. The signal word *therefore* is used to clarify relationships and make smooth transitions between ideas. The sixth sentence is a major detail because it states a major rule of discipline: *be consistent and reasonable*. Finally, the last sentence concludes the paragraph.

Remember that body paragraphs provide the content of an essay. Each paragraph should be unique, including different facts and opinions as appropriate. Like any paragraph, body paragraphs must be unified around a main idea and arranged coherently. You can use different types of details to support your main idea.

PRACTICE EXERCISE 5: WRITING BODY PARAGRAPHS

On the lines below, complete the main ideas as they relate to each thesis statement. Then choose one thesis statement and use the blank form that follows to plan out your details. Write a body paragraph for each main idea.

1. *Thesis Statement:*   In some ways, I really enjoyed high school but, in other ways, it was really a drag.

   Main Idea 1:   The aspect of school that I liked best was

   _____

   Main Idea 2:   The aspect of school that I liked least was

   _____

2. *Thesis Statement:*   I know that sometimes I am very patient and at other times I'm not.

   Main Idea 1:   One situation when I am usually very patient is

   _____

Main Idea 2:   I really lose my patience when

_____

3. *Thesis Statement:*

Main Idea 1:

Details:

Main Idea 2:

Details:

Conclusion of an Essay

The purpose of a conclusion is to leave readers with a good impression, a sense of completeness, and hopefully the desire to continue to think about the topic. The essay's conclusion is usually in the form of a short, single paragraph. There are many ways to create interesting conclusions; however, they should not give more information about the topic. Everything in your conclusion should follow logically from the body.

The beginning of the conclusion can be a restatement of the thesis. You can use signal words, such as *in conclusion, in summary, in brief*, or *in closing* to let the reader know this is the concluding paragraph. You can then restate your thesis statement in different words. Then, write some thought-provoking comments about your topic stating your opinion, judgment, or recommendations.

Here is an example of a concluding paragraph:

[1]With proper discipline at home and at school, our children can be controlled. [2]Parents and teachers can do the job before police action is necessary. [3]Maybe many of our children are out of control because not enough people take the responsibility seriously. [4]In conclusion, I believe that controlling children is one of the most important responsibilities for adults in our society.

The first sentence of the concluding paragraph is a partial restatement of the thesis statement. The second sentence is a conclusion that clarifies the thesis. The third sentence is an opinion about the nature of our society. It may motivate some readers to read more about this topic. Finally, the paragraph ends with a concluding remark about the importance of this topic.

PRACTICE EXERCISE 6: WRITING CONCLUDING PARAGRAPHS

In Practice Exercise 5 you wrote body paragraphs for one of the thesis statements below. Reread your body paragraphs and then write a concluding paragraph for the thesis you chose.

1. In some ways, I really enjoyed high school but, in other ways, it was really a drag.
2. I know that sometimes I am very patient and at other times I'm not.

Here is a list summarizing the elements of an essay.

ELEMENTS OF AN ESSAY

- Topic
- Thesis Statement
- Introductory Paragraph
- Body Paragraphs
- Concluding Paragraph

PRACTICE EXERCISE 7: RECOGNIZING ELEMENTS OF AN ESSAY

Read this essay. Then answer the questions about the elements of the essay.

BROTHERLY INFLUENCE

1 I was raised in an environment where many people influenced my behavior. However, no one has influenced my behavior more than my brother. My brother has been my best friend and a model for learning values.

2 My brother was my best friend. We grew up together although he was two years older and many years wiser. Fortunately, he always had time for me. He even let me hang around with him when he was with his friends. As a result, I felt important and wanted.

3 Most importantly, my brother taught me the value of learning—about myself and my world. For example, he taught me that knowledge is power and knowing oneself is personal power. I now know that learning should continue for a lifetime.

4 In summary, my brother has played a major role in shaping my behavior and values throughout my life. Everyone should try to establish a lasting relationship with an older brother or sister. If you do not have a sibling, try to find a cousin or neighbor as a model to help you grow in a positive way.

1. Underline the thesis statement.
2. The introduction is in paragraph number _____.
3. What is the purpose of the first sentence in paragraph 1?

   _____

4. What is the purpose of the second sentence in paragraph 1?

   _____

5. Underline the main idea of paragraph 2.
6. Underline the main idea of paragraph 3.
7. Underline the sentence in paragraph 4 that restates the thesis.
8. What recommendation is made in the conclusion of this essay?

   _____

Revising an Essay

As you put the elements of an essay together, you will find the need to go back and rewrite various parts. In the first draft, you will probably focus on what you want to say. When you review, you can focus on how to organize your ideas. Revising is the process of reviewing and rewriting your essay to make your ideas more logical, understandable, and interesting to your readers.

Revising a draft involves crossing out some material, adding other material, and rearranging material. It depends on your own evaluation and feedback you get from others.

There are two main aspects of the revision process: 1) revision through reading and 2) revision through collaboration.

Revision through Reading

Reading your essay to yourself is a good way to start the revision process. As you do this, keep in mind your purpose for writing. Also, keep in mind your audience, so you can make your essay as interesting and understandable as possible. With each rereading you will probably find some ways to improve your writing.

During the revision process, make sure you have all of the elements of an essay, as discussed on pages 173–184. The following checklist will help:

1. Is the entire essay organized around a thesis?

2. Is the thesis stated clearly and precisely?

3. Is there an introductory paragraph with an adequate attention-getter and bridge to the thesis statement?

4. Is there enough discussion in the body paragraphs?

5. Does each supporting body paragraph have a main idea that clearly follows from the thesis?

6. Is there sufficient clarification and support for each main idea in the form of definitions, explanations, and examples? (See pages 123–129.)

7. Are the details in each paragraph clearly related to the main idea? (See pages 79–80.)

8. Are the body paragraphs arranged logically? (See pages 138–143.)

9. Is there a concluding paragraph?

10. Do you use signal words appropriately to make transitions? (See pages 123–129.)

11. Are there errors in grammar, punctuation, capitalization, spelling, or usage? (See Correct English Handbook.)

Revision through Collaboration

Collaboration is a way of finding out what other readers think about your essay. You can find out if you have expressed your ideas clearly. Also, you may become aware of problems you have not noticed and get specific suggestions about how to improve your essay. Therefore, getting constructive criticism from other students is an important part of the revision process.

Following are some general questions you may ask yourself when giving feedback to other students:

1. What did you like most about the essay?

2. What did you like least about the essay?

3. What more would you like to know about it?

4. What would you like to change?

In addition, you may want to make some suggestions for improving organization and clarity of ideas, including grammar, punctuation, spelling, and usage (see Correct English Handbook).

Following is the first draft of a short essay written by a student. Note the constructive criticism appearing below it. Then, read the revised draft written by the same student. Notice how the student improved the essay by following the suggestions. Keep in mind that the actual revision process may include a series of readings, collaborations, and rewritings.

First Draft

THE FOOD OF MY FAMILY

Spanish people eat similar kinds of food. Rice, beans, chicken, bananas, plantains, and pork are traditional foods. To me, food is one of the most important aspects of family life.

I particularly like the way my mother makes my favorite dish, "arroz y habichuela" (rice and beans). She takes time to prepare it just right. She soaks and cooks the finest black beans. She grinds seasonings into a wonderfully savory powder. She cooks the rice to just the right firmness. She combines all of the ingredients. Sometimes she adds some jalapeno peppers to enhance the flavor. Always, it has a nice ebony-colored finish as the black skin from the beans casts its color.

Spanish people love to eat chicken. They often have their own special recipes. My uncle prepares the best chicken. He always starts with a fresh whole chicken. He washes and cleans the chicken inside and out. He prepares a special seasoning that still remains his little secret. He sprinkles the seasoning all over the chicken to give it a nice color and a great taste. It's placed in the oven at just the right temperature and for just the right time, so it is never over or under cooked. Since it's a whole chicken, it takes more than an hour to cook well. Roasted chicken is very popular among Puerto Ricans, especially when accompanied with "arroz y habichuela."

Some types of traditional Spanish food come from the land or are grown on trees. Other types of food come from livestock, which is raised on our farms.

Here are some comments written by a student during a collaboration session.

What did you like most about the essay?

The topic is very interesting to me. I enjoyed reading about different kinds of food. The description was good. It made me hungry. Also, it made me think about the kind of food my Mom used to make for me.

What did you like least about the essay?

I liked everything about it. Maybe it was a little too short.

What would you like to know more about?

I'd like to know about more of the dishes of Spanish people. How about the desserts? Also, I'd like to know about your family and how you get along with them. This may not be related to the topic, but it could be included in the introduction.

What would you like to change?

Just tell more about the topic.

What questions do you have about it?

Is the food very spicy? Are the peppers very hot? Do you like it that way?

How can it be improved?

Introduction seems a little choppy. I didn't notice any signal words in this essay. Maybe the sentences should not all start with "She" in the second paragraph. I think you need a concluding paragraph.

Revised Draft

THE FOOD OF MY FAMILY

To me, food is one of the most important aspects of family life. In Puerto Rico, where my family is from, we enjoy many types of traditional Spanish foods. Even though many Spanish people eat similar kinds of food, some of us prepare our food in a special way that has been passed from generation to generation.

I particularly like the way my mother makes my favorite dish, "arroz y habichuela" (rice and beans). She takes time to prepare it just right. First, she soaks and cooks the finest black beans. Second, she grinds seasonings into a wonderfully savory powder. Then, she cooks the rice to just the right firmness. Finally, she combines all of the ingredients. Sometimes she adds some jalepeno peppers to enhance the flavor. Always, it has a nice ebony-colored finish as the black skin from the beans casts its color.

On special occasions, when the entire family goes to visit my uncle, he prepares another of my favorite dishes—roasted chicken. He always starts with a fresh whole chicken. First, he washes and cleans the chicken inside and out. Second, he prepares a special seasoning that still remains his little secret. Third, he sprinkles the seasoning all over the chicken to give it a nice color and a great taste. Then, it is placed in the oven at just the right temperature and for just the right time, so it is never over or under cooked. Since it's a whole chicken, it takes over an hour to cook well. Roasted chicken is very popular among Puerto Ricans, especially when accompanied with "arroz y habichuela."

Every culture emphasizes traditional types of food. Eating the cuisine of my country, Puerto Rico, is one of my greatest passions. In conclusion, I hope that the special meals prepared by my family will continue to be passed on to future generations.

PRACTICE EXERCISE 8: REVISING AN ESSAY

As you read the following student essay, write any comments in the margins about how it should be revised. Use the revision checklist to guide you in the process. Then, answer the questions below. You may collaborate with others in your class to discuss your ideas about revising this draft of the essay.

MARRIAGE

Marriage is one of the most important cultural facts in any society. It involves two persons who officially or on common grounds agree to live together for a lifetime for the best or for the worst. However if getting married is quite easy, is being married an easy task? What does it require? And so what can you do to have a happy marriage?

One of the most important things to make a marriage successful is comprehension. Because, as a human being, we can always make a mistake. In this connection, if we are not comprehensive, every time that our partner commits an error, we feel frustrated. And this frustration can end in a quarrel. For example, your husband or your wife can have some natural behavior you don't like. And, as we know, natural behaviors are always taken out spontaneously. Therefore, if you don't settle a good understanding between you, you feel often hurt in your love. This can lead to a divorce from an unhappy marriage. So only comprehension can prevent you from being adamant. To settle comprehension between you, you must keep a permanent conversation: whenever you face a difficulty, you must stick together to get over this difficulty. You must keep an adequate consultation. You must not make free to take unilateral decisions. All decisions are to be taken by consulting each other. If you follow these instructions you can have a happy marriage. So we can assure that comprehension is one of the major factors which can amend some wrongdoings in a marital home and bring happiness in a marriage.

In addition, frankness guarantee a stable and a happy marriage. Suppose you have to deal with a person who never tells the truth, even if you are really in love with her or him, you can't rely on her or him. Hence, a lack of confidence that usually reigns in many marriages with its harmful consequences. Once you know that your husband or wife is seeing another person, you feel affronted and you can't count on him or her any more. Therefore, frankness is important.

In fact a marriage involves two persons. Two persons who have two different tempers. And two tempers are either compatible or incompatible. Compatible tempers lead to a successful marriage. On the other hand, incompatible tempers lead to an unhappy marriage. In order to make two tempers compatible, we deem that comprehension and frankness are the two most relevant factors.

Answer the following questions about the essay above.

1. What did you like most about the essay?

2. What did you like least about the essay?
3. What more would you like to know about it?
4. What would you like to change?

PRACTICE EXERCISE 9: WRITING AN ESSAY

Before Writing

Discover. How strong an influence has each of the following people had in your life? Put a check mark in the appropriate column.

Relationship	Strong Influence	Less Strong Influence	No Influence
Mother			
Father			
Other family members (Identify)			
Friend			
Neighbor			
Co-worker			

Organize. From the chart, choose the person who had the strongest influence on your life. How did that person affect your life? What important activities did you share? How did that person teach you what is important in life?

Write a precise thesis statement about the person who influenced you most. Make a list of at least two main ideas to develop your thesis.

Writing

Draft. Start by writing an introductory paragraph in which you state your thesis. Then, write a paragraph for each main idea. Finally, write a concluding paragraph.

After Writing

Collaborate. Working in a small group, read aloud the draft you have written. After each draft is read, discuss the draft and give some feedback. Helpful feedback might include the following:

- What do you like most about the essay?
- Was the relationship of the person to the writer described clearly?
- Does the essay include an introductory paragraph, body, and conclusion?
- Is the thesis stated clearly and precisely in the introductory paragraph?
- Do all the main ideas follow from the thesis statement?
- Is each main idea developed in a body paragraph?
- Is each main idea supported with enough details (examples, explanations, and so forth)?
- Does each paragraph have unity and coherence?
- Are signal words used appropriately to make transitions?
- What questions do you want to ask the writer about the essay?

Revise: Based on your reading and feedback you have received through collaboration, revise your essay. Use the checklist on pages 185–186 to help you decide what you want to keep, add, and delete from your first draft. Can you improve the organizational structure of this essay?

Proofread: Check your final paper for grammar, punctuation, and organization. Use the editing material in The Correct English Handbook if you need help.

PRACTICE EXERCISE 10: TOPICS FOR WRITERS

Following are some suggested topics for writing essays.

- Select a major problem in society today (for example, divorce, discrimination, poverty, crime). Describe the problem and explain how it affects our country.
- Which sport is the most difficult to play? Explain your answer.
- In your opinion, why is divorce so common in our culture? Discuss at least three reasons.
- What is the value of a college education?
- Should we limit immigration in the United States? Support your answer.

Summarizing Passages

Knowing how to summarize is important for both readers and writers. Readers summarize in order to make large amounts of material more manageable, for example, when taking notes, studying for a test, or collecting information for a report. Summarizing after you read helps you organize your thoughts and can be helpful in planning an essay. Writers may summarize to give readers a condensed (that is, shorter) version of an essay or a book.

A summary is a short version of the original writing. In fact, a short summary can be just a sentence or two. Summarizing requires the ability to find the thesis statement, identify the main ideas, and locate the most important supporting details.

Following are some suggestions for writing a good summary of a passage:

- Read carefully for main ideas and most important details.
- Combine the main ideas of the paragraphs into one or two sentences.
- Try to use your own words, but do not change the meaning of what you are reading.
- If there is an interesting detail or a key phrase, you may include it.
- Do not add your own ideas or reactions. A summary, like a main idea, includes only what the author tells you about the topic.

The following excerpt is about fatherly advice. As you read, try to get the main idea of each paragraph.

When I was young, and my father could see that something was bothering me, he used to suggest that I might try saying a prayer. . . . Later, when I began making a living as a journalist, he often suggested that if something disturbed me, I might try writing about it. Keeping a journal helped him a great deal, he said. Putting experience down on paper made it seem less chaotic, less depressing, more sympathetic. "I write to make sense of my life," he used to say.

So in the autumn of 1981, when we found out that my father was going to die soon, it seemed natural that I should write about this. I did, and it helped.

(Susan Cheever. *Home Before Dark*,
Houghton Mifflin, 1984, pp. ix–x.)

The main idea of paragraph 1 is, "My father suggested I keep a journal to help me when something disturbed me." The main idea of paragraph 2 is, "Keeping a journal when my father was dying helped me." A summary of both paragraphs follows:

The author's father suggested keeping a journal to help get through difficult times in life. She found it a helpful technique when her father was dying.

Here is a passage about child care. Underline the main idea of each paragraph.

I found that some patterns of child care are almost universal. Babies across all countries—except the United States—sleep in the same room with their parents and most often in the same bed. Most babies are also held most of the time. Moreover, parents from many cultures respond to infant cries in seconds and protect them from harm.

But even more striking are the major differences across cultures. Parents in some cultures refuse to speak much to their babies, thinking such activity will produce a high-strung, selfish, obnoxious adult. The Gusii women of Africa, for example, hold babies close, answer their cries with soothing mumbles and offer a breast, but they do not chat. Navajo babies are swaddled tightly and prevented from moving about in an attempt to maintain calm. In both cases, babies are stimulated visually as they are carried about all day on someone's hip or back. In contrast,

> Western cultures are devoted to verbal stimulation and believe it is imperative to talk to babies to encourage cognitive development. And yet parents in these cultures also leave their babies in playpens or car seats, ignoring the importance of physical contact.
>
> (Meredith Small, *Making Connections*, Information Access Company, 1997.)

The main idea of paragraph 1 is, "Some patterns of child care are almost universal." The main idea of paragraph 2 is, "There are major differences in patterns of child care." A summary of this selection follows:

> Some patterns of child care, such as holding a baby most of the time, are almost universal, while other patterns, such as talking to a baby, are not.

PRACTICE EXERCISE 11: RECOGNIZING SUMMARIES

For each of the following passages, choose the summary you think is best.

> 1   In many societies, married men spend a good deal of time in special men's houses. Food is handed in to them by wives and children, who are themselves forbidden to enter. Men also sleep and work in these "club-houses" although they may on occasion bed down with their wives and children. Among the Fur of the Sudan, for example, husbands usually sleep apart from their wives in houses of their own and take their meals at an exclusive men's mess. One of the most interesting cases of the separation of cooking and eating occurs among the Ashanti of West Africa. Ashanti men eat their meals with their sisters, mothers, and maternal nephews and nieces, not with their wives and children. But it is the wives who do the cooking. Every evening in Ashanti land one sees a steady traffic of children taking their mother's cooking to their father's sister's house.
>
> (Marvin Harris, *Cultural Anthropology*, 4th ed., HarperCollins, 1995, p. 103.)

a. Ashanti men eat their meals with their sisters, mothers, and maternal nephews and nieces, but their wives do the cooking.
b. Husbands and wives behave differently in different cultures.
c. It is not uncommon in many societies for men to sleep, work, and eat with other men and away from their wives.
d. Ashanti husbands and wives don't get along.

> 2   Sociolinguistics is concerned with the ethnography of speaking, that is, with cultural and subcultural patterns of speech variation in different social contexts. The sociolinguist might ask, for example, what kinds of things one talks about in casual conversation with a stranger. A foreigner may know English vocabulary and

grammar well but may not know that one typically chats with a stranger about the weather or where one comes from, and not about what one ate that day or how much money one earns. A foreigner may be familiar with much of the culture of a North American city, but if that person divulges the real state of his or her health and feelings to the first person who says, "How are you?" he or she has much to learn about "small talk" in North American English. Similarly, North Americans tend to get confused in societies where greetings are quite different from ours. People in some other societies may ask as a greeting, "Where are you going?" or "What are you cooking?" Some Americans may think such questions are rude; others may try to answer in excruciating detail, not realizing that only vague answers are expected, just as we don't really expect a detailed answer when we ask people "How are you?"

(Ember & Ember, *Anthropology: A Brief Introduction*, Prentice-Hall, 1998, p. 181, 183, adapted.)

a. A foreigner may be familiar with the English language but not with the appropriate topics for making small talk.
b. North Americans may not respond appropriately to greetings in other societies.
c. Sociolinguists are interested in how speech is used in different cultures and different social contexts, such as in making small talk and greeting people.
d. Conversation differs around the world.

3   Healthy interactions between family members are vital to a family's well-being, said Linda Wark of Ohio State University's College of Human Ecology. When those interactions aren't at their best, the whole family can suffer, Wark said.

Wark, an assistant professor of family relations and human development, talks about these interactions in terms of "boundaries." . . . They can be "clear," "rigid" or "diffuse." When family members respect each other's individuality but are still involved with each other, they have "clear" boundaries. "The clear boundary is the kind you want," Wark said. "Family members with clear boundaries have good communication. They meet each other's needs and at the same time allow each other to be individuals."

But sometimes relationships don't have such a happy balance. Family members can have too much separateness, known to family researchers as "rigid" boundaries. Family members may not be aware of each other's feelings, or could have a lot of secrets from each other.

On the other hand, sometimes family members become too closely related to each other's lives. With these "diffuse" boundaries, members lose their individuality and can be easily influenced by too-strong family ties.

(www.ag.ohio-state.edu/~ohioline/lifetime/lt4-2d.htm)

a. Two types of boundaries in families are "diffuse" and "rigid."
b. There are several reasons why some families have diffuse boundaries.

   c. Family interactions have been classified as either clear, rigid, or diffuse, with clear boundaries being the most desirable.

   d. Families with clear boundaries have good communication and meet each other's needs.

4   Children of all ages and all races recognize the power of media in their lives. They look to the media for role models—imitating the way their favorite characters dress, the way they talk, how they do their hair. From the shag haircuts of the women on *Friends* to the baggy fashions of the hip hop music scene, the influence of media on today's children can be seen everywhere. And beyond superficial messages about style and appearance, children are getting more formative messages from the media. The characters they admire—and the news stories they watch—send both subtle and explicit signals about their value, their families, and their race.

Today's children will be the first generation to come of age in an America where racial minorities are the numeric majority. Our future will depend upon their ability to develop positive racial identities and an appreciation of diversity. To help build bridges across racial lines, children will need to expand their conceptions of race and race relations in ways their parents never knew. Clearly, media are only one of the many influences in our children's lives, but young people believe that the media have both the power to break down stereotypes and the potential to build greater understanding.

   a. Children are getting powerful messages from the media.

   b. The media can be educational for children.

   c. Children need to learn to appreciate racial diversity.

   d. The media can help children learn to appreciate racial diversity.

5   The early years are the time to begin helping children form strong, positive self-images and grow up to respect and get along with people who are different from themselves. We know from research that children between 2 and 5 start becoming aware of gender, race, ethnicity, and disabilities. They also begin to absorb both the positive attitudes and negative biases attached to these aspects of identity by family members and other significant adults in their lives. If we want children to like themselves and value diversity, we must learn how to help them resist the biases and prejudices that are still far too prevalent in our society.

Bias based on gender, race, disability, or social class creates serious obstacles to all young children's healthy development. In order to develop healthy self-esteem, they must learn how to interact fairly and productively with different types of people. Naturally, children's curiosity will lead them to ask questions: "Why is her skin so dark?" "Why does he speak funny?" We may hide our own negative feelings, or hope that children simply won't notice, but our avoidance actually teaches children that some differences are not acceptable. We must face our own biased attitudes and change them in order to help foster all children's growth.

Building a healthy self-identity is a process that continues all our lives. Help children get a head start by teaching them to resist bias, and to value the differences between people as much as the similarities.

(Copyright © 1997 by National Association for the Education of Young Children.)

a. Parents should help their children resist bias.
b. Teaching young children to respect differences among people will contribute to their own healthy development.
c. Answering children's questions about different types of people should be avoided.
d. There are several things a parent can do to help build healthy self-identity in his or her child.

PRACTICE EXERCISE 12: WRITING SUMMARIES

Write a summary for each of the following short selections.

1   From where I stood at the window, I could see into the apartment across the way. A man and a woman and some children lived there. I had observed them before at various times. I had seen them in bathrobes, in evening clothes, and in ordinary, everyday wear. I had never seen these people do anything interesting—not exchange a kiss, not have what looked like a quarrel. They were always just passing through this room, as if it were a way station. Now it was empty of people. I could see a sofa, two chairs, and a wall of books. How luxurious, I thought, to have an empty room in your house, a room that nobody really needed. And isn't that what everyone in the world should have—more than was needed, one more room than you really need in your house? Now a question I would put to Mariah, for she felt just the opposite. She had too much of everything, and so she longed to have less; less, she was sure, would bring her happiness. To me it was a laugh and a relief to observe the unhappiness that too much can bring; I had been so used to observing the result of too little.

(Jamaica Kincaid, *Lucy*, Penguin, 1990, pp. 86–87.)

_____

_____

2   Miss Vera Brown, she wrote on the blackboard, letter by letter in flawlessly oval Palmer method. Our teacher for the fifth grade. The name might as well have been graven in stone.

As she called the roll, her voice was as gentle as the expression in her beautiful dark brown eyes. She reminded me of pansies. When she called on Alvin Ahrens to recite and he said, "I know but I can't say," the class snickered but she said, "Try," encouragingly, and waited, to be sure that he didn't know the answer, and then said, to one of the hands waving in the air, "Tell Alvin, what one-fifth of three-eighths is." If we arrived late to school, red-faced and out of breath and bursting with the excuse we had thought up on the way, before we could speak she said, "I'm sure you couldn't help it. Close the door, please, and take your seat." If she kept us after school it was not to scold us but to help us past the hard part.

(William Maxwell, "Love," in *Billie Dyer and Other Stories*, Penguin, 1992, pp. 36–37.)

_____

_____

_____

_____

3   Loneliness is caused not by being alone, but by being without close relationships. It is an unpleasant, at times acutely painful, feeling of isolation. Aloneness, on the other hand, is a state of being that can be growth-producing and desirable. "Being alone" is not the same experience as feeling separated from others; it is not the empty feeling of being lonely. We all need "time out" from others. It is important to include alone time in your busy college schedule.

Loneliness can result from rejection, misunderstanding, separation, illness, or tragedy. Certain personal characteristics increase the level of loneliness a person may experience. These include poor social skills, negative attitudes, low self-esteem, insecurity, and mistrust.

To deal effectively with loneliness, you must first admit to yourself that you are lonely. Then you can try to understand what would help alleviate it. Though loneliness itself may cause stress and anxiety, the anxiety of loneliness increases if you attempt to eliminate it by constantly keeping busy or seeking activity with others. Being out of touch with yourself and your needs only prolongs the pain of loneliness.

Take the initial step to reach out to someone; this helps you avoid feeling hopeless and powerless. Look for the similarities between you and those around you rather than dwelling on the differences. Loneliness may provide the catalysts to lead you to new and fulfilling relationships and a more complete life.

(http://www.uiuc.edu/departments/mckinley/health-info/hlthpro/relation/lonely.html)

_____

_____

_____

4   Researchers (have) found that the act of listening to someone else—part and parcel of good, active communication—is actually a relaxing activity. Two researchers from the University of Pennsylvania demonstrated the necessity for relaxation in an experiment in which patients were asked first to read, then to stare at a blank wall, then to sit quietly and watch fish swimming around in a tank.

Blood pressures were monitored throughout the experiments. As expected, the blood pressure readings were highest while the people were reading out loud. But, unexpectedly, the blood pressure readings were lower while the people sat watching fish swim in a tank than when they were sitting staring at a blank wall. Why? Paying calm attention to something outside yourself brings your blood pressure down and enhances overall well-being. Listening, then, is a great boost for better health.

(Robert Ornstein & David Sobel, *The Healing Brain: Breakthrough Discoveries about How the Brain Keeps Us Healthy*, Simon & Schuster, 1987.)

_____

_____

_____

5   Being a student and being in a committed relationship can present you with important life roles that sometimes feel incompatible and in conflict and at other times feel quite harmonious. Your relationship can provide you with important emotional support as you cope with the stresses of school and work, but at the same time represent additional responsibilities and demands on your time. Not surprisingly, trying to fill both roles can be a confusing and frustrating experience.

Couples who derive satisfaction from both their relationship and their academic pursuits tend to understand what the other's expectations are, reduce or modify certain expectations as needed, and then learn how to establish fairly clear approaches and routines for fulfilling those readjusted expectations.

(adapted from http://www.odos.uiuc.edu/ Counseling_Center/comrel.htm)

_____

_____

_____

Types of Essays and Passages

In previous sections we showed you how to write and summarize an essay. In this section we help you develop an essay by using essay patterns. As a reader, recognizing essay patterns helps you understand the author's purpose. It also helps you comprehend and remember what you read. As a writer, essay patterns help you organize your ideas effectively.

The pattern of an essay is determined by your purpose for writing. For example, you may want to discuss an issue or describe a person or place. You may want to persuade a reader to accept your point of view about an issue. Or you may simply want to entertain the reader with an interesting story.

College writing assignments usually dictate what type of essay to write. Therefore, you need to be familiar with several essay patterns. As long as you are clear about your purpose, you will be able to stay on the topic and include only those ideas that are related to it.

There are a number of patterns you can use to organize your ideas in an essay. These patterns include the following:

- description
- narration
- cause–effect
- comparison–contrast
- problem–solution
- persuasion

Essays often contain combinations of these patterns. For example, you may want to *narrate* a story which contains a *description*, or *compare and contrast* two *solutions* to a problem, or list *reasons* for an *opinion* in a persuasive essay.

Now let's look at these patterns in closer detail.

Description

The main purpose of a *descriptive essay* is to create a picture of a person, place, or object. People often use description when they tell others about themselves and their experiences. For example, a doctor may ask you to describe your problem, or a friend may ask you to describe the woman or man you are dating. Most writing contains some form of description.

Using Descriptive Language. Writing good description means using your sensory experiences as vividly as possible. Descriptive language includes all five senses. Here are the five senses with an example of descriptive language for each.

THE FIVE SENSES

Sense	Examples of Sensory Description
1. Sight	The *pudgy* instructor with *brown* hair entered the room.
2. Hearing	The *loud roar* of the ocean disturbed me.
3. Smell	The *musty* odor came from the attic.
4. Taste	The *spicy* food was also *sweet* and *sour*.
5. Touch	The *furry* cat had a *smooth* coat.

Good description helps readers form a vivid impression of what you are trying to communicate. Here is an example of both a bland description and a vivid description. How many senses are involved in each description?

Bland version: The boxer looked to be in bad condition as the round ended.

Vivid version: The salty sweat glistened as it dripped down from the cleanly shaved head of the beaten boxer. Low-pitched moans emanated from his bloodied lips. A musty smell was in the air as he hobbled weakly toward his chair in the far corner of the ring.

The bland description involves only one sense—sight. In addition to many visual features, the vivid description entails taste (salty), smell (musty), and hearing (low-pitched moans). Furthermore, you can form a mental picture of the boxer from the vivid description.

PRACTICE EXERCISE 13: READING DESCRIPTIVE LANGUAGE

This paragraph was used to introduce a passage about an Indonesian tribesman who had just started a fire to clear some land. As you read, try to form a mental image of the scene. Underline the descriptive words that help you picture the scene described.

Abdur Rani hunkered on the ground behind his home, little more than a box he'd nailed together from raw timber, and gazed across the still smoldering terrain at the acreage he'd just burned bare. For miles around this scorched field in southern Kalimantan, the Indonesian portion of the island of Borneo, the rolling land was baked black and crisp, dusted with feathery white ash. Tendrils of smoke curled from the peat ground cover and floated into the chrome yellow sky. Here and there charred and shattered tree trunks punctured the horizon, remnants of what had once been a dense tropical rain forest. The stillness of the sweltering afternoon was broken only by the rumbling and gear-growling of trucks hauling hardwood logs to the nearby Java Sea coast over roads that slashed the wilderness like red scars. In this landscape I could see only death and destruction. Abdur Rani saw opportunity, a new cycle, life itself.

(Lewis & Simon, "Indonesia's Plague of Fire,"
National Geographic, August 1998, p. 100.)

PRACTICE EXERCISE 14: READING A DESCRIPTIVE ESSAY

In the following passage, the author describes the experience of a group of migrant farm laborers. As you read, underline the words that make you feel as if you are out in the fields with the workers. Then answer the questions that follow the reading.

After many more bad leads and a lot of arguments about the gas, they found work . . . south of Bakersfield, at the foot of the great mountains between Bakersfield and Los Angeles. There, in Kern County, one of the richest farmlands in the world, they found plenty of work, and they worked at the melons, one of the physically hardest of all farm labors. Starting with the first light of day, they would straddle a row, bend down, and pick with heavy sacks on their backs. There were six men on each side of each truck, and every man would have his own row and he would walk along bent over, move the leaves, select only the large, three-quar-ter-size, ripe melons, pick them, toss them over his shoulder into his sack, fill the sack, and trot quickly to the truck, race up the two-by-twelve ramp which dragged along behind the truck, dump his sixty or eighty pounds of melons, race down the other board, jump over the rows of melons, get to his own row, straddle it, bend over, and start selecting, picking, and tossing them over his shoulder, filling his sack quickly. The faster the better, for soon the sun would be too hot, and they were getting paid so much per truck.

Then it was ten in the morning and the sun was hot and the men didn't run anymore. They began to walk, to lug up the ramp, flip-flop down the ramp, wipe the dripping sweat out of their eyes, line up at the five-gallon water tank tied to the side of the truck, take the empty can of Coors with a wire tied to it like a handle, fill it half up with ice-cold water, rinse, spit, drink, pass it to the next man, and return to the field. Refreshed. And so they would briskly walk out two or three or six rows, straddle, bend over, and begin selecting. Now it was truly hot. It was eleven, and all the melons were beginning to look bad. Too green. Too small. Too burned by the sun. And, for these bad ones, one didn't get paid. They'd get thrown out at the packing shed. Only the good ones were taken from the truck, boxed, and shipped, and one got paid by the number of boxes shipped per truck.

(Victor Villasenor, *Macho!* Delta, 1991, p. 180.)

1. What main idea about melon picking did you understand from reading this description?

   _____

2. What feelings did you experience as you read this passage?

   _____

   _____

3. What descriptive words in the passage gave you those feelings?

_____

_____

Writing a Descriptive Essay. As with all essays, writing a descriptive essay involves planning and organizing around a thesis statement. The thesis statement should reveal the main person, place, or object to be described, as well as the purpose of the description. Two examples follow:

DESCRIPTIVE THESIS STATEMENTS

1. My mother was a beautiful woman who made me feel I was loved.
2. This college has many unique buildings that are both beautiful and comfortable.

The first thesis statement could lead to several body paragraphs describing things the writer's mother did to make her feel loved. The second thesis statement might introduce an essay in which each paragraph describes one of the college's buildings.

PRACTICE EXERCISE 15: WRITING DESCRIPTIVE THESIS STATEMENTS

For each of the topics below, write a thesis statement that you could imagine developing into a descriptive essay.

1. The neighborhood playground

_____

2. My favorite study area

_____

3. The best teacher I ever had

_____

PRACTICE EXERCISE 16: WRITING A DESCRIPTIVE ESSAY

Write a descriptive essay using one of the topics from Practice Exercise 15 or a topic from the list below. Be sure to include introductory and concluding paragraphs.

The street on which you live
A favorite place or hangout

Your favorite musical or artistic piece
The president of the United States
A scientific experiment

Narration

A narrative relates events that have happened. In other words, narratives tell a story and are a large part of everyday conversation. People enjoy telling and listening to stories about all types of things—work, family, friends, school, or travel. Most television shows and movies involve narration. Even academic textbooks contain narration. For example, a history textbook may tell you the story of a great leader, or a medical textbook may tell you what happens to a person with a certain disease.

Narratives have certain common elements, most of which will be present in any narrative you write. Narratives typically offer answers to the following questions:

- *Who* is involved? (characters)
- *What* happens to the characters? (plot or events)
- *Where* does the story take place? (place)
- *When* does the story happen? (time)
- *Why* does it happen? (motives or reasons)
- *How* does it turn out? (climax and conclusion)
- *What* does it mean? (thesis or point)

If you have ever read a story or seen a movie in which you were left feeling that you wanted more information about some aspect of the story, it's possible that the author neglected to include an important element. Keep in mind that readers often look for the answers to these questions. Therefore, you should address as many of these questions as you can when you write a narrative.

Here is an example of narration:

NARRATION

The car drew in around them like a room. Their breaths fogged the windows. Earlier the air conditioner had been running and now some artificial chill remained, quickly turning dank, carrying with it the smell of mildew. They shot through an underpass. The rain stopped completely for one blank, startling second. Sarah had a little gasp of relief, but even before it was uttered, the hammering on the roof resumed. She turned and gazed back longingly at the underpass. Macon sped ahead, with his hand relaxed on the wheel.

(Anne Tyler, *The Accidental Tourist*,
Berkeley Books, 1985.)

Here are answers to the narrative questions:

Who: The characters are Sarah and Macon.

What: The car just went through an underpass. Sarah seems disturbed by the constant pounding of the rain, and relieved while the car goes through the underpass. Macon, on the other hand, seems quite relaxed and content.

Why: From this limited part of the story, we cannot determine the characters' motives or reasons for their actions or feelings.

Where: The story takes place in a car.

PRACTICE EXERCISE 17: READING NARRATIVES

The following narrative essay is from a biography of the author John Cheever, written by his daughter. She describes an alcoholism rehabilitation unit in New York where her father once stayed.

1   Theoretically, anyone at Smithers can walk right out the wrought-iron gates and around the corner to a bar or restaurant and order a drink. Smithers is a voluntary rehabilitation center. But everyone at Smithers knows that the ones who walk out almost always come back again—only the second time they are in even worse shape. The ones inside tell stories about the walkouts who don't come back, too: automobile accidents, fatal heart attacks, "accidental" deaths. By the time they get to Smithers, most people don't have anywhere else to go.

2   Communication with the outside world is made difficult at Smithers. For the forty to fifty patients, there is one pay telephone mounted on the wall at the busy second-floor landing. The first week my father spent at Smithers, he called me on this telephone every morning to say that he couldn't stand it anymore.

3   I was working as an editor at *Newsweek* by then, and the calls came into my brightly lit, windowless office down the hall from the noisy hubbub and wire-clacking sounds of the news desk. My father spoke to me in his broken Italian, so that he would not be overheard and understood.

4   "Non posso, cara," he would say. "Non posso stare qui." He whispered when anyone passed in the hall, and his voice was breaking. I tried to comfort him. I tried to explain why he should stay at Smithers, but really I was terrified. The next call from him, I was sure, would be from some bar around the corner on Madison Avenue—or it would be from the police or from a hospital. I made a reservation for him at Silver Hill, a gentler rehabilitation center in Connecticut, and I parked my car near the *Newsweek* office on Forty-ninth and Madison so that when the call *did* come I would be able to pick him up and get him the care he needed without wasting any time. Every day he sounded worse.

(Susan Cheever, *Home Before Dark*, Houghton Mifflin, 1984, pp. 194–195.)

1. Fill in the table with information from the essay.

Who is involved?	
Where does it take place?	
What happens?	
Why is the writer's father there?	

2. Do you feel sympathy for either the writer or her father? Which one? Why do you feel sympathy for that person?

_____

_____

_____

_____

3. Paragraph 4 begins with words spoken in Italian by the father. If you don't know Italian, what do you think the words mean?

_____

_____

4. What do you think happens next to the father in the story? (You may want to check this book out of your local library and read it to find out what actually happens.)

_____

_____

_____

5. Write a short summary of the essay.

_____

_____

_____

Writing a Narrative Essay. In a narrative essay, you tell an interesting story in the order in which events happened. Like every essay, a narrative has a thesis. The thesis of a narrative is usually the point of the story, and the events you choose to include should contribute to the reader's understanding of your essay's thesis. The thesis can be the main thing that happens to the character or the major motive of the character. It lets readers know exactly what idea or feeling to look for. For example:

NARRATIVE THESIS STATEMENTS

What happened:	During the time I worked for my father, I became a complete wreck.
Main motive:	Mr. Jones, my writing teacher, certainly tried to help me become a better writer.

PRACTICE EXERCISE 18: WRITING NARRATIVE THESIS STATEMENTS

Write a thesis statement for each of these topics. State the main character and the main point you want to make.

1. My first date

_____

2. My favorite trip

_____

3. An exciting news story

_____

Dialogue. To make the story more lively and vivid, narratives often contain dialogue or conversation. Dialogue is often included in a narrative because the words a person uses reveal a lot about that person. Therefore, you may want to include some dialogue between the people you write about. Here is an example of dialogue between two characters in a story. Notice how the dialogue helps us understand the characters and their relationship.

As Mary entered the apartment, she greeted her mother.

"Hi, Mom," Mary said, "I hope you have dinner ready because I'm really starved."

"Really," responded her mother, "Do you think of me as your personal slave? Why don't you get your own dinner for a change?"

"I don't want to be a problem for you tonight," consoled Mary. "Something is really bugging you, Mom. Let's sit down and talk about it."

"You are right about that," admitted Mother. "You won't believe what happened to me today."

Following are some tips for writing dialogue:

- Use quotation marks to set off direct quotations (the actual words of the speaker).
- Do not use quotation marks when you present what a person is saying indirectly. For example:

     Mother said that I should come home earlier.

- Write people's words exactly as they say them, including slang, dialect, and any unusual expressions.

PRACTICE EXERCISE 19: CREATING DIALOGUE

These activities will give you some practice in writing dialogue.

1. Spend about half an hour in a public area, such as a restaurant. Record the conversations of people around you. Then, write sentences using quotes for the exact words. If you do not know the people's real names, make them up.
2. Choose one of these situations and write a short dialogue between the characters:
   a. A husband and wife planning an evening out.
   b. A man and woman on their first date.
   c. A person being interviewed for a job.

PRACTICE EXERCISE 20: WRITING A NARRATIVE ESSAY

Choose one of the following topics and write a narrative essay. Try to include enough information so that a reader will find answers to the questions who, where, what, and why. Think about the thesis and how you want to state it. Also, before writing, you may want to brainstorm your ideas about the topic you choose so you can put the story in correct time order.

- A family member or friend who acted in an unexpected way toward you.
- A time when you learned something important about yourself.

- Pretend that you are a news reporter for a newspaper. Write a narrative about something that happened in your neighborhood, city, or country.
- An incident involving conflict or a clash between people of different cultures.
- Your favorite character from history, a book, or a movie. Be imaginative, but try to capture the character's actual personality in the action and dialogue.

Cause–Effect

Cause–effect relationships are part of our everyday world. Everything you do has causes or reasons, as well as effects or results. You will often have to analyze causes and effects in college assignments. For example, what are the causes and effects of the following:

- the American Civil War?
- drug addiction?
- a hurricane?
- crime?
- inflation?
- the Industrial Revolution?

In an essay, you may discuss the causes of something, the effects of something, or both the causes and the effects. Usually, there are multiple causes and effects. One cause may have many effects (for example, the effects of crime), and one effect may have many causes (for example, the causes of war). Also, causes and effects can occur in chains where an effect can become a cause for something else. For example, the effect of a poor grade in school may be low self-esteem. Feeling bad about yourself may cause you to drop out of school. Dropping out may cause you to feel even worse about yourself, and so on.

Before you begin writing about a topic with causes and effects, you can ask yourself some questions.

Causes	**Effects**
Why did it happen?	What happened as a result?
What are the reasons?	What are the consequences?
	How did one thing affect or change another?

For example, if you want to examine divorce, you can ask the following questions:

- Why do so many people get divorced in the United States? (causes)
- What happens as a result of divorce? (effects)
- How does divorce affect children? (effects)

You can brainstorm, create a map, or freewrite about any topic to get started. It will be helpful to make a list of the possible causes and effects for your topic. Putting causes and/or effects into a table is a good idea. Then, you can decide which ideas you want to use as supporting details in your essay. For example, you might brainstorm the following list of causes and effects in preparation for writing an essay about divorce.

DIVORCE

Causes	**Effects**
infidelity	children
incompatibility	financial situation
drug abuse	job performance

Writing a Thesis Statement for a Cause–Effect Essay. The thesis statement of a cause–effect essay should state the subject and whether causes, effects, or both will be examined. For example, the following thesis statements would help you get started on an essay about divorce.

CAUSE–EFFECT THESIS STATEMENTS

1. The *reasons* people get divorced are as varied as the people themselves.
2. The most serious *effect* of divorce is on the children.
3. There are many *causes* of divorce, and the *consequences* are felt for a lifetime.

The first thesis statement is about the causes of divorce, the second one focuses on effects, and the last one includes both causes and effects. Notice that signal words are used to help readers recognize the cause–effect relationship (*reasons, effects, consequences*). You will find a list of cause–effect signal words on page 129.

PRACTICE EXERCISE 21: WRITING CAUSE–EFFECT THESIS STATEMENTS

Write a cause–effect thesis statement for each of these topics. Indicate the subjects and whether you will be discussing causes, effects, or both.

1. Disciplining children

   _____

2. Living at home with your parents

   _____

3. Getting good grades

   _____

4. Dieting

   _____

5. Remaining single

_____

6. The American Revolutionary War

_____

7. Inflation

_____

8. A thunderstorm

_____

Arranging Supporting Details for a Cause–Effect Essay. In a cause–effect essay, details can be arranged in various ways. If you are including both causes and effects, you may want to present all of the causes before the effects, or the effects before the causes. To discuss each cause or effect, organize a body paragraph around a single cause or effect. In this case, introduce each cause or effect in the main idea sentence of the paragraph and support it with details. The following plan shows this method:

ARRANGING CAUSES–EFFECTS INTO BODY PARAGRAPHS

Thesis:	The *reasons* people get divorced are as varied as the people themselves.
Main Idea Sentence (Paragraph 1):	Among the problems in marriages, infidelity is the leading *cause* of divorce.
Main Idea Sentence (Paragraph 2):	*Also,* incompatibility is a *reason* that so many couples decide to get divorced.
Main Idea Sentence (Paragraph 3):	*Finally,* few couples can stay together when one of the partners is using illegal drugs.

Notice the signal words that are used to indicate cause (*reasons* and *cause*). Also, the signal words for a list, *also* and *finally*, are used to make transitions between body paragraphs.

Model Cause–Effect Essay. The following essay was written by Anne Roiphe, the author of *Up the Sandbox!*, a book about relationships. In this essay, she presents causes for failed marriages.

How does the title, "Why Marriages Fail," indicate the cause–effect pattern?

_____

As you read through it, underline all the causes you can find.

WHY MARRIAGES FAIL

Anne Roiphe

1   These days so many marriages end in divorce that our most sacred vows no longer ring with truth. "Happily ever after" and "Till death do us part" are expressions that seem on the way to becoming obsolete. Why has it become so hard for couples to stay together? What goes wrong? What has happened to us that close to one-half of all marriages are destined for the divorce courts? How could we have created a society in which 42 percent of our children will grow up in single-parent homes? If statistics could only measure loneliness, regret, pain, loss of self-confidence and fear of the future, the numbers would be beyond quantifying.

2   Even though each broken marriage is unique, we can still find the common perils, the common causes for marital despair. Each marriage has crisis points and each marriage tests endurance, the capacity for both intimacy and change. Outside pressures such as job loss, illness, infertility, trouble with a child, care of aging parents and all the other plagues of life hit marriage the way hurricanes blast our shores. Some marriages survive these storms and others don't. Marriages fail, however, not simply because of the outside weather but because the inner climate becomes too hot or too cold, too turbulent or too stupefying.

3   When we look at how we choose our partners and what expectations exist at the tender beginnings of romance, some of the reasons for disaster become quite clear. We all select with unconscious accuracy a mate who will recreate with us the emotional patterns of our first homes. Dr. Carl A. Whitaker, a marital therapist and emeritus professor of psychiatry at the University of Wisconsin, explains, "From early childhood on, each of us carried models for marriage, femininity, masculinity, motherhood, fatherhood and all the other family roles." Each of us falls in love with a mate who has qualities of our parents, who will help us rediscover both the psychological happiness and miseries of our past lives. We may think we have found a man unlike Dad, but then he turns to drink or drugs, or loses his job over and over again or sits silently in front of the T.V. just the way Dad did. A man may choose a woman who doesn't like kids just like his mother or who gambles away the family savings just like his mother. Or he may choose a slender wife who seems unlike his obese mother but then turns out to have other addictions that destroy their mutual happiness.

4   A man and a woman bring to their marriage bed a blended concoction of conscious and unconscious memories of their parents' lives together. The human way is to compulsively repeat and recreate the patterns of the past. Sigmund Freud so well described the unhappy design that many of us get trapped in as the unmet needs of childhood, the angry feelings left over from frustrations of long ago, the limits of trust and the recurrence of old fears. Once an individual senses this entrapment, there may follow a yearning to escape, and the result could be a broken, splintered marriage.

5   Of course people can overcome the habits and attitudes that developed in childhood. We all have hidden strengths and amazing capacities for growth and creative change. Change, however, requires work—observing your part in a rotten pattern, bringing difficulties out into the open—and work runs counter to the basic myth of marriage: "When I wed this person all my problems will be over. I will have achieved success and I will become the center of life for this other person and this person will be my center, and we will mean everything to each other forever." This myth, which every marriage relies on, is soon exposed. The coming of children, the pulls and tugs of their demands on affection and time, place a considerable strain on that basic myth of meaning everything to each other, of merging together and solving all of life's problems.

6   Concern and tension about money take each partner away from the other. Obligations to demanding parents or still-depended-upon parents create further strain. Couples today must also deal with all the cultural changes brought on in recent years by the women's movement and the sexual revolution. The altering of roles and the shifting of responsibilities have been extremely trying for many marriages.

7   These and other realities of life erode the visions of marital bliss the way sandstorms eat at rock and the ocean nibbles away at the dunes. Those euphoric, grand feelings that accompany romantic love are really self-delusions, self-hypnotic dreams that enable us to forge a relationship. Real life, failure at work, disappointments, exhaustion, bad smells, bad colds and hard times all puncture the dream and leave us stranded with our mate, with our childhood patterns pushing us this way and that, with our unfulfilled expectations.

8   The struggle to survive in marriage requires adaptability, flexibility, genuine love and kindness and an imagination strong enough to feel what the other is feeling. Many marriages fall apart because either partner cannot imagine what the other wants or cannot communicate what he or she needs or feels. Anger builds until it erupts into a volcanic burst that buries the marriage in ash.

9   If we sense from our mate a need for too much intimacy, then we tend to push him or her away, fearing that we may lose our identities in the merging of marriage. One partner may suffocate the other partner in a childlike dependency.

10   A good marriage means growing as a couple but also growing as individuals. This isn't easy. Richard gives up his interest in carpentry because his wife, Helen, is jealous of the time he spends away from her. Karen quits her choir group because her husband dislikes the friends she makes there. Each pair clings to each other and are angry with each other as life closes in on them. This kind of marital balance is easily thrown as one or the other pulls away and divorce follows.

11   Sometimes people pretend that a new partner will solve the old problems. Most often extramarital sex destroys a marriage because it allows an artificial split between the good and the bad—the good is projected on the new partner and the bad is dumped on the head of the old. Dishonesty, hiding and cheating create

walls between men and women. Infidelity is just a symptom of trouble. It is a symbolic complaint, a weapon of revenge, as well as an unraveler of closeness. Infidelity is often that proverbial last straw that sinks the camel to the ground.

12 All right—marriage has always been difficult. Why then are we seeing so many divorces at this time? Yes, our modern social fabric is thin, and yes the permissiveness of society has created unrealistic expectations and thrown the family into chaos. But divorce is so common because people today are unwilling to exercise the self-discipline that marriage requires. They expect easy joy like the entertainment on TV, the thrill of a good party.

13 Divorce is not an evil act. Sometimes it provides salvation for people who have grown hopelessly apart or were frozen in patterns of pain or mutual unhappiness. Divorce can be, despite its initial devastation, like the first cut of the surgeon's knife, a step toward new health and a good life. On the other hand, if the partners can stay past the breaking up of the romantic myths into the development of real love and intimacy, they have achieved a work as amazing as the greatest cathedrals of the world. Marriages that do not fail but improve, that persist despite imperfections, are not only rare these days but offer a wondrous shelter in which the face of our mutual humanity can safely show itself.

(*Family Weekly*, February, 1983.)

Suggestions for Writing Cause–Effect Essays. It will be helpful to keep in mind the following suggestions when writing cause–effect essays:

1. Before writing, make a list of causes and effects.

2. Then, decide which causes and/or effects you want to include in your essay.

3. Write a clear thesis statement indicating your topic and noting whether you will be discussing causes, effects, or both.

4. Make an outline for each paragraph indicating the main idea and the significant details you want to include.

5. Use signal words to help the reader follow your pattern of organization.

6. Be sure to proofread and revise your essay.

PRACTICE EXERCISE 22: WRITING CAUSE–EFFECT ESSAYS

Write at least one cause–effect essay. You may use any of the topics in Practice Exercise 21. Following are some additional topics.

Fad diets are rarely successful. Most people gain the weight back. Discuss the reasons for the failure.

How do you succeed in college? Discuss the causes for success in college.

Why do people have children? How do children affect people's lives?

How does growing up in a small or large family affect the way you are as an adult?

> Why do people get married?
> What are the causes and/or effects of smoking cigarettes?
> Why does the U.S. government have three branches?
> What is the effect of stress on the body?
> How would winning the lottery affect your life?
> Why do people commit crimes?

Comparison–Contrast

The purpose of comparison–contrast is to bring two or more persons, places, objects, or ideas together for closer examination. *Compare* means to consider similarities or differences; *contrast* means to consider only differences. Comparison–contrast means to consider both similarities and differences.

You use comparison–contrast often in everyday life when you make decisions about what products to buy. For example, you may compare prices from many stores before you buy a new television, stereo, or computer. You may have compared different colleges before you chose the one you attend.

Writing Supporting Details for a Comparison–Contrast Essay. Various types of supporting details may be used in comparison–contrast essays. For example, if you are comparing two paintings, you might use vivid description. Also, examples would be given to support your point. If you are comparing two politicians, you might want to give examples of what they have done for the people. Or, you might use narration to help make a comparison. For example, when comparing two events, as in "My twentieth birthday was better than my thirtieth," you might narrate the events at each occasion. The important point is to select your details as they relate to your purpose.

Writing Thesis Statements for a Comparison–Contrast Essay. The thesis statement in a comparison–contrast essay usually states the subjects being examined and the general nature of the comparison–contrast. Here are some examples:

Comparison–Contrast Thesis Statements

The French Revolution and the U.S. Revolution were fought for the *same* reasons; *however*, the *differences* were striking.

Freud and Rogers used *different* theories of psychology in their practice of psychotherapy.

My brother and sister turned out to be very *similar* in personality.

Notice that the thesis states whether the comparison–contrast will include similarities, differences, or both. Also, notice the signal words for comparison–contrast that are used to make the point clear (*same* and *similar, however, different*). Signal words for comparison–contrast were listed and discussed on page 126–127.

Suggestions for Writing Comparison–Contrast Essays. Before you write your first draft, it is a good idea to make a list of the similarities and differences you want to include in your essay. A two-column table or chart is a good way to list them, as in this example:

Sigmund Freud	**Carl Rogers**
Pessimistic about human nature	Optimistic about human nature
Believed humans are driven by instincts	Believed humans are driven by self-actualization
Focused on causes of mental illness	Focused on well-adjusted behavior
Analyzed patients' behavior	Listened to patients

Then, you can decide on the order to present the items in your list. Since you will have at least two subjects, you will have to decide on the order in which to present them in your essay. Here are two ways to arrange your body paragraphs. This example is based on a thesis statement from above (Freud and Rogers used *different* theories of psychology in their practice of psychotherapy).

- *Organize by subject:* arrange the details (similarities and differences) around each subject in separate paragraphs:
    1. Sigmund Freud (body paragraph 1)
        a. Pessimistic about human nature
        b. Believed humans are driven by erotic instincts
        c. Focused on causes of mental illness
        d. Analyzed patients' behavior
    2. Carl Rogers (body paragraph 2)
        a. Optimistic about human nature
        b. Believed humans are driven by desire for self-actualization
        c. Focused on well-adjusted behavior
        d. Listened to patients describe their behavior

- *Organize around related details:* present details on your list for one subject, followed by the related details for the other subject:
    1. Views on human nature (body paragraph 1)
        a. Freud was pessimistic about human nature. He believed that humans are driven by deep, dark, and sinister passions, mostly sexual in nature.
        b. Rogers was optimistic about the nature of humans. He wrote about positive self-regard.
    2. Views on motivation (body paragraph 2)
        a. Freud believed that basic erotic instincts drive all human behavior.
        b. Rogers believed that the desire to be self-actualized motivates humans to behave as well as they can.

The second method, organizing around related details, usually makes your essay easier to follow. If you are presenting both similarities and differences, it may be a good idea to discuss all of the similarities followed by all of the differences, or vice versa.

PRACTICE EXERCISE 23: WRITING COMPARISON–CONTRAST THESIS STATEMENTS

Write a comparison–contrast thesis statement for each of these pairs of subjects. Indicate the subjects and whether you will be discussing similarities, differences, or both.

1. TV and reading

   _____

2. Two members of your family

   _____

3. The 1980s and the 1990s

   _____

4. Married life and single life

   _____

5. A book (you have read) with the movie version (you have seen)

   _____

6. Life before a great invention with life after the invention (such as cars, trains, airplanes, telephones, computers)

   _____

7. Living in a developed nation (like the United States, Canada, Japan, or Europe) with living in an emerging nation (like Colombia, Haiti, Indonesia, or Rwanda)

   _____

8. Living in a city with living in a suburb

   _____

9. Teenagers and adults

   _____

10. People and computers

   _____

Model Comparison–Contrast Essay. Following is an essay written by a student in which she contrasts the behavior of Americans with Chinese. *In the following table, list all the differences and similarities you find as you read the essay.*

Differences	Similarities

LIFE IN CHINA COMPARED TO LIFE IN THE UNITED STATES

A Chinese friend who was living in New York once said, "I feel comfortable here because I don't have to care about other people. Unlike in China, nobody criticizes me, whatever I wear or however I behave." Her comment can be explained by the differences in characteristics between Americans and Chinese. Generally speaking, Americans are individualistic, while the Chinese are communal.

Americans think the important thing is whether they feel comfortable. No one is expected to behave the same way. This tendency can be observed in every aspect of life. For example, Americans choose their clothes freely without caring about other people. As a result, we can see people in torn jeans and T-shirts and people dressed formally at the same place. Also, even older Americans wear vivid colors. Some elderly ladies wear elaborate make-up and have manicured hair and nails. I was surprised to see an old lady wearing red lipstick. I never see such a scene in China. For Chinese, other people's eyes become the standard for our behavior. Chinese tend to dislike being different from each other. If a 70-year-old woman wore red in China, she would be criticized for not acting her age, and she would stop wearing it immediately.

In America no one puts pressure upon us because of age. In China, however, our surroundings make us constantly conscious of our age. For instance, we have a marriageable age. When someone, especially a woman, remains single beyond that age, people refer to her as an "old maid." One of my friends got married unwillingly only because she didn't want people to regard her as an old maid. These extreme examples show how much our behavior is influenced by our concern for what others will think of us.

Chinese tend to speak and act with consideration of others' feelings and points of view. However, Americans express their opinions in a self-assertive way. One day recently, I observed an interesting incident in a movie theater. During the movie a baby burst into tears. In spite of the complaints of others, the mother insisted on her right to stay in the theater. According to her, she had a right to see the movie because she had paid for it. As the baby kept crying, some people began to shout at her to leave. They emphasized their right to see the movie in peace. Because of this dispute, many viewers were not able to enjoy the movie. I was surprised at the self-centered conduct of the mother and those who created a disturbance. People who cursed each other never thought of other viewers. What was important to them was to protect their own right.

Americans and Chinese live under very different cultural influences. But we should be able to take control over our behavior and modify it when necessary. Having lived in two different cultures, I want to accept the good aspects of both. Without going to extreme "me-ism," I want to be an autonomous person who isn't excessively concerned about what others think of me.

Suggestions for Writing a Comparison–Contrast Essay.

1. Before writing, make a list of similarities and differences, and decide which ones you want to include in your essay.
2. Write a clear thesis statement indicating your subjects and noting whether you will be comparing, contrasting, or both.
3. Decide the way you want to organize the details—by subject or related details.
4. Make an outline for each paragraph indicating the details you want to include.
5. Use signal words to help readers recognize the similarities and differences.
6. Be sure to proofread and revise your essay.

PRACTICE EXERCISE 24: WRITING COMPARISON–CONTRAST ESSAYS

Write at least one comparison–contrast essay. You may use any of the topics in Practice Exercise 23. Following are some additional topics.

- Compare and contrast two different religions.
- Compare and contrast two different study techniques.
- Compare and contrast two authors.
- Compare and contrast two diets.
- Compare and contrast two college courses.

Problem–Solution

Problems are part of life. For example, there are personal, family, job-related, school-related, social, and political problems. Sometimes instructors will ask you to write essays about problems and solutions as part of an exploration of issues about which you are learning. The ability to write a problem-solution essay involves careful analysis, planning, and organization.

Analyzing a problem. Although this process can seem complicated, proceeding step by step will make your task easier. Sometimes, you will need to gather additional information through discussion and readings. In most cases, the following questions will help you analyze and solve problems:

1. What is the type of problem? Is it personal, social, psychological, economic, political, or other?
2. What is my goal or objective? Why do I need to solve this problem?
3. What are the possible solutions? Without judging, think of all the alternative solutions you can. Brainstorming ideas will be helpful at this point.
4. What are the advantages and disadvantages of each solution? Use a two-column table to keep track of the advantages and disadvantages of each solution.
5. Which solution is best and why? This is your opinion based on the analysis of advantages and disadvantages. Your objective is to maximize advantages and minimize disadvantages. Also, consider the seriousness of possible disadvantages.
6. How do I know how well my solution will work? Has it ever been tried? How can it be implemented and evaluated?

Here is an example of a problem–solution analysis:

Problem: How can we solve the crime problem or at least lower the crime rate?

1. Nature of the Problem: Crime is a serious problem in the United States. It affects us personally, socially, economically, and politically.
2. Objectives: Although it may not be possible to eliminate crime completely, it needs to be reduced so we can have an orderly society. There are many different kinds of crime. I will focus on violent crime that causes harm to innocent people and creates fear. Therefore, my objectives are to (1) identify the causes of crime, (2) propose a solution to reduce crime and fear, and (3) show how the solution can be implemented.
3. Alternative Solutions: (1) build more prisons, (2) give harsher sentences, (3) end or reduce parole, (4) make prison life harder, (5) hire more police, (6) improve police and community relations, (7) implement stricter gun control laws, (8) legalize drugs, and (9) provide more social welfare programs and recreational programs.
4. Advantages and Disadvantages: The advantages and disadvantages of each alternative solution should be listed. Here is an example of how a two-column chart can help analyze possible solutions:

SOLUTION 1
Build More Prisons

Advantages	Disadvantages
Gets violent offenders off the street	Costs too much money
Reduces overcrowding in jails so prisoners do not have to be released before serving full sentence	Doesn't affect the causes of crime (unemployment, drugs, delinquency, so on)
Prisoners can be rehabilitated in prison.	Most prisoners become better criminals and more violent after serving a prison sentence.

5. Best Solution: Based on a comparison–contrast of the advantage and disadvantage charts for each solution, it appears that two solutions have the fewest disadvantages: (1) improve police and community relations, and (2) provide more social welfare programs and recreational programs. Therefore, in my opinion, a combination of these alternatives is the best solution.

6. Evaluation: This solution can be implemented in any neighborhood. It has been tried in some areas and studies have shown that the crime rate went down. Also, people feel safer when police show some interest in their community.

Writing Thesis Statements for a Problem–Solution Essay. After analyzing the problem and proposing a solution, you need to create a thesis statement. The thesis of a problem–solution essay states the problem to be solved. Limit your problem to just the aspect you will be solving, as in the following example:

Although crime cannot be completely eliminated, the crime rate can be lowered through a combination of new policing methods and more attention to social and recreational programs.

PRACTICE EXERCISE 25: WRITING PROBLEM–SOLUTION THESIS STATEMENTS

Write a thesis statement for each of these problems. Identify the aspect of the problem you want to write about, and complete your statement with a possible solution.

1. Care of the elderly

_____

2. Drug abuse

_____

3. Violence in the home

_____

4. Coping with natural disasters

_____

5. Racial discrimination

_____

Writing Problem–Solution Essays. Like every essay, problem–solution essays contain an introductory paragraph, body paragraphs, and a concluding paragraph. The introduction emphasizes the importance of the problem. For example:

> Crime is rampant in the United States. Most Americans do not feel safe in their own home.

In the body paragraphs, you can discuss each proposed solution. It is a good idea to start by presenting some of the solutions you do not like and explaining why you rejected them. Then, include at least one paragraph describing your solution in detail. Explain why you think it will work best. Finally, end with a concluding paragraph that stresses the need for your solution and the possible consequences if it is not implemented.

Model Problem–Solution Essay. Here is an example of an essay written by a student who had read newspaper articles about homeless people. The writer analyzes the advantages and disadvantages of programs for the homeless in several cities. For each of the cities listed in the table following the reading, describe the author's solution to the problem of homelessness. Include the advantages and disadvantages of each program.

HOMELESSNESS

For many years, the number of homeless people has been rising greatly. As a matter of fact, three million homeless live in the United States. Some of them have lost their homes for various reasons, and many are mentally ill. Homelessness is a very difficult problem to solve. Although we may never be able to eliminate the problem completely, government action is required to help reduce the number of homeless and make them more comfortable.

New York City has a major problem with homelessness. In the past, the city has tried to solve the problem by converting unused city buildings like armories into large shelters. This solution has some advantages like getting many homeless off the city streets. However, herding the homeless into large areas causes many difficulties. Many homeless people have been attacked. Also, there has been a lot of theft, drug abuse, and disease.

In Westchester County, directly north of New York City, the number of homeless has been increasing. Westchester tried to build permanent housing for their homeless. However, people complained and the State prohibited the County from moving homeless into the housing. As a result, the County placed the homeless in motels. This cost $56 million in one year alone. If the money were spent properly, the homeless problem would be less severe in Westchester County.

San Francisco has innovative programs for the homeless. For example, the Bay Area Group Innovative Housing program helps place homeless into houses and apartments as roommates. This saves money since the housing is already established. Funds are used to supplement the cost of rent. This program is very successful because it keeps people off welfare and avoids the trouble in big shelters.

Los Angeles provides educational programs for the children of the homeless. They set up schools in the shelters. The children were able to learn and even compete with the children in the neighborhood schools. The homeless children felt happier and had an increase in their self esteem.

Recently, New York City has been trying to solve the problem by establishing special programs for the homeless. For example, last year, Mayor Dinkins proposed a plan to place the homeless in small shelters. He plans to spend $200 million to improve the living conditions of the homeless. The plan is to move them off the street, out of the large city shelters, and into smaller city shelters and even permanent housing. He plans to provide them with additional services. For example, they are given three meals a day. A local school district, P.S. 194, provides education for the children of the homeless. This is a decent solution which should reduce the number of people living on the streets of New York City.

Homelessness is a serious problem in the United States. Some cities have tried to reduce the number of homeless through special programs. Most programs have mixed results. The most successful programs have created small, safe, and clean areas to house the homeless. The San Francisco Innovative Housing program should be considered a model. The important thing is that the people in the neighborhood accept the homeless. They can live in vacant apartments. I think the local neighborhood should provide needed services like education. With education, job training, and health care, the homeless can contribute to the community.

City	Solution	Advantages	Disadvantages
New York City Past			
New York City Recent			
Westchester County			
San Francisco			
Los Angeles			

PRACTICE EXERCISE 26: WRITING PROBLEM–SOLUTION ESSAYS

Write at least one problem–solution essay. You may use any of the topics in Practice Exercise 25 or one of the topics below. Remember to analyze the problem using the steps suggested earlier.

1. Students in U.S. schools are doing poorly.
2. The environment is being polluted.
3. Completing study for a college degree is difficult.
4. Stress-related diseases like high blood pressure are on the increase.
5. Losing weight and keeping it off is often difficult.

Persuasive Essays

Persuasion is an attempt to convince others to share your opinion or point of view. In today's society we are almost constantly bombarded with attempts at persuasion. For example, advertisements and commercials try to convince us to buy certain products, and politicians try to convince us to vote for them. Many of the essays you are asked to write in college will be persuasive in nature.

It is natural to want others to adopt your point of view. For your writing to be convincing, you need to support your opinion with facts and reasons.

Suggestions for Writing Persuasive Essays.

1. State your opinion or position on an issue as the thesis statement. (It is usually best to put the thesis statement in the introductory paragraph.)

2. Make a list of the reasons to convince your readers that your position is correct or true.

3. Present each reason as the main idea statement for a body paragraph.

4. As with all essays, end your essay with a concluding paragraph.

The following persuasive essay was written by a student at Youngstown State University in Ohio. Notice the author's use of personal experience and examples to support his thesis about women in sports. Then, answer the questions that follow.

A MAN'S GAME

A tall blonde wearing purple gym shorts and a Youngstown State sweatshirt nervously stands in a corner of the volleyball court. The score is twenty to sixteen, and her team is behind two games to one. She already has one fault, and if they lose the serve, they will surely lose the game. She hits the ball, but it does not get enough height and crashes into the net. An angry voice from the crowd yells, "That's what you get when you let a woman play a man's game." All too often I have heard thoughtless fans criticize quality women players because of their sex. In my experience with coeducational sports, I have found that pound for pound women are just as tough as men.

I can remember when I was younger and played football in the sandlot next to my house. The only thing unusual about the games was that one of our players was named Sally, and happened to be a girl. Sally was no more a tomboy than any of the other girls in the neighborhood and really only played to escape boredom. She relied on her quickness and agility instead of trying to use brute force, which proved that she was more intelligent than the rest of us. I can remember the other teams laughing at her until she streaked by them for a touchdown; then it was her turn to laugh. Sally proved that she was as good an athlete as any of us.

Last summer I further learned how formidable a female opponent can be. I was playing tennis with my sister-in-law, who happens to be ten years older than I am. After a relaxed volley, we played a set in earnest. Her first serve was a bomb to my backhand. She aced me. Every shot she made was a powerhouse. Left, right, net, baseline—she ran me ragged and beat me handily 6–2. Frankly, I think she gave me two games to salvage my male ego.

Another example of women athletes performing well is still fresh in my mind because it happened this winter. I was captain of an intramural volleyball team and we needed some practice, so we were looking for a team to scrimmage. After about a week, a friend found a team that was willing to play us. The name of the team was the Bruisers, so we were expecting a mean game. However, when we entered the gym, we saw six cute girls practicing serves and doing warmups. They were wearing black and blue shirts with the name "Bruisers" printed across the chest, and we thought for sure someone was playing a joke on us. When we told them we thought it was a joke, they became furious and said that by the end of the game, an ambulance would have to carry us away. Laughingly, we accepted the challenge. I told the guys to take it easy on them because they were only girls. What a mistake! By the end of the game, we were fighting for our lives. When the final bell sounded, they had beaten us three games to two. The most embarrassing play of the game occurred when Lisa showed me just how tough she was. The ball was just above the net, and we both went for it; before I knew what was happening, the ball bounced off my face and sent me reeling to the ground. Even though my nose felt broken, my ego was damaged more.

Ever since that day I have never underestimated a female opponent. Playing with and against females has taught me to admire and respect them. The idea of women as the weaker sex is a figment of some man's imagination.

What do you think the author is trying to persuade you to believe?

_____

_____

_____

_____

Do you think this essay is convincing? Why or why not?

_____

_____

_____

_____

PRACTICE EXERCISE 27: READING A PERSUASIVE ESSAY

Would you have attended school when you were younger if you did not have to? In the following essay the author expresses his views on compulsory education.

1   A decline in standardized test scores is but the most recent indicator that American education is in trouble.

2   One reason for the crisis is that present mandatory-attendance laws force many to attend school who have no wish to be there. Such children have little desire to learn and are so antagonistic to school that neither they nor more highly motivated students receive the quality education that is the birthright of every American.

3   The solution to this problem is simple: Abolish compulsory-attendance laws and allow only those who are committed to getting an education to attend.

4   This will not end public education. Contrary to conventional belief, legislators enacted compulsory-attendance laws to legalize what already existed. William Landes and Lewis Solomon, economists, found little evidence that mandatory-attendance laws increased the number of children in school. They found, too, that school systems have never effectively enforced such laws, usually because of the expense involved.

5   There is no contradiction between the assertion that compulsory attendance has had little effect on the number of children attending school and the argument that repeal would be a positive step toward improving education. Most parents want a high school education for their children. Unfortunately, compulsory attendance hampers the ability of public school officials to enforce legitimate educational and disciplinary policies and thereby make the education a good one.

6   Private schools have no such problem. They can fail or dismiss students, knowing such students can attend public school. Without compulsory attendance, public schools would be freer to oust students whose academic or personal behavior undermines the educational mission of the institution.

7   Has not the noble experiment of a formal education for everyone failed? While we pay homage to the homily, "You can lead a horse to water but you can't make him drink," we have pretended it is not true in education.

8   Ask high school teachers if recalcitrant* students learn anything of value. Ask teachers if these students do any homework. Ask if the threat of low grades motivates them. Quite the contrary, these students know they will be passed from grade to grade until they are old enough to quit or until, as is more likely, they receive a high school diploma. At the point when students could legally quit, most choose to remain since they know they are likely to be allowed to graduate whether they do acceptable work or not.

9   Abolition of archaic attendance laws would produce enormous dividends.

* *recalcitrant* means disobedient

10   First, it would alert everyone that school is a serious place where one goes to learn. Schools are neither day-care centers nor indoor street corners. Young people who resist learning should stay away; indeed, an end to compulsory schooling would require them to stay away.

11   Second, students opposed to learning would not be able to pollute the educational atmosphere for those who want to learn. Teachers could stop policing recalcitrant students and start educating.

12   Third, grades would show what they are supposed to: how well a student is learning. Parents could again read report cards and know if their children were making progress.

13   Fourth, public esteem for schools would increase. People would stop regarding them as way stations for adolescents and start thinking of them as institutions for educating America's youth.

14   Fifth, elementary schools would change because students would find out early that they had better learn something or risk flunking out later. Elementary teachers would no longer have to pass their failures on to junior high and high school.

15   Sixth, the cost of enforcing compulsory education would be eliminated. Despite enforcement efforts, nearly 15 percent of the school-age children in our largest cities are almost permanently absent from school.

16   Communities could use these savings to support institutions to deal with young people not in school. If, in the long run, these institutions prove more costly, at least we would not confuse their mission with that of schools.

17   Schools should be for education. At present, they are only tangentially so. They have attempted to serve an all-encompassing social function, trying to be all things to all people. In the process they have failed miserably at what they were originally formed to accomplish.

(Roger Sipher, "So That Nobody Has to Go to School If They Don't Want To," *New York Times*, December 19, 1977, p. 31, col. 1.)

_____ 1.   The main pattern of this persuasive essay is
   a.   persuasion
   b.   cause–effect
   c.   comparison–contrast
   d.   problem–solution

_____ 2.   The thesis is stated in paragraph(s)
   a.   1 and 2
   b.   2 and 3
   c.   1
   d.   3

_____ 3. The thesis is restated in paragraph
       a.   16
       b.   17
       c.   2
       d.   7

_____ 4. The author uses the following evidence to support his thesis:
       a.   Recalcitrant students don't learn anything of value.
       b.   Standardized test scores have declined.
       c.   Most parents want a high school education for their children.
       d.   Private schools can fail or dismiss students.

5. According to the author, what effect do students who do not want to learn have on other students?

_____

_____

_____

6. In a few sentences, write a summary of this article.

_____

_____

_____

_____

7. Has the author persuaded you to support his opinion? Explain.

_____

_____

_____

_____

PRACTICE EXERCISE 28: WRITING A PERSUASIVE THESIS STATEMENT

Write a thesis statement that gives your opinion about each of the topics below. For example:

Topic: Open Admissions to Community Colleges
Thesis Statement: All students who apply to a community college
                        should be accepted.

1. *Topic:*   Divorce

   Thesis Statement: _____

2. *Topic:*   Sex Education in Public Schools

   Thesis Statement: _____

3. *Topic:*   Gun Control

   Thesis Statement: _____

4. *Topic:*   Capital Punishment

   Thesis Statement: _____

5. *Topic:*   Whether to Have Children Earlier or Later in Life

   Thesis Statement: _____

PRACTICE EXERCISE 29: WRITING A PERSUASIVE ESSAY

Write a persuasive essay using one of the thesis statements from Practice Exercise 28 or one of the thesis statements below. You may take the opposing view on any of these issues.

1. Health care should be nationalized in the United States.
2. Smoking should be prohibited from all public places.
3. People on welfare should be forced to work.
4. College education should be free to all American citizens.
5. The government should run free child care centers.

Mixed Patterns

Most essays you read and write will contain a combination of the patterns discussed. Once you identify your topic and purpose for writing, you can choose the combination of patterns that will help you write most effectively.

In the following essay, the author combines several of the patterns we have introduced. As you read, write in the margin any patterns you recognize.

DON'T LET STEREOTYPES WARP YOUR JUDGMENTS

Robert Heilbroner

1   Is a girl called Gloria apt to be better-looking than one called Bertha? Are criminals more likely to be dark than blond? Can you tell a good deal about someone's personality from hearing his voice briefly over the phone? Can a person's nationality be pretty accurately guessed from his photograph? Does the fact that someone wears glasses imply that he is intelligent?

2   The answer to all these questions is obvious: "No."

3   Yet, from all the evidence at hand, most of us believe these things. Ask any college boy if he'd rather take his chances with a Gloria or a Bertha, or ask any college

girl if she'd rather blind date a Richard or a Cuthbert. In fact, you don't have to ask: college students in questionnaires have revealed that names conjure up the same images in their minds as they do in yours—and for as little reason.

4   Look into the favorite suspects of persons who report suspicious characters and you will find a large percentage of them to be "swarthy" or "dark and foreign-look-ing" despite the testimony of criminologists that criminals do *not* tend to be dark, foreign or "wild-eyed." Delve into the main asset of a telephone stock swindler and you will find it to be a marvelously confidence-inspiring telephone "personality." And whereas we all think we know what an Italian or a Swede looks like, it is the sad fact that when a group of Nebraska students sought to match faces and nationalities of 15 European countries, they were scored wrong in 93 percent of their identifications. Finally, for all the fact that horn-rimmed glasses have now become the standard television sign of an "intellectual," optometrists know that the main thing that distinguishes people with glasses is just bad eyes.

5   Stereotypes are a kind of gossip about the world, a gossip that makes us pre-judge people before we ever lay eyes on them. Hence, it is not surprising that stereotypes have something to do with the dark world of prejudice. Explore most prejudices (note that the word means *prejudgment*) and you will find a cruel stereo-type at the core of each one.

6   For it is the extraordinary fact that once we have typecast the world, we tend to see people in terms of our standardized pictures. In another demonstration of the power of stereotypes to affect our vision, a number of Columbia and Barnard students were shown 30 photographs of pretty but unidentified girls, and asked to rate each in terms of "general liking," "intelligence," "beauty" and so on. Two months later, the same group were shown the same photographs, this time with fictitious Irish, Italian, Jewish and "American" names attached to the pictures. Right away the ratings changed. Faces which were now seen as representing a national group went down in looks and still farther down in likeability, while the "American" girls suddenly looked decidedly prettier and nicer.

7   Why is it that we stereotype the world in such irrational and harmful fashion? In part, we begin to type-cast people in our childhood years. Early in life, as every parent whose child has watched a TV Western knows, we learn to spot the Good Guys from the Bad Guys. Some years ago, a social psychologist showed very clear-ly how powerful these stereotypes of childhood vision are. He secretly asked the most popular youngsters in an elementary school to make errors in their morning gym exercises. Afterwards, he asked the class if anyone had noticed any mistakes during gym period. Oh, yes, said the children. But it was the unpopular members of the class—the "bad guys"—they remembered as being out of step.

8   We not only grow up with standardized pictures forming inside of us, but as grown-ups we are constantly having them thrust upon us. Some of them, like the

half-joking, half-serious stereotypes of mothers-in-law, or country yokels, or psy-chiatrists, are dinned into us by the stock jokes we hear and repeat. In fact, without such stereotypes, there would be a lot fewer jokes. Still other stereotypes are per-petuated by the advertisement we read, the movies we see, the books we read.

9   And finally, we tend to stereotype because it helps us make sense out of a highly confusing world, a world which William James once described as "one great, blooming, buzzing confusion." It is a curious fact that if we don't *know* what we're looking at, we are often quite literally unable to *see* what we're looking at. People who recover their sight after a lifetime of blindness actually cannot at first tell a triangle from a square. A visitor to a factory sees only noisy chaos where the superintendent sees a perfectly synchronized flow of work. As Walter Lippmann has said, "For the most part we do not first see, and then define; we define first, and then we see."

10   Stereotypes are one way in which we "define" the world in order to see it. They classify the infinite variety of human beings into a convenient handful of "types" towards whom we learn to act in stereotyped fashion. Life would be a wearing process if we had to start from scratch with each and every human con-tact. Stereotypes economize on our mental effort by covering up the blooming, buzzing confusion with big recognizable cut-outs. They save us the "trouble" of finding out what the world is like—they give it its accustomed look.

11   Thus the trouble is that stereotypes make us mentally lazy. As S. I. Hayakawa, the authority on semantics, has written: "The danger of stereotypes lies not in their existence, but in the fact that they become for all people some of the time, and for some people all the time, *substitutes for observation.*" Worse yet, stereotypes get in the way of our judgment, even when we do observe the world. Someone who has formed rigid preconceptions of all Latins as "excitable," or all teenagers as "wild," doesn't alter his point of view when he meets a calm and deliberate Genoese, or a serious-minded high school student. He brushes them aside as "exceptions that prove the rule." And, of course, if he meets someone true to type, he stands tri-umphantly vindicated. "They're all like that," he proclaims, having encountered an excited Latin, an ill-behaved adolescent.

12   Hence, quite aside from the injustice which stereotypes do to others, they impoverish ourselves. A person who lumps the world into simple categories, who type-casts all labor leaders as "racketeers," all businessmen as "reactionaries," all Harvard men as "snobs," and all Frenchmen as "sexy," is in danger of becoming a stereotype himself. He loses his capacity to be himself—which is to say, to see the world in his own absolutely unique, inimitable and independent fashion.

13   Instead, he votes for the man who fits his standardized picture of what a can-didate "should" look like or sound like, buys the goods that someone in his "situ-ation" in life "should" own, lives the life that others define for him. The mark of the

stereotyped person is that he never surprises us, that we do indeed have him typed. And no one fits this strait-jacket so perfectly as someone whose opinions about *other people* are fixed and inflexible.

14   Impoverishing as they are, stereotypes are not easy to get rid of. The world we type-cast may be no better than a Grade B movie, but at least we know what to expect of our stock characters. When we let them act for themselves in the strangely unpredictable way that people do act, who knows but that many of our fondest convictions will be proved wrong?

15   Nor do we suddenly drop our standardized pictures. Sharp swings of ideas about people often just substitute one stereotype for another. The true process of change is a slow one that adds bits and pieces of reality to the pictures in our heads, until gradually they take on some of the blurriness of life itself. Little by little, we learn not that Jews and Negroes and Catholics and Puerto Ricans are "just like everybody else"—for that, too, is a stereotype—but that each and every one of them is unique, special, different and individual. Often we do not even know that we have let a stereotype lapse until we hear someone saying, "all so-and-so's are like such-and-such," and we hear ourselves saying, "Well—maybe."

16   Can we speed the process along? Of course we can.

17   First, we can become *aware* of the standardized pictures in our heads, in other people's heads, in the world around us.

18   Second, we can become suspicious of all judgments that we allow exceptions to "prove." There is no more chastening thought than that in the vast intellectual adventure of science, it takes but one tiny exception to topple a whole edifice of ideas.

19   Third, we can learn to be wary of generalizations about people. As F. Scott Fitzgerald once wrote: "Begin with an individual, and before you know it you have created a type; begin with a type, and you find you have created—nothing."

20   Most of the time, when we type-cast the world, we are not in fact generalizing about people at all. We are only revealing the embarrassing facts about the pictures that hang in the gallery of stereotypes in our own heads.

(Robert Heilbroner. "Don't Let Stereotypes Warp Your Judgments."
Think Magazine, June 1961.)

In the following list, put a check by any essay pattern you noted.

1. _____   description

2. _____   narration

3. _____   cause–effect

4. _____   comparison–contrast

5. _____   problem–solution

PRACTICE EXERCISE 30: READING A MIXED PATTERN ESSAY

Read the short essay below and answer the questions.

TEENAGERS AND BOOZE

Carl Rowan

1   America's young people have found a potent, sometimes addictive, and legal drug. It's called alcohol.

2   Drinking is nothing new for teen-agers. In fact, it's a kind of ritual of youth. In recent years, however, a great many youngsters from all walks of life have turned to drugs like marijuana, heroin and barbiturates. Reports coming in now from schools and national studies tell us that there's a change occurring. The newest way for kids to turn on is an old way—with alcohol.

3   Listen to these words of a high school senior in Brooklyn, as told to a reporter from *Newsweek* magazine: "A lot of us used to smoke pot, but we gave that up a year or two ago. Now my friends and I drink a lot . . . and in my book, a high is a high."

4   Why are youngsters rediscovering booze? One reason is pressure from other kids to be one of the gang. Another is the ever-present urge to act grown-up. For some, it eases the burden of problems at home or at school. And it's cheaper. You can buy a couple of six-packs of beer for the price of three joints of pot.

5   Perhaps the main reason is that parents don't seem to mind. They tolerate drinking—sometimes almost seem to encourage it. In part this may be due to the fact that parents themselves drink; in part it's because they're relieved to find that their children are "only" drinking, and are not involved with pot, LSD or other drugs.

6   What these parents may not realize is that alcohol is also a drug, and a potentially dangerous one. Furthermore, few are aware just how young the drinkers are these days. The National Council on Alcoholism reports that in 1972 the age of the youngest alcoholics brought to its attention dropped from fourteen to twelve. Other studies have found that three fourths of senior-high students have used alcohol—an increase of 90 per cent in three years. And 56 per cent of junior-high students have tried alcohol.

7   The Medical Council on Alcoholism warns: The potential teen-age drinking problem should give far more cause for alarm than drug addiction. Many schools have reacted to teen-age drinking. They've started alcohol-education programs. But a lot of experts feel that teenagers are not going to stop drinking until adults do.

(Carl T. Rowan, *Just Between Us Blacks*,
Random House, 1974, pp. 95–96.)

1. The major pattern of this essay is problem–solution. The problem is

_____

2. The problem is stated in paragraph _____.

3. The reasons for the problem are stated in paragraph(s) _____.

4. There are _____ reasons stated for the problem.

5. The author states the solution to the problem in paragraph _____.

6. Write a summary of the thesis of this essay.

_____

_____

_____

PRACTICE EXERCISE 31: WRITING THESIS STATEMENTS

For each of the topics below, write a thesis statement using the pattern listed.

1. *Topic:*   Obesity
   Pattern: Cause–Effect

   Thesis Statement: _____

2. *Topic:*   My Community's Worst Problem
   Pattern: Problem–Solution

   Thesis Statement: _____

3. *Topic:*   The Difference between Having a Male or Female
                     as a Friend
   Pattern: Comparison–Contrast

   Thesis Statement: _____

4. *Topic:*   Television Watching Can Make You Lazy
   Pattern: Persuasion

   Thesis Statement: _____

5. *Topic:*   Stereotypes in the Movies
   Pattern: Your Choice

   Thesis Statement: _____

PRACTICE EXERCISE 32: WRITING AN ESSAY

Write an essay using one of the thesis patterns discussed in this chapter. Before you begin writing a first draft, brainstorm by listing or mapping the ideas you want to include in your essay. The following questions may help you plan the essay.

- What is your purpose for writing the essay?
- What essay pattern(s) will be most effective in conveying your thesis?
- What technique will you use to get the reader's attention in the introductory paragraph?
- At what point will you state your thesis?
- What main ideas do you want to write about?
- Are your main ideas relevant to the thesis? Do they help support your point?

Application

Textbook Selections
Relationships

Before Reading

According to the psychologist Abraham Maslow, once people have satisfied their needs for food and safety, they can turn their attention to a desire to be part of a relationship with others. Maslow called this the need for belonging and love.

Part of human behavior is the desire to create a family. Anthropologists study, among other topics, the variety of family structures found all over the world. Following are excerpts about families and relationships from several anthropology textbooks. Because you are a member of a family and have had many relationships in your own life, you should find these readings interesting.

Freewrite for a few minutes about your own family. Who is in your family? How many generations live together in one dwelling? Which member of your family do you feel closest to? Which member of your family do you like the least? The most?

During Reading

Types of Family Groups

1   The "typical American family" so thoroughly incorporated into our ideology consists of a husband, a wife, and two or more children, all of whom live in a single detached household. However, this image does not typify families in American society today. There are single parents with children, and there may be other relatives living with the family. If we look at families in other societies, we find that the American ideal is, in fact, rather rare worldwide.

2   The **nuclear family** is composed of a man, a woman, and their children. . . . The nuclear family group is most often found in segments of societies like the United States where housing is not in short supply and where social mobility, the hunt for jobs and improved social status, and the existence of specialized support systems (such as schools and nursing homes) reduce the central caring role of the family.

(Howard, *Contemporary Cultural Anthropology*,
HarperCollins, 1996, p. 225.)

1. Paragraph 1 contrasts _____
   with _____ .

2. The signal word that indicates the contrast is _____ .
3. Underline the main idea in paragraph 1.
4. Paragraph 2 gives several reasons for the existence of nuclear families in societies like the United States. List those reasons below.

   _____

   _____

   _____

   _____

This Tibetan woman (wearing the veil) is being married to the two men on the left, who are brothers.

3   Next we must consider whether the combination father-mother-child has the same functional significance where either father or mother is married to and is living with more than one spouse at a time. This question is important because *polygamy* (plural marriage) occurs to some extent in at least 90 percent of all cultures. In one form, called *polygyny*, several wives share a husband; in another, a much less common form called *polyandry*, several husbands share a wife.

4   Do people who have polygamous families also have nuclear families? O. P. Murdock suggested that nuclear families do exist in such situations. The man or woman simply belongs to more than one nuclear family at a time. But Murdock overlooked the fact that plural marriages create domestic situations that differ significantly from those created by monogamous (one husband, one wife) marriages.

(Harris, *Culture, People, Nature: An Introduction to General Anthropology*, Longman, 1997, p. 246.)

5. Underline the definitions in paragraph 3.

6. Polygyny and polyandry are kinds of _____.

7. In what ways do you think life would differ in a plural marriage as compared to a monogamous marriage?

_____

_____

_____

_____

_____

8. If you were in a polygamous marriage, which aspects that you listed above would you find acceptable or even advantageous? Which would you be unwilling to accept?

	Polygamous Marriage
Acceptable	1. 2. 3.
Not Acceptable	1. 2. 3.

5   Polygamous sexual arrangements, for example, imply a more relaxed attitude toward sharing sexual partners than one expects in monogamous marriages. The mode of reproduction is also different, especially with polygyny, because the spacing of births is easier to regulate through abstinence.

6   Further, distinctive patterns of nursing and infant care arise when the mother sleeps alone with her children while the father sleeps with a different wife each night. From the point of view of child rearing, special psychological effects are associated with a father who divides his time among several mothers. The monogamous nuclear family places the focus of adult attention on a small group of full siblings. In a polygynous household, a dozen or more half-siblings must share the affection of the same man. Furthermore, the presence of co-wives or co-husbands changes the burden of child care a particular parent must bear. Industrial-

age parents are troubled by the question of what to do with children when both parents go to work or visit friends. Polygynous families, however, have a built-in solution to the babysitting problem in the form of co-wives. From a first wife's point of view, additional wives are welcome because they help spread the work load and increase the productivity and prestige of the household.

(Harris, *Culture, People, Nature: An Introduction to General Anthropology*, Longman, 1997, p. 246.)

In Senegal, Islamic law permits this man to take one more wife to fill his quota of four.

9. Paragraphs 5 and 6 contrast polygynous and monogamous households in all of the following ways *except*
   a. mode of reproduction.
   b. prestige.
   c. psychological effects on children.
   d. child care.

7 There are also various forms of extended family groups, in which two or more families of at least two generations live together. . . . Extended family groups play a significant economic role in the adaptive strategies of many societies today. In Africa, for example, extended families provide important support services in the face of economic hardship and political upheaval. The growing number of individuals who depend on the few members able to earn a living, however, places considerable strain on the structure. Commenting on this stress in the face of Africa's almost overwhelming problems, Blaine Harden (1991) says of the extended family: "Like a bridge that has borne too much high-speed traffic for too many years, its foundations are cracking."

8 Finally, there are **joint family groups** in which two or more relatives of the same generation and their spouses and children live together. The *fraternal joint*

family group is a common example of this type; it consists of at least two brothers and their wives and children.

9   While one or two of these family groups may represent the normative ideal of a society, in practice many of these forms may coexist in the same social setting. In Kekchi villages in southern Belize, it is common to find nuclear families, various extended and joint family groups, and even an occasional polygynous family group (usually curers who have inherited wives from deceased patients). In each case, the pattern reflects the strategies of people in relation to their broader social environment—the size of the village, factionalism, the social network of the married couple, and how long they have lived in a village.

(Howard, *Contemporary Cultural Anthropology*,
HarperCollins, 1996, pp. 226–227.)

10. What conclusion can you draw from the statement, "The growing number of individuals who depend on the few members able to earn a living, however, places considerable strain on the structure"? (paragraph 7)
    a. More and more people in Africa are unwilling to earn a living.
    b. More and more people in Africa are living longer.
    c. Extended families in Africa are too large.
    d. Relationships in extended families are strained.

11. What relatives, other than brothers, might form a joint family group, as described in paragraph 8?

_____

12. Underline the main idea of paragraph 9.

10   Once a couple is married, where will they reside? In our own society, the ideal residence is their own dwelling, which may or may not be near either set of parents. We refer to such a practice as **neolocal** residence. . . . Neolocal residence is associated not only with geographical mobility but also with financial independence. A newly married couple who are poor or unemployed or who otherwise lack the capital to support themselves often reside with one set of parents until their financial situation improves, but in general the goal of a married couple remains living on their own.

11   Neolocality is not a universal residential preference. In many societies newly married couples do not aspire to owning their own homes and living independently. In societies where social bonds among closely related males are important, the couple usually resides with the husband's group and even in the same household as other male relatives of the husband. Wives in such situations may find themselves cut off from their natal group (group of birth) and may become permanent members of their husband's group instead. We refer to such a pattern as **patrilocal** residence.

(Howard, *Contemporary Cultural Anthropology*,
HarperCollins, 1996, pp. 221–222.)

13. Complete the following cause–effect relationship as expressed in paragraph 10.

Cause   _____

Effect   married and living with parents

14. Underline the main idea sentence in paragraph 11.

After Reading

1. Vocabulary in Context

Listed below are words from the textbook selections you have read on families. Reread the sentences in which these words are located and then write the meaning you think each word has. Then write a dictionary definition for each word.

Word and Paragraph	My Guess at Meaning	Dictionary Definition
ideology (1)		
mode (5)		
abstinence (5)		
siblings (6)		
prestige (6)		
borne (7)		
normative (9)		
mobility (10)		
aspire (11)		

2. Topics for Writers

Listed below are some types of marital residences found throughout the world.

Arrangement	Place Where Married Children Live
Neolocality	Apart from either husband's or wife's relatives
Patrilocality	With husband's father
Matrilocality	With wife's mother
Avunculocality	With husband's mother's brother
Amitalocality	With wife's father's sister

(adapted from Harris, *Culture, People, Nature: An Introduction to General Anthropology*, Longman, 1997, p. 247.)

Write an essay about one of the following:

- Which arrangement do you think would be the easiest for you to have as a married person? Why?
- Which arrangement do you feel would be the most difficult? Why?
- Compare the arrangement you like best with the one you like least.

Additional Reading
POEM FOR A DIVORCED DAUGHTER
Horace Coleman

Before Reading

Write about your relationship with your father or the person who has been a father figure in your life. Describe the person and how you feel about him.

During Reading

From the dialogue in the following "Poem for a Divorced Daughter," can you figure out how the father feels about his daughter?

if some nosey body asks "well,
is you got a daddy?"
give them the look that
writes "fool" on their face.

if that aint enough & they
got to say "where he at?"
tell em "where he be!"

& if they *so* simple they
haven't got it yet
& try to stay in your business

to the degree of "well,
if he love you then how
come he aint here?"
you just sigh

poke your lip out low
ball your hands up
on your hips and let it slip:
"he loves me where he *is*"
cause I do
where I am

(*Between a Rock and a Hard Place*, Kansas City, MO:
BKMK Press, 1977.)

After Reading

1. **Comprehension Check**

_____ 1) The father probably thinks that the question "well, is you got a daddy?" is foolish because
   a. his daughter does not know where her daddy is.
   b. the answer should be obvious.
   c. her parents are divorced.
   d. the nosey body has bad grammar.

_____ 2) The attitude which the father is suggesting when he says "poke your lip out low ball your hands up on your hips and let it slip" is
   a. assertiveness.
   b. cheerfulness.
   c. pessimism.
   d. optimism.

_____ 3) What does the father mean by "'he loves me where he *is*,' cause I do where I am"?
   a. They communicate often.
   b. He loves his daughter even if he's not with her.
   c. She does not want to see her father again.
   d. He lives too far away to visit.

2. **Topics for Writers**

1) Has one of your parents ever disappointed you in some way? Describe the circumstances and how you felt.

2) Have you ever loved someone even though that person was located in a distant place? Who is the person and how did you maintain a relationship?

Chapter Summary

Elements of an Essay	An essay is a group of related paragraphs and is usually organized around three sections: (1) introduction, (2) body, and (3) conclusion.
Thesis and Thesis Statement	The thesis is the main idea of the entire essay. The thesis statement is the sentence that states the thesis.
Introduction to an Essay	The introduction is the first part of an essay and may begin with an attention-getter, followed by a bridge leading to the thesis statement.
Body of an Essay	The body of an essay is usually a series of paragraphs that develop the idea expressed in the thesis statement.
Conclusion of an Essay	The conclusion of an essay, usually in the form of a short, single paragraph, should leave the readers with a sense of completeness.
Revising an Essay	Revising is the process of reviewing and rewriting your essay to make your ideas more logical, understandable, and interesting to your readers.
Revision through Reading	Reading your essay to yourself is a good way to start the revision process.
Revision through Collaboration	Collaboration is a way of finding out what other readers think about your essay.
Summarizing Passages	Summarizing is a useful skill for reading and studying. To summarize a passage, combine the main ideas of each paragraph into one or two sentences.
Types of Essays and Passages	When you write an essay, you should have a purpose for writing it. Your purpose may be to discuss an issue or to persuade or entertain the reader.
Description	When the main purpose of the writing is to create a picture of a person, place, or object. it is called a descriptive essay.
Narration	A narrative relates events that have happened. It usually contains answers to the questions *who, what, where, why, how,* and *when.*

Cause–Effect	In a cause–effect essay you explore reasons and results.
Comparison–Contrast	Compare means to consider similarities and differences; contrast means to consider only differences.
Problem–Solution	In a problem–solution essay you analyze issues in order to solve problems.
Persuasive Essays	Persuasion is an attempt to convince others to share your opinion or point of view.
Mixed Patterns	Most essays will contain a combination of patterns. You should choose the combination of patterns that will help you communicate most effectively.

 Journal

In the space below, write one thing you know now that you didn't know before reading this chapter. Do you think it will be useful to you in the future? Why or why not?

_____

_____

_____

_____

_____

_____

_____

_____

_____

_____

_____

_____

_____

_____

_____

_____

_____

_____

_____

_____

_____

_____

_____

_____

Go Electronic!

For additional readings, exercises, and Internet activities, visit the Longman English pages at:

http://longman.awl.com/englishpages

If you need a user name and password, please see your instructor.

Take a Road Trip to the Statue of Liberty

Be sure to visit the Patterns of Organization module in your Reading Road Trip CD-ROM for multimedia tutorials, exercises, and tests.

Practice Your Writing Skills

For additional practice with your writing skills, use the Writer's ToolKit CD-ROM included with this text.

CHAPTER 6

Making Inferences

Theme: Belonging

What You Will Find in This Chapter

- Making Inferences from Experience
- Making Inferences about Causes and Effects
- Making Inferences about Tone
- Making Inferences about Motive and Character
- Textbook Selections on Socialization, Social Structure, and Conformity
- Additional Readings about an Illegal Alien and a Shocking Experiment

Have you ever done something because other people were doing it? What was it? Was it something you would have chosen to do anyway?

_____

_____

_____

_____

Often people will behave in particular ways because they want to be accepted by others. Sometimes this acceptance is more important than their personal convictions about whether or not their actions are right.

We discuss the importance of being accepted by other people in this chapter, as we continue looking at the need for love and belonging. We've included an excerpt from a sociology textbook, a short story, and a report of an interesting psychological experiment. The skill of making inferences when reading is also introduced.

Making Inferences from Experience

Writers often work at two levels—literal and inferential. At the *literal* level, authors make direct statements. They say exactly what they mean. "You look terrific" and "I don't enjoy hot weather" are examples of literal statements.

But authors also assume that readers will be able to figure out some things for themselves. So they leave some important ideas unsaid, and it is up to you to "read between the lines" and draw conclusions. When you reach a conclusion that is not directly stated by the author, you are making an inference.

We make inferences based on our own prior knowledge and experience all the time, often without realizing that we're doing it. For example, if you look at a photograph of a person wearing dirty overalls while bent over the open hood of a car, you may infer that he is an auto mechanic. If you see a man dressed in shabby clothes sleeping on the sidewalk, you may infer that he is homeless. If you see a well-dressed woman carrying a briefcase on the train or bus in the early morning, you may infer that she is going to work. All of these inferences are based on your understanding of the world and your past experiences. Of course, it is possible that some of your inferences may be wrong; there is usually some element of uncertainty when you make an inference. Although inferences are not necessarily correct, they should be consistent with your experience and with whatever evidence you have.

Practice Exercise 1: Making Inferences from Experience

The first sentence in each item of this exercise states a common observation. The next sentence (or two) tells you that an obvious inference is incorrect. Can you make another inference for each situation? Write your inferences on the lines provided. The first one is done for you.

1. A person wearing dirty overalls is bent over the open hood of a car. He's not an auto mechanic. <u>Instead, he's a bank executive who enjoys working on his automobile during his free time.</u>

2. A man, dressed in shabby clothes, is sleeping on the sidewalk. He's not homeless. Instead, _____

   _____

   _____

3. A well-dressed woman is carrying a briefcase on the train or bus in the early morning. She's not going to work. Instead, _____

   _____

   _____

4. The sky becomes dark. It is not nighttime; it is the middle of the afternoon. The sun did not set yet. Instead, _____

   _____

   _____

5. You go into a friend's house to find that all of the clocks are set one hour behind the time on your wristwatch. The electricity did not go off in the house. Instead, _____

   _____

   _____

6. Every day, you see the same woman walking three dogs. This woman does not own a dog. Instead, _____

   _____

   _____

Readers often need to make inferences about

- causes and effects
- tone
- motive and character

Let's examine each of these, and see how to use a reading to make accurate inferences.

Making Inferences about Causes and Effects

One type of inference involves cause and effect (which we read about in Chapters 4 and 5). Sometimes you experience a situation in which you infer possible effects, outcomes, or results. For example, if you see large, dark clouds in the sky, you may conclude that it is going to rain.

Cause	Inferred Effect
Dark clouds	Rain

Also, you may infer the cause of an event. For example, if you see a student in your class dozing, you may infer that the student did not get enough sleep the night before—or that she is bored.

Inferred Cause	Effect
Not enough sleep, boredom	Sleeping in class

After reading the following excerpt about a child named Genie, what inferences can you make about the effects of child abuse on future behavior?

Genie was almost completely isolated from contact with anyone for 12 years, from the time she was a year and a half old. She saw only her father, mother, and brother, and such brief encounters only occurred when they came to feed her baby food. Genie's father, who spent most of his time at home, did not allow his wife or Genie to leave the house or have anyone visit them. Genie was kept in a back room where she was either strapped to a child's potty chair or placed in a sleeping bag that limited her body movements. Her contact even with her family was minimal, since she only saw them when they came to feed her. The family always spoke in whispers; isolated in a back room, Genie rarely heard any conversation. If she made noises her father punished her severely.

1. Infer the possible effects of this kind of treatment on Genie's future behavior.

_____

_____

_____

_____

_____

By studying cases such as this one, sociologists can make valuable inferences concerning the impact of *socialization* (the lifelong process by which people learn how to behave in a culture). Here is the rest of the story about Genie. What additional inferences can you make?

When Genie was 13, her mother took her and fled the house. According to accounts by people who saw her shortly afterward, Genie was unable to control her bowels, eat solid food, cry, or even talk. Because of her tight confinement, she had not even learned to focus her eyes beyond twelve feet. She was constantly salivating and spitting, and had little use of her arms or legs.

Gradually Genie learned some of the minimal social behavior expected of a 13-year-old. For example, she became toilet trained and learned to wear clothes. Although intelligence tests did not indicate reasoning disability, even after five years of concentrated effort on the part of a foster mother, social workers, and medical doctors, she never learned to speak beyond the level of a four-year-old, and did not engage others in conversation. Although she responded positively to people who treated her with sympathy and concern, Genie's social behavior remained severely underdeveloped. She never became a fully socialized adult member of society.

(Applebaum & Chambliss, *Sociology*, HarperCollins, 1995, p. 106.)

2. Why did Genie and her mother flee the house?

_____

_____

_____

3. Why was Genie unable to speak beyond the level of a four-year-old?

_____

_____

_____

4. Based on this example, what can you conclude about the process of socialization?

_____

_____

_____

_____

Making Inferences about Tone

You can tell how a speaker feels by his or her tone of voice. For example, an angry person usually speaks loud and uses a high pitched voice. Similarly, writers use tone to express feelings and attitudes about the characters and situations they write about. They create tone through their choice of words and the details they include. For example:

When Mrs. Smith walked into the bedroom and saw her husband sleeping, she yelled, "Get out of bed already and get to work! Do I have to do all the work around here? I'm sorry I ever married you."

Mrs. Smith is upset with her husband. Her tone is angry *(she yelled)*, resentful *(Do I have to do all the work?)*, and regretful *(sorry I ever married you)*.

Here are some more examples of words used to describe tone:

anxious	distressed	logical	rejecting
bitter	forgiving	loving	sad
compassionate	formal	matter-of-fact	sarcastic
confident	gloomy	objective	serious
critical	humorous	optimistic	surprised
cruel	informal	pessimistic	sympathetic
depressed	joyous	pleading	sorry

Many different tones can be revealed as a piece of writing develops. In each of the two examples that follow, the writer's tone may become apparent to you as you read. Check your ideas about each writer's tone with our explanations.

Mommy got the address and went to the place herself.

It was a dilapidated housing project near St. Nicholas Avenue, with junkies and winos standing out front. Mommy stepped past them and walked through a haze of reefer smoke and took the elevator to the eighth floor. She went to the apartment door and listened. There was music playing on a stereo inside, and the voice of someone on the phone. She knocked on the door. The stereo lowered. "Who is it?"someone asked. It sounded like Helen.

"I'm here to see Helen," Mommy said.

Silence.

"I know you're there, Helen," Mommy said.

Silence.

"Helen. I want you to come home. Whatever's wrong we'll fix. Just forget all of it and come on home." From down the hallway, a doorway opened and a black woman watched in silence as the dark-haired, bowlegged white lady talked to the closed door.

"Please come home, Helen."

The door had a peephole in it. The peephole slid back. A large black eye peered out.

"Please come home, Helen. This is no place for you to be. Just come on home." The peephole closed.

(James McBride, The Color of Water: A Black Man's Tribute to His White Mother, New York: Berkeley, 1996, p. 78.)

In this example, the author has used words such as *dilapidated* and *haze of reefer smoke* to create a tone for the physical surroundings. Tone about the characters is conveyed through the word *silence* and the fact that when the mother spoke to her daughter, she *talked to the closed door*, and *a large black eye peered out*. The mother is sad and pleading with her daughter to return home, whereas the daughter seems to reject her mother.

Here is another example:

I tell him I'm thinking about getting a new cat.

"No way," he says, like this is not negotiable. As if I haven't paid half the rent since grad school, and all the cat costs, including the spiffy new cat door installed next to the fridge.

I say I've been to the Animal Rescue League and they have seventeen adorable kittens—all colors. "You get to pick the color," I say.

"Hold it," he says. He lines up his sharp accountant's pencil across the top of his crossword, cracks the knuckles of his right hand. "I do not want another cat. What's wrong with the three we've got?"

The three we've got hear our voices rising and pad into the kitchen to see what's going on. The Persian, Jeanette, threads back and forth through my legs, her long hair flying, while gray-striped Fitzhugh leaps onto the fridge and blinks down at us. Sweetpeach, the calico, jumps into my lap and kneads my chenille stomach. Not a cat goes near Roy.

"There's nothing wrong with the three we've got," I say.

"So forget a new cat," he says, and turns back to his crossword.

(Pamela Painter, "I Get Smart," from The Company of Cats, edited by Michael J. Rosen. New York: Doubleday, 1991.)

Although the couple in this excerpt are disagreeing about adopting another cat, the tone is not threatening or gloomy. The author manages to convey the tone of the woman with phrases like *as if I haven't paid half the rent since grad school* and *you get to pick the color*. She seems rather confident about persuading her partner to agree with her. He, on the other hand, seems to be logical (*what's wrong with the three we've got?*), neat and organized (*he lines up his sharp accountant's pencil*), and dismissive of her suggestion (*so forget a new cat*). From the tone of this excerpt, do you think the woman will get another cat?

Now read the following excerpt to see if you can detect the tone of the person speaking.

I could've been somebody, you know? my mother says and sighs. She has lived in this city her whole life. She can speak two languages. She can sing an opera. She knows how to fix a T.V. But she doesn't know which subway train to take to get downtown. I hold her hand very tight while we wait for the right train to arrive.

She used to draw when she had time. Now she draws with a needle and thread, little knotted rosebuds, tulips made of silk thread. Someday she would like to see a play. She borrows opera records from the public library and sings with velvety lungs powerful as morning glories.

Today while cooking oatmeal she is Madame Butterfly until she sighs and points the wooden spoon at me. I could've been somebody, you know? Esperanza, you go to school. Study hard. That Madame Butterfly was a fool. She stirs the oatmeal. Look at my compadres. She means Izaura whose husband left and Yolanda whose husband is dead. Got to take care all your own, she says shaking her head.

Then out of nowhere:

Shame is a bad thing, you know. It keeps you down. You want to know why I quit school? Because I didn't have nice clothes. No clothes, but I had brains.

Yup, she says disgusted, stirring again. I was a smart cookie then.

(Sandra Cisneros, The House on Mango Street,
New York: Vintage, 1998, pp. 90–91.)

You will need to make inferences to answer the following questions.

1. Which word does *not* describe the mother in this story?
   a. intelligent
   b. regretful
   c. despondent
   d. lazy

2. For each of the characteristics listed in question 1 that you believe describes the mother, write some words and phrases from the story that support your opinion.

   _____

   _____

   _____

   _____

3. Why do you think the mother does not know which subway train to take to get downtown?

   _____

   _____

   _____

   _____

Making Inferences about Motive and Character

Have you ever said to yourself, "I wonder why she did that?" Most of the time our friends and relatives don't tell us the reasons for their actions. We infer the reasons by using all the information we have about them, their personalities, and our past experiences with them. We infer a great deal about the people we know and the possible reasons for their actions. For instance, a child may not admit to having eaten a cookie that his parent told him not to eat. If you know that the parent often spanks the child for disobeying, the reason for the child's behavior (to avoid a spanking) can be inferred.

When we read fiction, making inferences about the characters and their motives often helps us better understand real people in our everyday lives.

The following selection is about an American who went to live and work in Japan. She had an unexpected surprise while she was there.

FAMOUS IN THE FAR EAST

Before graduation from the University of Virginia, I sent my resume to African embassies and consulates, trying to find a position teaching English. But I didn't find a school in all the continent that would guarantee employment. In desperation, I applied to the Japanese Ministry of Education and Ministry of Foreign Affairs to teach English in Japan, which became my only offer.

But the more I thought about going to Japan, the more apprehensive I became. I knew nothing of the history or culture, and I didn't speak the language. I worried that facing prejudice in a foreign country would be extremely frustrating.

Arriving at Sakura Nishi High School, about 40 minutes from Tokyo, I was relieved to find that everyone, from my principal to the PTA mothers, treated me with kindness and respect. But I discovered that while Japanese teens respected me as an American, they idolized me because I was Black.

While I was in Japan, trendy department stores advertised Bobby Brown posters, Cross Colours gear and X caps in their windows. Rappers from Ice-T to Ice Cube toured, and *Malcolm X* was at the major theaters. On Saturday nights Shibuya ward, Tokyo's hub of hip-hop and high fashion, was packed with students in baggy jeans, "Doc" Martens, Chicago Bulls caps, permed Afros and dreadlocks. To them, my being African-American meant I was *kakoi*, cool. And before long I was a star.

At a track-and-field event in Tokyo, I was one of only a few foreign spectators. I hadn't been there ten minutes when a screaming mob of young girls swarmed around me like bees, waving pens, notebooks and T-shirts in my face, shouting, "Sign, sign, sign!" I was petrified. Then it dawned on me that they thought I was an athlete. I couldn't explain in Japanese that I was only a spectator, so I surrendered.

That day was only the first of many incidents of mistaken identity and instant stardom. Nightclub managers let me in free, knowing my presence would attract patrons, and security guards at rap concerts gave me backstage passes. To be young, single and Black in Tokyo in the nineties was surely as exciting and romantic as the pre–World War II Spain Hemingway knew.

But I wanted to say to the Japanese, "You must understand, being Black is more involved than just wearing an X cap. It means being committed to furthering our race and nurturing our children. Being Black runs deeper than just having rhythm. It means possessing a history of more than 300 years of fighting for freedom and equality. And as a people, we are more diverse than our hairstyles. Our talents and interests vary as much as our shades of brown." I wished I could have said what I really should have been telling myself all along, rather than defining myself by our images as either sports stars and performers or criminals and victims.

(excerpted from Elizabeth Ridley, "Famous in the Far East," *ESSENCE*, August 1994, p. 38.)

1. What was the author's reason for going to Japan?

_____

_____

_____

2. How did the author feel about going to Japan?
   a. desperate
   b. nervous
   c. disappointed
   d. frustrated

3. The author was treated like a star in Japan because
   a. she was a famous athlete.
   b. she was a famous rapper.
   c. she was an American.
   d. she was Black.

4. Support these conclusions with details from the passage.
   a. The author was really determined to find a job in Africa.

_____

_____

   b. Many Japanese believe that all Blacks who visit Japan are famous athletes.

_____

_____

c. The author did not actually tell anyone the ideas about being Black that she mentions in the last paragraph.

_____

_____

PRACTICE EXERCISE 2: MAKING INFERENCES

Following is an excerpt from a story by Joyce Carol Oates titled "Happy." Read the story to find out about the relationship among the characters. Then answer the questions that follow.

HAPPY

She flew home at Christmas, her mother and her mother's new husband met her at the airport. Her mother hugged her hard and told her she looked pretty, and her mother's new husband shook hands with her and told her, Yes she sure did look pretty, and welcome home. His sideburns grew razor sharp into his plump cheeks and changed color, graying, in the lower part of his face. In his handshake her hand felt small and moist, the bones close to cracking. Her mother hugged her again, God I'm so happy to see you, veins in her arms ropier than the girl remembered, the arms themselves thinner, but her mother was happy, you could feel it all about her. The pancake makeup on her face was a fragrant peach shade that had been blended skillfully into her throat. On her left hand she wore her new ring: a small glittering diamond set high in spiky white-gold prongs.

They stopped for a drink at Easy Sal's off the expressway, the girl had a club soda with a twist of lime (*That's* fancy, her mother said), her mother and her mother's new husband had martinis on the rocks, which were their "celebration" drinks. For a while they talked about what the girl was studying and what her plans were and when that subject trailed off they talked about their own plans, getting rid of the old house, that was one of the first chores, buying something smaller, newer, or maybe just renting temporarily. There's a new condominium village by the river, the girl's mother said, we'll show you when we drive past; then she smiled at something, took a swallow of her martini, squeezed the girl's arm, and leaned her head toward hers, giggling. Jesus, she said, it just makes me so happy, having the two people I love most in the world right here with me. Right here right now. A waitress in a tight-fitting black satin outfit brought two more martinis and a tiny glass bowl of beer nuts. Thanks sweetheart! her mother's new husband said.

(*Vanity Fair*, December 1984.)

1. What physical characteristics did the daughter notice about her mother when they met at the airport?

_____

_____

_____

2. From the daughter's observation of her mother, she probably thought her mother
   a. looked beautiful.
   b. looked younger than she remembered.
   c. looked older than she remembered.
   d. looked sick.

3. Which of the following inferences can you make from the story? Support your choices with information from the story.

True or False	**Support**
a. The daughter was not enthusiastic about her mother's remarriage.	_____ _____ _____
b. The mother and her new husband were very happy about their relationship.	_____ _____ _____
c. Her mother had remarried.	_____ _____ _____
d. Her mother was more interested in herself than she was in her daughter.	_____ _____ _____

PRACTICE EXERCISE 3: MAKING INFERENCES

As you read the following story, "Love Poems," try to figure out whom the main character loves.

LOVE POEMS

He has written her a St. Valentine's Day love poem. It is very beautiful; it impresses, embodies a passionate, genuine emotion, emotion of a sort he hardly realized himself capable of, tenderness that is like the tenderness of a better man. At the same time, the imagery is hard, diamond clear, the form intricate yet unobtrusive. He says the poem out loud to himself over and over. He cannot believe it, it is so good. It is the best poem he has ever written.

He will mail it to her tonight. She will open it as soon as it arrives, cleverly timed, on St. Valentine's Day. She will be floored, she will be blown away by its beauty and passion. She will put it away with his other letters, loving him for it, as she loves him for his other letters. She will not show it to anyone, for she is a private person, which is one of the qualities he loves in her.

After he has mailed the poem to her, written out in his interesting hand, he types up a copy for his own files. He decides to send a copy to one of the more prestigious literary magazines, one into which he has not yet been admitted. He hesitates about the dedication, which could lead to embarrassment, among other things, with his wife. In the end he omits the dedication. In the end he decides to give a copy also to his wife. In the end he sends a copy also to a woman he knows in England, a poet who really understands his work. He writes out a copy for her, dedicated to her initials. It will reach her a few days late, she will think of him thinking of her a few days before St. Valentine's Day.

(Lon Otto, *A Nest of Hooks*, University of Iowa Press, 1978.)

1. The main character had written a poem for
   a. his wife.
   b. a literary magazine.
   c. a lover.
   d. a poet in England.

2. Check the word below which you think best describes the character in the story.
   a. egocentric
   b. passionate
   c. loyal

   Meet in small groups to discuss your choice. Support each of your answers with information from the story.

In the following section of this chapter you will read about socialization, the process that makes it possible for us to function in society. You will have a chance to do more work with inferences as you read through these selections.

Application

Textbook Selection 1
SOCIALIZATION

Before Reading

Listed below are the major headings of an excerpt from a sociology textbook that appears on pages 261 to 272. Put a 1 next to the topic that sounds most interesting to you, and a 4 next to the one you think sounds least interesting.

I. Introduction: Education in Japan   _____

II. Socialization: A Lifelong Process   _____

III. Agents of Socialization   _____

IV. Gender Socialization   _____

Why does the heading you numbered 1 appeal to you the most?

_____

_____

_____

During Reading

Remember to turn headings into questions before reading each section of the following textbook excerpts. (If necessary, review Chapter 2.) This will give you a purpose for reading. Also underline all definitions and main ideas.

Introduction: Education in Japan

1   The 45 students in the first homeroom class of the ninth grade were all seated at their desks when the opening notes of the Brahms symphony roared from the loudspeaker at precisely 8:30 a.m. Soon the violins faded, and a slow, synthesized pulse spread across the room, numbing the mind with its smooth, hypnotic gait. The room was cold and slightly dank. No sun shone through the plate glass windows overlooking the balcony. The clouds, like the students, were still.

2   In a moment, a soothing, resonant voice began to speak. "Good morning, boys and girls. Let's begin another *wonderful* day. Please close your eyes. . . ."

3   For ten minutes every morning the students at Sano Junior High sat in quiet meditation to prepare themselves for the day ahead. The principal, *Sakamoto-sensei*, had introduced this system, known as Method Training, several years earlier in order to quell the growing incidence of school "violence," mainly minor scuffles and hair violations. The program consisted of a sequence of 25 tapes for total mental and physical conditioning. Each day a different tape was played. . . .

4   After ten minutes the music dissolved, the voice disappeared, and Mrs. Negishi—standing erect before the class—took control of the homeroom meeting.

5   "Stand up," she commanded, and the students rose to their feet.

6   "Attention," she said, and they dropped their arms to their thighs.

7   "Bow."

8   It was 8:42 in the morning.

9   People who are born and grow up in different cultures act and think very differently from one another. Bruce Feiler, an American who taught school in Japan, was struck by the ways in which Japanese schools socialized their students to become adult members of Japanese society. Deep respect for authority, long hours of focused learning, appropriate modes of dress, even proper ways to bow—all of these were central aspects of Japanese education that would be virtually unthinkable in most American schools today. Japanese educational practices, in turn, reflect widely shared norms and values that are found in Japanese families, workplaces, and indeed throughout Japanese culture.

(Applebaum & Chambliss, *Sociology*, HarperCollins, 1995, p. 104.)

1. The main idea of paragraph 9 is
   a. Japanese educational practices reflect widely shared norms and values that are found throughout Japanese culture.
   b. Bruce Feiler was struck by the ways in which Japanese schools socialized their students.
   c. people from different cultures act and think differently from one another.
   d. central aspects of Japanese education would be virtually unthinkable in most American schools.

2. Using the following chart and paragraphs 1–9, list the values of the Japanese educational system in the left-hand column. In the right-hand column write the values you feel are part of the American system.

Japanese Educational Values	American Educational Values

3. What differences do you think there would be in adults from Japan and the United States as a result of their experiences in the educational system of their countries?

_____

_____

_____

_____

_____

_____

Socialization: A Lifelong Process

10   For a society to endure across generations, its members must devise ways to pass their culture along to one another. Sociologists refer to the ways in which people acquire their society's core beliefs and practices as **socialization**, the _lifelong process through which people learn the values, norms, and roles of their culture, and thereby develop their sense of self_. Socialization occurs throughout a person's lifetime, beginning with birth and ending with death. It is an active process in which individuals select among different cultural influences to construct their sense of who they are and how they should think and act as members of their culture.

11   As we shall see below, the principal agents of socialization often exert an enormous influence on the members of a society, particularly during the early years of

life. Parents, teachers, television, and even friends constantly convey cultural norms and values. Although socialization involves a measure of conscious choice, much occurs "behind our backs"—it is carried in the language we speak, the roles we are given to play, and virtually every facet of our social interaction.

Agents of Socialization

12   Although socialization occurs throughout a person's lifetime, sociologists regard some sources of socialization to be especially important. These include family, schools, peer groups, workplaces, and the mass media.

The Family and Socialization

13   The family, a central institution in all societies, plays a key role in reproducing members' norms, values, and overall cultural understandings. It is a primary group in which children are physically and emotionally dependent on adult members during the earliest years of their lives. As a result, the family is the first and usually foremost source of socialization in all societies.

14   In most societies children are raised in families consisting of blood-related parents and siblings. There are, however, important variations in the structure of family relations. In some cultures, for example, the mother's brother is the most important adult figure and is responsible for socializing his sister's children (Whiteford and Friedl, 1992). In other cultures "the family" consists of an extended group of people, including aunts, uncles, cousins, and in-laws.

15   In the United States, family socialization differs somewhat depending on race and ethnicity (Starrels, 1992; Harrison et al., 1990). For example, African-American families typically share responsibility for child-rearing among a broader range of family members than do white families, reflecting a sense that children are the responsibility of extended families and even neighbors (Lubeck, 1985). This has also been found true of Afro-Caribbean immigrants (Ho, 1993), as well as the European-origin Amish of Pennsylvania.

16   Because of the diversity of U.S. culture, it is difficult to describe the "typical American family". . . . Family patterns are changing rapidly, partly the result of a significant increase in divorce, separation, or remarriage (Brody et al., 1988; Cherlin et al., 1991; Courter et al., 1984; DeLoache et al., 1987; Dornbusch et al., 1985; Emery, 1988; Furstenberg et al., 1983; Guidubaldi et al., 1987; Norton and Click, 1986). The average number of children in a family has declined in the last 30 years. Mothers are much more likely to be employed at a full-time job out of the

home than was the case in the past. More and more children are being raised by single parents as well. An increasing number of same-sex couples are raising children. Such changes directly affect the socialization process.

17   Child-rearing practices also tend to differ among families of different social classes. Parents whose jobs require them to be subservient to authority and follow orders without raising questions typically emphasize the importance of obedience and respect for authority within the family. On the other hand, parents whose work gives them considerable freedom to make their own decisions and be creative are likely to socialize their children into norms of creativity and spontaneity as well. Since most working-class jobs demand conformity while middle- and upper-middle-class jobs are more likely to emphasize independence, such workplace differences are strongly associated with social class (Kohn, 1965, 1976, 1977).

4. Underline the definition in paragraph 10.

5. List the agents of socialization in paragraph 12.

_____

_____

_____

_____

6. Underline the main idea of paragraph 13.

7. Circle the signal words that indicate cause–effect in paragraph 13.

8. Of the following, which is the cause and which is the effect?

   The child is physically dependent on the adult. _____

   The family is the first source of socialization. _____

9. Underline the main idea sentence in paragraph 14.

10. How many examples are given in paragraph 16 to illustrate the main idea? _____

11. Paragraph 17 makes a comparison. Circle the signal words that indicate a comparison. Then underline the explanation of what the comparison is about.

12. The following chart shows the topics of paragraphs 14–17. First determine the paragraph for each topic. Then write the main idea and an example of it for each paragraph.

Topic	Par.	Main Idea	Example
Child rearing and social class			
Factors contributing to changes in American family structures			
Differences in family relations			
Effects of race and ethnicity on family patterns in American families			

The School and Socialization

18   Prior to the twentieth century most Americans lived and worked on family farms; school was far less important than family as an agent of socialization. Children in rural America started school relatively late in life, spent fewer hours in the classroom, and were out of school for longer periods during the harvest and planting seasons. In the urbanized, industrialized world of today, however, the school and education have taken on a much more important role in socialization. Children often begin "schooling" when they enter day care or preschool at age two or three, and they stay in school for longer hours each day and for more days each year than was the case a hundred years ago.

19   The importance of education as socialization for entering the workforce has vastly increased as well. Few urban children learn skills from parents that will enable them to make a living. Such socialization extends well beyond such basic intellectual skills as reading, writing, and arithmetic. Today schools are also expected to teach manners, cleanliness, and respect for authority and to develop inquiring attitudes and basic social skills, although whether this is appropriate (indeed, whether it is possible) is a subject of considerable controversy today. Indeed, some sociologists describe this as the **hidden curriculum**, *unspoken classroom socialization to norms, values, and roles* that a school provides along with the "official" curriculum.

13. Circle the signal word(s) indicating a contrast in paragraph 18. What is being contrasted?

_____

14. Following are several inferences one might make after reading paragraphs 18 and 19. Support each inference with information from the paragraphs.

a. In the 1800s young children helped their parents farm.

_____

_____

b. Children are not at home as much today as they were in the 1800s.

_____

_____

c. Parents have relinquished to the schools some of the responsibility for teaching values to their children.

_____

_____

Peers and Socialization

20   In American society adolescents spend far more time with their **peers**, *people of the same age, social standing, and class*, than they do with their family. This process of socialization begins with the first peer contacts outside the family, when the child begins to play with other children during the first year of life. The intensity and importance of peer group interactions increases during adolescence and into adulthood (Sebald, 1992). So important are peer contacts that sociological theories often focus on this period of life to account for a wide variety of adult behavioral patterns such as career choices, ambition, and deviant behavior (Garden et al., 1986; Sebald, 1992; Sutherland, 1966; Cohen, 1958).

21   During adolescence, new language variations, new values, standards of dress, taste in popular culture (music, sports, and films), and new interpersonal allegiances develop. Children who learned at home to be polite often find other standards applied to their behavior by their adolescent peers. Rebellion against adult authority or, in the case of oppressed groups, against society at large, may become more important than the values learned at home.

22   From the point of view of socialization, not all peers are equal. Friendship groups constitute the most important peer associations that influence the socialization process. Because children cannot always choose their friends any more than their family, peer socialization depends in part on the friends they "happen to have." This, in turn, reflects circumstances over which children typically exercise little control, such as where they live or attend school. Of course, the attractiveness of some friends rather than others is also influenced by what children learn in their family, including their self-concept. In a study of college students, for example, it

was found that people preferred to befriend others who validated their self image through favorable responses (Chambliss, 1965).

23   People do not need to actually belong to a particular peer group for it to affect their socialization. Sociologists use the term **anticipatory socialization** to describe *adopting the behavior or standards of a group one hopes to emulate or join.* You may aspire to join a club, fraternity, or sorority, and so use its standards of dress or behavior as a guide to shape your own. Or you may train to become a better athlete in order to join your favorite team. A teenager may dress and act in ways that run counter to his family socialization, in order to be accepted by a particular group or "crowd." Anticipatory socialization is oriented toward future expectations, rather than to present experience.

15. Following are several inferences one might make after reading paragraphs 20–23. Support each inference with information stated in the paragraphs.
   a. Teenagers would probably prefer taking a vacation with friends more than with family.

   _____

   _____

   b. The friends one has as a teenager probably have some influence over whether or not one engages in criminal behavior as an adult.

   _____

   _____

   c. Teenagers who had been well-behaved when younger often become discipline problems at home.

   _____

   _____

   d. Attending high school in a neighborhood where the majority of students are college-bound makes it more likely you will attend college.

   _____

   _____

   _____

   e. It is likely that your friends will tell you something positive about yourself.

   _____

   _____

   _____

16. If you are about to enter college and change the way you dress to be more like other college students, your behavior is an example of

_____

_____

17. How many examples of anticipatory socialization are given in paragraph 23? _____

Work and Socialization

24 For most Americans, the most immediate postadolescent experience with socialization occurs when they enter the workforce. We have previously noted that workplace norms calling for conformity or independence frequently extend into the home as well. Workforce expectations often differ substantially from those experienced in primary relationships such as the family and peer groups. While primary relations may develop around the workplace, the initial encounters are likely to be more impersonal.

25 People taking jobs for the first time realize that if they are to succeed, they often must balance opposing or contradictory role expectations. On the one hand, the employer will want them to work as hard as they can to produce as much as they can in as short a period of time as possible. In many work settings, people who work too long or too many hours can create similar work expectations that affect their coworkers. If this occurs, other employees will indicate rather clearly (and at times forcefully) that they expect everybody to work at a comfortable pace. Such informal norms that develop in the workplace have long been known to be extremely powerful agents of socialization (Mayo, 1977, orig. 1933; Homans, 1950).

26 Employment also often involves socialization into the wider aspects of the social role itself, as well as learning the details of how to get the job done. Becoming a teacher, cook, factory worker, professor, lawyer, or thief involves learning the norms and values associated with each role, along with the specific skills the role requires. A professor is not only socialized into the proper way to lecture, grade papers, or give examinations but also into appropriate ways of dressing, interacting with other professors and administrators, and behaving in front of students.

18. The contradictory role expectations discussed in paragraph 25 concern those of the _____ versus those of _____.

19. What are one skill and one value you will need to be successful in the profession you are planning to pursue?

_____

_____

The Mass Media and Socialization

27   In modern society, much of what we experience is filtered through the lens of **mass media**, *forms of communication that permit a one-way flow of information from a single source to a wide audience.* . . . Newspapers, magazines, movies, radio, and television are all examples.

28   It is commonplace to read about the negative effects of the mass media on the socialization of children and teenagers. Children's television programs, for example, are blamed for everything from violence to the breakdown of cultural norms and values. Since the average American child spends from three to four hours a day in front of the television set, it seems reasonable to conclude that the content of television programming has a major effect on socialization. By the time the typical young American reaches 18, he or she will have seen 22,000 hours of television (Donnerstein et al., 1987, 1993; Huston et al., 1992; Staples and Jones, 1985).

29   Television exposes children to definitions of reality and fantasy, to heroes and villains, role models and fools (Bierman, 1990). It informs children about how they can have fun and what they must buy to be happy. Children learn what it means to be a boy or girl, a man or woman. They learn about music and style, sex and violence (Donnerstein et al., 1993; Bierman, 1990; Huston et al., 1992; Tangney and Feshbach, 1988; Tracy, 1990; Waley et al., 1992).

30   During the past few years, the impact of media violence on children and young adults has received considerable attention. Five to six violent acts are depicted each hour on supposedly family-oriented prime-time television alone; all told, there are nearly two hundred such acts each week (Gerbner and Signorielli, 1990). By the time a child reaches junior high school, he or she has witnessed as many as 8,000 murders (Donnerstein et al., 1993). Three major media studies conducted during the past 20 years have all come to the same conclusion: media violence socializes many children, teenagers, and even adults into a greater acceptance of real-life violence. This is true of both males and females, whites and nonwhites (Donnerstein et al., 1993; Huston et al., 1992). Much media violence is directed against women, and a large body of research supports the conclusion that it helps socialize some men into condoning sexual violence, including rape (Donnerstein, Linz, & Penrod, 1987; Linz, Donnerstein, and Adams, 1989; Linz, Donnerstein, and Penrod, 1988; Linz, 1989).

20. Which one of these conclusions is *not* supported by the research discussed in paragraphs 27–30?
    a. A large proportion of media violence is directed against women.
    b. Because of the effects of media, people are less upset by real violence.
    c. Nonwhites are more prone to the violent effects of media.
    d. The content of television has an enormous effect on the behavior of children.

21. Which of these is the implied main idea of paragraph 29?
    a. Television exposes children to reality.
    b. Television has an impact on every aspect of a child's life.
    c. Sex and violence are learned from television.
    d. Television is fun and makes you happy.

22. Check all of the following that you find in paragraph 27.

    ■ examples   _____

    ■ cause–effect   _____

    ■ definition   _____

    ■ comparison   _____

    ■ signal words   _____

23. Which of the mass media mentioned in paragraph 27 do you believe has influenced you the most?

    _____

24. Following are several inferences one might make after reading paragraphs 28 and 29. Support each inference with information from the paragraphs.

    a. Children in families without television tend to play more with toys and other children.

    _____

    _____

    b. There is less violence in primitive societies in which people do not watch television than in societies in which television is common.

    _____

    _____

Gender Socialization

31   An important aspect of socialization concerns the learning of culturally defined gender roles. . . . We are not born into our gender roles but rather learn them. Boys learn to be boys and girls learn to be girls, according to cultural norms and values. Such learning involves all the agents of socialization we have just reviewed: family, peers, schools, work, and media. By the time children have become teenagers, they have usually learned to do the sorts of things deemed appropriate for males or females in their culture.

32   Within the family, parents often hold stereotypical notions of how boys and girls should "be," and reinforce those behaviors in countless subtle and not-so-subtle ways (Marini, 1990; Katz, 1986; Jacklin et al., 1984; Ross and Taylor, 1989; Mosheretal, 1988; Siegal, 1987; Eccles et al., 1990). A girl may be treated as delicate or fragile, a boy as rough-and-tumble. Parents often serve as role models for "appropriate" gender roles, leading some sociologists to describe the home as a "gender factory" (Waite and Goldscheider, 1992).

33   Peer group gender socialization begins in young children's playgroups, where boys and girls characteristically engage in different activities reflecting cultural notions of gender-appropriate behavior (Cahill, 1989; Eisenhart and Holland, 1983). Although there is evidence that gender stereotyping is somewhat less pronounced among some racial or ethnic groups than others (for example, among African Americans; see Grant, 1983), such stereotyping is common throughout American culture.

34   Gender stereotypes are reproduced on television and other forms of the media, helping to socialize children from an early age. From children's cartoons to prime-time television, from advertisements to MTV, much television programming depicts males and females in stereotyped ways. Teenage girls, for example, are likely to be depicted as boy-crazy and obsessed with their looks; teenage boys as active and independent (Cantor, 1987; Condry, 1989; Glazer, 1980; Silverstein et al., 1986; Steenland, 1988; Women's Institute for Freedom of the Press, 1986).

(Applebaum & Chambliss, *Sociology*, HarperCollins, 1995, pp. 104–117.)

25. Underline the main idea of paragraph 31.
26. Underline the main idea of paragraph 32.
27. Underline the main idea of paragraph 33.
28. Underline the main idea of paragraph 34.
29. True _____ or False _____: People of all ethnic groups are equally susceptible to gender stereotyping.

After Reading

1. **Topics for Writers**

    1) What effect have television programs had on your socialization? Would you let your children watch the programs you watch? Why or why not?

    2) Compare two values that you learned from your parent(s) with those you learned from your peers.

    3) Which one of the agents of socialization had the greatest effect on you? Which one had the least effect on you? Explain your choices.

4) Describe a peer who had a strong influence on you as you were growing up. (You may want to refer to the section on writing descriptive essays on page 199 in Chapter 5.)

5) Describe the agent of socialization that influenced you most in terms of your role as a man or a woman.

6) Write an essay comparing the influence of family with that of peers on the process of socialization.

7) Do you believe that schools should teach manners, cleanliness, and respect for authority? Write a persuasive essay on this issue.

2. **Vocabulary in Context**

Listed below are words from the preceding section. The numbers in parentheses indicate the paragraphs in which the words can be found. Find the words in the selection and, using the context of the sentences, write a meaning for each word.

Word	My Definition
synthesized (1)	
gait (1)	
dank (1)	
resonant (2)	
quell (3)	
subservient (17)	
spontaneity (17)	
deviant (20)	
allegiance (21)	
validate (22)	
emulate (23)	
aspire (23)	
condone (30)	

Textbook Selection 2
SOCIAL STRUCTURE

Before Reading

Listed below are four words you are going to read about in the next section from a sociology text. Choose two of the words you are most familiar with and, on the lines provided, write whatever comes to your mind when you think about these words.

institutions

_____

status

_____

roles

_____

groups

_____

During Reading

Institutions

1   . . . We defined social structure as *the underlying regularities in how people behave and interrelate with one another.* One of the central insights of sociology is that social structures help to shape social life in important ways.

2   Sociologists analyze social structure in terms of the institutions, groups, statuses, and roles that make it up. These terms are key conceptual building blocks in sociology. . . . **Institutions** are *clusters of relatively stable rules that govern social activities in a society, which at the same time provide shared understandings of the cultural meaning of those activities.* The law is one such institution in most societies. It consists of a set of rules that the members of a society generally share and understand. The institution of law in modern society contains written rules governing behavior, as well as punishments for their violation. In societies without a written language, laws are passed down through parables, stories, and word of mouth. The family is another institution that exists in every society. Family relationships vary tremendously from one society to the next. In some societies the cousins, uncles, grandparents, and aunts may be as important as mothers and fathers; in

others, only the biological parents will do. In the United States, some families have one parent, and some have two. Among two-parent families, each parent is usually a different sex, although same-sex parents are becoming increasingly common as well. Yet despite these variations, "the family" as an institution is a fundamental part of every society, even though the particular relationships that constitute a family vary from society to society and over time within a single society (Brown, 1991; Brody et al., 1988; Dornbusch et al., 1985; Thompson et al., 1992). Other institutions that exist in every society include politics, education, economics, medicine, and religion.

1. Underline the definition and central insight of sociology in paragraph 1.

2. Underline the definition of institutions in paragraph 2.

3. In the column labeled "Institutions," list the seven institutions mentioned in paragraph 2. In the column labeled "Rank," number the institutions, with 1 having the strongest influence in your life and 7 having the least influence.

Institutions	Rank
1)	
2)	
3)	
4)	
5)	
6)	
7)	

Status

3   Institutions such as the family, education, and law are built around **statuses—** *established social positions in society that vary in terms of prestige.* In the institution of education, for example, the different statuses include teachers, students, principals, and college presidents. All individuals occupy many different statuses, organized around the family, work, education, religion, and the other institutions in which they participate. A student may also be a floor advisor in a dorm, an employee at a bookstore, and a campus politician. A judge may also be a wife, a mother, and a

daughter. Sometimes people use the term "status" to mean "high prestige." Among sociologists, however, the term does not have this evaluative aspect, although one might sociologically describe a status as "low" or "high" in terms of the prestige accorded it in a particular society.

4   The fact that everyone occupies many statuses is a source of potential conflict. Sociologists refer to this as **status inconsistency**, *a situation where a person occupies two or more statuses of different rank*. This can often occur as a result of the enormous geographical mobility that occurs in the world today. Many people have left their native countries in search of political freedom or greater economic opportunity. Once they arrive in their new homeland, however, they may find that they have a vastly different status from that which they enjoyed before they migrated.

5   One recent study, for example, found that Korean immigrants to southern California experienced such status inconsistency with regard to their occupation. Although many had worked in high-status professional occupations in Korea, once they arrived in Los Angeles their immigrant minority status severely limited their range of occupational choice. Many found themselves running liquor stores, grocery stores, and other small businesses in low-income, high-crime neighborhoods. They felt they were overworked in their new occupations, in constant physical danger, and looked down upon by their customers. Needless to say, this made adjustment to their new situation extremely difficult (Min, 1990).

6   People in modern societies typically experience many different **achieved statuses**, *statuses acquired by virtue of the social positions that people occupy*. Achieved statuses can change over time, as people move from one social position to another. The status of student gives way to that of worker; the status of doctor is replaced by that of retired person. Some statuses, however, are based almost entirely on personal characteristics over which we have little control. **Ascribed statuses** are *those that are given for life at the moment of birth*. In modern societies two of the most common bases for ascribing status are race and sex, two attributes that are unlikely to change regardless of other changes that might occur during a person's lifetime. Although statuses tend to be achieved rather than ascribed in modern society, the continued attribution of status on the basis of such unchanging personal characteristics as race and sex remains an important source of discrimination and inequality today.

4. Underline the definitions in paragraphs 3, 4, and 6.

5. Paragraph 3 states that people have more than one status. List all the statuses you hold.

_____

_____

_____

6. Now write the statuses you listed in question 5 in the correct column below.

Achieved Statuses   **Ascribed Statuses**

_____   _____

_____   _____

_____   _____

_____   _____

_____   _____

Roles

7   A **role** is _the expected behavior associated with a particular status._ The status of student, for example, carries with it certain role expectations: students are expected to attend class, read books, write papers, and socialize with other students. Some behaviors associated with a role may be highly specific and may even be written down as rules and regulations. At many universities, for example, the role of professor is spelled out in highly legal terms governing such things as the terms of employment, classroom responsibilities, and outside income. Yet there are many aspects of the role of professor that are highly vague and undefined. Although a professor may be expected to act and dress in a certain way, the numerous exceptions to this rule suggest that there is considerable leeway in this particular aspect of the professor's role. The role of student is especially undefined, as you will realize if you try to define a consistent set of role expectations that supposedly govern your behavior as student.

8   Just as statuses may contradict one another, so too may roles. **Role conflict** exists when _two or more roles contain contradictory behavioral expectations._ The role of parent may conflict with the role of full-time worker; it is difficult to find the time to be a "good" father or mother when one is working full-time to pay the bills or advance one's career. Students often experience role conflict when the expectations of their role as daughter, son, or companion conflict with the expectations of their role as student. Should I cram for the exam tonight, or help celebrate my best friend's birthday?

9   Sometimes the source of conflict is not between two roles but is rather within a single role. **Role strain** occurs when _contradictory expectations exist within a given role._ Professors are expected to be approachable, friendly, and supportive of students. They also are expected to judge the students and give them grades based on performance, which may make being friendly and supportive quite difficult.

10   Role conflict and role strain are examples of how larger social structures can create problems experienced at the personal level. Such problems originate in the ways in which social roles are defined within a particular society. Once people come to occupy social roles, they find themselves experiencing conflicts and strains that are structured into the roles themselves. Understanding the relationship between individual experience and social structure—between our own lives and the larger social forces that help to shape them—is an example of what is called the "sociological imagination". . . (Mills, 1959).

(Applebaum & Chambliss, *Sociology*, HarperCollins, 1995, pp. 81–83.)

7. In your own words, describe the difference between *role conflict* and *role strain*.

_____

_____

_____

_____

After Reading

Topics for Writers

1. Write a descriptive essay about one of the statuses you listed in question 6.
2. Describe a conflict that exists between two roles in your life. How do you deal with the conflict?
3. Discuss the similarities and differences between the institution of law and the institution of family.
4. The text states: "The role of student is especially undefined." Discuss the role expectations that govern your behavior as a college student. What events in your life contributed to these expectations?

Textbook Selection 3
CONFORMITY

In this chapter you have been reading about the effects of different social influences on our roles, expectations, and behavior. Sometimes these influences are so strong that we behave in ways we never thought possible. In the following selection you will read about two research studies in which people behaved in surprising ways because of the social influences around them.

Before Reading

Describe a situation in which you changed the way you normally behave because of the pressure of others.

During Reading

1   One of the most direct forms of social influence occurs when we modify our behavior, under perceived pressure to do so, so that it is consistent with the behavior of others, a process referred to as **conformity**. Although we often think of conformity in a negative way, to conform is a natural and often desirable process. Conformity helps make social behaviors efficient and, at least to some degree, predictable.

2   When he began his research, Solomon Asch believed that people are not very susceptible to social pressure when the social situation is clear-cut and unambiguous. Asch hypothesized that subjects would behave independently of group pressure when there was little question that their own judgments were accurate, and he developed an interesting technique for testing his hypothesis (Asch, 1951, 1956).

3   A subject in Asch's procedure would join a group seated around a table. In the original study, the group consisted of seven people. Unknown to the subject, the six others were confederates of the experimenter; that is, they were "in on" the experiment. The subjects were led to believe that the study dealt with the ability to make perceptual judgments. A participant had to do nothing more than decide which of three lines was the same length as a standard line. The experimenter showed each set of lines to the group and then collected responses, one by one,

In Asch's study, the lone dissenter (here, on the right) begins to doubt his judgment and looks again at the card, even though the correct answer is obvious.

from each member of the group. There were 18 sets of lines to judge, and the real subject was always the last one to respond.

4   It is important to note that each of the 18 judgments the subjects made involved unambiguous stimuli. The correct answer was always obvious. However, on 12 of the 18 trials, the confederates gave a unanimous, but *incorrect* answer. What would the subjects do now? How would they resolve this conflict? Their perceptual experience was telling them what the correct answer was, but the group was saying something else. Should they trust the judgments of the others, or should they trust their own?

5   The results of his initial study surprised Asch, because they did not confirm his original hypothesis. Across the critical trials (when the confederates gave "wrong" answers), conformity occurred 37 percent of the time. That is, subjects responded with an incorrect answer that agreed with the majority on more than one-third of the critical trials. Moreover, three-quarters of Asch's subjects conformed to the group pressure at least once.

6   In subsequent studies, Asch tried several variations of his original procedure. In one experiment, he varied the size of the unanimous, incorrect majority. As you might expect, the level of conformity increased as the size of the majority increased, leveling off at about three or four people (Asch, 1956; Knowles, 1983). Subjects gave an erroneous judgment only 4 percent of the time if only one incorrect judgment preceded their own. In another study, subjects gave an erroneous judgment only 10 percent of the time when there was just one dissenter among the six confederates who voiced an accurate judgment before the subjects gave theirs. In other words, when the subjects had any social support for what their eyes had told them, they tended to trust their own judgment. Other experiments have shown that a minority opinion (say, one dissenter) can have significant effects on conformity if that position is maintained consistently (e.g., Moscovici et al., 1969, 1985; Nemeth, 1986).

7   Conformity involves yielding to the perceived pressure of a group. In most circumstances, it is assumed that group members are peers, or at least similar to the conformer. When one yields to the pressure of a perceived authority, the result is obedience. It is to *obedience* that we turn next.

(Gerow, *Essentials of Psychology*, 2nd ed.,
HarperCollins, 1996, pp. 490–491.)

1. Underline the definition of *conformity* in paragraph 1.

2. What does *unambiguous* mean as used in paragraphs 2 and 4?

   _____

3. Paragraph 4 states that the stimuli were unambiguous. What does that tell you about the stimuli?

   _____

   _____

4. What does *confederates* mean in paragraph 3?

   _____

5. Using the context, what is the meaning of the word *hypothesis* as used in paragraph 2?

   _____

6. What was Asch's original hypothesis?

   _____

7. Did the results of the study support Asch's hypothesis? Explain your answer.

   _____

   _____

8. Which one of these statements is true based on the results of Asch's first study?
   a. The majority of subjects were unable to determine which line was the same length as the standard line.
   b. The majority of subjects gave an incorrect answer.
   c. People are not very susceptible to group pressure.
   d. Thirty-seven percent of the subjects conformed to group pressure.

9. Following are several inferences. First, indicate whether each statement is true or false based on the results of Asch's experiments. Then, find the paragraph containing information that supports your judgment of each inference.

Inference	True or False	Par.
Most people are susceptible to group pressure in situations that are clear-cut.		
The level of conformity is directly proportional to the size of the majority.		
Subjects in Asch's first study would have felt less pressure to conform if only one of the confederates of the experimenter gave an incorrect judgment.		

Obedience to Authority

8   The participants in Asch's studies took the procedure seriously, but the consequences of either conforming or maintaining independence were rather trivial. At worst, Asch's subjects might have experienced some discomfort as a result of sticking to their independent judgments. There were no rewards or punishments for their behavior, and there was no one telling them how to respond. Stanley Milgram (1933–1984), a social psychologist at Yale University, went beyond Asch's procedure. Milgram's experiments pressured subjects to comply with the demand of an authority figure—a demand that was both unreasonable and troubling (Milgram, 1963, 1965, 1974).

9   All of Milgram's studies involved the same basic procedure. Subjects arrived at the laboratory to discover that they would be participating with another person (again, a confederate of the experimenter). The experimenter explained that the research dealt with the effects of punishment on learning, and that one subject would serve as a teacher while the other would act as learner. The two roles were assigned by a rigged drawing in which the actual subject was always assigned the role of teacher, while the confederate was always the learner. The subject watched as the learner was taken to the next room and wired to electrodes that would be used for delivering punishment in the form of electric shocks.

10   The teacher then received his instructions. First, he was to read to the learner a list of four pairs of words. The teacher was then to read the first word of one of the pairs, and the learner was to supply the second word. The teacher sat in front of a

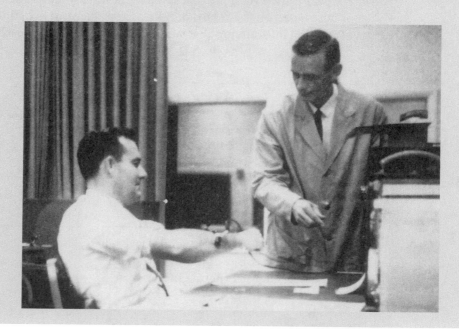

rather imposing electric "shock generator" that had 30 switches, each with its voltage level labeled. From left to right, the switches increased by increments of 15 volts, ranging from 15 volts to 450 volts. Labels were printed under the switches on the generator. These ranged from "Slight" to "Moderate" to "Extreme Intensity" to "Danger: Severe Shock." The label at the 450-volt end simply read "XXX."

11   As the task proceeded, the learner periodically made errors according to a prearranged schedule. The teacher had been instructed to deliver an electric shock for each incorrect answer. With each error, the teacher was to move up the scale of shocks, giving the learner a more potent shock with each new mistake. (The learner, remember, was part of the act, and no one was actually receiving any shocks.)

12   Whenever the teacher (subject) hesitated or questioned if he should continue, the experimenter was ready with a verbal prod, such as "Please continue," or "The experiment requires that you continue." If the subject protested, the experimenter would become more assertive and offer an alternative prod: "You have no choice; you must go on," he might say. The degree of obedience was determined by the level of shock at which the teacher refused to go further.

13   Milgram was astonished by the results of his study, and the results continue to amaze us 30 years later. Twenty-six of Milgram's 40 subjects—65 percent—obeyed the experimenter and went all the way to the highest shock and closed all the switches. In fact, no one stopped prior to the 300-volt level, the point at which the learner pounded on the wall in protest. One later variation of this study added vocal responses from the learner, who delivered an increasingly stronger series of demands to be let out of the experiment. The level of obedience in this study still was unbelievably high, as 25 of 40 subjects, or 62.5 percent, continued to administer shocks to the 450-volt level.

14   It is important to note that all of the subjects (teachers) experienced genuine and extreme stress in this situation. Some fidgeted, some trembled, many perspired profusely. Several subjects giggled nervously. In short, the people caught up in this unusual situation showed obvious signs of conflict and anxiety. Nevertheless, they continued to obey the orders of the authoritative experimenter even though they had good reason to believe that they might well be harming the learner.

15   Milgram's first study used only male subjects ranging in age from 20 to 50. A replication with adult women produced precisely the same results: 65 percent obeyed fully. Other variations uncovered several factors that could reduce the extent of obedience. Putting the learner and teacher in the same room, or having the experimenter deliver his orders over the telephone, for example, reduced obedience markedly. When the shocks were delivered by a team consisting of the subject and two disobedient confederates, full-scale obedience dropped to only 10 percent.

16   Upon first hearing about these rather distressing results, there is a tendency for many people to think that Milgram's obedient subjects were cold, callous, unfeeling, or downright cruel and sadistic people (Safer, 1980). Nothing could be further from the truth. The participants in this research were truly troubled by what was

happening. If you thought that Milgram's subjects must be strange or different, perhaps you were a victim of . . . attribution error. That is, you were willing to attribute the subjects' behavior to (internal) personal characteristics instead of recognizing the powerful situational forces at work.

17   In reading about Milgram's research, it should have occurred to you that putting people in such a stressful experience could be considered ethically objectionable. Milgram himself was concerned with the welfare of his subjects. He took great care to debrief them fully after each session had been completed. He told them that they had not really administered any shocks and explained why deception had been necessary. Milgram reported that the people in his studies were not upset over having been deceived and that their principal reaction was one of relief when they learned that no electric shock had in fact been used. Milgram also indicated that a follow-up study performed a year later with some of the same subjects showed that no long-term adverse effects had been created by his procedure.

18   Despite these precautions, Milgram was severely criticized for placing people in such an extremely stressful situation. Indeed, one of the effects of his research was to establish in the scientific community a higher level of awareness of the need to protect the well-being of human research subjects. It is probably safe to say that because of Milgram's experience, no one would be allowed to perform such experiments today.

(Gerow, *Essentials of Psychology*, 2nd ed.,
HarperCollins, 1996, pp. 491–494.)

10. According to paragraph 7, how are conformity and obedience similar? What is the difference between them?

_____

_____

11. How were Milgram's experiments different from Asch's?

_____

_____

12. What does the label "XXX" mean as used in paragraph 10?

_____

_____

13. The purpose of Milgram's experiment was to
    a. study how people learn to memorize pairs of words.
    b. study how cruel people can be.
    c. find out what happened in Nazi Germany ten years earlier.
    d. learn about the nature of conformity.

14. How was the degree of obedience determined?

_____

15. From the results of Milgram's studies, we can conclude that
    a. most people obey orders even when they believe they are harming another person.
    b. Milgram's subjects were cold and cruel.
    c. men deliver more severe punishment than women.
    d. people are just as likely to obey orders over the telephone as when the authority is present.

16. True _____ or False _____: Most subjects stopped giving shocks to learners who screamed.

17. Underline the main idea of paragraph 16.

18. Why would an experiment such as Milgram's no longer be allowed?

_____

_____

Additional Reading 1

LA MIGRA
Sasha Gregory Lewis

As you read this account of an illegal alien's experience living in New York City, think about the different statuses he holds, both achieved and ascribed.

A man from Ecuador works in a Brooklyn restaurant washing dishes. He works twelve hours each day except Monday and earns about two dollars per hour, from which are deducted his meals and his rent for the restaurant basement space he shares with two other men. His boss, for a 5 percent fee, sees to it that his letters and his money are sent home to his wife. He considers himself lucky because he has been able to work at the same restaurant for three years. His boss has helped him, and once, when there was a raid by immigration inspectors, the boss found him a place to hide until they were gone. If he can hold out for two more years, he says, his family will have enough money for a decent house and to start a small business. He misses his family very much, and from the damp walls of the basement droop a few precious photographs of his wife and four children.

Aside from his boss and the two others who share his cement-walled basement, he has spoken to no one for three years except a Catholic priest. Even though he was grateful to see the priest, he asked that the priest not come back. The man has not left the restaurant and its basement even once for the entire three years he has worked there. He has not seen daylight for those three years. The lack of daylight has taken its toll even on his deep brown skin, giving it a yellow pallor like a soil once rich and dark but overplanted and drained of life.

The Ecuadorian dishwasher chooses to stay inside, in what has become a kind of prison, because he fears La Migra, the immigration authorities. If they found him, they would return him home before he could finish accumulating the grubstake that might make his family's life a bit better than it was. His fear of La Migra is so great that when he needs medicines, rather than telling his boss and asking him to go, for fear his boss will fire him, he waits until his wife can send them. This way, he says, he can be more secure for the two more years it will take until he has made the money he thinks he needs and can return home from exile.

Not all undocumented workers go to such extremes as the dishwasher, but they live with the same fear. It is a fear that builds so much tension, community workers say, that it often brings illness. And the fear keeps them in hiding, going out only to their jobs, to buy food, and perhaps to attend an occasional mass. They trust no one they do not know. For no one knows who will call La Migra. If they are beaten or robbed, they will not complain to the police for fear of La Migra. If they are sick, they will not go to the hospital for fear of La Migra. If they need help, they get it from friends they can trust, and not from public agencies set up to help the poor. They are a people in hiding, and, as such, invisible to most Americans. They hide because no matter how difficult their life in the U.S., their poverty at home is much worse. At home, as they watched their children go hungry, their meager earnings never quite enough to fill a belly, there was no hope. In America, even in fear and hiding, at least there is hope.

(Sasha Gregory Lewis, *Slave Trade Today*,
New York: Beacon Press, 1979.)

After Reading

1.   Comprehension Check

_____ 1) The man has had the same job for
   a. three years.
   b. twelve years.
   c. two years.
   d. can't tell from the story.

_____ 2) The man's family
      a. lives with him.
      b. lives in another country.
      c. is hiding.
      d. lives in a decent house.

_____ 3) The man's boss
      a. wants to report him to the authorities.
      b. is kind to him.
      c. will not talk to him.
      d. keeps him a prisoner in a basement.

_____ 4) The man came to this country in order to
      a. work as a dishwasher in a restaurant.
      b. hide in a basement apartment.
      c. make money for his family.
      d. get away from his children.

5) In the chart below, list all the man's statuses you are able to identify. Then identify whether each status is achieved or ascribed.

Status	Achieved	Ascribed

2. **Topics for Writers**

1) Discuss any role conflicts between the statuses, whether ascribed or achieved, of the character in this essay.

2) In your opinion, should the number of immigrants to the United States be limited? Give reasons for your opinion.

Additional Reading 2
OBEDIENCE TO AUTHORITY
Stanley Milgram

Following is a description of the "shock generator" used by Dr. Milgram in the experiments described in the sociology textbook excerpt you read earlier (pages 282–284).

The real focus of the experiment is the teacher. After watching the learner being strapped into place, he is seated before an impressive shock generator. The instrument panel consists of thirty level switches set in a horizontal line. Each switch is clearly labeled with a voltage designation ranging from 15 to 450 volts. The following designations are clearly indicated for groups of four switches, going from left to right: Slight Shock, Moderate Shock, Strong Shock, Very Strong Shock, Intense Shock, Extreme Intensity Shock, Danger: Severe Shock. (The two switches after this last designation are simply marked XXX.)

When a switch is depressed, a pilot light corresponding to each switch is illuminated in bright red; an electric buzzing is heard; a blue light, labeled "voltage energizer," flashes; the dial on the voltage meter swings to the right; and various relay clicks sound off.

The upper left-hand corner of the generator is labeled SHOCK GENERATOR, TYPE ZLB, DYSON INSTRUMENT COMPANY, WALTHAM, MASS. OUTPUT 15 VOLTS–450 VOLTS.

(Stanley Milgram, *Obedience to Authority*, New York: Harper & Row, 1974, p. 218.)

Using a blank piece of paper, draw the generator, including labels, according to the description given.

Here is an actual transcript of what took place between one subject and the experimenter. Your instructor may ask you and a few other students to play the parts of "Teacher," "Learner," and "Experimenter" and read the text out loud.

Fred Prozi's reactions, if more dramatic than most, illuminate the conflicts experienced by others in less visible form. About fifty years old and unemployed at the time of the experiment, he has a good-natured, if slightly dissolute, appearance, and he strikes people as a rather ordinary fellow. He begins the session calmly but becomes tense as it proceeds. After delivering the 180-volt shock, he pivots around in his chair and, shaking his head, addresses the experimenter in agitated tones:

PROZI: I can't stand it. I'm not going to kill that man in there. You hear him hollering?

EXPERIMENTER: As I told you before, the shocks may be painful, but . . .

PROZI: But he's hollering. He can't stand it. What's going to happen to him?

EXPERIMENTER (his voice is patient, matter-of-fact): The experiment requires that you continue, Teacher.

PROZI: Aaah, but, unh, I'm not going to get that man sick in there—know what I mean?

EXPERIMENTER: Whether the learner likes it or not, we must go on, through all the word pairs.

PROZI: I refuse to take the responsibility. He's in there hollering!

EXPERIMENTER: It's absolutely essential that you continue, Prozi.

PROZI: (indicating the unused questions): There's too many left here, I mean, Jeez, if he gets them wrong, there's too many of them left. I mean, who's going to take the responsibility if anything happens to that gentleman?

EXPERIMENTER: I'm responsible for anything that happens to him. Continue, please.

PROZI: All right. (Consults list of words.) The next one's "Slow—walk, truck, dance, music." Answer, please. (A buzzing sound indicates the learner has signaled his answer.) Wrong. A hundred and ninety-five volts. "Dance." (Zzumph!)

LEARNER (yelling): Let me out of here! My heart's bothering me!

(Teacher looks at Experimenter.)

EXPERIMENTER: Continue, please.

LEARNER (screaming): Let me out of here! You have no right to keep me here! Let me out of here, my heart's bothering me, let me out!

PROZI (shakes head, pats the table nervously): You see, he's hollering. Hear that? Gee, I don't know.

EXPERIMENTER: The experiment requires . . .

PROZI (interrupting): I know it does, sir, but I mean—hunh! He don't know what he's getting in for. He's up to 195 volts! (Experiment continues, through 210 volts, 225 volts, 240 volts, 255 volts, 270 volts, at which point Prozi, with evident relief, runs out of word-pair questions.)

EXPERIMENTER: You'll have to go back to the beginning of that page and go through them again until he's learned them all correctly.

PROZI: Aw, no. I'm not going to kill that man. You mean I've got to keep going up with the scale? No sir. He's hollering in there. I'm not going to give him 450 volts.

EXPERIMENTER: The experiment requires that you go on.

LEARNER: Ohhh. I absolutely refuse to answer anymore. (Shouting urgently now.) Let me out of here! You can't hold me here! Get me out. Get, me-out-of-here!

EXPERIMENTER: Continue. The next word is "Green," please.

PROZI: "Green–grass, hat, ink, apple." (Nothing happens. No answering buzz. Just gloomy silence.)

PROZI: I don't think he is going to answer.

EXPERIMENTER: If the learner doesn't answer in a reasonable time, about four or five seconds, consider the answer wrong. And follow the same procedures you have been doing for wrong answers. Say, "Wrong," tell him the number of volts, give him the punishment, read him the correct answer. Continue, please.

PROZI: "Green–grass, hat, ink, apple." Answer, please. (More silence. Subject just sits there.)

EXPERIMENTER: Go on with the procedure, please.

PROZI: Three hundred and fifteen volts. The answer is "ink." (Zzumph!)

LEARNER: Ohh . . . Ooohh.

PROZI: (relieved to hear response): Next one . . .

LEARNER: I absolutely refuse to answer.

PROZI: You got to. You get a shock if you don't answer. (Experiment continues with learner refusing to answer, and, finally, failing even to grunt or groan. At 375 volts, the subject stands up.)

PROZI: I think something's happened to that fellow in there. I don't get no answer. He was hollering at less voltage. Can't you check in and see if he's all right, please?

EXPERIMENTER (with same detached calm): Not once we've started. Please continue, Teacher.

PROZI (sits down, sighs deeply): "Cool—day, shade, water, paint." Answer, please. Are you all right in there? Are you all right?

EXPERIMENTER: Please continue, Teacher. Continue, please. (Subject pushes lever. Zzump!)

PROZI (swiveling around in his chair): Something's happened to that man in there. (Swiveling back.) Next one. "Low—dollar, necklace, moon, paint." (Turning around again.) Something's happened to that man in there. You better check in on him, sir. He won't answer or nothing.

EXPERIMENTER: Continue. Go on, please.

PROZI: You accept all responsibility?

EXPERIMENTER: The responsibility is mine. Correct. Please go on. (Subject returns to his list, starts running through words as rapidly as he can read them, works through to 450 volts.)

PROZI: That's that.

EXPERIMENTER: Continue using the 450 switch for each wrong answer. Continue, please.

PROZI: But I don't get anything!

EXPERIMENTER: Please continue. The next word is "white."

PROZI: Don't you think you should look in on him, please?

EXPERIMENTER: Not once we've started the experiment.

PROZI: What if he's dead in there? (Gestures toward the room with the electric chair.) I mean, he told me he can't stand the shock, sir. I don't mean to be rude, but I think you should look in on him. All you have to do is look in on him. All you have to do is look in the door. I don't get no answer, no noise. Something might have happened to the gentleman in there, sir.

EXPERIMENTER: We must continue. Go on, please.

PROZI: You mean keep giving him what? Four-hundred-fifty volts, what he's got now?

EXPERIMENTER: That's correct. Continue. The next word is "white."

PROZI: (now at a furious pace): "White—cloud, horse, rock, house." Answer, please. The answer is "horse." Four hundred and fifty volts. (Zzumph!) Next word, "Bag—paint, music, clown, girl." The answer is "paint." Four hundred and fifty volts. (Zzumph!) Next word is "Short—sentence, movie . . ."

EXPERIMENTER: Excuse me, Teacher. We'll have to discontinue the experiment.

(Abridged and adapted from Stanley Milgram, *Obedience to Authority*, New York: Harper & Row, 1974, pp. 219–223.)

After Reading

1. **Comprehension Check**

_____ 1) The experimenter insisted that Prozi continue administering shocks to the learner because

   a. he was mean.

   b. he enjoyed seeing people suffer.

   c. it was part of the experiment.

   d. the subject did not answer the question correctly.

2) How did Prozi feel as the experiment continued?

_____

_____

_____

_____

3) What reasons might there have been for Prozi to follow the experimenter's instructions as the experiment continued?

_____

_____

_____

4) What do you think you would have done if you had participated in this experiment as a teacher?

_____

_____

_____

2. **Topics for Writers**

1) The text states: "In reading about Milgram's research, it should have occurred to you that putting people in such a stressful experience could be considered ethically objectionable." In what ways is this experiment objectionable? Should researchers be allowed to conduct studies of this type? State the reasons for your opinions.

2) Do you think the findings of these studies on conformity justify the potential ill effects subjects may experience?

Chapter Summary

Making Inferences from Experience	Making an inference is also called "reading between the lines." You make an assumption that is not stated directly by the author. We make inferences based on our own prior knowledge and experience all the time, often without realizing that we're doing it.
Making Inferences about Causes and Effects	Sometimes you experience a situation in which you may infer possible causes or results.
Making Inferences about Tone	Tone is the way the author conveys feelings about characters and situations.
Making Inferences about Motive and Character	When reading fiction, making inferences about the characters and their motives often helps us better understand real people in our everyday lives.

Journal

Now that you have read some topics from a sociology textbook, do you think you would want to enroll in a sociology course at your college? Why or why not?

_____

_____

_____

_____

_____

_____

_____

_____

_____

_____

_____

_____

_____

_____

_____

_____

_____

_____

_____

_____

_____

_____

Go Electronic!

For additional readings, exercises, and Internet activities, visit the Longman English pages at:

http://longman.awl.com/englishpages

If you need a user name and password, please see your instructor.

Take a Road Trip to the Great Lakes and the American Southwest

Be sure to visit the Inference and Critical Thinking modules in your Reading Road Trip CD-ROM for multimedia tutorials, exercises, and tests.

Practice Your Writing Skills

For additional practice with your writing skills, use the Writer's ToolKit CD-ROM included with this text.

Additional Readings

Included in This Section

HOW I LEARNED TO READ AND WRITE

Frederick Douglass

- List four times you looked at printed material of any kind today. These printed materials might include such things as advertisements, books, or newspapers.
- List four times you wrote something today. Your writings might include a telephone number, a note to someone, or a bank check.
- In what ways would your day be different if you were not able to read and write the things you listed?

The following passage is from the autobiography of Frederick Douglass, *Narrative of the Life of Frederick Douglass*. Born into slavery in the United States in 1817, learning to read and write for Douglass was extremely dangerous. In this excerpt Douglass tells how he learned to read and write despite many obstacles. After escaping from slavery, Frederick Douglass became a great statesman and champion of black rights.

VOCABULARY	
Word	**Definition**
compelled (2)	forced
indispensable (2)	absolutely necessary or essential, needed
denunciation (6)	an open or public criticism
vindication (6)	a clearing from accusation or suspicion
abhor (6)	hate, detest
wretched (6)	miserable, awful
animate (6)	alive, able to move voluntarily
tedious (7)	dull, long, and tiring

1   Very soon after I went to live with Mr. and Mrs. Auld, she very kindly commenced to teach me the A, B, C. After I had learned this, she assisted me in learning to spell words of three or four letters. Just at this point of my progress, Mr. Auld found out what was going on, and at once forbade Mrs. Auld to instruct me further, telling her, among other things, that it was unlawful, as well as unsafe, to teach a slave to read. To use his own words, further, he said, "If you give a nigger an inch, he will take an ell. A nigger should know nothing but to obey his master—to do as he is told to do. Learning would *spoil* the best nigger in the world. Now," said he, "*if* you teach that nigger (speaking of myself) how to read, there would be no keeping him. It would forever unfit him to be a slave. He would at once become unmanageable, and of no value to his master. As to himself, it could do him no good, but a great deal of harm. It would make him discontented and unhappy." These words sank deep into my heart, stirred up sentiments within

Frederick Douglass

that lay slumbering, and called into existence an entirely new train of thought. It was a new and special revelation, explaining dark and mysterious things, with which my youthful understanding had struggled, but struggled in vain. I now understood what had been to me a most perplexing difficulty to wit, the white man's power to enslave the black man. It was a grand achievement, and I prized it highly. From that moment, I understood the pathway from slavery to freedom. It was just what I wanted, and I got it at a time when I the least expected it. Whilst I was saddened by the thought of losing the aid of my kind mistress, I was gladdened by the invaluable instruction which, by the merest accident, I had gained from my master. Though conscious of the difficulty of learning without a teacher, I set out with high hope, and a fixed purpose, at whatever cost of trouble, to learn how to read. The very decided manner with which he spoke, and strove to impress his wife with the evil consequences of giving me instruction, served to convince me that he was deeply sensible of the truths he was uttering. It gave me the best assurance that I might rely with the utmost confidence on the results which, he said, would flow from teaching me to read. What he most dreaded, that I most desired. What he most loved, that I most hated. That which to him was a great evil, to be carefully shunned, was to me a great good, to be diligently sought; and the argument which he so warmly urged, against my learning to read, only served to inspire me with a desire and determination to learn. In learning to read, I owe almost as much to the bitter opposition of my master, as to the kindly aid of my mistress. I acknowledge the benefit of both. . . .

2   I lived in Master Hugh's family about seven years. During this time, I succeeded in learning to read and write. In accomplishing this, I was compelled to resort to various stratagems. I had no regular teacher. My mistress, who had kindly commenced to instruct me, had, in compliance with the advice and direction of her husband, not only ceased to instruct, but had set her face against my being instructed by any one else. It is due, however, to my mistress to say of her, that she did not adopt this course of treatment immediately. She at first lacked the depravity indispensable to shutting me up in mental darkness. It was at least necessary for her to have some training in the exercise of irresponsible power, to make her equal to the task of treating me as though I were a brute.

3   From this time I was most narrowly watched. If I was in a separate room any considerable length of time, I was sure to be suspected of having a book, and was at once called to give an account of myself. All this, however, was too late. The first step had been taken. Mistress, in teaching me the alphabet, had given me the *inch*, and no precaution could prevent me from taking the *ell*.

4   The plan which I adopted, and the one by which I was most successful, was that of making friends of all the little white boys whom I met in the street. As many of these as I could, I converted into teachers. With their kindly aid, obtained at different

times and in different places, I finally succeeded in learning to read. When I was sent on errands, I always took my book with me, and by going one part of my errand quickly, I found time to get a lesson before my return. I used also to carry bread with me, enough of which was always in the house, and to which I was always welcome; for I was much better off in this regard than many of the poor white children in our neighborhood. This bread I used to bestow upon the hungry little urchins, who, in return, would give me that more valuable bread of knowledge. I am strongly tempted to give the names of two or three of those little boys, as a testimonial of the gratitude and affection I bear them: but prudence forbids; not that it would injure me, but it might embarrass them; for it is almost an unpardonable offence to teach slaves to read in this Christian country. It is enough to say of the dear little fellows, that they lived in Philpot Street, very near Durgin and Bailey's shipyard. I used to talk this matter of slavery over with them. I would sometimes say to them, I wished I could be as free as they would be when they got to be men. "You will be free as soon as you are twenty-one, but *I am a slave for life!* Have not I as good a right to be free as you have?" These words used to trouble them; they would express for me the liveliest sympathy, and console me with the hope that something would occur by which I might be free.

5   I was now about twelve years old, and the thought of being *a slave for life* began to bear heavily upon my heart. Just about this time, I got hold of a book entitled "The Columbian Orator." Every opportunity I got, I used to read this book. Among much of other interesting matter, I found in it a dialogue between a master and his slave. The slave was represented as having run away from his master three times. The dialogue represented the conversation which took place between them, when the slave was retaken the third time. In this dialogue, the whole argument in behalf of slavery was brought forward by the master, all of which was disposed of by the slave. The slave was made to say some very smart as well as impressive things in reply to his master—things which had the desired though unexpected effect; for the conversation resulted in the voluntary emancipation of the slave on the part of the master.

6   In the same book, I met with one of Sheridan's mighty speeches on and in behalf of Catholic emancipation. These were choice documents to me. I read them over and over again with unabated interest. They gave tongue to interesting thoughts of my own soul, which had frequently flashed through my mind, and died away for want of utterance. The moral which I gained from the dialogue was the power of truth over the conscience of even a slaveholder. What I got from Sheridan was a bold denunciation of slavery, and a powerful vindication of human rights. The reading of these documents enabled me to utter my thoughts, and to meet the arguments brought forward to sustain slavery; but while they relieved me of one difficulty, they brought another even more painful than the one of which I was relieved. The more I read, the more I was led to abhor and detest my enslavers. I could regard them in no other light than a band of successful robbers, who had left

their homes, and gone to Africa, and stolen us from our homes, and in a strange land reduced us to slavery. I loathed them as being the meanest as well as the most wicked of men. As I read and contemplated the subject, behold! that very discontentment which Master Hugh had predicted would follow my learning to read had already come, to torment and sting my soul to unutterable anguish. As I writhed under it, I would at times feel that learning to read had been a curse rather than a blessing. It had given me a view of my wretched condition, without the remedy. It opened my eyes to the horrible pit, but to no ladder upon which to get out. In moments of agony, I envied my fellow-slaves for their stupidity. I have often wished myself a beast. I preferred the condition of the meanest reptile to my own. Any thing, no matter what, to get rid of thinking! It was this everlasting thinking of my condition that tormented me. There was no getting rid of it. It was pressed upon me by every object within sight or hearing, animate or inanimate. The silver trump of freedom had roused my soul to eternal wakefulness. Freedom now appeared, to disappear no more forever. It was heard in every sound, and seen in every thing. It was ever present to torment me with a sense of my wretched condition. I saw nothing without seeing it, I heard nothing without hearing it, and felt nothing without feeling it. It looked from every star, it smiled in every calm, breathed in every wind, and moved in every storm.

7   The idea as to how I might learn to write was suggested to me by being in Durgin and Bailey's ship-yard, and frequently seeing the ship carpenters, after hewing, and getting a piece of timber ready for use, write on the timber the name of that part of the ship for which it was intended. When a piece of timber was intended for the larboard side, it would be marked thus—"L." When a piece was off the starboard side, it would be marked thus—"S." A piece for the larboard side forward, would be marked thus—"L. F." When a piece was for starboard side forward, it would be marked thus—"S. F." For larboard aft, it would be marked thus—"L. A." For starboard aft, it would be marked thus—"S. A." I soon learned the names of these letters, and for what they were intended when placed upon a piece of timber in the ship-yard. I immediately commenced copying them, and in a short time was able to make the four letters named. After that, when I met with any boy who I knew could write, I would tell him I could write as well as he. The next word would be, "*I* don't believe you. Let me see you try it." I would then make the letters which I had been so fortunate as to learn, and ask him to beat that. In this way I got a good many lessons in writing, which it is quite possible I should never have gotten in any other way. During this time, my copy-book was the board fence, brick wall, and pavement; my pen and ink was a lump of chalk. With these, I learned mainly how to write. I then commenced and continued copying the Italics in Webster's Spelling Book, until I could make them all without looking on the book. By this time, my little Master Thomas had gone to school, and learned how to write, and had written over a number of copy-books. These had been brought home, and shown to some of our near neighbors, and then laid aside. My mistress

used to go to class meeting at the Wilk Street meetinghouse every Monday after-noon, and leave me to take care of the house. When left thus, I used to spend this time writing in the spaces left in Master Thomas's copy-book, copying what he had written. I continued to do this until I could write a hand very similar to that of Master Thomas. Thus, after a long, tedious effort for years, I finally succeeded in learning how to write.

(Douglass, Frederick. "How I Learned to Read and Write," from
Narrative of the Life of Frederick Douglass,
An American Slave, 1987.)

1.   Comprehension Check

_____ 1) The main idea of this essay is
   a. Frederick Douglass was a slave.
   b. Frederick Douglass learned to read and write despite overwhelming hardships he endured as a slave.
   c. Mr. and Mrs. Auld did not want Douglass to learn to read and write.
   d. Douglass learned to write from studying letters written on pieces of timber in a shipyard.

_____ 2) Mr. Auld did not want Douglass to learn how to read because
   a. he wanted Douglass to be happy.
   b. it would make Douglass dissatisfied being a slave.
   c. it was difficult to learn.
   d. it was a dark and mysterious thing.

_____ 3) What represented "the pathway from slavery to freedom" for Frederick Douglass (paragraph 1)?
   a. Running away.
   b. Following the master's orders.
   c. Reading and writing.
   d. Organizing a slave revolt.

_____ 4) Which one of the following is *not* true about how Frederick Douglass reacted to Mr. Auld's conversation with his wife?
   a. He was upset that his mistress could not teach him anymore.
   b. He hated and dreaded his master.
   c. He learned a great lesson.
   d. He was grateful to his master for forbidding him to learn to read.

_____ 5) Frederick Douglass got the white boys from the neighborhood to help him learn to read by
   a. asking them.
   b. giving them bread.
   c. paying them money.
   d. promising to play with them.

_____ 6) What did Frederick Douglass think was unusual about the conversation in "The Columbian Orator"?
   a. The slave was freed by the master.
   b. The slave ran away three times and was returned each time.
   c. The slave said some very smart things.
   d. The master had a conversation with his slave.

_____ 7) Douglass's reaction to reading Sheridan's speeches can be described as
   a. interested.
   b. tormented.
   c. bored.
   d. calm.

8) In what way was reading for Douglass a "curse rather than a blessing"?

_____

_____

_____ 9) From this selection you can conclude that Douglass was
   a. lazy.
   b. intelligent.
   c. cruel.
   d. selfish.

_____ 10) This passage is developed principally by means of
   a. a comparison.
   b. a listing.
   c. explanation.
   d. cause–effect.

2. Vocabulary

Listed below are eight sentences from the essay by Frederick Douglass. Each sentence contains an underlined word. Read each sentence and circle one of the three words found below the sentence that means the same as the underlined word.

   1) Very soon after I went to live with Mr. and Mrs. Auld, she very kindly <u>commenced</u> to teach me the A, B, C. (paragraph 1)

   a. refused   b. agreed   c. began

   2) These words sank deep into my heart, stirred up <u>sentiments</u> within that lay slumbering, and called into existence an entirely new train of thought. (paragraph 1)

   a. memories   b. feelings   c. anger

3) I now understood what had been to me a most <u>perplexing</u> difficulty. . . . (paragraph 1)

    a. confusing   b. interesting   c. complicated

4) That which to him was a great evil, to be carefully shunned, was to me a great food, to be <u>diligently</u> sought. . . . (paragraph 1)

    a. unhappily   b. constant in effort c. slowly

5) She at first lacked the <u>depravity</u> indispensable to shutting me up in mental darkness. (paragraph 2)

    a. love   b. money   c. wickedness

6) I read them over and over again with <u>unabated</u> interest. (paragraph 16)

    a. continued   b. little   c. no

7) I <u>loathed</u> them as being the meanest as well as the most wicked of men. (paragraph 6)

    a. doubted   b. envied   c. hated

3. **Topics for Writers**
   1) How could reading make a person discontented and unhappy?
   2) How can reading and writing be a pathway to freedom?
   3) Discuss three events Douglass describes in his essay that had a profound effect on his learning to read and write.
   4) Explain why Mr. Auld prohibited his wife from teaching Douglass to read and write.
   5) Describe Douglass' reaction to having read "The Columbian Orator."
   6) Imagine you are a friend of Mr. Auld. Enumerate reasons to convince Mr. Auld to allow Douglass to learn to read and write.

Cesar Chavez and La Causa

What is one injustice you are aware of that is part of life in the United States?

Have you ever done anything to try to change that injustice in some way? If yes, what was it? If no, explain why.

_____

_____

_____

_____

_____

_____

	Vocabulary
Word	**Definition**
shunted (2)	shoved or turned out of the way
apostle (8)	a pioneer of a reform movement
pelt (8)	attack someone or something with repeated blows or missiles
beset (11)	surround

1   In early April 1962, a 35-year-old community organizer named Cesar Estrada Chavez set out to singlehandedly organize impoverished migrant farm laborers in the California grape fields. He, his wife, and their eight children packed their belongings into a dilapidated 9-year-old station wagon, and moved to Delano, California, a town of 12,000 that was the center of the nation's table-grape industry. Over the next two years, Chavez spent his entire lifetime savings of $1200 creating a small social service organization for Delano's field laborers; it offered immigration counseling, citizenship classes, funeral benefits, credit to buy cars and homes, assistance with voter registration, and a cooperative to buy tires and gasoline. As the emblem of his new organization, the National Farm Workers Association, Chavez chose a black Aztec eagle inside a white circle on a red background.

2   Chavez's sympathy for the plight of migrant farmworkers came naturally. He was born in Yuma, Arizona, in 1927, one of five children of Mexican immigrants. When he was 10 years old, his parents lost their small farm; he, his brothers and sisters, and his parents hoed beets, picked grapes, and harvested peaches and figs in Arizona and California. There were times when the family had to sleep in its car or camp under bridges. When young Cesar was able to attend school (he attended more than 30 schools as a child), he was often shunted into special classrooms set aside for Mexican-American children.

3   In 1944, when he was 17, Chavez joined the Navy and served for two years on a destroyer escort in the Pacific. After World War II ended, he married and spent

Cesar Chavez

two and a half years as a sharecropper raising strawberries. That was follow by work in apricot and prune orchards and in a lumber camp. Then in 1952 his life took a fateful turn. He joined the Community Service Organization (CSO), which wanted to educate and organize the poor so that they could solve their own social and economic problems. After founding CSO chapters in Madera, Bakersfield, and Hanford, California, Chavez became the organization's general director in 1958. Four years later, he broke with the organization when it rejected his proposal to establish a farmworkers' union.

4   Most labor leaders considered Chavez's goal of creating the first successful union of farmworkers in U.S. history an impossible dream. Not only did farm laborers suffer from high rates of illiteracy and poverty (average family earnings were just $2000 in 1965), they also experienced persistently high rates of unemployment (traditionally around 19 percent) and were divided into a variety of ethnic groups (Mexican, Arab, Filipino, and Puerto Rican). Making unionization even more difficult were the facts that farmworkers rarely remained in one locality for very long, and they were easily replaced by inexpensive Mexican day laborers, known as *braceros*, who were trucked into California and the Southwest at harvest time.

5   Moreover, farmworkers were specifically excluded from the protection of the National Labor Relations Act of 1935. Unlike other American workers, farmworkers were not guaranteed the right to organize, had no guarantee of a minimum wage, and had no federally guaranteed standards of work in the fields. State laws requiring toilets, rest periods, and drinking water in the fields were largely ignored.

6   In September 1965, Chavez was drawn into his first important labor controversy. The Filipino grape pickers went on strike. "All right, Chavez," said one of the Filipino grape pickers' leaders, "are you going to stand beside us, or are you going to scab against us?" Despite his fear that the National Farm Workers Association was not sufficiently well organized to support a strike (it had less than $100 in its strike fund), he assured the Filipino workers that members of his association would not go into the field as strikebreakers. *Huelga!*—the Spanish word for strike—became the grape pickers' battle cry.

7   Within weeks, the labor strike began to attract national attention. Unions, church groups, and civil rights organizations offered financial support for *La Causa*, as the farmworkers' movement became known. In March 1966, Chavez led a 250-mile Easter march from Delano to Sacramento to dramatize the plight of migrant farm laborers. That same year, Chavez's National Farm Workers Association merged with an AFL-CIO affiliate to form the United Farm Workers Organizing Committee.

8   A staunch apostle of nonviolence, Chavez was deeply troubled by violent incidents that marred the strike. Some growers raced tractors along the roadside, covering the strikers with dirt and dust. Others drove spraying machines along the edges of their fields, spraying insecticide and fertilizer on the picketers. Local police officers arrested a minister for reading Jack London's definition of a scab ("a two-legged animal with a corkscrew soul, a water-logged brain, and a combination backbone made of jelly and glue"). Some strikers, in turn, intimidated strikebreakers by pelting them with marbles fired from slingshots and by setting fire to packing crates. One striker tried to drive a car into a group of growers.

9   In an effort to quell the escalating violence and to atone for the militancy of some union members, Chavez began to fast on February 14, 1968. For five days he kept the fast a secret. Then, in an hour-long speech to striking workers, he explained that continued violence would destroy everything the union stood for. He said that the "truest act of courage, the strongest act of manliness, is to sacrifice ourselves for others in a totally nonviolent struggle for justice." For 21 days he fasted; he lost 35 pounds and his doctor began to fear for his health. He finally agreed to take a small amount of bouillon and grapefruit juice and medication. On March 11, he ended his fast by taking communion and breaking bread with Senator Robert F. Kennedy.

10   The strike dragged on for three years. To heighten public awareness of the farmworkers' cause, Chavez in 1968 initiated a boycott of table grapes. It was the boycott that pressured many of the growers into settling the strike. An estimated 17 million American consumers went without grapes in support of the farmworkers' bargaining position. By mid-1970, two-thirds of California grapes were grown under contract with Chavez's union.

11   In the years following its 1970 victory, Chavez's union has been beset by problems from within and without. Union membership dwindled from a high of more than 60,000 in 1972 to a low of 5000 in 1974. (It has since climbed back to around 30,000.) Meanwhile, public concern for the plight of migrant farmworkers declined.

12   Chavez died in 1993, at age 66. To commemorate his legacy, 25,000 people marched for more than two and a half hours to the spot where he had founded the United Farm Workers Union. As a result of Chavez's efforts, the most back-breaking tool used by farmworkers, the short hoe, was eliminated, and the use of many dangerous pesticides in the grape fields was prohibited. His efforts also brought about a 70 percent increase in real wages from 1964 to 1980, and establishment of healthcare benefits, disability insurance, pension plans, and standardized grievance procedures for farmworkers. He helped secure passage of the nation's first agricultural labor relations act in California in 1975, which prohibited growers from firing striking workers or engaging in bad-faith bargaining. Thanks to his efforts, migrant farm laborers won a right held by all other American workers: the right to bargain collectively.

(Martin, James, R. Roberts, S. Mintz, L. McMurry & J. Jones. *America and Its People: A Mosaic in the Making,* Vol. 2. Longman, 1997, pp. 1062–1063.)

1. **Comprehension Check**

_____ 1) The main idea of this selection is
   a. the United Farm Workers Union helped thousands of migrant workers to attain important rights.
   b. Chavez organized a union and led migrant workers in a struggle for a better life.
   c. Chavez had a very difficult life.
   d. Chavez led a strike against grape growers that lasted three years.

_____ 2) Chavez left the Community Service Organization because
   a. he didn't feel appreciated.
   b. he wanted to educate and organize the poor.
   c. the organization rejected his dream of a farmworkers union.
   d. he didn't like his job as general director.

_____ 3) All of the following were true about the farmworkers when Chavez started working for them *except*
   a. they were not guaranteed the right to organize.
   b. most could not read.
   c. they could always find work.
   d. they earned very little money.

_____ 4) Cesar probably attended more than 30 schools as a child because
   a. he could not speak English and failed classes.
   b. he had to help his parents work on farms.
   c. he did not like school.
   d. he needed a school that had special classrooms set aside for Mexican-American children.

_____ 5) The farmworkers' movement was known as
   a. La Causa.
   b. the Easter march.
   c. AFL-CIO.
   d. the National Labor Relations Act.

_____ 6) Chavez began a fast in 1968
   a. as a way to lose weight.
   b. in protest of the violence during the strike.
   c. in an effort to end the violence during the strike.
   d. in an effort to destroy the union.

_____ 7) The boycott of table grapes was successful in getting the growers to settle the strike because
   a. the growers were not earning a living.
   b. people wanted to buy the grapes.
   c. the growers were afraid of further violence.
   d. the strike lasted so long.

_____ 8) Chavez was responsible for achieving all of the following *except*

    a. the first labor relations act in California.

    b. the prohibition of many dangerous pesticides in the grape fields.

    c. an increase in wages for farmworkers.

    d. the use of the short hoe.

2. Vocabulary

Match the words in Column A with the correct definitions in Column B. Then write, on a line, each word from Column A that has the same number of letters as the number of spaces provided. When you are finished, the letters in the parentheses will form a word from the article.

Column A: Words	Column B: Definitions
scab	blemish, ruin, spoil
quell	frighten, scare
mar	decayed, run-down
dilapidated	silence, crush, calm
intimidated	firm, loyal, strong
staunch	a worker who takes a striker's job
commemorate	honor, observe

```
__ __ (  ) __ __ __ __ __ __ __
       __ (  ) __
       __ (  ) __ __
__ __ __ __ __ __ __ __ (  ) __ __
       __ (  ) __ __ __
          (  ) __ __ __ __ __ __
__ __ __ __ __ __ __ (  ) __ __ __
```

3. Topics for Writers

1) Compare and contrast Douglass and Chavez in terms of their backgrounds, motives, and achievements.

2) Write about a hardship in your life you had to overcome.

3) Discuss a goal you want to reach and ways you plan to achieve it.

4) Imagine you are participating in a strike against your employer. Write a persuasive essay to convince someone not to purchase the products or services provided by the company.

5) Enumerate and discuss the importance of the benefits Chavez was able to attain for farmworkers over the years.

6) Trace the development of Chavez's work from the establishment of the National Farm Workers Association to the end of the grape pickers' strike.

7) Explain why organizing the migrant farmworkers was so difficult.

IT'S NOT EASY BEIN' GREEN
Joe Raposo

Have you ever wished you were someone else? Have you ever felt that you would never want to be anyone but who you are? On the lines below list a few drawbacks and advantages to being who you are.

Drawbacks   **Advantages**

_____   _____

_____   _____

_____   _____

In this song the author finds both disadvantages and advantages to his situation.

It's not that easy being green;
Having to spend each day the color of leaves.
When I think it could be nicer being red, or yellow or gold—
or something much more colorful like that.

It's not that easy being green.
It seems you blend in with so many other ordinary things.
And people tend to pass you over 'cause you're
not standing out like flashy sparkles in the water—
or stars in the sky.

But green's the color of Spring.
And green can be cool and friendly-like.
And green can be big like an ocean, or important
like a mountain, or tall like a tree.

When green is all there is to be
It could make you wonder why, but why wonder,
I am green and it'll do fine,
it's beautiful!
And I think it's what I want to be.

1.   **Comprehension Check**

_____ 1) What does the color "green" represent in the poem?
   a. a distinguishing characteristic of a person
   b. the color of leaves
   c. an ocean or a mountain
   d. jealousy

_____ 2) Being green is not easy for all the following reasons *except*
   a. there is no choice.
   b. green is ordinary.
   c. green is the color of spring.
   d. green is not noticeable.

_____ 3) The author's purpose in writing this poem is
   a. to complain about being green.
   b. to comment on why it would be better to be a different color.
   c. to brag about being green.
   d. to give both the disadvantages and advantages of being green.

_____ 4) At the conclusion of the poem the tone is
   a. optimistic.
   b. pessimistic.
   c. depressed.
   d. sarcastic.

_____ 5) True or False: The author feels he has no choice about being green.

_____ 6) Which of the following proverbs expresses the main idea of the poem?
   a. The grass is always greener on the other side of the fence.
   b. All that glitters is not gold.
   c. The best things are hard to come by.
   d. Beauty is in the eye of the beholder.

2. Topics for Writers

   1) Do you prefer to stand out in a crowd or blend in with others? How does your behavior with others reflect your preference?

   2) If you could choose any color to represent you, what color would you be? Explain your reasons for choosing that color.

LOVING YOUR ENEMIES
Martin Luther King, Jr.

Write about a time someone did you harm, either emotionally or physically. Did you forgive that person? Why or why not? If you did, do you usually forgive? If you did not, do you ever forgive?

This passage by Martin Luther King, Jr. is about love. Dr. King explains why and how we should love our enemies.

Let us be practical and ask the question, *How do we love our enemies?*

1   . . . First, we must develop and maintain the capacity to forgive. He who is devoid of the power to forgive is devoid of the power to love. It is impossible even

to begin the act of loving one's enemies without the prior acceptance of the necessity, over and over again, of forgiving those who inflict evil and injury upon us. It is also necessary to realize that the forgiving act must always be initiated by the person who has been wronged, the victim of some great hurt, the recipient of some tortuous injustice, the absorber of some terrible act of oppression. The wrongdoer may request forgiveness. He may come to himself, and, like the prodigal son, move up some dusty road, his heart palpitating with the desire for forgiveness. But only the injured neighbor, the loving father back home, can really pour out the warm waters of forgiveness.

2   Forgiveness does not mean ignoring what has been done or putting a false label on an evil act. It means, rather, that the evil act no longer remains as a barrier to the relationship. Forgiveness is a catalyst creating the atmosphere necessary for a fresh start and a new beginning. It is the lifting of a burden or the cancelling of a debt. The words "I will forgive you, but I'll never forget what you've done" never explain the real nature of forgiveness. Certainly one can never forget, if that means erasing it totally from his mind. But when we forgive, we forget in the sense that the evil deed is no longer a mental block impeding a new relationship. Likewise, we can never say, "I will forgive you, but I won't have anything further to do with you." Forgiveness means reconciliation, a coming together again. Without this, no man can love his enemies. The degree to which we are able to forgive determines the degree to which we are able to love our enemies.

3   Second, we must recognize that the evil deed of the enemy-neighbor, the thing that hurts, never quite expresses all that he is. An element of goodness may be found even in our worst enemy. Each of us is something of a schizophrenic personality, tragically divided against ourselves. A persistent civil war rages within all of our lives. Something within us causes us to lament with Ovid, the Latin poet, "I see and approve the better things, but follow worse," or to agree with Plato that human personality is like a charioteer having two headstrong horses, each wanting to go in a different direction, or to repeat with the Apostle Paul, "The good that I would I do not: but the evil which I would not, that I do."

4   This simply means that there is some good in the worst of us and some evil in the best of us. When we discover this we are less prone to hate our enemies. When we look beneath the surface, beneath the impulsive evil deed, we see within our enemy-neighbor a measure of goodness and know that the viciousness and evilness of his acts are not quite representative of all that he is. We see him in a new light. We recognize that his hate grows out of fear, pride, ignorance, prejudice, and misunderstanding, but in spite of this, we know God's image is ineffably etched in his being. . . .

5   Third, we must not seek to defeat or humiliate the enemy but to win his friendship and understanding. At times we are able to humiliate our worst enemy. Inevitably, his weak moments come and we are able to thrust in his side the spear of defeat. But this we must not do. Every word and deed must contribute to an

Martin Luther King, Jr.

understanding with the enemy and release those vast reservoirs of goodwill which have been blocked by impenetrable walls of hate.

6   The meaning of love is not to be confused with some sentimental outpouring. Love is something much deeper than emotional bosh. Perhaps the Greek language can clear our confusion at this point. In the Greek New Testament are three words for love. The word *eros* is a sort of aesthetic or romantic love. In the Platonic dialogues *eros* is a yearning of the soul for the realm of the divine. The second word is *philia*, a reciprocal love and the intimate affection and friendship between friends. We love those whom we like, and we love because we are loved. The third word is *agape*, understanding and creative, redemptive goodwill for all men. An overflowing love which seeks nothing in return, *agape* is the love of God operating in the human heart. . . . At this level, we love the person who does an evil deed, although we hate the deed that he does. . . .

7   Let us move now from the practical *how* to the theoretical *why: Why should we love our enemies?* The first reason is fairly obvious. Returning hate for hate multiplies hate, adding deeper darkness to a night already devoid of stars. Darkness cannot drive out darkness; only light can do that. Hate cannot drive out hate; only love can do that. Hate multiplies hate, violence multiplies violence, and toughness multiplies toughness in a descending spiral of destruction. . . . Have we not come to such an impasse in the modern world that we must love our enemies—or else? The chain reaction of evil—hate begetting hate, wars producing more wars—must be broken, or we shall be plunged into the dark abyss of annihilation.

8   Another reason why we must love our enemies is that hate scars the soul and distorts the personality. Mindful that hate is an evil and dangerous force, we too often think of what it does to the person hated. This is understandable, for hate brings irreparable damage to its victims. We have seen its ugly consequences in the ignominious deaths brought to six million Jews by a hate-obsessed madman named Hitler, in the unspeakable violence inflicted upon Negroes by bloodthirsty mobs, in the dark horrors of war, and in the terrible indignities and injustices perpetrated against millions of God's children by unconscionable oppressors.

9   But there is another side which we must never overlook. Hate is just as injurious to the person who hates. Like an unchecked cancer, hate corrodes the personality and eats away its vital unity. Hate destroys a man's sense of values and his objectivity. It causes him to describe the beautiful as ugly and the ugly as beautiful, and to confuse the true with the false and the false with the true.

10   Dr. E. Franklin Frazier, in an interesting essay entitled "The Pathology of Race Prejudice," included several examples of white persons who were normal, amiable,

and congenial in their day-to-day relationships with other white persons but when they were challenged to think of Negroes as equals or even to discuss the question of racial injustice, they reacted with unbelievable irrationality and an abnormal unbalance. This happens when hate lingers in our minds. Psychiatrists report that many of the strange things that happen in the subconscious, many of our inner conflicts, are rooted in hate. They say, "Love or perish." . . .

11   A third reason why we should love our enemies is that love is the only force capable of transforming an enemy into a friend. We never get rid of an enemy by meeting hate with hate; we get rid of an enemy by getting rid of enmity. By its very nature, hate destroys and tears down; by its very nature, love creates and builds up. Love transforms with redemptive power.

12   Lincoln tried love and left for all history a magnificent drama of reconciliation. When he was campaigning for the presidency one of his arch-enemies was a man named Stanton. For some reason Stanton hated Lincoln. He used every ounce of his energy to degrade him in the eyes of the public. So deep rooted was Stanton's hate for Lincoln that he uttered unkind words about his physical appearance, and sought to embarrass him at every point with the bitterest diatribes. But in spite of this Lincoln was elected President of the United States. Then came the period when he had to select his cabinet which would consist of the persons who would be his most intimate associates in implementing his program. He started choosing men here and there for the various secretaryships. The day finally came for Lincoln to select a man to fill the all-important post of Secretary of War. Can you imagine whom Lincoln chose to fill this post? None other than the man named Stanton. There was an immediate uproar in the inner circle when the news began to spread. Adviser after adviser was heard saying, "Mr. President, you are making a mistake. Do you know this man Stanton? Are you familiar with all of the ugly things he said about you? He is your enemy. He will seek to sabotage your program. Have you thought this through, Mr. President?" Mr. Lincoln's answer was terse and to the point: "Yes, I know Mr. Stanton. I am aware of all the terrible things he has said about me. But after looking over the nation, I find he is the best man for the job." So Stanton became Abraham Lincoln's Secretary of War and rendered an invaluable service to his nation and his President. Not many years later Lincoln was assassinated. Many laudable things were said about him. Even today millions of people still adore him as the greatest of all Americans. H. G. Wells selected him as one of the six great men of history. But of all the great statements made about Abraham Lincoln, the words of Stanton remain among the greatest. Standing near the dead body of the man he once hated, Stanton referred to him as one of the greatest men that ever lived and said "he now belongs to the ages." If Lincoln had hated Stanton both men would have gone to their graves as bitter enemies. But through the power of love Lincoln transformed an enemy into a friend. It was this same attitude that made it possible for Lincoln to speak a kind word about the South during the Civil War when feeling was most bitter. Asked by a shocked

bystander how he could do this, Lincoln said, "Madam, do I not destroy my enemies when I make them my friends?" This is the power of redemptive love. . . .

13   The relevance of what I have said to the crisis in race relations should be readily apparent. There will be no permanent solution to the race problem until oppressed men develop the capacity to love their enemies. The darkness of racial injustice will be dispelled only by the light of forgiving love. For more than three centuries American Negroes have been battered by the iron rod of oppression, frustrated by day and bewildered by night by unbearable injustice, and burdened with the ugly weight of discrimination. Forced to live with these shameful conditions, we are tempted to become bitter and to retaliate with a corresponding hate. But if this happens, the new order we seek will be little more than a duplicate of the old order. We must in strength and humility meet hate with love. . . .

(King, Martin Luther, Jr. *Strength to Love.* PA: Fortress Press, 1963, pp. 49–57, adapted.)

1.   **Comprehension Check**

_____ 1) Each of the following is suggested by Dr. King as a way to love our enemies *except*
   a. gain understanding.
   b. develop the capacity to forgive.
   c. find an element of goodness.
   d. ignore any evil that was done.

_____ 2) Why does Dr. King consider forgiveness an important part of love?
   a. It helps us forget.
   b. It helps us create a false label.
   c. It helps us lift the burden.
   d. It can be used as a mental block.

_____ 3) What did Plato mean by "human personality is like a charioteer having two headstrong horses, each wanting to go in a different direction"?
   a. We should forgive our enemies.
   b. There is a combination of good and evil in everyone.
   c. Forgiveness must be initiated by the person who has been wronged.
   d. Making decisions is very difficult.

_____ 4) According to the Greek New Testament "eros" is
   a. romantic love.
   b. intimate affection.
   c. love of God.
   d. friendship.

_____ 5) According to the Greek New Testament "agape" is
   a. romantic love.
   b. intimate love.
   c. love of God.
   d. friendship.

_____ 6) Each of the following is suggested by Dr. King as a reason we should love our enemies *except*
  a. hate damages its victim.
  b. hate drives out hate.
  c. love transforms an enemy into a friend.
  d. returning hate multiplies hate.

_____ 7) Which of the following is an example of the third reason we should love our enemies?
  a. H.G. Wells' statement about Lincoln being one of the six great men of history.
  b. Lincoln's appointment of Stanton as Secretary of War.
  c. Dr. E. Franklin Frazier's example of white persons who could not talk about racial injustice.
  d. Martin Luther King's belief in utopia.

_____ 8) The purpose of this passage is to
  a. inform.
  b. persuade.
  c. entertain.
  d. narrate a story.

2. Vocabulary

In the chart below, first try to figure out the meaning of each word from the context. Write it in the third column. Then, using a dictionary, write the correct definition in the fourth column. Finally, if you know any other words that are similar in spelling or meaning to the word, write it in the fifth column.

Word	Par.	Guessed Meaning	Dictionary Meaning	Other Words
tortuous	1			
catalyst	2			
reconciliation	2			
impenetrable	5			
abyss	7			
annihilation	7			

Word	Par.	Guessed Meaning	Dictionary Meaning	Other Words
ignominious	8			
amiable	10			
congenial	10			
diatribes	12			
laudable	12			
retaliate	13			

3. Topics for Writers

1) What do you believe is the nature of racial problems in this country?

2) How can an understanding of our need for belonging and love help solve some of the problems discussed by Martin Luther King?

3) Write about a time you either forgave or could not forgive someone who hurt you in some way.

4) Dr. King concludes this essay with an appeal for love and nonviolence in race relations. In what ways do you agree and/or disagree with Dr. King's solution to race problems?

5) Compare and contrast the various types of love defined by Martin Luther King. How are they a part of your experience?

6) Explain why it is important to be able to forgive according to Martin Luther King.

SUNDAY IN THE PARK
Bel Kaufman

Have you ever been intimidated by a bully?

Why do you think someone would choose to bully people?

_____

_____

_____

In this story a husband and wife experience an unpleasant encounter while spending a peaceful afternoon in the park with their son.

VOCABULARY	
Word	**Definition**
stolid (1)	unemotional
impassive (1)	without emotions, apathetic, calm
deftly (2)	skillfully, nimbly
tentative (3)	unsure, hesitant
insolent (10)	boldly rude or disrespectful, insulting
suffused (11)	pervade, overspread with
impotent (11)	lacking power or ability, unable to do something
rapt (18)	deeply engrossed or absorbed

1   It was still warm in the late-afternoon sun, and the city noises came muffled through the trees in the park. She put her book down on the bench, removed her sunglasses, and sighed contentedly. Morton was reading the *Times Magazine* section, one arm flung around her shoulder; their three-year-old son, Larry, was playing in the sandbox: a faint breeze fanned her hair softly against her cheek. It was five-thirty of a Sunday afternoon, and the small playground, tucked away in a corner of the park, was all but deserted. The swings and seesaws stood motionless and abandoned, the slides were empty, and only in the sandbox two little boys squatted diligently side by side. *How good this is*, she thought, and almost smiled at her sense of well-being. They must go out in the sun more often; Morton was so city-pale, cooped up all week inside the gray factorylike university. She squeezed his arm affectionately and glanced at Larry, delighting in the pointed little face frowning in concentration over the tunnel he was digging. The other boy suddenly stood up and with a quick, deliberate swing of his chubby arm threw a spadeful of sand at Larry. It just missed his head. Larry continued digging; the boy remained standing, shovel raised, stolid and impassive.

2   "No, no, little boy." She shook her finger at him, her eyes searching for the child's mother or nurse. "We mustn't throw sand. It may get in someone's eyes and hurt. We must play nicely in the nice sandbox." The boy looked at her in unblinking expectancy. He was about Larry's age but perhaps ten pounds heavier,

a husky little boy with none of Larry's quickness and sensitivity in his face. Where was his mother? The only other people left in the playground were two women and a little girl on roller skates leaving now through the gate, and a man on a bench a few feet away. He was a big man, and he seemed to be taking up the whole bench as he held the Sunday comics close to his face. She supposed he was the child's father. He did not look up from his comics, but spat once deftly out of the corner of his mouth. She turned her eyes away.

3   At that moment, as swiftly as before, the fat little boy threw another spadeful of sand at Larry. This time some of it landed on his hair and forehead. Larry looked up at his mother, his mouth tentative; her expression would tell him whether to cry or not.

4   Her first instinct was to rush to her son, brush the sand out of his hair, and punish the other child, but she controlled it. She always said that she wanted Larry to learn to fight his own battles.

5   "Don't *do* that, little boy," she said sharply, leaning forward on the bench. "You mustn't throw sand!"

6   The man on the bench moved his mouth as if to spit again, but instead he spoke. He did not look at her, but at the boy only.

7   "You go right ahead, Joe," he said loudly. "Throw all you want. This here is a *public* sandbox."

8   She felt a sudden weakness in her knees as she glanced at Morton. He had become aware of what was happening. He put his *Times* down carefully on his lap and turned his fine, lean face toward the man, smiling the shy, apologetic smile he might have offered a student in pointing out an error in his thinking. When he spoke to the man, it was with his usual reasonableness.

9   "You're quite right," he said pleasantly, "but just because this is a public place . . . . "

10   The man lowered his funnies and looked at Morton. He looked at him from head to foot, slowly and deliberately. "Yeah?" His insolent voice was edged with menace. "My kid's got just as good right here as yours, and if he feels like throwing sand, he'll throw it, and if you don't like it, you can take your kid the hell out of here."

11   The children were listening, their eyes and mouths wide open, their spades forgotten in small fists. She noticed the muscle in Morton's jaw tighten. He was rarely angry; he seldom lost his temper. She was suffused with a tenderness for her husband and an impotent rage against the man for involving him in a situation so alien and so distasteful to him.

12   "Now, just a minute," Morton said courteously, "you must realize . . . ."

13   "Aw, shut up," said the man.

14   Her heart began to pound. Morton half rose; the *Times* slid to the ground. Slowly the other man stood up. He took a couple of steps toward Morton, then stopped. He flexed his great arms, waiting. She pressed her trembling knees

together. Would there be violence, fighting? How dreadful, how incredible. . . . She must do something, stop them, call for help. She wanted to put her hand on her husband's sleeve, to pull him down, but for some reason she didn't.

15   Morton adjusted his glasses. He was very pale. "This is ridiculous," he said unevenly. "I must ask you . . . ."

16   "Oh, yeah?" said the man. He stood with his legs spread apart, rocking a little, looking at Morton with utter scorn. "You and who else?"

17   For a moment the two men looked at each other nakedly. Then Morton turned his back on the man and said quietly, "Come on, let's get out of here." He walked awkwardly, almost limping with self-consciousness, to the sandbox. He stooped and lifted Larry and his shovel out.

18   At once Larry came to life; his face lost its rapt expression and he began to kick and cry. "I don't *want* to go home, I want to play better, I don't *want* any supper, I don't *like* supper. . . ." It became a chant as they walked, pulling their child between them, his feet dragging on the ground. In order to get to the exit gate they had to pass the bench where the man sat sprawling again. She was careful not to look at him. With all the dignity she could summon, she pulled Larry's sandy, perspiring little hand, while Morton pulled the other. Slowly and with head high she walked with her husband and child out of the playground.

19   Her first feelings was (*sic*) one of relief that a fight had been avoided, that no one was hurt. Yet beneath it there was a layer of something else, something heavy and inescapable. She sensed that it was more than just an unpleasant incident, more than defeat of reason by force. She felt dimly it had something to do with her and Morton, something acutely personal, familiar, and important.

20   Suddenly Morton spoke. "It wouldn't have proved anything." "What?" she asked.

21   "A fight. It wouldn't have proved anything beyond the fact that he's bigger than I am."

22   "Of course," she said.

23   "The only possible outcome," he continued reasonably, "would have been—what? My glasses broken, perhaps a tooth or two replaced, a couple of days' work missed—and for what? For justice? For truth?"

24   "Of course," she repeated. She quickened her step. She wanted only to get home and to busy herself with her familiar tasks; perhaps then the feeling, glued like heavy plaster on her heart, would be gone. *Of all the stupid, despicable bullies,* she thought, pulling harder on Larry's hand. The child was still crying. Always before she had felt a tender pity for his defenseless little body, the frail arms, the narrow shoulders with sharp, winglike shoulder blades, the thin and unsure legs, but now her mouth tightened in resentment.

25   "Stop crying," she said sharply. "I'm ashamed of you!" She felt as if all three of them were tracking mud along the street. The child cried louder.

26   *If there had been an issue involved*, she thought, *if there had been something to fight for. . . . But what else could he possibly have done? Allow himself to be beaten? Attempt to educate the man? Call a policeman? "Officer, there's a man in the park who won't stop his child from throwing sand on mine. . . ."* The whole thing was as silly as that, and not worth thinking about.

27   "Can't you keep him quiet, for Pete's sake?" Morton asked irritably.

28   "What do you suppose I've been trying to do?" she said.

29   Larry pulled back, dragging his feet.

30   "If you can't discipline this child, I will," Morton snapped, making a move toward the boy.

31   But her voice stopped him. She was shocked to hear it, thin and cold and penetrating with contempt. "Indeed?" she heard herself say. "You and who else?"

(Kaufman, Bel. "Sunday in the Park," as printed in The Available Press/PEN Short Story Collection, Ballantine, 1985.)

1. **Comprehension Check**

_____ 1) Choose the statement which best expresses the main idea of the story.
   a. It doesn't pay to fight with people who are bigger and stronger than you.
   b. Husbands disappoint their wives.
   c. Life is not always the way it seems.
   d. Children cause problems for parents.

_____ 2) At the end of the story the wife was angry because
   a. her son was crying.
   b. her husband did not stand up to the man who threatened him.
   c. her son had sand thrown in his hair.
   d. she had to prepare supper when she got home.

_____ 3) Morton probably did not want to fight with the man who threatened him because
   a. he was afraid his glasses would get broken.
   b. the man was bigger than he.
   c. he thought the man was right.
   d. he didn't want his son to see him fight.

_____ 4) You can conclude from this story that the wife and husband
   a. probably fight all the time.
   b. have only been married a few months.
   c. visit the park every Sunday.
   d. have some problems in their marriage they have not discussed.

2.   **Topics for Writers**

1) Describe a time you tried to use reason to settle a dispute. Were you successful?

2) In what situations do you think the use of brawn (physical strength) is more appropriate than the use of intellect (reason)?

3) Write about a time when you realized that life is not a "Sunday in the park."

4) What reasons do you think Morton might have had for acting as he did?

5) *If you are a female*, how would you feel if your husband or boyfriend acted as Morton did? *If you are a male*, what would you do in a situation as described in this story?

6) Suppose Morton had decided to fight for his rights. Write a narration based on how you think it would have turned out.

HARVEST BOUND
Ramón "Tianguis" Pérez

If you could pack your suitcase and move anywhere you want, where would you go? How do you think you would feel when you arrived there?

The following excerpt is from the diary of an illegal immigrant who earns money as a migrant farm worker.

1   On days when there is work, I talk to the other guys. Some of them tell me that the harvest season is coming in northern California, and they say that one can earn good money there. Things haven't gone so badly in the car wash, but one afternoon I give the manager my thanks for having hired and promoted me, and with a little suitcase that night I board a Greyhound headed north. My ticket is made out for San Francisco, but I don't plan to go that far. I plan to ride until I find a place where people are harvesting, and to get off the bus there.

2   I sleep on the bus for a few hours that night, and in the morning, when I awake, I don't know where we are. I get up from my seat and walk down the bus aisle, looking for a Mexican or Chicano to tell me our location, but oddly enough, I don't see any among the passengers, who are all white-skinned. I pay attention to the road signs we pass, but they are not of much help. I can read the town names, but I don't know where the towns lie. A map would help me, and I decide to buy one at our next stop. Lots of things are for sale at the bus stop's gift shop, but there are no maps. I direct myself towards the shop's operator, but I run into the language barrier. The operator is an Anglo, and when I speak to him in Spanish, he says that he doesn't understand. I try to practice my very precarious English with

Migrant Workers in Field

him, but it's of no use. I have a rough idea of the sound of the words that I want to say, but I can't pronounce them right. I make signs, signaling a big piece of paper and say "from California," but he turns into a question mark, with eyes wide open, arms raised and hands extended. "Map," I say, but I don't pronounce the word very well. "Freeways, streets," I add, but he still doesn't understand. He points out chewing gum, candies, pieces of cake, sandwiches, soft drinks, and cigarettes, trying to guess what I'm asking for. But he doesn't show me any maps. Finally, I back out of the store, and as I leave I hear him say, "I'm sorry."

3   A little before the bus leaves, I run into a Mexican-American in a hallway and I immediately ask him to help me find a map of California. We go back to the store. The Chicano asks for a map. "Ahh! Ahaaa!" the operator exclaims. Then he goes to a corner of his shelves and takes out what I'd been asking for. While I am paying him, he talks to the Chicano in a joyful tone. With the map in my hands, I give the Chicano my thanks, and he explains that the store-keeper thought that I was asking if he needed anybody to clean the floor or "mop."

(Pérez, Ramón "Tianguis". *Diary of an Undocumented Immigrant*,
Texas: Arte Publico Press, 1991, pp. 178–179.)

1.   Comprehension Check

_____ 1) The writer decided to leave his job and go to northern California because
    a. his boss didn't like him.
    b. things were going badly in the car wash.
    c. he thought he could earn more money.
    d. there wasn't always work.

_____ 2) The writer wanted a map because
    a. he was lost.
    b. he couldn't read the road signs.
    c. he wanted to know where he was in relation to the entire trip.
    d. he wanted to find his way back to the car wash.

_____ 3) You can infer that
    a. the owner of the shop did not want to sell the writer a map.
    b. the writer was fired from the car wash.
    c. the writer is a migrant worker.
    d. the writer was traveling with a friend who could speak English.

2.   **Topics for Writers**

1) Do you think it is important for immigrants living in the United States to learn English? Why?

2) Write about a time you had difficulty communicating with someone who did not speak your language.

NO SPEAK ENGLISH
Sandra Cisneros

Have you ever been in a situation where you felt you did not belong? Describe the situation and how you dealt with it.

In "Harvest Bound" you read about a man who tried to communicate in English, a language he did not know very well. In this story you will read about a woman who also does not know English very well. How is this woman different than the man in the previous story?

1   Mamacita is the big mama of the man across the street, third-floor front. Rachel says her name ought to be *Mamasota*, but I think that's mean.

2   The man saved his money to bring her here. He saved and saved because she was alone with the baby boy in that country. He worked two jobs. He came home late and he left early. Every day.

3   Then one day Mamacita and the baby boy arrived in a yellow taxi. The taxi door opened like a waiter's arm. Out stepped a tiny pink shoe, a foot soft as a rabbit's ear, then the thick ankle, a flutter of hips, fuchsia roses and green perfume. The man had to pull her, the taxicab driver had to push. Push, pull. Push, pull. Poof!

4   All at once she bloomed. Huge, enormous, beautiful to look at, from the salmon-pink feather on the tip of her hat down to the little rosebuds of her toes. I couldn't take my eyes off her tiny shoes.

5   Up, up, up the stairs she went with the baby boy in a blue blanket, the man carrying her suitcases, her lavender hatboxes, a dozen boxes of satin high heels. Then we didn't see her.

6   Somebody said because she's too fat, somebody because of the three flights of stairs, but I believe she doesn't come out because she is afraid to speak English, and maybe this is so since she only knows eight words. She knows to say: *He not here* for when the landlord comes, *No speak English* if anybody else comes, and *Holy smokes*. I don't know where she learned this, but I heard her say it one time and it surprised me.

7   My father says when he came to this country he ate hamandeggs for three months. Breakfast, lunch and dinner. Hamandeggs. That was the only word he knew. He doesn't eat hamandeggs anymore.

8   Whatever her reasons, whether she is fat, or can't climb the stairs, or is afraid of English, she won't come down. She sits all day by the window and plays the Spanish radio show and sings all the homesick songs about her country in a voice that sounds like a seagull.

9   Home. Home. Home is a house in a photograph, a pink house, pink as hollyhocks with lots of startled light. The man paints the walls of the apartment pink, but it's not the same you know. She still sighs for her pink house, and then I think she cries. I would.

10   Sometimes the man gets disgusted. He starts screaming and you can hear it all the way down the street.

11   Ay, she says, she is sad.

12   Oh, he says, not again.

13   Cuándo, cuándo, cuándo? she asks.

14   ¡Ay, Caray! We *are* home. This *is* home. Here I am and here I stay. Speak English. Speak English. Christ!

15   ¡Ay! Mamacita, who does not belong, every once in a while lets out a cry, hysterical, high, as if he had torn the only skinny thread that kept her alive, the only road out to that country.

16   And then to break her heart forever, the baby boy who has begun to talk, starts to sing the Pepsi commercial he heard on T.V.

17   No speak English, she says to the child who is singing in the language that sounds like tin. No speak English, no speak English, and bubbles into tears. No, no, no as if she can't believe her ears.

(Cisneros, Sandra. *The House on Mango Street*, Vintage Books, 1989, pp. 76–78.)

1.   Comprehension Check

_____ 1) The main idea of this story is
   a. the woman didn't leave her apartment because she was self-conscious about her weight.
   b. the man wanted his wife to live with him in this country.
   c. children of immigrant parents in the United States want to learn English.
   d. it is difficult to adjust to a new culture.

_____ 2) You can infer that Mamacita's husband painted the walls of the apartment pink because
   a. it was Mamacita's favorite color.
   b. so she wouldn't feel so homesick.
   c. her son wanted that color.
   d. Mamacita saw it in a photograph.

_____ 3) You can infer that Mamacita did not want her son to speak English because
   a. she thought English was an ugly language.
   b. she could not understand what he was saying.
   c. he had difficulty learning it.
   d. she did not want him to assimilate into the new culture.

_____ 4) Mamacita does not come out of her apartment for all the following reasons *except*
   a. she is too fat.
   b. she is afraid to speak English.
   c. she does not have any friends.
   d. she cannot climb the three flights of stairs.

2. **Topics for Writers**

   1) Have you ever been homesick? Write about how you felt and what you did to make yourself feel less homesick.

   2) Describe Mamacita's appearance. What does that tell you about her as a person?

The Correct English Handbook

To be a good writer, you need to write clear and correct sentences. You can develop this ability by learning the basics of standard English—grammar, punctuation, capitalization, and usage. In this handbook we provide explanations, examples, and practice exercises in these important aspects of English.

This handbook is designed to be a workbook and a handy reference for correct English. To use it as a workbook, you may study the material and write your answers to the practice exercises. Also, you may refer to a particular section when you want to check any aspect of the standards of English. You will find this material particularly helpful during the proofreading stage.

Grammar instruction (Sections 1 through 9) is arranged sequentially to help you master the basics before moving on to more complex structures. The remainder of this handbook deals with the mechanics of writing and word usage. In Section 14 you will find a checklist to help guide you through the sentence proofreading process. Here is what you will find in this handbook:

- Types of words (parts of speech) that make up a sentence (Section 1)
- Sentence relationships and agreement (Sections 2 and 3)
- Complex pronoun structures (Section 4)
- Sentence voice (Section 5)
- Types of phrases (Section 6)
- Types of clauses (Section 7)
- Avoiding common problems with sentences (Section 8)
- Parallel structures (Section 9)
- Punctuation (Section 10)
- Capitalization (Section 11)
- Spelling (Section 12)
- Usage (Section 13)
- Proofreading sentences (Section 14)

[1] Parts of Speech

Parts of Speech

There are eight parts of speech in English:

Parts of Speech

- Noun
- Pronoun
- Adjective
- Verb
- Adverb
- Preposition
- Conjunction
- Interjection

Knowing the parts of speech will help you understand the function of each word in a sentence. Also, the parts of speech give you the basic knowledge you need to combine words to form richer and more descriptive sentences.

[1a] Nouns

Nouns name a person (for example, *man* or *John*), place (for example, *city* or *New York City*), object (for example, *desk*), or idea (for example, *justice*). Nouns are important because they tell you *who* and *what* you are reading or writing about. They may be general topics or specific terms, concrete or abstract. **Concrete nouns** can be seen or touched (for example, *book*). **Abstract nouns** cannot be seen or experienced directly (for example, *science*). A **proper noun** is the actual name of someone or something. The following table contains some examples of nouns.

Types of Nouns

Abstract	Concrete	Proper
motivation	building	Chrysler Building
life	country	America
peace	student	John Smith
communication	telephone	Bell Atlantic
justice	lawyer	Miss Jones
science	planet	Earth
health	pill	Tylenol

PRACTICE EXERCISE 1: IDENTIFYING NOUNS

Underline all the nouns in each of the following sentences.

1. Martin Luther King fought for justice for every person in America.

2. Free speech must be communicated through a free press.

3. Unless an audience can be assembled, speakers might as well keep silent.

4. Elections have little meaning when candidates cannot express their opinions without fear of punishment.

5. Our meeting was held in the Sears Building in Chicago.

6. Freedom of religion is guaranteed by two clauses in the First Amendment.

[1b] Pronouns

A pronoun is a word that takes the place of a noun. There are several categories of pronouns. Since the following categories are based on the way a pronoun is used in a sentence, some pronouns will appear in more than one category.

- **Personal pronouns** refer to people (*I, you, he, she, it, me, him, we, they, us*, and *them*).

- **Possessive pronouns** show ownership (*my, mine, your, yours, his, her, hers*, and *its*). For example:

  My duty is done.
  His work is finished.
  That book is *hers*.

- **Indefinite pronouns** (*someone, everyone, all, many, each*, etc.) refer to indefinite individuals or groups. They are used when we are not specific about the noun to which we refer, and they are pronouns only when used in place of nouns (see Sections 3c and 4).

- **Relative pronouns** (*that, which, whichever, who, whose, whoever, whom*, and *whomever*) introduce a group of words that give more specific information about a noun in the sentence (see Section 7b, Dependent Clauses). For example:

  The book *that* my teacher gave me is on the table.
  The man *whom* I admire will be our guest speaker.
  Mt. Everest, *which* I climbed, is one of the highest mountains in the world.

- **Interrogative pronouns** (*who, whom, whose, what*, and *which*) are used to ask questions. For example:

  Who wrote the poem?
  What did you say about my mother?
  Which course is your favorite?

  With one exception (*what*), the interrogative pronouns we have listed can also be used as relative pronouns.

- **Demonstrative pronouns** point out other nouns (*this, these, that*, and *those*). For example:

  This is my best friend.
  Come here and try one of *these*.
  That is my first choice.

  The pronoun *that* can also be used as a relative pronoun.

- **Reflexive pronouns** refer to oneself or others (*myself, himself, yourself, itself*, etc.). They are formed by adding -*self* to the end of a possessive pronoun. For example:

I choose *myself* for the position.
My teacher is not *himself* today.

A complete list of pronouns follows.

Pronouns

Personal	Possessive and Reflexive (-self)	
I, me	my, mine, myself	
you	your, yours, yourself	
he, she, him, her, it	his, hers, its, himself herself, itself	
we, us	our, ours, ourselves	
they, them	their, theirs, themselves	

Relative	Interrogative	Demonstrative
who, whose, whoever, whom, whomever	who, whom, whose	this, these, those
which, whichever	which	
that	that	that

Indefinite
anyone, anybody, someone, somebody, everyone, everybody, no one, one, other, each other, another, either, neither, both, many, few, several, others, all, some, most, much, none, any

Pronoun Antecedents. All pronouns refer to nouns. The noun for which a pronoun stands is called its *antecedent*. The antecedent may be stated in the same sentence as the pronoun. For example:

John informed *his* teacher that *he* would be late.

Both pronouns *his* and *he* refer to John, which is the antecedent. The antecedent also may appear in a different sentence than the pronoun, often a previous sentence. For example:

John was caught in traffic. *He* called his teacher from *his* cellular phone to report that *he* would be late.

All of the pronouns in the second sentence refer to John, the antecedent.

Some pronouns may be used as another part of speech. For example, in the sentence, "*Some* books are good to read," *some* is used to describe the books. To be a pronoun, the word must replace the noun—as in "*Some* are good to read."

The use of pronouns is discussed more thoroughly in Sections 3c, Singular and Plural Pronouns, and Section 4, Using Pronouns Properly.

PRACTICE EXERCISE 2: RECOGNIZING PRONOUNS AND THEIR ANTECEDENTS

Underline the pronoun in each sentence. Then, write the antecedent for the pronoun on the line.

1. _____ John was out of control after he began the diet.

2. _____ The people are the most important part of our democracy.

3. _____ Even though they try their best, some students need extra help.

4. _____ The play was a great success. I really enjoyed it.

5. _____ Lawyers often become judges. Being a judge is considered a promotion for them.

[1c] Adjectives

Adjectives are used to describe or modify a noun or pronoun. To *modify* means to *change* in some way. Adjectives are important because they clarify our understanding of nouns and pronouns.

Adjectives may answer three types of questions: (1) What kind? (2) Which one? and (3) How much or how many?

Adjectives

What Kind?	Which One?	How Much or How Many?
large	this	two
happy	these	few
smart	that	several
blue	those	no

America is a proper noun (see Section 1a). With small changes in the word endings, most proper nouns may also be converted into adjectives (called *proper adjectives*), for example, *American* citizen. *American* is an adjective because it answers the question, "What kind of citizen?" Since proper adjectives are formed from proper nouns, they are also capitalized. For example:

Proper Nouns	Proper Adjectives
Russia	Russian capital
Queen Elizabeth	Elizabethan literature
Europe	European countries

Adjectives may also be used to compare and contrast. The **comparative form** of an adjective is used when two things are being compared. This form is created by placing the letters *-er* at the end of the adjective. Another way to create a comparative is to place the word *more* before the adjective. For example:

Comparative Forms

John is *smarter* than his brother.
He feels *more important* than his sister.

When something is being compared to more than two other things, the **superlative form** is used. You can create the superlative form by placing the letters *-est* at the end of the adjective. Also, you can put the word *most* before an adjective. As a rule, you use the words *more* and *most* with adjectives of more than two syllables.

Superlative Forms

Ted is the *smartest* student in the class.
He thinks that he is the *most important* person at school.

Following are some examples of comparison forms of adjectives:

Adjective Comparisons

Adjective	Comparative Form	Superlative Form
smart	smarter	smartest
tall	taller	tallest
happy	happier	happiest
sad	sadder	saddest
important	more important	most important
ignorant	more ignorant	most ignorant

Some adjectives have irregular comparison forms. For example:

Irregular Comparison Forms

Adjective	Comparative Form	Superlative Form
good	better	best
bad	worse	worst
many	more	most
little	less	least

PRACTICE EXERCISE 3: ADJECTIVES

Underline the adjectives in the sentences below.

1. The Constitution of the United States is our most important document; however, it still contains serious flaws.

2. The idea of individual rights is the oldest and most traditional of American values.

3. Despite harsher laws, average people today are no safer from violent crime than before.

4. A religious person in a free country can hold any belief.

5. With beautiful mountains with green trees, America is a great land where poor and wealthy people live together without governmental interference.

[1d] Verbs

Verbs can seem quite complicated. However, if you understand the aspects of verbs that we introduce here, you will be able to handle this important part of every sentence.

A verb shows action or states that someone or something exists. There are two kinds of verbs—action and linking. **Action verbs**, like *jump*, *write*, and *think*, show some type of action. **Linking verbs** show existence (being) and include all forms of the word *be*. In addition, some other verbs may be used as linking verbs.

Some action verbs are listed below:

Action Verbs

jump	think	watch
listen	look	play
read	study	hit
write	walk	feel

The linking verbs are listed below:

Linking Verbs

Forms of the Verb *Be* (shows proper use of pronouns)		Other Linking Verbs
(I) am	would be	appear
(he, she, it) is	might be	look
(you, we, they) are	can be	become
(I, he, she, it) was	could be	seem
(you, we) were	has been	taste
be	have been	feel
being	might have been	smell

Forms of the Verb *Be* (*continued*)		**Other Linking Verbs** (*continued*)
been	would have been	sound
shall be	could have been	remain
should be	should have been	stay
will be		

Verbs are often accompanied by **helping verbs**, which come before the main verb. The most commonly used helping verbs are forms of *be* and *have*, as in the sentence, "New York City *is growing* at a fast pace." The main verb, *growing,* is accompanied by the helping verb, *is.* Here is a list of commonly used helping verbs:

Helping Verbs

be (is, are, was, etc.)	shall
have (has, had)	will
do (did, does)	can
must	may
might	could

Verb Forms. Every verb has four forms that can be used in various ways in sentences. The correct use of verbs involves understanding the principal parts and how to use them. The four **principal parts of verbs** are present, present participle, past, and past participle.

- The **present** is the basic verb form (for example, *jump*).
- The **present participle** is always formed by adding *-ing* to a verb (for example, *jumping*).
- The **past** is usually formed by adding *-ed* or *-d* to the end of a verb (for example, *jumped*). However, many verbs do not follow this rule. Exceptions to this rule are called *irregular verbs* (for example, *ran* is the past tense of *run*).
- The **past participle** is always used with a form of the helping verb *have* (*has* and *had*). For regular verbs, the past participle is the same as the past. For example:

My teacher *has helped* me with my homework.

Following are some examples of the principal parts of regular verbs:

Principal Parts of Regular Verbs

Present	Present Participle	Past	Past Participle
help	helping	helped	(have or had) helped
murder	murdering	murdered	(have or had) murdered
play	playing	played	(have or had) played
discuss	discussing	discussed	(have or had) discussed

The past participles of irregular verbs are formed in a different way than regular verbs. For example, the past participle of *write* is *written*:

John *has written* three essays in this class.

Following are some examples of irregular verbs. Mistakes often arise in the use of past and past participle forms of some verbs because of irregularities. Studying this list will help you avoid mistakes. In addition, you should practice using irregular verbs in sentences.

Principal Parts of Irregular Verbs

Present	Past	Past Participle
be (am, is, are)	was, were	been
begin	began	begun
break	broke	broken
bring	brought	brought
choose	chose	chosen
do	did	done
drink	drank	drunk
eat	ate	eaten
fall	fell	fallen
forget	forgot	forgotten
give	gave	gotten
go	went	gone
have, has	had	had
hurt	hurt	hurt
know	knew	known
lay	laid	laid
lead	led	led
lie	lay	lain
meet	met	met
pay	paid	paid
quit	quit	quit
raise	raised	raised
rise	rose	risen
ride	rode	ridden
run	ran	run
see	saw	seen
set	set	set
shine	shone	shone
sing	sang	sung
sit	sat	sat

speak	spoke	spoken
steal	stole	stolen
swim	swam	swum
take	took	taken
throw	threw	thrown
write	wrote	written

PRACTICE EXERCISE 4: PRINCIPAL PARTS OF IRREGULAR VERBS

Write three sentences (one for each principal part in the previous list) for each of the following irregular verbs. The following suggestion will help you with this exercise. For the present form, start your sentence with the words, right now. *For the past form, begin your sentence with* yesterday. *For the past participle form, start with* many times. *For example:*

Right now, I *begin* my day with a nice breakfast.
Yesterday, I *began* my day with a nice breakfast.
Many times, I have *begun* my day with a nice breakfast.

bring

Right now, _____.

Yesterday, _____.

Many times, _____.

choose

Right now, _____.

Yesterday, _____.

Many times, _____.

eat

Right now, _____.

Yesterday, _____.

Many times, _____.

forget

Right now, _____.

Yesterday, _____.

Many times, _____.

go

Right now, _____ .

Yesterday, _____ .

Many times, _____ .

know

Right now, _____ .

Yesterday, _____ .

Many times, _____ .

speak

Right now, _____ .

Yesterday, _____ .

Many times, _____ .

steal

Right now, _____ .

Yesterday, _____ .

Many times, _____ .

write

Right now, _____ .

Yesterday, _____ .

Many times, _____ .

Verb Tenses. Verbs, whether action or linking, indicate the time in which something takes place. Verbs express time through verb tense. The verb tenses are simple, perfect, progressive, or perfect progressive. In each of these categories, action may take place in the past, present, or future. Based on these combinations, there are twelve verb tenses. In this section, we will describe and show examples of each of the verb tenses. All are formed by using the four principal parts of verbs.

Simple Verb Tenses. The simple verb tenses are present, past, and future. Present tense is often used in topic sentences because it shows action in a general way. For example, "Higher education is the road to success," is a general statement in the present tense. The present and past forms of verbs are used to make simple tenses.

1. The **simple present tense** takes place in the present moment. For example:

   The lawyer *makes* the opening statement.
   Fathers *help* children to be successful.
   The student *studies* hard to pass the test.

2. The **simple past tense** refers to action or a state of being that is already completed. For example:

   The lawyer *made* the opening statement.
   Fathers *helped* their children to be successful.
   The student *studied* earlier in the day.

3. The **simple future tense** makes a statement about something that will be completed in the future. Future tenses can usually be made by adding the helping verb *will* to the present tense of a main verb. For example:

   The lawyer *will make* the opening statement.
   Fathers *will help* their children to be successful.

Perfect Verb Tenses. Perfect tenses show action or being that occurs over a period of time in the present, past, or future. Perfect tenses use the past participle form of the main verb along with a form of the helping verb *have* (*has, had, will have*).

1. The **present perfect tense** states an action that has been going on but is now completed. It uses the *present* tense of the helping verb *have*. For example:

   The lawyer *has made* the opening statement and is ready to proceed.
   Many times, fathers *have helped* their children.
   The student *has studied* long enough.

2. The **past perfect tense** states an action that started in the past and, after a period of time, ended in the past. It uses the *past* tense of the verb *have*. For example:

   The lawyer *had made* the opening statement while I was outside the courtroom.
   Many people became successful because their fathers *had helped* them when they were children.
   The student *had studied* all day yesterday.

3. The **future perfect tense** states an action that has started and will be completed some time in the future. Use the helping verb *will* in addition to *have*.

   The lawyer *will have made* the opening statement by the time I get home.
   The fathers *will have helped* their children to be successful by the time they become adults.
   By midnight, the student *will have studied* long enough to pass the test.

Progressive Verb Tenses. Progressive tenses show action or being that continues in the present, past, or future. They use the present participle (*-ing*) form of a main verb along with a form of the verb *be* as a helping verb.

1. The **present progressive tense** gives an action that is still going on at the present moment. It uses the *present* tense of *be* plus the present participle of the verb. For example:

   The lawyer *is making* the opening statement at this time.
   As we speak, the fathers *are helping* their children.
   The student *is studying* right now.

2. The **past progressive tense** states an action that started in the past but was uncompleted at that time. It uses the *past* tense of *be* plus the present participle of the verb. For example:

   The lawyer *was making* the opening statement when I arrived.
   The fathers *were helping* their children. We hope they will continue.
   The student *was studying* for a test.

3. The **future progressive tense** states an action that will continue for a period of time in the future. It uses the helping verb *will* along with the helping verb *be* and the present participle of the verb. For example:

   Soon, the lawyer *will be making* the opening statement.
   Some day, all fathers *will be helping* their children to be successful.
   The student *will be studying* all day today.

Perfect-Progressive Verb Tenses. These tenses are a combination of perfect and progressive forms. They indicate action that continues for a longer time than the perfect tenses alone. However, the action is limited to a period of time in the present, past, or future. Perfect-progressive tenses have three parts: (1) a form of the helping verb *have* (*have, has,* or *had*), a form of the verb *be* (*been*), and the present participle form of a main verb (*-ing*):

1. The **present perfect-progressive tense** describes an action that has been continuing for a long period of time. It uses the present forms of *have* and *been* and the present participle of the verb. For example:

   The lawyer *has been making* the opening statement for over an hour.
   For a long time, the fathers *have been helping* their children.
   The student *has been studying* for most of the day.

2. The **past perfect-progressive tense** states an action that started in the past, had continued for a period of time, and was completed. Use two helping verbs, *had* and *been*, before the main verb in the progressive form, *-ing*. For example:

The lawyer *had been making* the opening statement. When I arrived, he was
  finished.
The fathers *had been helping* their children. We hope they will do it again
  next week.
The student *had been studying* all day yesterday.

3. The **future perfect-progressive tense** states an action that started and will
   continue for a long time into the future. This form uses three helping verbs,
   will have been, before the main verb with the *-ing* ending. For example:

   If his energy continues, the lawyer *will have been making* the opening state
     ment for the entire day.
   If they continue, the fathers *will have been helping* their children longer than
     they ever have before.
   By midnight, the student *will have been studying* for the entire day.

PRACTICE EXERCISE 5: USING VERB TENSES

*Write one sentence for each verb tense using the suggested verb form. Then, write a
second sentence in the same verb tense using any verb of your choice.*

1. **Present**
   (drink) _____
   (any verb) _____

2. **Past**
   (broke) _____
   (any verb) _____

3. **Future**
   (will eat) _____
   (any verb) _____

4. **Present Perfect**
   (has seen) _____
   (any verb) _____

5. **Past Perfect**
   (had sung) _____
   (any verb) _____

6. **Future Perfect**
   (will have ridden) _____

(any verb) _____

7. **Present Progressive**

(is forgetting) _____

(any verb) _____

8. **Past Progressive**

(was quitting) _____

(any verb) _____

9. **Future Progressive**

(will be helping) _____

(any verb) _____

10. **Present Perfect Progressive**

(has been stealing) _____

(any verb) _____

11. **Past Perfect Progressive**

(had been discussing) _____

(any verb) _____

12. **Future Perfect Progressive**

(will have been writing) _____

(any verb) _____

[1e] Adverbs

Like adjectives, adverbs are used to describe or modify. Adverbs usually modify verbs; however, they may also modify adjectives or even another adverb. Adverbs are often formed by adding *-ly* to the end of adjectives. Here are some examples of adverbs and the types of words they may modify:

Adverbs

Modify Verbs	**Modify Adjectives**	**Modify Adverbs**
ran *quickly*	*very* good show	*more* quickly
write *daily*	*hardly* visible	*most* haphazardly
turned *left*	*especially* beautiful	*very* rarely
never fail	*extremely* talented	*not* very well
will *not* be	*usually* happy	*quite* logically

Adverbs answer these questions:

- Where? (*there, here, up*)
- When? (*hourly, then, next*)
- How? (*carefully, quickly*)
- To what extent? (How much or how long?) (*all, never, hardly*)

Following are some examples of adverbs used in sentences with the question given after each.

Adverbs in Context	**Questions That Adverbs Answer**
The judge arrived *early*.	(*When* did the judge arrive?)
The suspect fell *down*.	(*Where* did the suspect fall?)
The man drove *wildly* down the street.	(*How* did the man drive?)
John was *barely* upset.	(*To what extent* was John upset?)

PRACTICE EXERCISE 6: RECOGNIZING ADVERBS

Underline the adverbs in these sentences.

1. Food travels down the esophagus on its way to the stomach.

2. He studied extremely hard for the exam.

3. Yesterday, John wrote his best paper.

4. You should be very happy about your grade.

5. I was especially grateful for your advice.

6. John wrote the paper too quickly.

7. Extreme motivation is required to read and write effectively.

8. The judge quickly decided the case.

9. The emotional trauma has never subsided.

10. Down went the pill that I swallowed.

[1f] Prepositions

Prepositions show relationships between a noun or pronoun and some other word in the sentence. The following examples show various relationships between a man and a tree.

Prepositions Showing Relationships

The man was standing *under* the tree.
The man was standing *on* the tree.
The man was standing *near* the tree.

The following is a list of commonly used prepositions:

Prepositions

about	behind	from	since
above	below	in	through
across	beside	into	to
after	between	like	toward
against	beyond	near	under
along	by	of	until
among	down	off	up
around	during	on	with
at	except	over	within
before	for	past	without

Prepositions appear in groups of words called *prepositional phrases*. For more about prepositions and how they are used in sentences, see Section 6.

PRACTICE EXERCISE 7: RECOGNIZING PREPOSITIONS

Underline the prepositions in these sentences.

1. At the end of the semester, most students are highly motivated.

2. During the trial the lawyer spoke about the case with great passion.

3. Without enough water the food will not pass comfortably through your intestines.

4. For a small charge you can hire a private tutor for help in your courses.

5. The class will be held across the street from the college for one week while the building is under construction.

[1g] Conjunctions

Conjunctions are used to join or connect words or groups of words in a sentence. This section will help you recognize conjunctions. Later, we will show you how they are used to create different types of sentences (Section 7, p. 387).

There are four types of conjunctions:

1. **Coordinating conjunctions** (*and, or, but, yet, so,* and *for*). Coordinating conjunctions are used to join two or more words, groups of words, or sentences. For example:

Joining Words

The man bought *and* fixed the car.
John *or* Mary will come to help.
He liked the tall *yet* thin woman best.

Joining Groups of Words

He went across the room *and* through the kitchen.
Dieting *but* not eating an adequate amount of food is very dangerous.

Joining Sentences

The man was arrested, *but* he was innocent.
John was arrested, *so* he had to hire a lawyer.

2. **Conjunctive adverbs.** Conjunctive adverbs are used to connect related sentences. The following adverbs can serve as conjunctions: *however, therefore, consequently, nevertheless, meanwhile, rather, as a result, on the contrary,* and *similarly.* For example:

The Constitution is for all of the people; *however,* some people still feel left out.

3. **Correlative conjunctions** (*either/or, neither/nor, not only/but also*). Correlative conjunctions are used in pairs to make compound forms. For example:

You can have *either* a cat *or* a dog for a pet.

4. **Subordinating conjunctions** (*because, if, although, since, while*). Subordinating conjunctions are used to join parts of a sentence. For example:

Because he passed the final exam, the student celebrated.
The lawyer was paid in full *although* he lost the case.

PRACTICE EXERCISE 8: RECOGNIZING CONJUNCTIONS

Underline the conjunctions in these sentences.

1. John and his friend led the fight to locate and analyze the evidence.

2. The student passed the midterm and the final; consequently, he passed the course.

3. Either you get motivated to succeed or you will fail.

Copyright © 2000 Addison-Wesley Educational Publishers Inc.

4. If you work hard, you will achieve your goals.

5. You ate the whole meal, but you did not drink enough liquids.

[1h] Interjections

Interjections are used to express strong emotion or exclamation. They are often set off from the rest of the sentence with a comma. But sometimes an interjection is a one-word sentence. In this case it is set off by an exclamation point (!). For example:

Oh, I had a hard day.
Well, I am really tired!
Wow! I really passed that test.
Shucks! Someone took my umbrella, and it is raining.

PRACTICE EXERCISE 9: RECOGNIZING INTERJECTIONS

Underline the interjections in these sentences.

1. Oh, I can't carry so many books to class.

2. Boy, this assignment is really difficult.

3. Rats! The police are right behind us.

4. My, we better hurry or we will be late.

5. It is snowing in July. Crazy!

[1i] Multiple Parts of Speech

Many words can be used as more than one part of speech, depending on how they are used in the sentence. Take, for example, the word *play*.

The *play* was really entertaining. (noun)
The boys *play* very hard. (verb)

Another example is the word *handle*.

The *handle* on the suitcase is broken. (noun)
John will *handle* my case. (verb)

You can check in a dictionary for part of speech whenever you are unsure about how to use a word properly in a sentence.

PRACTICE EXERCISE 10: RECOGNIZING MULTIPLE PARTS OF SPEECH

Each italicized word can be used as more than one part of speech depending on how it is used in each sentence. On the line before each sentence, write the part of speech of the italicized word.

1. _____ The baseball player scored a *run*.

2. _____ John will *run* in the marathon.

3. _____ After the fight I had a *sore* nose.

4. _____ I have a *sore* on my foot from wearing those tight shoes.

5. _____ The *pilot* flew the plane.

6. _____ The astronauts *pilot* the shuttle back to Earth.

The following table contains a summary of the eight parts of speech, their functions in a sentence, and some examples.

Summary Table: The Parts of Speech

Parts of Speech	Functions	Examples
Noun	Names a person, place, thing, or idea	*judge, John, city, New York, table, freedom*
Pronoun	Takes the place of (refers to) a noun	*I, me, mine, you, it, he, him, his, they, their, them, we, us, ours*
Adjective	Modifies a noun or pronoun	*red, happy, careful, reliable*
Verb	Shows action or state of being	*run, think, is, were, have*
Adverb	Modifies a verb, adjective, or adverb	*quickly, extremely, faster, not*
Preposition	Shows how a noun or pronoun and another part of the sentence are related	*in, on, over, with, to, of*
Conjunction	Joins words or groups of words	*and, or, but, because, however, although*
Interjection	Shows strong emotion	*wow, oh, well*

PRACTICE EXERCISE 11: REVIEWING PARTS OF SPEECH

Directly over each italicized word, write its part of speech as used in the sentence. Use the following abbreviations: N *(noun),* Pro *(pronoun),* Adj *(adjective),* V *(verb),* Adv *(adverb),* Prep *(preposition),* Conj *(conjunction), and* Inter *(interjection). For example:*

         Adj   V   N
The *conscientious* student *did* his *homework.*

1. Mary *felt* weak because *she* dieted for *too* long.

2. *Either* the student *or* the *teacher* left the briefcase *in* the desk.

3. *Yesterday*, we *stayed* at a *beautiful* but *expensive* hotel *on* the corner.

4. *Her* desk was *very far* from the *front* of the *room.*

5. *Great*! We *finally* won the writing *contest.*

6. The *Sahara Desert* has *very little* rainfall.

7. *Our* stomach *contracts* when we feel hungry.

8. *Who* wrote *that* book *about* losing weight *quickly*?

9. I must go to school *five* days *each* week.

10. *Goodness, everyone* has *been* reading *quietly* for over an *hour.*

[2] Sentence Components

Sent

A sentence is a group of words expressing a complete thought or idea. All sentences have two main parts. First, the **subject** names the person or thing that the sentence is about. Second, the **predicate**, which contains the verb, is the rest of the sentence and tells about the subject.

Usually, the predicate contains an additional element, called a **complement**, that completes the thought begun by the subject and verb. For example, "The student passed *the test*" or "Mr. Jones is *my teacher*."

The subject, verb, and complement are the basic parts of a sentence. Together, they make the *core* of the sentence. In fact, all sentences can be reduced to their core parts. The reader's job is to recognize the core parts, whereas the writer's job is to expand on the core parts. For example,

Core Parts of a Sentence

Subject	Verb	Complement
Boy	hit	ball
Student	wrote	paper
Judge	settled	case

The relationships between these core parts of a sentence will be discussed in this section.

[2a] Subjects

Subjects

The *judge* told the defendant to sit down.

The district *court* is in my hometown.

He took me to court.

The **simple subject** of a sentence is a noun or pronoun that tells you who or what the sentence is about. You can find the simple subject by asking *who* or *what* the sentence is about. If there is an action verb, the simple subject will answer the question, *Who or what does (did) the action?* For example, in the first sentence above, the *judge* is the simple subject of the sentence. Notice that the sentence contains an action verb, *told*. The simple subject will tell you who or what did the action (*judge told*). The second sentence is about the *court*. This sentence contains no action because it has a linking verb, *is*. Still, *court* is the simple subject because something is said about the court, that is, it *is in my hometown*. In the third example the simple subject is a pronoun, *he*.

The **complete subject** of a sentence includes the subject plus anything that describes the subject. In the second example above, *the district court* is the complete subject because *the district* describes the subject. Sometimes the simple subject and the complete subject are the same. In the third example above, *he* is the simple and complete subject because *he* did the action *took*.

PRACTICE EXERCISE 12: RECOGNIZING SUBJECTS

Circle the simple subjects and underline the complete subjects.

1. My best friend was elected to the highest office in the land.

2. The diet that I just completed did not work.

3. My lost sister has just called.

4. The Constitution of the United States contains some very elegant words.

5. Innocence of the heart was my best trait.

[2b] Predicates

The predicate is the part of the sentence that tells you something about the subject. The **simple predicate** is the *verb* (and any helping verbs). You can identify the predicate by asking, "What is the author telling about the subject?" For example, "The boy hit the ball over the fence" is made up of a subject (*boy*) and a simple predicate (*hit*).

The **complete predicate** includes any words or phrases that modify the verb or complete the thought begun by the verb. In the following examples, the simple subjects and simple predicates are in italics.

Complete Subjects	**Complete Predicates**
The *boy*	*hit* the ball over the fence.
The high-priced *lawyer*	*is making* the opening statement.
All good *fathers*	*will help* children to be good citizens.
The dangerous *criminal*	*will have thrown* away the gun.

As these examples show, all sentences can be divided into these two parts—complete subject and complete predicate.

Subjects usually come before predicates, but not always. Sometimes the predicate will appear before the subject. It is also possible for the subject to come in the middle of the predicate. For example:

Predicates before Subjects

(Predicate)   (Subject)
On the bench at the front of the room is the judge.

(Predicate)   (Subject)   (Predicate)
During the off season, many lawyers *take a vacation*.

In the first example, the complete predicate (*on the bench at the front of the room is*) comes before the subject (*the judge*). In the second example, the complete subject, *many lawyers*, interrupts the two parts of the predicate, *during the off season* and *take a vacation*.

PRACTICE EXERCISE 13: RECOGNIZING SUBJECTS AND PREDICATES

In the sentences below, underline the complete subjects once and underline the complete predicates twice. Also, circle the simple subjects (nouns and pronouns) and the simple predicates (verbs and helping verbs). For example:

The (book) (was submitted) to the publisher on time.

1. Schools occasionally deny students a diploma as punishment for misconduct.

2. The alleged offense was committed on school property.

3. A parent was notified, and a school official stayed with the student until the parent arrived.

4. Law enforcement authorities had questioned the student at his school.

5. You have the right to remain silent according to constitutional law.

6. He was highly motivated to attend the conference.

7. The dieting program on television is very expensive.

8. High-calorie food makes you fat.

9. The speech was given before an audience.

10. Yesterday afternoon, the lawyer pleaded my case before the jury.

[2c] Complements

A complement is the third core part of a sentence. It extends the thought started by the subject and verb. Although some verbs do not need complements—for example, "The wind blew strongly," most verbs need a complement to complete the thought begun by the verb. For example, "John bought" is a subject and a verb. However, it is not complete without a complement—for example, "John bought *the book*." There are two kinds of complements, *object* and *subject*.

Object Complements. Object complements are nouns or pronouns. Object complements show relationships with action verbs. There are two types of object complements, direct and indirect.

Direct objects receive the action of the verb or name the result of the action. Consider the following examples of direct objects:

Direct Objects
The policeman fired the *gun* in the air.
The judge removed the *lawyer* from the courtroom.
The professor made a new *test*.

Gun is the direct object of the first sentence because it receives the action of the verb *fired*. The *gun* is what the policeman fired. The direct object of the second sentence, *lawyer*, receives the action *removed*. *Test* is the direct object of the third sentence because it is the result of the action of the verb *made*.

Direct objects answer the questions *what?* or *who?* The policeman fired *what?* He fired the *gun*. The judge removed *whom?* The judge removed the *lawyer*. The professor made *what?* The professor made a *test*.

Sometimes sentences contain additional words that may describe object complements. If you keep in mind that the object itself is always a noun or pronoun, excess words will not be a problem when identifying objects.

Direct objects can be easily identified by using a simple procedure. First, identify the subject and verb. Then, to find the direct object, ask yourself *what* or *whom* directly after the subject and verb. The answer to this question will be the direct object. For example:

Subject   Verb
The *student wrote* a long and elegant argument about the rights of animals.
Student—wrote—*what?* The student wrote an *argument.*

Asking the question, "Student wrote *what?*" leads you to the direct object, *argument.*

PRACTICE EXERCISE 14: RECOGNIZING DIRECT OBJECTS

Underline the simple subjects once and the verbs twice. Put the direct objects into brackets. For example:

The lawyer has defended his [client] very well.

1. The dieter ate the raw vegetables for dinner.
2. The student left class early.
3. Scientists have discovered dinosaur bones under the rocks.
4. Concentration helps students to do better work.
5. Martin Luther King safely led the freedom marchers to Montgomery, Alabama.

Indirect objects come before the direct object and answer one of the following about the action of the verb:

- to whom or to what
- for whom or for what

Consider these examples of indirect objects:

Indirect Objects

Our government gave the *people* the right of free speech.
The congressman bought my *house* a new roof because the storm had destroyed the old roof.

People is the indirect object of the first sentence because it tells *to whom* our government gave the right of free speech. *The right of free speech* is the direct object because it answers the question, "Our government gave the people *what?*" In the second example, *house* is the indirect object. It tells *for what* the congressman bought the new roof. It precedes the direct object *roof.*

Similar to direct objects, indirect objects can be identified by a simple strategy. First, identify the subject, verb, and direct object. Then, ask yourself *to whom, to what, for whom,* or *for what.* For example:

Subject Verb   Direct object
The *boy tossed* me the *ball.*
boy—tossed—ball—*to whom?* The boy tossed *me* the ball.

The question *boy—tossed—ball—to whom?* leads directly to the indirect object *me.*
Indirect objects should not be confused with prepositional phrases, although they may serve the same function in a sentence. For example, compare the following pair of sentences.

My friend sent *me* a present for my birthday.
My friend sent a present *to me* for my birthday.

The meaning of these sentences is the same. However, the sentence components are different. In the first sentence *me* is the indirect object because it answers the question, *friend sent present to whom?* Although the second sentence contains the same word, *me,* notice that it is preceded by a preposition, *to.* Therefore, the group of words *to me* is not an indirect object but a prepositional phrase (see Section 6a).

PRACTICE EXERCISE 15: RECOGNIZING DIRECT AND INDIRECT OBJECTS

Underline the simple subjects once and the verbs twice. Put the direct and indirect objects into brackets and label them. (Not all the sentences have indirect objects.) For example:

S   V   IO   DO
Mary brought [me] the [medicine] to help me feel better.

1. John's friends gave him good advice.

2. The student gave her friends the answers to the test.

3. The speaker delivered the farewell address to the audience.

4. The neighbor felt deep emotion for my friend.

5. My boss sent me out of the country.

6. Mary completed her paper in time.

7. The teacher showed the students a map of the world.

8. The trainer threw the bird a piece of bread.

9. We drove the car to school in order to be on time.

10. You should read a book every day.

Subject Complements. Object complements follow *action verbs* only. In contrast, subject complements complete the meaning of a sentence when there is a *linking verb*. There are two types of subject complements, predicate nominatives and predicate adjectives.

A **predicate nominative** is a noun or pronoun that gives another name for the subject. Here are several examples:

Predicate Nominatives

The governor is a *man* with the power to control the state.
The judge was a *woman*.
The boy became a *man*.

The predicate nominatives *man* and *woman* come after the linking verbs (*is* and *was*) and refer directly to the subjects of the sentences. The governor can be called a man, and the judge can be called a woman. In the third example, *became* is used as a linking verb. It links the subject *boy* to the predicate nominative *man*. (*Hint:* A verb is a linking verb if it can be easily replaced with a *being* verb. For example, the third sentence can be rewritten as, "The boy is a man," without changing the meaning.)

A **predicate adjective** is an adjective that describes the subject of a sentence that contains a linking verb. For example:

Predicate Adjectives

Our Constitution is *helpful* to most governments around the world.
The food seems *good*.

In the first example, the predicate adjective *helpful* describes the subject of the sentence, *Constitution*. In the second sentence *good* is a predicate adjective because it describes the subject, *food*. Both sentences contain a linking verb, *is* and *seems*, respectively.

PRACTICE EXERCISE 16: SUBJECT COMPLEMENTS

Underline the simple subjects once, the verbs twice, and put the subject complements in brackets. Write PN *or* PA *on the line depending on whether the complement is a predicate nominative or predicate adjective.*

1. _____ Mr. Jones is the best teacher in this school.

2. _____ The president seemed competent.

3. _____ The fruit tastes good.

4. _____ My goal is retirement.

5. _____ Some books are too long.

6. _____ Tomorrow is my birthday.

7. _____ Mr. Jones is a very competent judge.

8. _____ Your paper appeared especially well organized.

9. _____ After dieting, John looked good in his new suit.

10. _____ The best fruit was an apple.

Summary Table: Sentence Components

Component	Function	Example
Subject	Who or what sentence is about.	
Simple	Noun or pronoun	The *boy* hit the ball.
Complete	Includes everything that describes subject.	*The tall boy* hit the ball.
Predicate	Tells something about the subject.	
Simple	Verb and helping verbs	The boy *hit* the ball.
Complete	Includes everything that modifies the verb and completes the thought.	The boy *hit the ball over the fence.*
Complements		
Objective	Noun or pronoun	
Direct Object	Receives action of verb	The boy hit the *ball.*
Indirect Object	To whom or for whom the action of verb is directed.	The boy gave his *friend* a gift.
Subjective	Noun, pronoun, adjective with linking verb	
Predicate Nominative	Another name for subject	The boy was a good *player.*
Predicate Adjective	Describes subject	The boy was *great.*

[3] Subject and Verb Agreement

In English grammar, the term *number* means **singular** or **plural**. Nouns, pronouns, and verbs have both singular and plural forms. *Singular* number means one, and *plural* number means more than one.

In present tense sentences, subjects (nouns or pronouns) and verb forms must *agree* in terms of number. Specifically, singular subjects require singular verbs, and plural subjects require plural verbs. For example:

S/V
Agr

Subject and Verb Agreement

Singular Subject and Verb	Plural Subject and Verb

        S   V   S   V

The *boy strikes* the ball.   The *boys strike* the ball.

        S   V   S   V

The *man breaks* his arm.   The *men break* their arms.

      S   V   S   V

John swims.   *People swim.*

In the next section, we show you how to create singular and plural forms of verbs, nouns, and pronouns.

[3a] Singular and Plural Verbs

Verbs in the present tense have both singular and plural forms. Creating these forms is relatively simple. Verbs that are in the present principal form (see principal parts, p. 335–336) are generally in the plural form. To change this form to singular, add the letters -*s* or -*es* to the end of the verb. For example, to change the verb *talk* to the singular form, add an -*s* (*talks*). Two exceptions to the general rule (*I* or *you* as subject and the verb *be*) are discussed in the next sections.

The following table shows the forms of some common verbs.

Singular and Plural Verbs

Singular	Plural
helps	help
murders	murder
plays	play
discusses	discuss
begins	begin
breaks	break
brings	bring
chooses	choose
does	do
has	have

PRACTICE EXERCISE 17: RECOGNIZING SINGULAR AND PLURAL VERBS

Write the singular or plural form of each verb on the line.

Singular	Plural
1. writes	_____
2. _____	think

3. feels   _____

4. _____   continue

5. researches   _____

I and *You* **as Subjects.** When used as subjects, the pronouns *I* and *you* are exceptions to the general rule of agreement given above. Although it is singular, the pronoun *I* takes the present tense form of the verb that is without the -*s* or -*es* ending. The pronoun *you* may be singular or plural depending on how many people it refers to. In either case, when used as a subject, *you* takes the same form of the present tense verb—without the -*s* or -*es* ending. For example:

Singular	**Plural**
I help.	*We* help.
I discuss.	*We* discuss.
I do.	*We* do.
You help.	*You* help.
You discuss.	*You* discuss.
You do.	*You* do.

PRACTICE EXERCISE 18: *I* AND *YOU* AS SUBJECTS

Underline the form of the present tense verb that agrees with the subject.

1. I (*writes, write*) my essays in my journal.

2. You (*considers, consider*) me to be your best friend.

3. Because you left me, I (*feels, feel*) lonely.

4. You (*thinks, think*) very well under pressure.

5. I (*captures, capture*) the prisoner single handed.

The Verb *Be.* The verb *be* is a special case because it has irregular forms. It is helpful to learn forms of *be* in relation to the pronouns with which they must agree. The following table summarizes the correct present and past tense forms:

Forms of *Be* in Agreement with the Pronouns

Present Tense		**Past Tense**	
Singular	**Plural**	**Singular**	**Plural**
I *am*	we *are*	I *was*	we *were*
you *are*	you *are*	you *were*	you *were*
he *is*	they *are*	he *was*	they *were*

Present Tense		Past Tense	
Singular	**Plural**	**Singular**	**Plural**
she *is*	people *are*	she *was*	people *were*
John *is*		John *was*	
it *is*		it *was*	

The future tense of the verb *be* is *will be*. This form is the same for all subjects. For example:

I *will be* late.	You *will be* late.	She *will be* late.
He *will be* late.	It *will be* late.	They *will be* late.
We *will be* late.	John *will be* late.	People *will be* late.

The past participle of the verb *be* is *been*. In order to form the perfect tenses (see Section 1d), the helping verb *have* must be used. There are three forms of the verb *have*: the present (*have, has*), past (*had*), and future (*will have*). For example:

Present		Past		Future	
Singular	**Plural**	**Singular**	**Plural**	**Singular**	**Plural**
I *have*	We *have*	I *had*	We *had*	I *will have*	We *will have*
You *have*	You *have*	You *had*	You *had*	You *will have*	You *will have*
He *has*	They *have*	He *had*	They *had*	He *will have*	They *will have*
She *has*	People *have*	She *had*	People *had*	She *will have*	People *will have*
It *has*		It *had*		It *will have*	
John *has*		John *had*		John *will have*	

PRACTICE EXERCISE 19: SUBJECT–VERB AGREEMENT WITH *BEING* VERBS

Underline the form of the being *verb that agrees with the subject.*

1. I (*am, is, are*)

2. I (*have, has*)

3. We (*am, is, are*)

4. Peter (*am, is, are*)

5. You (*have been, has been*)

6. She (*have been, has been*)

7. The student (*am, is, are*)

8. New York City (*am, is, are*)

9. Lawyers (*am, is, are*)

10. The idea (*have been, has been*)

11. He (*am, is, are*)

12. I (*was, were*)

13. They (*am, is, are*)

14. I (*have been, has been*)

15. You (*am, is, are*)   18. The books (*was, were*)

16. She (*am, is, are*)   19. We (*was, were*)

17. You (*was, were*)   20. We (*have been, has been*)

[3b] Singular and Plural Nouns

A singular noun refers to *one* person, place, object, or idea. A plural noun refers to *more than one*. The general rule is to add an *-s* or *-es* to the end of a noun to make it plural. Here are some examples:

Singular and Plural Nouns

Singular	Plural
building	buildings
kiss	kisses
book	books

When used as the subject of a sentence in the present tense, the singular and the plural nouns must match the verb forms. For example:

Subject and Verb Agreement

Singular Subject	Plural Subject

                    s   v   s   v
The *building falls* to the ground.   The *buildings fall* to the ground.

          s   v   s   v
The *book costs* too much.   The *books cost* too much.

Irregular Noun Forms. Following are some exceptions to the general rule for creating plural nouns:

1. Some nouns change their spellings in unusual ways. For example:

Singular Nouns	Plural Nouns
man	men
woman	women
focus	foci
mouse	mice
child	children
foot	feet

2. When a noun ends with any *consonant* followed by the letter *-y*, create the plural form by changing the *y* to *i* before adding the letters *-es*. For example, *copy* becomes *copies*. Here are some more examples:

Singular	Plural
city	cities
company	companies
secretary	secretaries
duty	duties

Be careful not to use this rule when a *vowel* comes before the final letter *y*. Instead, use the general rule and just add *-s*. For example, the plural of *play* is *plays*.

3. For some words ending in *-f* or *-fe*, change the *f* to *v* before adding *-es*. For example:

Singular	Plural
shelf	shelves
wife	wives
half	halves
life	lives
leaf	leaves

4. Some nouns have the same form whether singular or plural. For example:

Singular	Plural
sheep	sheep
fish	fish
deer	deer

5. Some nouns are always in the plural form; yet, they are logically singular. For example, *measles, mumps, athletics, mathematics, economics,* and *news*. These nouns take a singular verb form. For example:

Mathematics *is* my favorite subject.
The news *comes* on after the movie.

PRACTICE EXERCISE 20: SINGULAR AND PLURAL NOUNS

Write the singular or plural form of each verb on the line.

Singular	Plural		Singular	Plural
1. man	_____		6. _____	women
2. _____	computers		7. dress	_____
3. life	_____		8. _____	deer
4. _____	companies		9. _____	measles
5. secretary	_____		10. wife	_____

More than One Subject. When a subject is composed of nouns or pronouns joined by the conjunction *and*, it takes a plural verb. For example:

John *and* Mary *write* the paper together.

This sentence has a plural verb (*write*) because the subject (*John and Mary*) includes two people.

Nouns or pronouns joined by *or, nor, either*, or *neither* agree with the subject nearest to the verb. For example:

John *or* Mary *writes* the paper.
Either John *or* his friends *write* the paper.
Neither the pencil *nor* the pen *works* very well.
Neither the pencil *nor* the pens *work* very well.

In all of the above sentences, the verb agrees with the subject closest to it.

Collective Nouns. A collective noun refers to a group of persons or things that are considered to be one unit. For example:

Collective Nouns

team	group
faculty	family
army	assembly
audience	public
crowd	herd

     A collective noun takes a singular verb when the noun is referred to as a single unit. For example:

The *crowd moves* slowly toward the demonstration site.
The *family receives* a package.

     A collective noun takes a plural verb when the individual parts or members of the group are referred to. For example:

The *crowd attack* the police from all directions.
The *family argue* among themselves.

In the above examples, the *crowd* and *family* are acting as individuals. Therefore, the verb forms (*attack* and *argue*) are plural.

PRACTICE EXERCISE 21: SUBJECT-VERB AGREEMENT (NOUNS)

For each sentence, write C (for "Correct") on the line if the subject and verb agree. If not, put I (for "Incorrect") on the line and correct the errors. For example:

help

   __I__   Good teachers helps students with their homework.

1. _____ The judge wants to try this case.

2. _____ The lawyers decides to drop their clients.

3. _____ Henry and John return to class.

4. _____ Either Mary or Jane help other students.

5. _____ Justice requires sacrifice on our part.

6. _____ Democracies springs up all over the world.

7. _____ The shelves is leaning toward the left.

8. _____ At this conference women speak about life in the home.

9. _____ The men continues to be upset.

10. _____ Together, the family eat out every night.

11. _____ The faculty argue among themselves.

12. _____ Both fish are in the bowl.

13. _____ The halves was good to eat.

14. _____ My feet stands firmly on the ground.

15. _____ Neither my teacher nor my parents has been helpful.

[3c] Singular and Plural Pronouns

Like nouns, pronouns may be singular or plural in number. The following table contains singular and plural forms of personal, possessive, and reflexive pronouns.

Singular and Plural Pronouns

Personal	Possessive and Reflexive (*-self*)
Singular	**Singular**
I, me	my, mine, myself
you	your, yours, yourself
he, him	his, himself
she, her	her, hers, herself
it	its, itself
Plural	**Plural**
we, us	our, ours, ourselves
they, them	their, theirs, themselves
you	your, yours

The present tense verb form must agree with the pronoun that is used as a subject. For example:

Singular	**Plural**
I am successful. *I write* well.	*We are* successful. *We write* well.
You are successful. *You write* well.	*You are* successful. *You write* well.
He is successful. *He writes* well.	*They are* successful. *They write* well.
It is successful. *It works* well.	

Pronoun agreement with the various forms of the verb *be* was discussed in the last section.

Indefinite Pronouns. Indefinite pronouns do not refer to a definite person, place, or thing. Some indefinite pronouns are singular, some are plural, and some may be either singular or plural depending on how they are used.

The following indefinite pronouns are singular and always take singular verbs.

Singular Indefinite Pronouns

each	everyone	anyone
either	everybody	anybody
neither	no one	someone
one	nobody	somebody

For example, "*Everyone is* in my class," has a singular verb (*is*) to agree with the indefinite pronoun *everyone*.

The following indefinite pronouns are plural:

Plural Indefinite Pronouns

both
many
few

For example, "*Few* of the students in my class *come* in late," has a plural verb *come* to agree with the plural indefinite pronoun *few*.

Some indefinite pronouns can be singular or plural:

Indefinite Pronouns That Are Singular or Plural

some
any
none
all
most
much

For these special words, the number of the subject is determined by context, specifically, the noun to which the pronoun refers (see Section 4b). If the context is singular, the pronoun is singular, and the verb must agree. If the context is plural, the verb must also be plural. For example:

Some of my apartments *are* for sale. (*Some* is plural because the word *apartments* refers to it.)
Some of my apartment *is* dirty. (*Some* is singular because *apartment* is singular.)
All of the apples *are* gone. (*All* is plural because of *apples*.)
All of the apple *is* rotten. (*All* is singular because of *apple*.)

PRACTICE EXERCISE 22: SUBJECT–VERB AGREEMENT (PRONOUNS)

In each sentence, underline the simple subject and circle the correct form of the verb.

1. He (*runs, run*) away from the police officer.

2. I (*eats, eat*) too much food.

3. Everyone (*is, are*) trying to pass this course.

4. Everybody (*gets, get*) an *A* for trying.

5. In this class few (*completes, complete*) the homework.

6. All of the food (*has, have*) been digested.

7. Some of my friends (*has, have*) left.

8. Someone (*is, are*) helping the teacher.

9. All of the apples (*is, are*) sweet.

10. None of the books (*is, are*) difficult.

PRACTICE EXERCISE 23: SUBJECT–VERB AGREEMENT (PRONOUNS)

In the paragraph below, underline simple subjects and circle the correct verb forms.

Everyone (*has, have*) the right to remain silent when questioned by the police. Many (*believes, believe*) that questions asked by the police must be answered. But even if someone (*tells, tell*) you that it is in your best interest to answer, you still have the right to remain silent. Some of your rights (*is, are*) violated when a police officer (*fails, fail*) to read you your rights. All of this (*is, are*) in the Constitution.

Sometimes a group of words may come in between the subject and verb. This complication is discussed in Section 6e.

[4] Using Pronouns Properly

Pronouns take the place of nouns. Therefore, every pronoun refers to a noun, which is usually stated in the same sentence or a previous sentence (see Section 1b for a discussion of pronoun antecedents). The form of a pronoun depends on its antecedent and how that pronoun is used in the sentence. Therefore, pronouns can be tricky business.

In this section we help you use pronouns properly. After introducing pronoun case, we discuss pronoun-antecedent agreement in number and person.

Pron

[4a] Pronoun Case

There are three different forms of pronouns (called *cases*). The cases are nominative, objective, and possessive.

Nominative Case. Nominative case is used when a pronoun serves in a sentence as a subject or subject complement. The nominative case pronouns are listed below:

Nominative Case Pronouns

Singular	Plural
I	we
he, she	they
you	you
it	

Here are some examples of nominative case pronouns used in a sentence:

She is the captain of the team. (Subject)
They helped me do my homework. (Subject)
The best student was *he*. (Subject complement)

The pronouns *she* and *they* are subjective case because they are used as the subjects of sentences. The pronoun *he* is subjective because it serves as the subject complement.

Objective Case. Objective case is used when a pronoun serves in a sentence as any kind of object. The objective case pronouns are listed below.

Objective Case Pronouns

Singular	Plural
me	us
him, her	them
you	you
it	

Here are some examples of objective pronouns used in sentences:

The teacher marked *him* absent. (Direct object)
The speaker gave *me* good advice. (Indirect object)
He gave the same advice to *them*, too. (Object of preposition)

In the first sentence, *him* is the direct object. In the second sentence, *me* is the indirect object. In the third sentence, an objective pronoun, *them*, is used because it is the object of the preposition *to* (see prepositional phrases, Section 6a).

Possessive Case. Possession means ownership. You can form the possessive case by adding the apostrophe (') after indefinite pronouns (*someone's, everybody's, nobody's;* see Section 1b for a complete list). However, do not use the apostrophe with possessive pronouns. Following is a list of possessive pronouns.

Possessive Pronouns

Singular	Plural
my, mine	our, ours
his, her, hers	their, theirs
you, yours	you, yours
its	

Following are some examples of possessive pronouns used in sentences.

My teacher is the best.
That is *our* book.
That is *ours*.
Someone's book is on my desk.
Its tail is still wagging.

All of these pronouns show possession or ownership. Notice that the apostrophe is added to the indefinite pronoun *someone*. Also, note that an *-s* is added to the possessive pronoun (*ours*) when the noun being possessed does not follow the pronoun. This can be seen in the third sentence above. In the second sentence, the possessive pronoun *our* is used because the noun being possessed (*book*) is stated after the pronoun.

Do not confuse the possessive forms *its*, *their*, and *yours* with the contractions *it's* (it is), *they're* (they are), and *you're* (you are).

PRACTICE EXERCISE 24: USING PRONOUN CASE

Underline the correct pronoun.

1. (*She, Her*) is the best student in the class.

2. John and (*he, him*) came to my rescue.

3. The judge told (*I, me*) to present my case.

4. The lawyer gave (*she, her*) the briefcase.

5. My favorite teacher was (*him, he*).

6. That grade was given to (*me, I*).

7. (*Our, Ours*) teacher is the best.

8. (*Your, Yours*) is the best diet (*I, me*) have ever tried.

9. John sat in (*his, him*) seat during class.

10. The book I found is (*their, theirs*).

Who, Whom, Whose. Understanding the difference between these pronouns can seem complicated. However, once you understand pronoun cases, you will be able to use them properly.

Who is in the nominative case (subjects). *Whom* is in the objective case (objects of verbs and prepositions). *Whose* is in the possessive case (ownership). All of them can be used as interrogative pronouns to ask questions. For example:

Who is your teacher? (Subject)
Whom do you like? (Direct object)
To *whom* did you give the book? (Object of preposition)
John is the student with *whom* I am working. (Object of preposition)
Whose book is that? (Possessive)

Sometimes these pronouns are used in complex sentences as relative pronouns (see Section 7b). In this case they will appear as part of a related group of words. This word group will contain a verb that is separate from the main subject and verb of the sentence. You must identify this group of words to determine the proper use of *who* or *whom*. If the relative pronoun is the subject of the word group, *who* is used. If it is the object of the group, *whom* is proper. For example:

Main Part   **Word Group**

S   V   S   V
John is the person *who* gave me the present.

Main Part   **Word Group**

S   V   O   S   V
John is the person *whom* I like.

In the first sentence, *who gave me the present* is the group of words begun by the relative pronoun. Since the relative pronoun is the subject of this word group, *who* is used. In the second sentence, the word group is *whom I like*. In this case *whom* is used because it is the object of the verb *like*.

PRACTICE EXERCISE 25: USING WHO, WHOM, AND WHOSE

In each sentence, underline the proper relative pronoun. Be prepared to give the reason you chose your answer.

1. (Who Whom) is the best teacher in school?

2. I want to thank Mr. Jones, (who whom) helped me the most.

3. (Whom Whose Who) car is the fastest?

4. Mr. Harvey is the worker (who whom) my family hired.

5. My boyfriend is the one to (who whom) I am writing.

[4b] Pronoun and Antecedent Agreement

In Section 3c, we discussed agreement between pronouns as subjects and their verbs. In this section we introduce another type of agreement—between pronouns and their antecedents. Pronouns must agree with their antecedents in terms of number and person.

Number. Every pronoun should agree with the noun to which it refers, called the *antecedent*. In other words, singular pronouns refer to singular nouns and plural pronouns refer to plural nouns. For example:

> The *boy* rushes to *his* class. *He* is late.
> The *boys* rush to *their* classes. *They* are late.
> The *car* lost *its* luster.

In the first sentence, the *boy* is a singular antecedent. Therefore, the pronouns *his* and *he* are also singular. In the second sentence, the antecedent *boys* is plural. Therefore, the pronouns *their* and *they* are plural. In the third sentence, the antecedent *car* is singular, and the pronoun *its* is also singular.

Person. There are three grammatical persons. The **first person** is the person(s) speaking (*I* and *we*). The **second person** is the person(s) that is being spoken to (*you*). The **third person** is the person, place, or object being spoken about (*he, she, it, they*). Actually, every noun used in a sentence is in the third person because it is being spoken about by the author. Additionally, some pronouns show whether the person is a male or female; that is, they indicate *gender*. For example, *he, him*, and *his* are male and *she, her*, and *hers* are female. Other pronouns can be used for males or females (for example, *you, we, I*, and *our*).

The following table shows the singular and plural forms for the three persons of the personal pronouns.

Pronoun Persons

First	Second	Third
Singular	**Singular**	**Singular**
I, me, my, mine	you, your, yours	he, him, his
		she, her, hers
		it, its
Plural	**Plural**	**Plural**
we, us, our, ours	your, yours	they, them, their, theirs

An important rule is that pronouns should agree with their antecedents in terms of number, person, and gender. For example:

> *I* was angry at *my* mother. (First person, singular)
> *We* must do *our* duty. (First person, plural)

You are *your* best judge. (Second person)

Mary is failing the class. *She* must do *her* homework. (Third person, singular, female)

John was on *his* diet for over a month. (Third person, singular, male)

John and Mary stayed in *their* room for hours. (Third person, plural)

The *book* fell from *its* shelf. (Third person, singular)

Everyone did *his* or *her* homework. (Third person, singular—Note: *everyone* is singular)

In all of the above examples, the pronouns in each sentence agree with their antecedents in terms of number, person, and gender.

PRACTICE EXERCISE 26: PRONOUN–ANTECEDENT AGREEMENT

Underline the correct pronouns in terms of case, number, person, and gender. Be prepared to explain your answer.

1. The school had to change (*her, his, its*) name.

2. Miss Jones is a teacher who really cares if (*her, his, their, its*) students will work hard.

3. (*He, Him, She, Her*) left the backpack in his closet.

4. Peter, Paul, and Mary are a popular singing group. (*They, Their, Its, Her, His*) albums are very good.

5. Joan, Mary, and I ate lunch in (*their, our, your, its*) cafeteria.

6. My computer broke (*its, my, his*) main disk drive.

7. People who stay on a diet too long may not realize that (*we, you, they*) are in danger.

8. Either Jim or John knows how (*he, they, it*) will do.

9. Mr. Jones gave the book to Jim, but he did not reveal (*his, its, their*) title.

10. Few students have stayed for (*his, her, their*) graduation.

PRACTICE EXERCISE 27: PRONOUN–ANTECEDENT AGREEMENT

Complete the paragraph by underlining the appropriate pronouns that agree with their antecedents.

Thomas Jefferson wrote the Declaration of Independence. In (*it, its*), (*she, he*) declared that "all men are created equal." (*Their, His*) belief was that everyone is endowed with life, liberty, and the pursuit of happiness. However, (*he, him*) did not mean to say that everyone was exactly alike. (*We, Us*) all have different abilities. (*Ours, Our*) ability depends on the amount of opportunity (*we, they*) have in life. Thomas Jefferson gave (*us, we*) hope. (*Us, We*) can all have an equal opportunity to develop our abilities. (*Their, His*) message was important. (*We, They*) still admire (*he, him*) for writing it.

[5] Active and Passive Voice

Voice

Voice is a way of controlling the basic relationship among the subject, verb, and object. In **active voice**, the subject does the action of the verb and the object receives the action. All of the examples we've shown so far have been in the active voice. In contrast, **passive voice** changes the basic relationship among the subject, verb, and object. It allows the subject to receive the action instead of the object. Look at this sentence:

John hit the ball.

This sentence is written in the active voice because *John*, the subject, is doing the action, *hit*, and the ball receives the action. Now, compare this sentence:

The ball is hit.

Now, the *ball*, the subject, is receiving the action, *is hit*. This sentence is written in the passive voice.

We may add the phrase *by the boy* to the previous example:

The ball is hit by the boy.

Now, the meaning of the active and passive versions are the same. Changing voice does not change the basic meaning of the sentence. It just alters the relationship between the subject and the verb.

To form the passive voice, use the past participle with a form of the verb *be* (*is, are, was, were, will be, have been*). Passive voice is not a verb tense, but it may appear in any verb tense with the exception of progressive tense. Here are some examples:

Active and Passive Voice

Active	Passive
The lawyer *made* the opening statement.	The opening statement *was made* by the lawyer.
The fathers *helped* their children.	The children *were helped* by their fathers.
The student *has read* the book.	The book *has been read* by the student.

Copyright © 2000 Addison-Wesley Educational Publishers Inc.

Notice that all of the main verbs are past participles. Also, all passive sentences have a form of the helping verb *be*. Examine the subject and object relationships in the active and passive sentences. In the active sentences the subjects (*lawyer, fathers,* and *student*) are doing the action. In the passive sentences, the subjects (*statement, children,* and *book*) are receiving the action.

Both active and passive voice are correct forms of English. In some instances passive voice may be desirable, especially when the person doing the action is unimportant or unknown. This may occur when reporting news or business events. For example:

The suspects were taken into custody for questioning.
The computers were placed on the shelves in time for the holiday sale.

However, in most cases passive voice is not an effective form of writing. Generally, it is a good idea to use the active voice whenever possible. Compare these pairs of sentences. Notice that sentences in the active voice are more direct and, therefore, more effective.

Passive	Active
To be married was finally decided by John and Mary.	John and Mary finally decided to be married.
The final exam was passed by everyone in Mr. Johnson's class.	Everyone in Mr. Johnson's class passed the final exam.

PRACTICE EXERCISE 28: RECOGNIZING VOICE

On the line in front of each sentence, put an A if the sentence is active and a P if passive. Next, for each active sentence, write the passive version on the line below the sentence. For each passive sentence, write the active version on the line.

1. _____ The digestive system dissolves food.

_____

2. _____ The Declaration of Independence was signed by John Hancock.

_____

3. _____ The student was disciplined by the principal for leaving class.

_____

4. _____ Motivation is required by the coach.

_____

5. _____ Peer pressure has controlled my every move.

_____

[6] Phrases

A phrase is a group of words that contains neither a subject nor a verb and acts as a single part of speech. Grouping words together is common in English. We have already seen that we can add helping verbs to main verbs to create verb phrases.

In this section you will see that phrases can be used as nouns, adjectives, and adverbs. First, we discuss prepositional phrases. Next, we examine three types of phrases based on verb forms: (1) participles, (2) gerunds, and (3) infinitives. We will show you how to combine phrases to create more complex word groups. Then we introduce the appositive phrase. Finally, we will show you how to deal with phrases that come between subjects and verbs.

[6a] Prepositional Phrases

Prepositions (see Section 1f) usually appear in phrases. A prepositional phrase is a group of words beginning with a preposition and ending with a noun or pronoun. The noun or pronoun at the end of the prepositional phrase is called the *object of the preposition*. An **adjective prepositional phrase** modifies a noun or pronoun. For example:

The Congress *of the United States* represents the people.

The prepositional phrase *of the United States* starts with the preposition *of* and ends with the noun (object) *United States*. The whole phrase acts as an adjective because it describes the noun, *Congress*.

One adjective phrase may follow another. For example:

Some people think that New York is the center *of the world of finance*.

The second phrase, *of finance*, describes the noun at the end of the first phrase, *world*. The phrase *of the world* describes the noun *center*. Therefore, both prepositional phrases are adjective phrases.

Prepositional phrases may also serve as adverbs when they modify a verb, adjective, or adverb. For example:

The court session begins *in the morning*.

In the morning is an adverb phrase because it modifies the verb *begins* by answering the question *when*?

Adverb prepositional phrases may exist in combination, too. For example:

He stabbed the man *in the back with a knife*.

Both of these prepositional phrases (*in the back, with a knife*) act as adverbs because they describe the verb *stabbed*. They answer the questions *where?* and *how?* the man was stabbed.

PRACTICE EXERCISE 29: RECOGNIZING PREPOSITIONAL PHRASES

Underline the prepositional phrases in these sentences. Then, circle the words being modified by each prepositional phrase. For example:

The (man) with the big hat is my teacher.

1. The group of students wrote their papers in the classroom.
2. In the evening the teacher of psychology went home early with a friend.
3. During the night the boys ran down the street along the sidewalk.
4. We traveled through the city of New York around midnight.
5. With effective social controls people will not challenge the police with violent acts.
6. Around nine o'clock in the morning, the jurors came through the door and into the courtroom.
7. Because the runner was near the finishing line, he ran with longer strides.
8. Everyone except John went to dinner with Mr. Richards.

PRACTICE EXERCISE 30: WRITING SENTENCES WITH PREPOSITIONAL PHRASES

Write a sentence using each of these prepositional phrases.

1. with the proper nutrition

_____

2. under control

_____

3. with pressure

_____

4. in the same way

_____

5. from another country

_____

[6b] Verbals

Sometimes words that appear to be verbs are not used as verbs in a sentence. These words are called verbals. They are forms of verbs used in a sentence as either adjectives or nouns. Verbals can be single words or phrases made from the principal parts of verbs. There are three types of verbals: *participles, gerunds*, and *infinitives*.

Participles. Participles are verbals that act as adjectives in a sentence. Both types of participles, past participle (*-ed, -d*, or irregular endings) and present participle (*-ing*), can be used this way. Be sure to use the correct form of the past participle, especially for irregular verbs. For example:

Adjective Participles

The *broken* toy was returned to the store. (*Broken* is the past participle of *break*. It is used as an adjective to describe *toy*.)

I turned off the *running* water. (*Running* is the present participle of *run*. It is used as an adjective to describe *water*.)

A **participial phrase** is a group of related words that acts as an adjective. It begins with a present or past participle and may include a complement and modifiers. These modifiers are often prepositional phrases. Here are some examples:

Participial Phrase with Modifiers

Tossed up and down in the pot, the spaghetti came to a boil.

Running on empty, the car came to a stop.

Tossed up and down in the pot is a participial phrase. The past participle of the verb *toss* introduces the phrase. The phrase includes two adverbs (*up* and *down*) and a prepositional phrase, *in the pot*. The entire participial phrase is used as an adjective to describe the noun, *spaghetti*. In the second example, *running on empty* is a participial phrase. It contains the present participle form of the verb *run* along with a prepositional phrase, *on empty*. The whole phrase is used to describe the car.

Participial Phrases with Complements

Eating the pie, Mary had a big smile on her face.

Writing the letter, John began to remember his experiences.

Eating the pie is a participial phrase that contains an object complement, *the pie* (eating *what?*). The entire phrase describes Mary. *Writing the letter* is a participial phrase that has a complement, *the letter*. The phrase acts as an adjective by describing John.

PRACTICE EXERCISE 31: RECOGNIZING PARTICIPIAL PHRASES

Underline the participial phrase in each sentence. Then, circle the noun or pronoun that it modifies. For example:

Playing in the sun, (we) became sunburned.

1. Traveling around the world, the man became a great leader.

2. The peasants, worked to the bone, complained about their conditions.

3. Horrified by what they saw, the men decided to leave the room.

4. The book sitting on the shelf was my favorite.

5. Having the best time of our lives, we had to come home.

6. Disgusted with this class, I decided to drop it.

7. The police investigating the accident stopped all traffic.

8. The student sleeping in class will miss a very important assignment.

9. I have an appointment with a therapist known to be compassionate.

10. Written on a computer, the essay looked professional.

Gerunds. Gerunds are verbals that act as nouns. To make a gerund, we use the present participle (*-ing*) form of a verb. Gerunds may be used as subjects, complements, and objects of prepositions. For example, "*Running* is healthy" has a gerund for its subject. *Running* is the present participle form of the verb *run*.

Gerunds often appear in phrases. These phrases are made by adding a complement, modifiers, or both. Here are some examples of **gerund phrases** serving as different parts of a sentence:

Gerund Phrases

Lying in the sun is dangerous to your health. (Subject)
The athletes tried *running in place*. (Object complement)
I wrote a book about *swimming in the ocean*. (Object of preposition)
John's problem was *opening the door*. (Subject complement)

Lying in the sun is a gerund phrase because it acts as a noun. It is the subject of the sentence. Also, it contains the prepositional phrase *in the sun*. In the second example, *running in place* is a gerund phrase. It acts as the object complement of *tried* (the athletes tried *what?*). In the third example, *swimming in the ocean* is the gerund phrase. It acts as the noun (a book about *what?*) and serves as the object of the preposition *about*. In the last example, *opening the door* is a gerund phrase. It acts as a subject complement. The entire gerund phrase serves as a noun because it is a predicate nominative in the sentence. *John's problem* and *opening the door* are connected by the linking verb *was.*

PRACTICE EXERCISE 32: RECOGNIZING GERUNDS

Underline the gerund phrases in these sentences. Determine the role of each gerund in the sentence by putting S *(subject),* DO *(direct object), or* OP *(object of preposition) on the line.*

1. _____ Studying hard is the best ingredient for success.

2. _____ You should try supporting your opinion with facts.

3. _____ By working in a group, you learn more.

4. _____ Reading a book will improve your skills.

5. _____ The women's group discussed collecting money for charity.

6. _____ Using a computer is the best way to write.

7. _____ My boss does not tolerate sleeping on the job.

8. _____ I really enjoy living in the United States.

Infinitives. Placing the word *to* before the present tense verb form creates an **infinitive phrase**. Infinitives can be used as nouns, adjectives, or adverbs. When used as nouns, infinitives may serve as subjects and complements. Infinitives always appear in phrases of at least two words (*to* + present form of verb). For example, *to run* and *to write* are infinitive phrases. Like other phrases, infinitive phrases may contain complements and modifiers.

Here are some examples of infinitive phrases:

Infinitive Phrases

Used as Nouns

To think deeply about life is important. (*To think* names *what* is important; it serves as the *subject.*)

I like *to eat* well. (*To eat* names *what* I like and serves as *direct object.*)

My goal is *to write* better. (*To write* names *what* is my goal and serves as *predicate nominative.*)

Used as an Adjective

You have the right *to remain silent.* (*To remain silent* describes the noun *right.*)

Used as an Adverb

The politician gave the speech *to get votes.* (*To get votes* describes the verb *gave* by answering the question *why?*)

PRACTICE EXERCISE 33: RECOGNIZING INFINITIVE PHRASES

Underline the infinitive phrases in each sentence. Write Adj *for adjective,* Adv *for adverb, or* N *for noun on the line depending on how the infinitive phrase is used in the sentence.*

1. _____ To be successful you have to read and write often.

2. _____ Our goal is to be free.

3. _____ The right to speak freely is protected by the Constitution.

4. _____ To keep weight off is more difficult than to lose it.

5. _____ It is embarrassing to be arrested by the police.

6. _____ The lawyer wanted to object to that statement.

7. _____ To be elected to office you need to campaign day and night.

8. _____ The students seemed happy to leave class early.

[6c] Expanding Phrases

You can make your phrases more descriptive by adding modifiers—adjectives or adverbs. Single words or additional phrases can make phrases more vivid. Here are some ways to expand sentences by using phrases.

Expanding with Prepositional Phrases. Sometimes prepositional phrases are found in a series. For example:

> The boy wrote the paper *for homework with great care on the computer in the afternoon.*

There are four prepositional phrases in this sentence: (1) *for homework,* (2) *with great care,* (3) *on the computer,* and (4) *in the afternoon.*

One or more prepositional phrases are often attached to verbals. For example:

Expanding Verbals with Prepositional Phrases

> The student, *feeling upset about failing the test,* went home crying. (participial phrase)
> *Eating a good breakfast with fruit juice in the morning* is good for your health. (gerund phrase)
> *To believe in justice for all* is important for all Americans. (infinitive phrase)
> I like *to read at night in the quiet of my room.* (infinitive phrase)

Each of the verbal phrases above has been expanded by attaching one or more prepositional phrases.

Expanding with Verbal Phrases. Participial or infinitive phrases may be attached to other phrases. For example:

Expanding Phrases with Other Phrases

Lying on the beach can be dangerous. (gerund phrase)
Lying on the beach *facing the sun* can be dangerous. (gerund phrase expanded with participial phrase)
I am not able *to put together the toy*. (infinitive phrase)
I am not able *to put together the toy broken in five pieces*. (infinitive phrase expanded with participial phrase)

[6d] Appositives

A noun phrase is any group of words that plays the role of a noun. The noun phrase can be used as a subject, complement, or object of a preposition. An appositive is another way to use a noun or noun phrase in a sentence. An appositive is a noun that comes directly after another noun in order to rename or identify it further. An **appositive phrase** consists of a noun along with any modifiers, for example:

Appositive Phrases

The judge, *an accomplished lawyer*, sits on the bench.
New York City, *the most densely populated city in the country*, is my hometown.
I finally finished writing the book, *a real accomplishment*.
My favorite possession, *a diamond ring*, is on the table.

In the first example, the appositive (*an accomplished lawyer*) is a noun phrase that further identifies the judge. In the second example, the appositive (*the most densely populated city in the country*) identifies New York City. Notice that the noun in an appositive (*city*) can be expanded with adverbs (*most densely*), adjectives (*populated*) and prepositional phrases (*in the country*). In the third example, *a real accomplishment* renames the book. In the last sentence, *a diamond ring* identifies the favorite possession.

PRACTICE EXERCISE 34: RECOGNIZING APPOSITIVES

Underline the appositives in each sentence.

1. Mr. Jones, my favorite teacher, helps me with my homework.

2. The Constitution, a masterpiece of writing, protects us in many ways.

3. The diet ended on May 23, my birthday.

4. The textbook *Sociology in Perspective* is difficult to understand.

5. The captain wrote a letter to his daughter Julia.

6. Everyone needs a good education, the great equalizer.

7. Fortunately, writing, a necessary skill, can be learned.

8. The necessary ingredients—salt and pepper—made the salad tasty.

PRACTICE EXERCISE 35: RECOGNIZING ALL TYPES OF PHRASES

Underline all of the phrases in this paragraph. Label each phrase in terms of type (preposition, participle, gerund, appositive, or infinitive) and role in the sentence (noun, adjective, or adverb).

Being motivated to succeed is one of the most important ingredients in life. However, after studying people with different degrees of motivation, Philip Zimbardo, a psychologist at Stanford University, has reached some interesting conclusions. He discovered an unusual relationship between motivation, task difficulty, and performance. For simple tasks, a higher degree of motivation increases the quality of performance. That is, to perform well on easy tasks, you should get into a highly aroused state. On the other hand, performing complex tasks is better when you are less motivated to succeed. That is, being too motivated will actually hinder your ability to perform complicated tasks like taking an exam. No matter what type of task you are asked to do, having too little or too much motivation seems to hurt your performance.

[6e] Phrases That Come between Subjects and Verbs

Sometimes phrases will come between a subject and its verb. You need to recognize this arrangement and make sure that the subject and verb agree in number. The rule is to ignore the words that interrupt the subject and verb. For example:

Phrases between Subject and Verb

John and Jim, *fired by the president*, remain on the job. (participial phrase between subject and verb)

The car *with good tires* is very expensive. (prepositional phrase between subject and verb)

The professor *teaching over a hundred students* works very hard. (participial phrase between subject and verb)

Mr. Jones, *to get the votes*, hires more assistants. (infinitive phrase between subject and verb)

Everybody *with three publications* is automatically hired. (prepositional phrase between subject and verb)

In the first sentence, *fired by the president* is a participial phrase that comes between the subject and the verb. The verb *remain* must be plural to agree with the plural subject *John and Jim* (see Section 3b). In the second sentence, the prepositional phrase *with good tires* interrupts the subject and verb. Since the subject (*car*) is singular, the verb (*is*) must also be singular. In the third sentence, *professor* is the singular subject and *works* is the singular verb. *Teaching over a hundred students* is a phrase that should be ignored when determining subject-verb agreement. In the fourth sentence, the verb *hires* must agree with the subject, *Mr. Jones*. The infinitive phrase *to get the votes* interrupts. In the last sentence, the subject *everybody* is singular. Therefore, the verb (*is hired*) is also singular even though it is interrupted by the prepositional phrase *with three publications*.

There is an exception to the rule given above. As we showed in Section 3c, some indefinite pronouns may be either singular or plural (*some, any, none, all, most*, and *much*). For these pronouns, number is determined by their antecedents. An antecedent may be found in a phrase that interrupts the pronoun and its verb. In this case, number *is* determined by the interrupting phrase. Here are some examples:

> *Some* of my *friends* are here. (*Some* is plural because *friends* is plural.)
> *All* of the *building* is under construction. (*All* is singular because *building* is singular.)

PRACTICE EXERCISE 36: PHRASES BETWEEN SUBJECT AND VERB

In each of the sentences below, circle the form of the verb that agrees with the subject.

1. Freedom of expression (is are) an important First Amendment right.
2. The right to speak, to write, to assemble, and to express our views without fear of government intrusion (constitutes constitute) the First Amendment right to free expression.
3. Specific rules about freedom of speech (makes make) us feel secure.
4. If a person (stands stand) on a street corner and (distributes distribute) pamphlets, the police cannot (asks ask) him to move unless traffic is being blocked.
5. Both conservatives and liberals (believes believe) there is a need to discuss religion in the public schools.

Summary Table: Phrases

Phrase	Function	Examples
Prepositional	Adjective Adverb	*to the store* *with the book* *on the desk*

Phrase	Function	Examples
Participial (*-ing*) (*-ed, -d*) (irregular)	Adjective	*Writing a letter,* John was busy.
		The boy, *helped by the teacher,* passed the test.
		Broken into pieces, the desk was discarded.
Gerund (*-ing*)	Noun	*Turning the key* was difficult.
		Lying down on the job will get you into trouble.
Infinitive (*to* + present tense verb)	Noun	*To run* fast is required.
	Adjective	The student was given an assignment *to write* an essay.
	Adverb	I play *to win.*
Appositive (noun)	Noun	My teacher, *Mr. Jones,* is here.
		New York, *a great state,* is my home.

[7] Clauses

Clauses

A clause is a group of words that contains both a subject and verb. Compare this to a phrase, which is also a group of words but does *not* contain a verb and a subject. There are two kinds of clauses, independent and dependent.

[7a] Independent Clauses

The independent clause (sometimes called the *main clause*) is a very important part of writing. Every sentence that you write *must* have an independent clause in order to be a complete sentence.

Independent clauses must have a subject and verb and often have a complement that completes the thought. In addition, the independent clause may contain any of the phrases discussed in Section 6. It may also have adjectives and adverbs either alone or in phrases. In every case the independent clause stands alone as a complete sentence. A sentence with one independent clause is called a **simple sentence**.

Here are a few examples with the sentence elements labeled:

Independent Clauses

Subject   Verb   Compound objects Prepositional phrase
The government maintains law and order in society.

Gerund phrase   Subject   Verb   Object
Running down the street, the policeman caught the man.

Prepositional phrases   Subject Verb Adjective Object
In the middle of the night, the child had a bad dream.

Two independent clauses may be combined to form a **compound sentence**. Each clause must have its own subject and verb and each must be able to stand alone as a complete sentence. Coordinating conjunctions (*and, or, but, yet, so*, and *for*) and conjunctive adverbs (*however, therefore*, etc.) can be used to join independent clauses (see Section 1g). Independent clauses may also be connected with a semicolon (;) to create a compound sentence. Here are some examples:

Compound Sentences

S   V   S   V
The judge read the verdict, and he sentenced the defendant to life in jail.

S   V   S V
The student passed the final exam; consequently, he passed the course.

S   V   S V
The diet was finally over; I lost 50 pounds.

Punctuation between Independent Clauses. Proper punctuation is necessary between two independent clauses. Both the semicolon and the comma are used in compound sentences. There are a few rules to follow.

1. Use the *semicolon* (;) to separate independent clauses under the following conditions:

   - If there is no conjunction between independent clauses, place the semicolon between the independent clauses. For example:

     John hit a mighty home run; he won the game single-handedly.

   - If you use a conjunctive adverb (see Section 1g) like *however, moreover, furthermore*, or *fortunately*, place a semicolon before it. Also, place a comma after the conjunctive adverb. For example:

     John hit a home run; *fortunately*, it was enough to win the game.

2. Use a *comma* to separate independent clauses when the independent clauses are joined by a coordinating conjunction (*and, but, or, nor, for, so, yet*). Place the comma before the conjunction. For example:

The mayor delivered the address, *but* he failed to impress anyone.
The student studied all night, *and* he passed the test.
John is my brother, *yet* he is my best friend.

3. Use no punctuation between independent clauses that are very short and closely related. For example:

Dogs bite and cats scratch.

More information about punctuation of independent clauses is found in Section 8c, on run-ons and comma splices. Also see Section 10, Punctuation.

PRACTICE EXERCISE 37: WRITING COMPOUND SENTENCES

Combine the two independent clauses in each group into a compound sentence. Use each method (coordinating conjunctions, adverbial conjunctions, or semicolons) at least once. Be sure to use the correct punctuation.

1. The trial was completed. We went home to eat dinner.

   _____

   _____

2. Studying for a long period of time can lead to a headache. Studying for too short a time can lead to a failing grade.

   _____

   _____

3. Some people are born leaders. Others are born to follow.

   _____

   _____

4. Dark clouds began to form in the sky. It began to rain.

   _____

   _____

5. The water was freezing. I lost all feeling in my feet and hands.

   _____

   _____

[7b] Dependent Clauses

Like an independent clause, a dependent clause (also called a *subordinate clause*) contains both a subject and a verb. However, *the dependent clause cannot stand alone as a complete thought. It is not a complete sentence unless it is connected to an independent clause.*

Attaching a dependent clause to an independent clause creates a **complex sentence**. Complex sentences have one independent (or main) clause and one or more dependent clauses. The dependent clause can be placed before, after, or in between parts of the main clause. In the following examples, the subjects and verbs of each dependent clause are labeled.

Positions of Dependent Clauses

Dependent Clause before Main Clause: *After he won his first case*, the lawyer became very popular.

Dependent Clause after Main Clause: The lawyer became very popular *after he won his first case.*

Dependent Clause inside Main Clause: The lawyer *who won his first case* became very popular.

Dependent clauses relate to some part of the main clause. In the first and second examples above, the dependent clause tells *when* the lawyer became so popular (*after he won his first case*). Adverbs answer the question *when?* (see Section 1e). Therefore, we can say that the dependent clauses in the first two examples are acting as adverbs. In the third example, the dependent clause (*who won his first case*) acts as an adjective. This entire clause describes the lawyer by telling us *which one.*

PRACTICE EXERCISE 38: RECOGNIZING DEPENDENT CLAUSES

Underline the dependent clauses in these sentences. Circle the subject and verb in each dependent clause.

1. Because she stayed on her diet, she lost the weight that she desired.
2. Judge Benson, who had recently retired, remained on the bench when my case came up for review.
3. Since you have a high level of motivation, you should succeed in this class.
4. The criminal case, which is the last of the day, is about to be heard.
5. You will feel better if you learn to control your temper.

There are three kinds of dependent clauses, classified by their relationship to the main clause. Those that act like adjectives are called **adjective clauses**, and those that act as adverbs are called **adverb clauses**. Dependent clauses that function as nouns are called **noun clauses**.

Adjective Clauses. Like words and phrases, clauses can act as adjectives. Following are some examples of the different ways that adjectives can be written.

Using Adjectives

Word	Phrase	Dependent Clause
red car	car *with the red finish*	car *that has the red finish*
intelligent student	student *with intelligence*	student *who has intelligence*

In each case the noun (*car* and *student*) is described. An adjective clause is a dependent clause that acts in the same way as an adjective, to modify a noun or pronoun. All of the adjectives above tell us *which one* or *what kind* of car and student. The dependent clause that serves as an adjective is usually introduced by a special type of pronoun, the **relative pronoun** (see Section 1b).

The Relative Pronouns for Adjective Clauses

that
which, whichever
who, whose, whoever
whom, whomever

Be careful when recognizing relative pronouns since they may be used in other ways. For example, the pronoun *who* can be used as an interrogative pronoun to ask a question. (*Who is absent?*) The pronoun *that* can serve as a demonstrative pronoun to point to another noun (*That is my book*). To be a relative pronoun, it must be in a dependent clause.

A dependent clause can never be a full sentence; it must be attached to an independent clause. Here are some examples of adjective clauses used in complete sentences:

Dependent Clauses That Act as Adjectives

The judge was a very intelligent woman *who graduated first in her class*. (which one?)

The document *that I signed* will protect me from legal action. (which one?)

That book, *which is a great novel*, was given to me as a present. (what kind?)

You can see in these examples that each dependent clause describes a noun in the sentence (shown by the arrows). The noun being described is part of the independent clause.

Some relative pronouns are preceded by a preposition. For example:

Adjective Clauses Preceded by a Preposition

The college *to which I wanted to go* was very expensive.
John, *for whom I brought the book*, was my best friend.
The doctor, *in whose office I was examined*, told me I was healthy.

As shown in these examples, it is better to place the preposition in the beginning of the dependent clause rather than at the end. That is, *to which I wanted to go* is better than *which I wanted to go to*.

PRACTICE EXERCISE 39: RECOGNIZING ADJECTIVE CLAUSES

Underline the adjective clauses in these sentences. Circle the relative pronoun. Then, draw an arrow to the noun or pronoun in the main clause that is being modified. For example:

The doctor (who) operated on me just arrived in the hospital.

1. The book that I just completed soon became a best-seller.

2. Mary or Jane, whoever comes first, will be my tutor for today.

3. The president of the United States, whom I respected very much, came to speak at my school.

4. Some people whom I cannot mention will be here soon.

5. The business started making money, which I really needed.

6. The senator for whom I voted will soon be in town to deliver a speech.

7. The artist whose painting was sold is now a rich man.

8. Mr. Richards, who teaches English, is a very good teacher.

Adverb Clauses. Like adverbs and adverb phrases, adverb clauses modify a verb, adjective, or another adverb. Here are some examples of adverbs using words, phrases, and dependent clauses.

Using Adverbs

Word	Phrase	Dependent Clause
sleep *regularly*	sleep *at night*	sleep *whenever the sun goes down*
sit *outside*	sit *on the front step*	sit *where the front step was fixed*

In each of these examples, the verb, *sleep* or *sit*, is described. Recall that adverbs answer the questions *when, where, how,* and *how much* (see Section 1e). Adverbial dependent clauses can also tell us *why, under what condition,* and *to what degree.* For example:

Adverb Dependent Clauses

When: *When you read the Constitution,* you will learn your rights.

Where: The White House is a place *where you should show respect.*

How: The president acts *as though he missed a night's sleep.*

Why: *Because you study hard,* you will pass the test.

Under What Condition: *Although he is the best,* the lawyer needs to prepare for each case.

Comparison: John worked harder *than Mary worked.*

You may have noticed that certain words are often used to introduce dependent clauses. These special words are called subordinating conjunctions (see Section 1g). **Subordinating conjunctions** indicate the relationship between the dependent clause and the main clause. Here is a list of some commonly used subordinating conjunctions:

Subordinating Conjunctions for Adverb Clauses

Time (when)	Place (where)	Manner (how)
after, as soon as, as long as, before, since, until, when, whenever, while	where, wherever	as, as if, as though

Subordinating Conjunctions for Adverb Clauses (continued)

Cause (why)	Condition	Comparison
because, since, so that	whether, although, even though, if, unless	as, than

PRACTICE EXERCISE 40: RECOGNIZING ADVERB CLAUSES

Underline the adverb clauses in these sentences. Circle the subordinating conjunction. Then, draw an arrow to the word or words in the main clause being modified. For example:

(Until) it was time for the operation, the doctor was resting.

1. If you don't stop this diet, you will have more health problems than I have.

2. We worked all night because we wanted to finish the paper.

3. When you complete the assignment, you may leave the class.

4. Some people become more motivated as soon as they begin to see success.

5. Since you came to this country, you have lived where you feel most comfortable.

6. You can leave class as soon as you complete the assignment.

7. Until you lose fifty pounds, you will stay on the diet.

8. The judge ruled in the defendant's favor because the lawyer argued the case very well.

Noun Clauses. Nouns can appear as single words (see Section 1a), groups of words (see Section 6), or dependent clauses. Noun clauses play the role of a noun. They may be introduced by the relative pronouns (*who, whoever, which, whichever, what,* and *whatever*—see Section 1b). Also, they may be connected to the main clause by such words as *that, when, where, why, how,* or *whether*. Here are some examples:

Noun Dependent Clauses

Subject:	*How the lawyer managed to win the case* is beyond me.
Direct Object:	I imagine *that he will run for re-election.*
Indirect Object:	I will give *whoever comes first* a hundred-dollar certificate.
Object of Preposition:	The application must be completed *by whoever comes to work.*
Predicate Nominative:	That man is *whom I met.*

PRACTICE EXERCISE 41: RECOGNIZING NOUN CLAUSES

Underline the noun clauses in these sentences. Circle the relative pronouns or any words that introduce the dependent clauses. Then, indicate the role of the noun clause by writing S for subject or O for object (including indirect object and object of preposition). For example:

> S
> (Whatever) you do will be all right with me.

1. I hope that I will become a good writer.

2. Why she stayed on the diet is difficult to understand.

3. How to write an essay will be discussed in the next chapter.

4. The money will be given to whoever arrives first.

5. You can go on whichever diet you like best.

6. That you will succeed is my greatest wish.

7. Do you know what ingredients are listed on the label?

8. Whether you are married or single, we will still be friends.

PRACTICE EXERCISE 42: RECOGNIZING COMPLEX SENTENCES

In the following paragraph, underline each dependent clause. Circle the subordinate conjunction, relative pronoun, or word that introduces the dependent clause. If the dependent clause is an adjective clause, write Adj over the clause. If the dependent clause is an adverb clause, write Adv over the clause. If the dependent clause is a noun clause, indicate the sentence relationship by putting over the clause an S for subject or O for object. For example:

> O
> Many people think (that) marriage is a good thing. (If) everyone believed
> Adv
> in it, the world would be a better place.

When most people marry in the United States, a beautiful ceremony is performed. The people who are married make a promise that is supposed to last a lifetime. How people feel about their marriage does make a difference. If everyone kept his or her marital promise, our society would be better.

Those who are affected most directly by the marriage commitment are the children. Children learn what it means to grow up in a loving family. They learn to feel good about themselves. On the contrary, children who grow up in a broken home have a more difficult time than other children have in making adjustments in life. However, if they can cope with their situation, most children of divorced parents will grow up just fine. The reason is that children adapt to whatever is their family life as long as it is loving.

Punctuation of Dependent Clauses. We've shown the punctuation of dependent clauses in the many examples provided in this section. For a complete guide to punctuation of dependent clauses, see Section 10, rules 4 and 5. The following summary of the rules for proper punctuation should be helpful.

1. *When the dependent clause is at the beginning of a sentence*, place a comma at the end of the dependent clause or between the dependent and main clauses. For example:

   Because John was prepared, he passed the course.

2. *When the dependent clause is at the end of a sentence or after the main clause*, punctuation between the clauses may not be necessary. For example:

   John saw the movie *after he read the book.*

3. *When the dependent clause is inside the main clause*, there are two ways to punctuate.

   ■ If the dependent clause is necessary to understand an element in the main clause, then do *not* set it off with commas. This type of dependent clause is called a **restrictive clause**. For example:

      The judge *who will try our case* just came in the room.

      The dependent clause tells you necessary information about the judge—he will try our case.

   ■ If the information in the dependent clause is not essential in the sentence, then set it off from the main clause with two commas. This type of dependent clause is called a **nonrestrictive clause**. For example:

      Mr. Jones, *who lives in New York*, is my new lawyer.

      The dependent clause (*who lives in New York*) is set off with commas because it does not give essential information.

   Of course, it is the writer's decision whether a dependent clause is essential or not. Following are examples of a restrictive clause and a nonrestrictive clause.

Restrictive and Nonrestrictive Clauses

Restrictive (no punctuation):   The gun *that was used in the murder* was placed into evidence.

Nonrestrictive (set off with commas):   The gun, *which is stored in my closet,* is a valuable antique.

The fact that the gun was used in a murder is essential to understanding why it was placed into evidence. Therefore, in the first sentence, this dependent clause is not set off from the main clause. However, the gun in the second example is valuable no matter where it is stored. Since the gun's location is not necessary for understanding the main clause, it is separated from the main clause with commas. Note that the relative pronoun *that* cannot be used in a nonrestrictive clause. The relative pronoun *which* may be used in a restrictive or nonrestrictive clause.

PRACTICE EXERCISE 43: WRITING COMPLEX SENTENCES

Make a complex sentence by adding a main clause to each of these dependent clauses. Put one line under the subject and two lines under the verb in each clause, dependent and independent. Punctuate each sentence properly.

1. when I began working on this project

   _____

2. because the paper was well written

   _____

3. that I like to eat

   _____

4. who taught me how to ride a bicycle

   _____

5. although I got off to a poor start

   _____

6. which made me gain weight

   _____

7. unless the weather changes

   _____

8. as if you are my boss

   _____

[8] Avoiding Common Errors

In this section we discuss how to recognize and correct some common errors: (1) misplaced and dangling modifiers, (2) sentence fragments, (3) run-on sentences, (4) comma splices, and (5) shifts of person and tense.

[8a] Misplaced and Dangling Modifiers

Adjectives, adverbs, phrases, and clauses are all modifiers. We have seen that words, phrases, and dependent clauses can serve as modifiers. Because modifiers change the meaning of parts of a sentence, it is necessary to place modifiers close to the words they modify. If a modifier is far enough away from the word it modifies to cause confusion, it is called a **misplaced modifier**. If the word being modified is not even present in the sentence, the modifier is called a **dangling modifier**.

Misplaced Modifiers. Misplaced modifiers are out of place in the sentence. Here are some examples:

Misplaced Modifiers

Misplaced Participle:	The professor left the room *tired.*
Corrected:	The *tired* professor left the room.
Misplaced Participial Phrase:	*Having no fuel,* the gasoline station was not far away from us.
Corrected:	*Having no fuel,* our car was not far from the gasoline station.
Misplaced Prepositional Phrase:	The man was reading about the trial *in the newspaper.*
Corrected:	The man was reading *the newspaper article* about the trial.
Misplaced Dependent Clause:	*After he went off the diet,* John thought Henry looked too thin.
Corrected:	*After he went off the diet,* Henry looked too thin according to John.

In the first example, the participle *tired* is used as an adjective. However, it was the professor who was tired, not the room. In the corrected version, the participle is placed right next to the word it modifies, *professor*. In the second example, the participial phrase *having no fuel* is misplaced; it does not describe the gasoline station. The car was out of fuel, not the gasoline station. In the third example, the prepositional phrase *in the newspaper* is misplaced because it describes where the man was reading, not where the trial was. Finally, in the last example, the dependent clause *after he went off the diet* does not describe John. It was Henry who went off the diet.

Misplaced modifiers can be corrected by rearranging the affected parts of the sentence. Sometimes it is helpful to rewrite the sentence to make it clear.

Dangling Modifiers. Dangling modifiers are missing the element that is being modified. Here are some examples:

Dangling Modifiers

Dangling Participle:	*Tired,* the class was finally over.
Corrected:	*Tired,* I finally was finished with the class.
Dangling Prepositional Phrase:	*While running for president,* many people were supportive.
Corrected Version 1:	*While running for president,* John was supported by many people.
Corrected Version 2:	*While John was running for president,* many people were supportive.

In the first example, the participle *tired* is dangling because we do not know who was tired. In the second example, *while running for president* is a dangling prepositional phrase. It is not clear who is running for president. Two ways to correct the problem are shown. In both correct versions, there is a reference to John because he is the one running for president.

Dangling modifiers are corrected by rearranging or adding words to the sentence. The goal is to place the modifiers close to the words being modified in order to make a clear connection.

PRACTICE EXERCISE 44: CORRECTING MISPLACED AND DANGLING MODIFIERS

Underline the misplaced or dangling modifiers in each sentence. Then, rewrite the sentence correctly.

1. Sprinkled with blue dye, the bank teller gave the money to the thief.

   _____

2. Eating between meals, my weight is too high.

   _____

3. Climbing down the mountain, lunch was waiting for us.

   _____

4. The judge resigned from the case that was prejudiced.

   _____

5. While preparing for the test, my friend tried to interrupt me.

   _____

6. John wrote the book that was damaged on a computer.

   _____

7. Broken in five pieces, John returned the radio to the store.

   _____

8. Everyone needs motivation for success that is required.

   _____

[8b] Sentence Fragments

For a sentence to be complete, it must have a subject, a verb and express a complete thought. Sentences that fail to meet these requirements are called fragments. Fragments are just parts of a complete sentence.

We often use fragments in speech, especially in response to a question. For example, in response to the question, "What did you do last night?" you might say, "Studied hard all night." In response to the question, "Where are you going?" you might answer with the prepositional phrase, "To the store." This is permissible in speech. However, unless you are writing dialogue, you should use complete sentences in your writing.

Here are some examples of fragments.

Sentence Fragments

With the great joy of having finished the course. (Prepositional phrases with no subject or verb)

Broken in three places. (Participial phrases with no subject or verb)

Responding to peer pressure. (Participial or gerund phrase with no subject or verb)

To become a good student. (Infinitive phrase with no subject or verb)

The lawyer who tried the case. (No verb)

The man eating the chicken stew. (Incomplete verb with no helping verb or adjective phrase)

Ran all the way home. (No subject)

Because I want to become the best. (Dependent clause that contains subject and verb but does not express a complete thought)

PRACTICE EXERCISE 45: RECOGNIZING FRAGMENTS

Determine whether each group of words is a sentence or a fragment. If it is a complete sentence, write S on the line. For fragments, write F on the line.

1. _____ Eating less to lose weight.

2. _____ The teacher helping me to do better.

3. _____ To join the most important club in the school.

4. _____ Searching students in school constitutes an illegal search.

5. _____ When taking a test that you need to pass.

6. _____ After brainstorming and identifying topics.

7. _____ Because she was a dedicated student.

8. _____ I enjoy reading good books.

9. _____ Her diet not very healthy.

10. _____ As you enter the building and find your classroom.

There are three common fragment types: phrase fragments, subject–verb fragments, and dependent clause fragments.

Phrase Fragments. Phrases are groups of words without a subject and a verb. Therefore, any type of phrase will be a sentence fragment if presented alone or in combination with other phrases.

Phrase fragments can be caused by confusion about verbals (words that come from a verb but are used as other parts of speech—see Section 6b). If a verbal is mistaken for a verb, a phrase fragment will often result.

Here are some examples of prepositional and verbal phrase fragments.

Phrase Fragments

With much regret for hurting your feelings. (Prepositional phrase)
Paralyzed from the neck down. (Participial phrase)
Hanging with the wrong crowd. (Gerund or participial phrase)
To have such a great opportunity to express myself. (Infinitive phrase)

To correct a phrase fragment, you need to create an independent clause with a subject and a verb. Following are the corrected phrase fragments from above.

Corrected Phrase Fragments

I am sending you this sympathy card *with much regret for hurting your feelings.*
Paralyzed from the neck down, Christopher Reeve is still a leader among men.
Hanging with the wrong crowd is a big mistake.
I am happy *to have such a great opportunity to express myself.*

PRACTICE EXERCISE 46: CORRECTING PHRASE FRAGMENTS

Write a complete sentence using each of these phrase fragments. Be sure to create an independent clause with a subject and verb.

1. On the side of the road.

   _____

2. Having no control over the situation.

   _____

3. Digested very quickly in my stomach.

   _____

4. Working on my paper for hours.

   _____

5. To get a passing grade on the test.

   _____

Subject–Verb Fragments. A sentence that lacks either a subject and verb is a fragment. Also, sentences with incomplete verbs (missing a required helping verb) are fragments. Subject-verb fragments often occur after an introduction or a question. For example:

What are you doing? *Writing a letter.* (No subject)
I just read the Bible. *A great book.* (No verb)

The first fragment has no subject. It is easy to correct by adding one. For example, "*I am* writing a letter." The fragment *a great book* refers to the Bible. It cannot stand alone as a sentence because it does not have a verb. You may correct this problem by creating an independent clause using "a great book" as the subject or the object of the sentence. For example, "A great book is hard to find" or "It is a great book."

Another way to correct the problem is to create an appositive. An appositive is a word or phrase that means the same thing as the noun or pronoun that it follows (see Section 6d). Appositives are usually set off by commas. Here is a corrected version of the example above using the fragment as an appositive:

I just read the Bible, *a great book.* (Appositive)

Another type of fragment contains a subject, but has an incomplete verb. Some verbs must have helping verbs to be complete. All present progressive verbs (*-ing* endings) appear with a form of the *be* verb (see Section 1d). For example:

Fragment—missing helping verb: *The boy running.*
Corrected version: The boy *is* running.

Without the helping verb (*is*), the sentence is a fragment.

Also, the perfect tenses use a form of the helping verb *have* to make them complete. Failure to use the helping verb is particularly common when an irregular verb is used as a past participle. For example, the past participle *broken* is needed in this sentence:

Fragment—missing helping verb: *Students broken most of the rules.*
Corrected version: Students *have* broken most of the rules.

PRACTICE EXERCISE 47: CORRECTING SUBJECT AND VERB FRAGMENTS

Correct each of these sentences by eliminating the fragment. You may choose to create an independent clause or attach a fragment as an appositive.

1. The group played prisoner. A game of social control.

   _____

2. My digestion never been better.

   _____

3. I enjoy living in New York City. The most densely populated city in the United States.

   _____

4. Working closely with me.

   _____

5. At school we saw a movie. A drama about the origin of life.

Dependent Clause Fragments. As we saw in Section 7b, dependent clauses have both a subject and a verb. For this reason, dependent clauses are sometimes written as sentences. However, dependent clauses do not express complete thoughts and cannot stand alone. They are sentence fragments. For example, *When John reads the story* is a fragment. Although it contains a subject (*John*) and a verb (*read*), it is not a complete thought (*what happens when John reads the story?*).

Dependent clauses are often introduced by subordinating conjunctions (*although, where, when, if*—see Section 1g) or relative pronouns (*who, whom, whose, which, that*—see Section 1b). Simply by adding one of these conjunctions or pronouns to a sentence, you can create this type of fragment.

Here are three ways to correct a dependent clause fragment:

1. Create an independent (main) clause and attach the dependent clause to it.
2. Remove the subordinating conjunction or replace the relative pronoun with a noun or pronoun.
3. Change the fragment into a question.

Here are some examples:

Dependent Clause Fragments

Fragment with Subordinate Conjunction:	*Because you worked so hard on the paper.*
Corrected by creating main clause:	*Because you worked so hard on the paper,* I gave you an A.
Corrected by removing conjunction:	*You worked so hard on the paper.*
Fragment with Relative Pronoun:	*Who won the best writer award.*
Corrected by creating main clause:	The student *who won the best writer award* was honored at the party.
Corrected by removing relative pronoun and replacing it with a noun:	The student *won the best writer award.*
Corrected by changing fragment to a question:	*Who won the best writer award?*

PRACTICE EXERCISE 48: CORRECTING DEPENDENT CLAUSE FRAGMENTS

Correct each of these fragments in two ways: (1) by adding a main clause and (2) by removing the subordinating conjunction or relative pronoun.

1. Because you continued to eat after being full.

   _____

   _____

2. Before the speaker began to talk.

   _____

   _____

3. While I was digesting my dinner.

   _____

   _____

4. That was running down the hall.

   _____

   _____

5. Who tried to help me with my writing.

   _____

   _____

[8c] Run-on Sentences and Comma Splices

A run-on sentence happens when a writer does not recognize the end of a sentence. The writer continues from one independent clause (see Section 7a) right into another independent clause without any punctuation. For example:

Run-on Sentence

The lawyer delivered the opening statement then he began to question the witnesses.

This sentence is a run-on because two independent clauses are joined without any punctuation.

Another common mistake is to place a comma between two independent clauses that are not joined by a coordinating conjunction (*and, or, but, yet, so, for*—see Section 1g). This mistake is called the comma splice. For example:

Comma Splice

The Constitution is our best protection, we need it to maintain order in society.

There are five ways to correct run-ons and comma splices:

1. Separate the independent clauses into two sentences.
2. Use a semicolon between the two independent clauses.
3. Connect the two independent clauses with a semicolon and conjunctive adverb (see Section 1g).
4. Connect the two independent clauses with a comma and a coordinating conjunction.
5. Change one of the independent clauses into a dependent clause by adding a subordinating conjunction and placing it before or after the main clause. Be sure to place a comma after the dependent clause when it is before the main clause.

Here is an example of each type of correction:

Correcting Run-on Sentences and Comma Splices

Run-on:	The lawyer delivered the opening statement then he began to question the witnesses.
Comma Splice:	The Constitution is our best protection, we need it to maintain order in society.
Correction 1: *(separate sentences)*	The lawyer delivered the opening statement. Then, he began to question the witnesses.
	The Constitution is our best protection. We need it to maintain order in society.
Correction 2: *(semicolon between clauses)*	The lawyer delivered the opening statement; he began to question the witnesses.
	The Constitution is our best protection; we need it to maintain order in society.
Correction 3: *(semicolon with conjunctive adverb)*	The lawyer delivered the opening statement; *then*, he began to question the witnesses.
	The Constitution is our best protection; *furthermore*, we need it to maintain order in society.
Correction 4: *(comma with coordinating conjunction)*	The lawyer delivered the opening statement, *and* he began to question the witnesses.
	The Constitution is our best protection, *and* we need it to maintain order in society.

> *Correction 5:*
> *(create a dependent clause*
> *by adding a subordinating*
> *conjunction)*

After the lawyer delivered the opening statement, he began to question the witnesses.

The Constitution is our best protection *because* we need it to maintain order in society.

PRACTICE EXERCISE 49: CORRECTING RUN-ON SENTENCES AND COMMA SPLICES

Some of the following sentences are run-ons or comma splices. Put an S on the line if the sentence is a complete sentence. Put an R on the line for run-on and a CS for comma splice. Then, rewrite each run-on and comma splice using one of the methods just described. Try to use all five correction methods at least once in this exercise.

1. _____ Criminal law, one of the most difficult specialties in the practice of law, is very demanding.

   _____

2. _____ A good diet is important, it is connected to our state of health.

   _____

3. _____ Every student should study for as long as needed to obtain good grades and complete the curriculum.

   _____

4. _____ The judge ordered the suspect to appear before the court and I hoped that he would go.

   _____

5. _____ Writing often and reading a lot are the best ways to become an effective reader and writer, you will need these skills to succeed.

   _____

6. _____ Becoming motivated in college is not an easy task for many of us have developed bad habits by the time we get to college.

   _____

7. _____ Most people want to be liked by other group members with whom they are affiliated.

   _____

8. _____ Social control mechanisms rarely work unless someone is in a position of authority but often nobody is in a position of authority and teenagers run wild.

_____

9. _____ People feel safer when police are on the street yet they cannot completely stop crime.

_____

10. _____ I was satisfied the student wrote the paper in class.

_____

[8d] Shifts of Person and Tense

Before you begin writing an essay, you need to decide the appropriate person (see Section 4b) and verb tense (see Section 1d). It is a good idea to stay in the same person and tense throughout the essay. In this section we discuss needless shifts and show you how to correct them.

Person. You may write in the first, second, or third person However, do not shift needlessly from one person to another in an essay. For example:

> Dieting can be dangerous. Before starting one, a *person* should always see *his* or *her* doctor. *He* or *she* must be in good health to be on a vigorous diet. Otherwise, *you* will lose your strength.

This essay starts in the third person (*person, his, her, he, she*). Then, it shifts into the second person (*you*). This shift of person is awkward and should be avoided. Either change the entire essay into the second person or stay in the third person.

A common mistake writers make is to shift into the first person to give a personal account of something. For example:

> Before *you* buy an expensive product, *you* should check out the reputation of the dealer. *I* always call the Better Business Bureau before *I* buy anything over $100.

This essay begins in the second person (*you*). However, it shifts into the first person (*I*). It is better to stay in the second person throughout the essay—*You should always call the Better Business Bureau before buying anything over $100.*

PRACTICE EXERCISE 50: AVOIDING SHIFTS OF PERSON

The following paragraph was originally written in the first person. Some of the personal pronouns have been shifted to the second or third person. Underline any shifts in person that appear awkward, and write the correct pronouns above them. You may also change verbs so that they agree with their pronoun subjects.

Stress is a reaction to stressors in our lives, that is, reactions to real or perceived threats to our sense of well-being. One source of your stress is frustration—the blocking or thwarting of your goal-directed behaviors. When something or someone in our environment blocks your goal-directed behaviors, we say that he is experiencing environmental frustration. When his goal-directed behaviors are thwarted by your own shortcomings, the frustration is referred to as personal frustration. The amount of stress they experience depends on both the importance of the goal we are seeking and the completeness or totality of the blocking or thwarting.

(Gerow, *Essentials of Psychology*, 2nd edition, HarperCollins, 1996, p. 403.)

Tense. Verb tenses indicate the time in which something takes place. In your writing, try to be consistent in verb tense; that is, avoid needless shifts. For example:

Shift in Verb Tense:	John *hits* the ball over the fence; then, he *ran* around the bases.
Correct:	John *hits* the ball over the fence; then, he *runs* around the bases.
Correct:	John *hit* the ball over the fence; then, he *ran* around the bases.
Shift in Verb Tense:	Mr. Jones *is afraid* of taking tests. Therefore, he *refused* to go to school.
Correct:	Mr. Jones *is afraid* of taking tests. Therefore, he *refuses* to go to school.
Correct:	Mr. Jones *was afraid* of taking tests. Therefore, he *refused* to go to school.

In both examples, the verb tense shifts from present tense (*hits, is*) to past tense (*ran, refused*). In the corrected versions, the verb tenses are consistent.

Although you should try to stay in the same verb tense, you may shift verb tenses with good reason. For example:

Because Maria *will start* her diet tomorrow, she *has been eating* like a pig all day.

PRACTICE EXERCISE 51: AVOIDING SHIFTS OF TENSE

This paragraph was originally written entirely in the past tense. Some of the verb tenses have been shifted. Underline any verbs that appear awkward, and write the correct verb forms above them.

In the 1960 presidential race Kennedy challenged his Republican opponent, Richard M. Nixon, to a series of television debates. At the time, Kennedy faces an uphill battle. Young, handsome, and wealthy, Kennedy is considered by many too young, too handsome, and too wealthy to make an effective president. His undistinguished political record stands in stark contrast to Nixon's work in Congress and his eight years as Eisenhower's vice president. In addition, Kennedy was Catholic, and Americans have never elected a Catholic president. Behind in the polls, Kennedy will need a dramatic boost. That was the reason for the challenge. Against the advice of his campaign manager, Nixon accepts.

(Martin, et al., *America and Its Peoples*, 3rd edition, HarperCollins, 1997, p. 1001.)

[9] Parallelism

Often, you will write sentences that contain a series of two or more elements (nouns, verbs, adjectives, phrases, clauses, and so on). Any series of elements connected by a conjunction (*and, or, but*) or part of a comparison must have the same grammatical form, called **parallelism**. For example:

Sentence 1

Wrong: I want to marry her because she is *kind, intelligent,* and *has* great beauty.

Correct: I want to marry her because she is *kind, intelligent,* and *beautiful.*

Correct: I want to marry her because she has *kindness, intelligence,* and great *beauty.*

Sentence 2

Wrong: For this class I need a *notebook, textbook,* and *to look for my dictionary.*

Correct: For this class I need a *notebook, textbook,* and *dictionary.*

Correct: For this class I need *to get a notebook and a textbook* and *to look for my dictionary.*

Sentence 3

Wrong: The sleepwalker went *down the hall, through the kitchen,* and *she opened the refrigerator.*

Correct: The sleepwalker went *down the hall, through the kitchen,* and *into the dining room.*

Correct: The sleepwalker went *down the hall* and *into the kitchen;* then, *she opened the refrigerator.*

Sentence 4

Wrong: Peter is a student *with great talent* and *who should be elected to the student council.*

Correct: Peter is a student *who has great talent* and *who should be elected to the student council.*

Correct: Peter is a student *with great talent;* therefore, *he should be elected to the student council.*

Sentence 5

Wrong: *Writing on a computer* is better than *when I wrote with a pen.*

Correct: *Writing on a computer* is better than *writing with a pen.*

Correct: *When I write on the computer,* it is better than *when I write with a pen.*

The first sentence is not parallel because *has great beauty* is not an adjective like *kind* and *intelligent*. This sentence can be corrected by changing all the elements into parallel adjectives or parallel nouns.

The series in the second sentence contains two nouns and an infinitive phrase. The first correct version has a parallel series of nouns. The second correct version has two infinitive phrases. When writing a series of infinitive phrases, you do not need to rewrite the word *to* before each phrase. For example:

I need *to* eat, (*to*) shower, and (*to*) dress.

The series in the third sentence starts with two prepositional phrases but ends with an independent clause. To correct this problem, we changed the independent clause into a parallel prepositional phrase. The sentence can also be corrected by changing it into a compound sentence.

In the fourth sentence, the prepositional phrase (*with great talent*) is followed by a noun clause with the relative pronoun *who*. The sentence can be corrected by changing the prepositional phrase into a noun clause (*who has great talent*). It can also be corrected by making it into a compound sentence by changing the noun clause into an independent clause.

The fifth sentence demonstrates the need for parallel structure of comparisons (*than*). The sentence can be made parallel by making both sides of the comparison into gerund phrases or dependent clauses.

PRACTICE EXERCISE 52: PARALLELISM

Underline the faulty parallelism that you find in each sentence. Then, rewrite the sentence correctly on the line. Some sentences may be correct. For example:

I really need more exercise and to diet.

I really need to exercise more and to diet.

1. My English teacher is considerate, very friendly, and will help me pass this course.

   _____

2. Your lawyer wants you to answer some questions, sign a few papers, and, most important, telling the truth.

   _____

3. I recommend the Pritikin Diet, the Adkins Diet, or eating less.

   _____

4. Most of our students learn to read, to write, and they study hard.

_____

5. Counting calories is not as good as when you cut down on the amount of fat you eat.

_____

6. The sleep researcher said that sleep is controlled by brain waves, that we need to sleep regularly, and to relax.

_____

7. John is a student with motivation and who will probably succeed.

_____

8. The couple should not get divorced because they are in love, because they have three children, and staying friends.

_____

9. Martin Luther King delivered his speech in the morning, before a large crowd, and with great emotion.

_____

10. The prisoner said, "Give me freedom, give me dignity, or I will die."

_____

[10] Punctuation

Punct

Punctuation is an important part of writing. Through punctuation, you tell the reader how to group words, where to pause or stop, and which words to emphasize. Without it, your writing would be confusing or even impossible to understand.

Punctuation is usually determined by the grammatical structure of the sentence. Therefore, it will be helpful to refer to the appropriate grammar sections.

We will introduce the following elements of punctuation:

- end marks
- the comma
- the semicolon
- the colon
- the apostrophe
- quotations
- the hyphen
- the dash
- parentheses
- italics

[10a] End Marks

Punctuation marks used to end a sentence are the period, the question mark, and the exclamation point.

The Period [.]. The period is used at the end of a sentence that is a statement (declarative), command (imperative), or indirect quotation. For example:

Statements:	Brenda, who started her diet yesterday, lost three pounds.
	John is my best friend.
	Writing essays is easier if you follow the writing process.
Commands:	Get to school on time.
	Release that prisoner.
	Meet me at Joe's restaurant.
Indirect Quotations:	My teacher asked me if I did my homework.
	John asked where I put his books.
	My mother asked us whether we will be home early.

The period is used at the end of most abbreviations. For example:

Dr. (Doctor)   ft. (foot)
Mr. (Mister)   Co. (Company)
N.Y.C. (New York City)   Sept. (September)
Cal. (California)   M. L. King (Martin Luther)
P.S.U. (Penn State University) etc. (et cetera)

However, do not use a period with postal abbreviations (NY, PA, FL), names of well-known companies or products (IBM, NASA, FBI, CD-ROM), television and radio stations (ABC, WFLN), and well-known shortened terms (TV, gym, lab, memo).

Three periods (ellipses) are used to note the omission of a word or words within a quotation. Three periods plus the appropriate end mark are used if the omission is at the end of the quotation. For example:

"We the People of the United States . . . do ordain and establish this Constitution for the United States of America."

"When, in the course of human events, it becomes necessary for one people to dissolve the political bonds. . . ."

Notice that the second sentence has four periods at the end of the quotation. The first is the regular end mark, followed by three periods (ellipses).

You may use a period at the end of a nonsentence. A nonsentence lacks a subject and a verb; however, it is a legitimate expression as long as it is not a fragment (see

Section 8b). Legitimate nonsentences include greetings, dialogue, and mild exclamations (see Conjunctions, Section 1g). For example:

Greeting:	Welcome to my class.
	Good morning.
Dialogue:	Where is my book? On the table.
Mild Exclamations:	Say there.
	Oh, my.

The Question Mark [?]. Use a question mark at the end of a direct question. For example:

Who is the greatest boxer who ever lived?
Have you ever met my favorite teacher?
That man hit you, didn't he?
Your teacher failed you?

Notice that the last sentence could also be a statement. The question mark is needed to signal that it is a question, not a fact.

Do not use a question mark after indirect questions (*He asked what time it was.*) or polite requests in question form (*Would you please send me a free sample.*).

The Exclamation Point [!]. The exclamation point is used after a word, phrase, or sentence that expresses excitement or strong feeling. For example:

Help!
Stop it!
Get out of here!
Watch out, that man has a gun!
You wrote the best play ever!

A command may be followed by an exclamation point if it is emphatic (shows strong feeling). For example:

Emphatic:	Come over here right now!
Polite:	Please come over here.

Some sentences may be emphatic statements or questions. Use either an exclamation point or a question mark; never use more than one end mark. For example:

Exclamation:	You shot a cop!
Question:	You shot a cop?

PRACTICE EXERCISE 53: END MARKS

Put the appropriate end mark at the end of each sentence.

1. Why do you want to get a good grade

2. Wow, I made the grade

3. Because you are my best friend, I will help you with the paper

4. Don't you know who I am

5. Stop the war

6. Please wait a minute

7. When David finishes this book, he wants me to read it, too

8. Would you send me the newest computer chip

9. Mr. Rogers asked if I would come in early today

10. It was Mr. Smith who called, wasn't it

[10b] The Comma [,]

Commas divide sentences into parts and indicate pauses within sentences. Have a reason for using each comma in your writing, and try to avoid using them carelessly. Use commas in the following situations:

1. between independent clauses in compound sentences

2. between items in a series

3. between adjectives

4. after introductory words, phrases, and clauses

5. to set off nonessential elements

6. to set off interrupters

7. to set off examples, contrasts, and question tags

8. in direct quotations

9. in dates and addresses

10. in letters

11. to prevent misunderstanding

1. Commas between Independent Clauses. Use a comma between two independent clauses that are joined by coordinating conjunctions (*and, but, or, nor, for, yet,* and *so*) to make a compound sentence (see Section 7a). Place the comma before the conjunction. For example:

Independent Clause Independent Clause
1. My family moved to Texas, *and* I joined them.
2. Diane started her diet, *but* she forgot to visit her doctor.
3. You may finish your homework in class, *or* you may do it at home.
4. The salesman was not very helpful, *nor* was he very friendly.
5. Alex was grateful for the handout, *for* he could not pay his rent without it.
6. Everyone left work early, *yet* the job was not done.
7. The jury selection is completed, *so* the trial can begin.

Do *not* use a comma under the following circumstances:

- When coordinating conjunctions are used to connect words or phrases. For example:

John *and* Mary were married in the church.
(*and* connects two words—compound subjects)

I came to visit my mother *but* not my father.
(*but* connects two phrases—compound objects)

In the morning *or* in the afternoon, we will get together.
(*or* connects two prepositional phrases)

My brother has a valuable stamp collection *yet* doesn't like to show it to anyone.
(*yet* connects two verbs, *has* and *doesn't*)

- When very short independent clauses are connected by a coordinating conjunction. For example:

He came *and* he conquered.
She is rich *but* he is poor.

- When independent clauses are *not* connected by a coordinating conjunction. For example:

Wrong: The teacher entered the room, we began working.

Correct: The teacher entered the room; we began working.

The first sentence is a comma splice (see Section 8c). To punctuate it properly, use a semicolon instead of a comma.

PRACTICE EXERCISE 54: COMMAS BETWEEN INDEPENDENT CLAUSES

Place a comma before coordinating conjunctions (and, but, or, nor, for, yet, and so) that connect independent clauses. Some sentences may not need a comma.

1. Everyone knows how important it is to find the right partner in marriage but many people fail in this regard.
2. Most people find their romance near where they live and they eventually get married.

3. Staying married requires commitment for those who take it lightly will probably fail.

4. Children of divorced parents are disadvantaged yet they usually survive.

5. Children of divorced parents and children of married parents seem to differ in important ways.

6. Children of divorced parents need a significant relationship with the same-sex parent so they will have a model for development.

7. Children of married parents need love and attention from both parents or they will suffer.

8. Marriage is important yet divorce is not the end of the world.

9. Make a wise decision about your mate and your chances will be better.

10. Love your children and they will achieve their dreams.

2. Commas between Items in a Series. Use a comma to separate words, phrases, and clauses in a series of three or more. Place the comma after each item in the series (except the last one). Sometimes the last comma before the conjunction (*and, or*) is omitted. However, for clarity it is better to use the final comma, especially in college writing. For example:

Words: *John, Jim,* and *Mary* took the same course. (Nouns)

Many students must *work, study,* and *sacrifice* to complete school. (Verbs)

Your essay was *concise, intelligent,* and *interesting.* (Adjectives)

The students worked *quietly, attentively,* and *willingly.* (Adverbs)

He, she, or *it* can be used as subjects. (Pronouns)

Phrases: The detective searched *under the desk, in the closet,* and *behind the chairs.* (Prepositional phrases)

The library books were *broken in two, ripped into shreds,* and *thrown into the trash.* (Verb phrases)

My goal is *to work hard, to accomplish my dreams,* and *to have fun in the process.* (Infinitive phrases)

Running in place, jumping over hurdles, and *climbing a rope* are required to pass physical education. (Gerund phrases)

Clauses: *John wrote the script, Jim directed the play,* and *John acted in the play.* (Independent clauses)

The detective wanted to know *what I did for a living, where I was on October 9th,* and *how I got home.* (Dependent clauses)

Do not use a comma in these situations:

■ when there are only two items connected by *and* or *or: Mr. Jones taught elementary school and secondary school.*

■ when all items in a series are connected by the conjunction *and* or *or*: *He wrote a book and a movie and a play.*

PRACTICE EXERCISE 55: COMMAS BETWEEN ITEMS IN A SERIES

In each sentence, place commas between items in a series. Some sentences may not need a comma.

1. Mary John and Sam attended the meeting.
2. In the afternoon in September and on a sunny day, we decided to take a trip.
3. She ate carrots peas and squash every day of the week.
4. As a result of her diet she lost weight felt better and improved her health.
5. Thoughtfully thoroughly and conscientiously, Mr. Jones taught his classes.
6. We stopped we looked and we listened before entering the intersection.
7. The wealthy famous and dedicated athlete signed a million-dollar contract.
8. My mother and my father and my brother are all here for Christmas.
9. Playing ball and studying for classes at the same time is difficult.
10. A student who does all of her homework gets good grades and participates in class sets a good example for other students.

3. Commas between Adjectives. Two or more adjectives in a series modifying the same noun are called *coordinate adjectives.* Separate the adjectives with commas, but do not put a comma between the last adjective and the noun. A good rule to follow is to put a comma wherever the word *and* seems to make sense. For example:

She delivered a *healthy, strong, beautiful* baby.
Happy, intelligent, fulfilled students fill these classes.
Deceitful, corrupt politicians run this county.

These sentences seem natural if you place *and* between each adjective. For example:

She delivered a healthy *and* strong *and* beautiful baby.
Happy *and* intelligent *and* fulfilled students fill these classes.
Deceitful *and* corrupt politicians run this country.

However, if it seems unnatural to put the word *and* between the adjectives, do not use commas to separate them. For example:

two kind old men (not two *and* kind *and* old men)
extra added caution (not extra *and* added caution)

PRACTICE EXERCISE 56: COMMAS BETWEEN COORDINATE ADJECTIVES

Place a comma where appropriate in each sentence.

1. A happy energetic handsome man entered the room.

2. The large hairy ugly rat scampered down the hall.

3. The quiet shy girl sat in back of the room.

4. The owner placed further financial demands on us.

5. The light green window shade was stunning when the sun shone through it.

6. Carlos married a strange mysterious woman.

7. The grumpy old man sat on my front step.

8. The man in torn tattered clothes needed a hand-out.

4. Commas after Introductory Words, Phrases, and Clauses. Place a comma after most introductory elements. For example:

Words:	*Well,* tell me the truth. (Interjection)
	Yes, my diet was successful. (Interjection)
	Finally, we came to visit. (Introductory adverb)
	However, the girls did better than the boys. (Conjunctive adverb)
	John, tell us how you like being back in school. (Direct address)
Phrases:	*Of course,* you can take your time. (Parenthetical expression)
	In the middle of the quiet afternoon, I took a nap. (Long prepositional phrase)
	Forced into submission, he put down his weapons. (Participial phrase)
	To win the prize, you need to write an essay. (Infinitive phrase)
Clauses:	*When you show some self-discipline,* you will be allowed back. (Dependent adverbial clause)
	Because you are my best friend, I will let you borrow my car. (Dependent adverbial clause)

The types of words shown in the examples are followed by commas. They include interjections (see Section 1h) such as *well, yes, no, oh, wow*; adverbs (*finally, first, next, then*); adverbial conjunctions (see Section 1g) such as *however, consequently,* and *otherwise;* and direct addresses. Direct addresses are names or other words that refer to a person who is being addressed (*Mary, Sir, Madam, Your Honor, Mr. President*).

Some phrases, called *parenthetical expressions,* may appear at the beginning of a sentence. *Parenthetical* means not essential to the meaning of the sentence. Therefore, they are separated by commas wherever they appear in the sentence (see Comma Rule 6). Here are some common parenthetical expressions:

of course	in my opinion
by the way	in fact
after all	for example
in a way	as a matter of fact

Long prepositional phrases and those in a series at the beginning of a sentence are followed by a comma. However, a short prepositional phrase at the beginning of a sentence usually is not set off with a comma. For example:

In the classroom the teacher is the boss.

An infinitive phrase (*to win the prize*) at the beginning of a sentence is set off with a comma. However, an infinitive phrase or a gerund phrase (see Section 6b) used as the subject of a sentence is not set off with a comma. For example:

To run for President is my dream. (Infinitive phrase as subject)
Writing a book is a big job. (Gerund phrase)

Dependent clauses at the beginning of a sentence (before the main clause) are set off with commas. However, dependent clauses at the end of a sentence are not set off by commas (see Section 7b).

PRACTICE EXERCISE 57: COMMAS AFTER INTRODUCTORY ELEMENTS

Place a comma as needed after introductory elements in each sentence. Some sentences may be correct.

1. Boy I better get out of here quickly.

2. In the center of the controversy Mr. Reyes seemed disturbed.

3. In my opinion we need to continue the strike.

4. Opening the door carefully the student tiptoed into the class.

5. To hold elections now would be foolish.

6. When the results of the essay contest are final we can celebrate.

7. Because Beth lost so much weight she can fit into her new dress.

8. If you invest properly you can earn interest on your money.

9. However the insurance policy will cover the damages.

10. Of course you get a passing grade in this course.

5. Commas to Set Off Nonessential Elements. Phrases and dependent clauses that act as adjectives (modify a noun or pronoun) in a sentence are sometimes set off by commas. It depends on whether the elements are essential or nonessential. Essential elements contain information that is necessary to the meaning of the sentence. Nonessential elements can be removed without changing the meaning of the sentence. Here are the rules:

Set off all nonessential modifiers (*called nonrestrictive modifiers*).
Do not set off essential modifiers (*called restrictive modifiers*).

To set off a modifier, place a comma before and after the element if it is in the middle of the sentence. If the element is at the end of the sentence, a comma is placed before it.

Here are some examples of proper punctuation of phrases and clauses that act as adjectives in a sentence. It may be helpful to review prepositional phrases (Section 6a), participial phrases (Section 6b), and appositive phrases (Section 6d). Punctuation of restricted and nonrestricted dependent clauses was discussed at length in Section 7b.

Phrases

Nonessential Phrase:	Psychology 100, *about human behavior,* is a difficult course. (Prepositional phrase—not essential to understand *which* course is difficult)
Essential Phrase:	The course *about human behavior* is difficult. (Prepositional phrase—essential to the meaning of the sentence because it tells *which* course is difficult)
Nonessential Phrase:	Francisco and Irene, *working in the first group,* finished their assignment. (Participial phrase—not necessary information)
Essential Phrase:	The students *working in the first group* finished the assignment. (Participial phrase—essential because it tells *which* students finished the assignment)
Nonessential Phrase:	*Of Mice and Men, a popular book,* was just made into a movie. (Appositive—not necessary to know *which* popular book was made into a movie)
Essential Phrase:	*The popular book Of Mice and Men* was just made into a movie. (Appositive—essential because it gives necessary information, that is, *which* book was made into a movie)

Clauses

Nonessential Clause:	Mr. Richards, *who came from Texas,* helped me with my studies. (Dependent clause—not necessary information)
Essential Clause:	The man *who came from Texas* helped me with my studies. (Dependent clause—necessary because it indicates *which* man helped)
Nonessential Clause:	Erika lost 50 pounds while on the Pritikin Diet, *which was made popular by Mr. Pritikin's book.* (Dependent clause—not necessary information because we know which diet Mary was on *without* the dependent clause)
Essential Clause:	Mary lost 50 pounds while on a diet *that was made popular by Dr. Pritikin's book.* (Dependent clause—necessary because it reveals *which* diet)
Nonessential Clause:	Philadelphia, *where I was born,* is a historic city. (Dependent clause—not necessary to understand the point)

You may have noticed that essential phrases and clauses usually answer the question *which one?* For example:

> The man helped me with my studies.
> *Which one? (The one) who is from Texas.*
> The man *who is from Texas* helped me with my studies.

Essential phrases and clauses help identify the noun preceding the phrase or clause. Therefore, they are written without commas.

Dependent clauses beginning with the relative pronoun *that* are always essential. The relative pronoun *which* may be used in an essential or nonessential clause.

PRACTICE EXERCISE 58: COMMAS TO SET OFF NONESSENTIAL ELEMENTS

Place commas to set off any nonessential phrases or clauses. Do not put commas before or after essential elements.

1. The lawyer believing in his client's innocence decided to pursue the case.

2. Mr. Jones my attorney was the best trial lawyer in the country.

3. The girl who is staying for dinner tonight requires a special diet.

4. Mrs. Richards who is sleeping at our house tonight needs special care.

5. The teacher encouraged by the reaction of her students assigned the play by Shakespeare.

6. The homework which was given to us by our teacher was difficult to do.

7. The scientist to whom the society gave the award came to visit our school.

8. The Golden Gate Bridge which is one of the longest bridges in the world sways in the wind.

9. The student who emigrated from Chile was on the dean's list.

10. Judge Howard wearing the traditional black robe sat on the bench during my hearing.

6. Commas to Set Off Interrupters. Use a comma to set off any expression that interrupts the flow of a sentence and is not essential to the meaning of the sentence. Sentence interrupters include parenthetical expressions, direct addresses, and adverbial conjunctions. As introductory elements, these types of interrupters were discussed in Comma Rule 4. Sometimes, adjectives can interrupt the flow of a sentence. Here are some examples of sentence interrupters.

The professor, *in my opinion,* is the best in the school.
(Parenthetical expression)

Please respond to our request, *Mr. Harris,* for this information.
(Direct address)

The test, *however,* was not on that subject.
(Adverbial conjunction)

The turkey, *fat and succulent,* was served with all the trimmings.
(Adjectives)

Some parenthetical expressions and adverbial conjunctions are not always set off by commas. For example:

You may succeed *after all.*
Most politicians *at least* do their job.

Since these expressions do not interrupt the flow of thought, they are not set off by commas.

PRACTICE EXERCISE 59: COMMAS TO SET OFF INTERRUPTERS

Place commas to set off interrupters in these sentences.

1. The paper by the way is almost finished.

2. Tell me Bob if you want to run for reelection.

3. The principal tough but fair kept order in our school.

4. Mr. Jones wants you to participate too.

5. The suspect to be sure was hard to find.

7. Commas to Set Off Examples, Contrasts, and Question Tags. Use commas to set off the following elements:

- Examples and other phrases introduced by the terms *especially, particularly,* and *such as:*

My whole family is overweight, *especially my brother.*
I need to take a social science course, *such as Psychology 100,* to graduate this year.
People should eat healthy food, *particularly when they're sick.*

- Contrasting phrases beginning with *not:*

My mother, *not my father,* is the head of this household.
Make a right turn, *not a left turn,* at the intersection.

- Question tags:

Mark McGwire broke the home run record, *didn't he?*
It is fortunate that you got your promotion, *isn't it?*

PRACTICE EXERCISE 60: COMMAS TO SET OFF EXAMPLES, CONTRASTS, AND QUESTION TAGS

Put commas in the appropriate places in each sentence.

1. The police searched everywhere for the evidence particularly in the closets.

2. All they found were clothes not evidence in the closets.

3. The police do expect to find something worthwhile don't they?

4. Exercising is an important part of dieting especially if you want to lose weight.

5. Exercising not dieting is the most important aspect of health.

6. Write often particularly to become a proficient writer.

7. Some baseball players such as Mark McGwire and Sammy Sosa work really hard at their sport.

8. I expect you to succeed not fail at this task.

8. Commas in Direct Quotations. A direct quotation includes the exact words of the speaker (see Section 10f). Use commas to set off names of speakers or other words that are not part of the exact words of the speaker. These words may appear before or after the quotation or interrupt it. For example:

Before: *John said,* "I am sorry to be late for this class."
After: "This is the start of something new," *I told my new girlfriend.*
Interrupt: "Eating disorders," *explained the teacher,* "can be cured."

As you can see in the last two examples, commas are placed *inside* quotation marks at the end of a quote ("This is the start of something new,") or at the end of one part of an interrupted quote ("Eating disorders,").

PRACTICE EXERCISE 61: COMMAS IN DIRECT QUOTATIONS

Use commas to set off the quotations in these sentences.

1. The teacher finally said "Get to work right now."

2. Harry replied quietly "You can eat all of the cake if you want."

3. "At least" said Mr. Frank "you make an effort to finish the work."

4. "That bomb may go off soon" warned the officer.

5. The author says "peace is at hand."

6. "Never look a gift horse in the mouth" suggested my friend.

7. "Eat more fruits and vegetables" urged the doctor "or you might get sick."

8. The announcer said "The event is about to begin."

9. Commas in Dates and Addresses. Use commas to set off dates and addresses. Place the comma before and after the year in a date. For example:

On *November 5, 1949,* the flood waters finally receded.
May 23, 1998, was a really good day.

Do not use a comma when just the month and year are given. For example:

I was born in *May 1970.*

Also, do not use a comma when the date is given as day-month-year. For example:

We will celebrate on *10 June 1999.*

Place a comma between parts of an address. For example:

> Our meeting will be held in *Philadelphia, Pennsylvania.*
> I live at *110 Johnson Street, Apt. 3, San Jose, California.*

Do not use a comma between a state and the zip code. For example:

> Come to *New York, New York 10007.*

PRACTICE EXERCISE 62: COMMAS IN DATES AND ADDRESSES

Place commas where needed in these sentences.

1. My party is at 450 Madison Avenue New York New York 10007.

2. San Francisco California is the vacation spot of the world.

3. Will you meet me at 202 First Street Apartment 9 Wilmington Delaware on December 22 1999?

4. The September 1999 semester starts on September 2 1999.

5. Our vacation begins on December 25 and ends on January 25 2000.

6. This class is over 6 May 2001.

7. June 9 1998 was the best day in my life.

8. How can I get to Dallas Texas by Saturday July 19 2000?

10. Commas in Letters. Use a comma after the greeting of a friendly letter and after the closing of any letter. For example:

Friendly Letter

Greetings	Closings
Dear John,	Sincerely yours,
Dear Mr. Jones,	Love,
Dear Mom,	As always,
Dear Dr. Smith,	Best wishes,

Business Letter

Closings

Very truly yours,
Sincerely yours,
Respectfully,
Cordially yours,

PRACTICE EXERCISE 63: COMMAS IN LETTERS

1. Write three greetings for a friendly letter, using correct punctuation.

    a. _____

    b. _____

    c. _____

2. Write three closings for a friendly letter, using correct punctuation.

    a. _____

    b. _____

    c. _____

3. Write three closings for a business letter, using correct punctuation.

    a. _____

    b. _____

    c. _____

11. Commas to Prevent Misunderstanding. Use commas when you need to separate words that may create a misunderstanding. Compare the three sentences in the following example:

1. Having helped Mary James was relieved.
2. Having helped, Mary James was relieved.
3. Having helped Mary, James was relieved.

The first sentence is confusing because we do not know who helped. The second sentence clearly reveals that Mary James helped someone and was, therefore, relieved. In the third sentence, it is clear that James helped Mary, and he was relieved.

Prepositions (see Section 6a) can be particularly confusing because they may seem to be part of words that come after them. However, sometimes, prepositions may not be part of a phrase. The proper use of the comma prevents misunderstanding. For example:

Nearby the tree and all its branches fell on the house.

Nearby is not part of a prepositional phrase (*Nearby the tree*). To prevent any misunderstanding, a comma is needed after the word *nearby*.

PRACTICE EXERCISE 64: COMMAS TO PREVENT MISUNDERSTANDING

Place commas in the following sentences to prevent misunderstanding.

1. Since leaving Joan Harris was able to find another apartment.
2. As the boys gathered around the speaker began to talk.
3. When we were sure Mr. Jones was through the door was opened.
4. After the class was invited to a party.
5. My diet finally over the waiter brought more food.
6. If the swimming pool business goes under the water will have to be removed from the pool.
7. Outside the house was a mess.
8. Long after the tragedy will be just a memory.

PRACTICE EXERCISE 65: REVIEW OF COMMA RULES

Place a comma wherever appropriate in the following sentences or groups of sentences. Use the comma rules to help you make your choices.

1. A newspaper headline from Friday October 25 1929 said "Worst stock crash stemmed by banks."
2. The National Bank a commercial bank was hit the hardest by the depression. Therefore it decided to change its location to 165 Main Street Madison Wisconsin.
3. Consumers stopped shopping for cars appliances jewelry and other expensive items when the Great Depression hit.
4. Because of the banking crisis many people were unable to secure loans. People who could not borrow any money went into debt and many of them lost their homes.
5. In November 1943 Roosevelt Churchill and Stalin met to discuss world conditions after World War II.
6. The tall fiery leader came to the front of the room. He was to be sure a dominant figure and he was about to make history.
7. Students waving the flags around campus were very patriotic.

8. My teacher Mr. Jones refused to take part in the parade. Mr. Jones who had fought in World War II sat on the steps of the building waved a flag and shouted slogans at the marchers.

9. Tell us Mr. Jones do you really want to participate?

10. Working with the committee the man with the red cap organized the event hired all participants and financed all costs especially the exorbitant ones.

[10c] The Semicolon [;]

The semicolon contains a comma and a period. It signals a stronger break in thought than the comma but not as strong as the period. It is closer to the period and often interchangeable with it. Basically, there are three rules for the semicolon.

1. Semicolon between Independent Clauses Not Connected by a Coordinate Conjunction. Use a semicolon to separate the independent clauses of a compound sentence when there is no coordinate conjunction (*and, but, or, nor, for, so, yet*). For example:

Many children grow up in poverty; this is an unfortunate condition in today's society.

Community colleges are an important part of our educational system; they are a good alternative for students who cannot attend a four-year college.

Alligators have round noses; crocodiles have pointed ones.

The semicolon helps show the close relationship between the independent clauses in these examples. As in the last example, the semicolon is particularly helpful to indicate contrast.

2. Semicolon between Independent Clauses Connected by a Conjunctive Adverb. Use a semicolon to separate independent clauses joined by an adverbial conjunction (*however, thus, then, furthermore, hence, therefore, consequently, accordingly*—see Section 1g). Place a comma *after* conjunctive adverbs that interrupt the sentence (see Comma Rule 6). For example:

I started writing this paper yesterday; *however,* I'm not finished yet.

Tom is a good student and a star athlete; *therefore,* he decided to run for student council president.

Copyright © 2000 Addison-Wesley Educational Publishers Inc.

Do not use a semicolon; instead, use a comma if the independent clauses are very short and closely related (see Comma Rule 1). For example:

The famous author came, he spoke, he left.

3. Semicolon between Independent Clauses and Items in a Series When There Are Commas within the Phrases or Clauses. This rule has two parts.

First, use a semicolon instead of a comma when independent clauses, connected by a coordinate conjunction, are already punctuated with commas. The purpose of the semicolon is to show the break between compound sentences more clearly than the comma. For example:

In the past banks were not able to sell stocks, trade bonds, or make any other market transactions; *but* today most banks offer a complete line of investment choices.

The semicolon indicates the break between independent clauses more clearly than a comma.

Second, use a semicolon to separate the items in a series when there are commas within individual items. For example:

The committee will meet on May 3, 1999; June 4, 2000; and July 5, 2001.

Again, the semicolon marks the break between items more clearly than a comma.

PRACTICE EXERCISE 66: USING THE SEMICOLON

Place a semicolon where appropriate in each sentence. You may change incorrect commas to semicolons; however, be aware that some sentences are correct.

1. John is the best athlete in school unfortunately, he is on academic probation.

2. I cannot seem to find the concert hall meanwhile, the concert is still in progress.

3. The books are on top of the desk the paper is inside the drawer of the desk.

4. The jury, of which I was a member, stayed overnight in The Marriott Hotel, a beautiful hotel in the heart of Manhattan however, by morning we had to reach a verdict.

5. We took a nice vacation that included Denver, Colorado Dallas, Texas San Francisco California and Tempe Arizona.

6. The party started late, yet it was over before eleven.

7. I arrived, I sat down, and I ate.

8. Teenagers today like to watch television, listen to the radio, and talk on the telephone but I used to sit and read a good book to pass the time.

9. Lawyers earn a lot of money teachers do not make as much.

10. The student council election results are John, president Harry, vice president and Mary, treasurer.

[10d] The Colon [:]

The colon is used to introduce something that follows, such as a list, a second clause that explains the first, a long or formal quotation, and the words of a speaker in a play. Also, colons are used in business letters, titles, and numbers.

1. Colons to Introduce Lists. Colons are used to formally introduce lists of items. Often, the words *as follows* or *the following* are used. For example:

> T*he following* material is required for this course: a textbook, a notebook, and a word processor.
>
> Take some medications on your trip *as follows:* aspirin, cough syrup, and antibiotic cream.
>
> Some discipline is necessary to diet successfully: eat fewer calories, exercise often, avoid eating at night, and get enough vitamins and minerals.
>
> One student stood out in my mind: John Smith. (one-item list)

Do *not* use a colon after introductory remarks (*like, such as, including*). For example:

> Mr. Jones bought us a good lunch *including* ham and eggs.

Also, do *not* use a colon if there is no break in thought before the list items. For example:

> We ordered eggs, bacon, and lettuce.

In this example, *eggs, bacon, and lettuce* are the object complements that complete the thought; hence, there is no colon.

2. Colons to Introduce a Second Clause That Explains the First. In a compound sentence, a colon may be used to separate the independent clauses if the second clause is an explanation of the first clause. For example:

> Keep your objective in mind at all times: stay in school until you graduate.

Copyright © 2000 Addison-Wesley Educational Publishers Inc.

3. Colon to Introduce Quotations. Colons may be used to introduce quotations when they are unusually long or formal. For example:

> In *The Declaration of Independence* Thomas Jefferson wrote: "When, in the course of human events, it becomes necessary for one people to dissolve the political bonds which have connected them with another . . ." (quotation continues)

4. Colons to Introduce the Words of a Speaker in a Play. In a play, colons are used after a speaker's name to introduce the exact words. For example:

> Juliet: Wherefore art thou, Romeo?

5. Colons in Business Letters, Titles, and Numbers. Colons are used in business letters after the greeting. For example:

> Dear Sir: Dear Mr. Jones: Gentlemen:

Also, colons may be used in titles. For example:

> *Psychology: An Introduction to Human Behavior*

Finally, colons may be used in numbers to express the time. For example:

> 10:30 a.m.   5:23 p.m.

PRACTICE EXERCISE 67: USING THE COLON

Put a colon in the appropriate places in these sentences. Some sentences are correct.

1. The teacher made an important announcement bring your books, essays, and writing journals to every class.
2. The picnic began at 5 00 in the afternoon.
3. To graduate, I still need the following courses biology, psychology, and history.
4. The following words are never spoken in class give up and resign.
5. Writing is easier if you do as follows use a computer.
6. You must show leadership, talent, and ability.
7. Scientists have discovered some fascinating creatures, such as amoebas and protozoans.
8. The following students should report to the gym Nancy, Jim, and John.
9. Their trip took them to Germany, Austria, and Italy.
10. Their expedition took them to three places the North Pole, the South Pole, and the jungles of Africa.

[10e] The Apostrophe [']

The apostrophe has two main uses: (1) to indicate ownership (possession) and (2) to show where letters or numbers have been left out of a contraction.

1. Apostrophe to Indicate Ownership. Apostrophes are used with singular and plural nouns to show possession.

To show possession of a singular noun, use an apostrophe and *s* (*'s*). For example:

John's car   a man's house
Mr. Robert's book   a country's honor
the class's room   one dollar's worth

To show possession of a plural noun ending in *s*, use an apostrophe after the final *s* (*s'*). For example:

students' desks   the classes' rooms
boys' rooms   countries' boundaries
books' covers   the doctors' equipment

There are two important exceptions to these rules. First, for plural nouns not ending in *s*, use *'s*. For example:

people's choice
women's votes
children's toys

Second, for singular names ending in *s*, use the apostrophe alone (*s'*) under the following conditions: (1) when the name has more than one syllable or (2) adding another *s* would make the name sound awkward. For example:

Mr. Rogers' house
Arynelis' dilemma

Note that personal possessive pronouns do not take an apostrophe. For example:

This house is *his, hers, yours, ours, mine,* or *theirs.*

However, indefinite pronouns (see Section 1b) do take an apostrophe. For example:

This is *everybody's, someone's,* or *anyone's* house.

In the case of compound nouns, add the apostrophe and *s* only to the last noun if both nouns possess the same thing. For example:

Ed and Mary's house is beautiful. (Ed and Mary own the same house.)

However, if each noun possesses a different thing, add an apostrophe at the end of each noun. For example:

Ed's and Mary's houses are both for sale. (Ed and Mary own different houses.)

2. Apostrophe in Contractions. Use an apostrophe where letters are left out of a contraction. For example:

don't (do not)	can't (cannot)
won't (will not)	what's (what is)
shouldn't (should not)	wouldn't (would not)
I'm (I am)	John's (John is)
summer of '68 (1968)	class of '99 (1999)

PRACTICE EXERCISE 68: USING THE APOSTROPHE

Place an apostrophe as required in these sentences.

1. The students notebook was on the desk.

2. The peoples exhibit was placed into evidence.

3. Doesnt the Joneses house look really clean?

4. Clean up the childrens toys.

5. The presidents cabinet wasnt sworn in yet.

6. During the fall 99 semester, well have more students than we can handle.

7. The two sisters appointments were canceled, werent they?

8. The womens rights group was on television.

9. Jim and Harrys apartment was a mess.

10. Marys and Sams stores were having a sale.

[10f] Quotations [" "]

Quotation marks are used to enclose a person's exact words, titles, and definitions of words.

1. Quotation Marks to Set Off a Direct Quotation. Put quotation marks before and after the exact words spoken by a person. Always capitalize the first word of the quotation. Be sure to identify the speaker of every direct quotation. For example:

Mr. Jones said, "Come pick up your homework."
My friend Tom remarked, "You better finish the job."
"It's time to stop work on the test," someone shouted over the loudspeaker.

A direct quotation may be interrupted or divided into parts. Use quotation marks around only the spoken words. If the second part of the quotation is in the *same* sentence, start it with a small letter. If the interrupted quotation begins a new sentence, start it with a capital letter. For example:

"Go straight to bed," demanded his mother, "or you will be punished."
"You haven't got a chance," said the attorney to his client, "to win this case."
"The homework will be due tomorrow," said the teacher. "Don't forget to do it." (Quote divided into two sentences)

Don't forget to set off speakers' names with commas (see Comma Rule 8).

A quotation may continue uninterrupted into another sentence. Use only one set of quotes. *Begin* the quotes before the exact words of the speaker in the first sentence and *end* the quotes after the speaker's words in the last sentence. Be sure to begin each new sentence with a capital letter. For example:

The judge replied, "This man is guilty. He will surely serve time for this crime."
My instructor said, "Work on pages 100 to 110 for tomorrow. Work on pages 110 to 120 for Wednesday. Then, finish the chapter for Thursday."

When writing dialogue, start a new paragraph for each change of speaker. In the following example of dialogue, notice the start of paragraphs and the proper placement of quotes in interrupted and uninterrupted quotes:

The test was finally over. On the way out I met Bob. Bob asserted, "I'm sure I passed this test. It wasn't so difficult."
I replied, "I think I passed with flying colors."
"Me, too," Larry said confidently, "but I thought it was really hard. I hope I'm not overconfident."

Use single quotation marks [' '] to set off a quotation within a quotation. For example:

My teacher asked, "Who said, 'I can't do it'?"

2. Quotation Marks to Set Off Titles. Place quotation marks before and after titles of short written works (short stories, poems, articles, essays, smaller units of a book like chapter names, and songs). For example:

My essay, "The Causes of Insomnia," was published in a magazine.
Chapter 5 of the book is called "John Makes It through College."
"All You Need Is Love" is my favorite song.

3. Quotation Marks to Set Off Definitions of Words. Place quotation marks around exact definitions and words used in a special way. For example:

In that sentence the word *mankind* means "all human beings."
We live right on the "strip" in Las Vegas.

4. The Placement of Other Punctuation Marks with Quotations. Punctuating quotations can be tricky. The following three rules clearly show the proper use of punctuation marks with quotations.

1. Place *commas* and *periods* inside closing quotation marks. For example:

"Most fad diets," the doctor said, "do not work."

2. Place colons and semicolons outside closing quotation marks. For example:

The defendant said, "Judge, I'm an innocent man"; yet the jury found him guilty. (Semicolon outside the quotations)
Three students said, "I didn't do my homework": Juan, Maria, and Sally.

3. Place question marks and exclamation points *inside* the quotation when they apply only to the quotation and *outside* when they apply to the entire sentence. For example:

Mom seemed serious when she asked, "When are you coming home?"
(Question mark inside quotation because it applies only to the quotation)

Why did John say, "I don't love you any more"?
(Question mark outside quotation because the entire sentence is a question)

"That's really great!" she exclaimed as soon as she arrived.
(Exclamation point inside quotation because it applies only to the quotation)

I felt completely overwhelmed when my baby said, "Mommy"! (Exclamation point outside quotation because it applies to the entire quotation)

PRACTICE EXERCISE 69: USING QUOTATION MARKS

Place quotation marks wherever needed in these sentences. Be sure to carefully follow the rules for other punctuation marks. Some sentences may be correct.

1. I'm sorry I called you in the middle of the night, apologized Arlene. I didn't know you were sleeping.

2. I asked the intruder, Why did you come to my house?

3. Did you feel threatened when the policeman asked, Where are you going, tonight?

4. Harry said with a frown on his face: I'll die without some food!

5. He said, Be careful or you will fall; however, we fell anyway.

6. Do your homework carefully, the teacher insisted, if you want to pass this course.

7. By the word *capture,* the author meant hold on to securely.

8. Ramon said, We better get to work right away. I think the boss is coming.

9. The suspect exclaimed, You'll never get me alive!

10. The Nutcracker Suite is a wonderful piece of music.

[10g] The Hyphen [-]

The hyphen is used to form compound words, join adjectives, connect prefixes and suffixes to avoid ambiguity, join numbers, indicate a spelling or hesitation, and divide a word at the end of a line. Here are the rules for the hyphen:

1. Hyphen to Form Compound Words. The hyphen may be used in some compound words. However, in English, there are three ways to make compound words:

- as whole words (rainbow, bedroom, moonlight)
- as separate words (sound stage, motion picture, dining room)
- as hyphenated words (sleepy-head, father-in-law, jack-o'-lantern)

The only way to be sure you are using hyphens properly to form compound words is to check your dictionary.

2. Hyphen to Join Adjectives. Use the hyphen to join words that act as a single adjective when they come before the noun or pronoun. For example:

I am a *happy-go-lucky* person.
Mr. Jones is a *well-known* teacher in this school.

Do *not* use the hyphen when the adjectives follow the noun or pronoun. For example:

Mr. Jones, my teacher, is *well known.*

Copyright © 2000 Addison-Wesley Educational Publishers Inc.

3. Hyphen to Connect Prefixes and Suffixes. Hyphens are often used with the following prefixes: *ex-, pre-, pro-, all-,* and *self-*. Also, use hyphens with the suffix *-elect*. For example:

ex-official	*all*-butter
pre-industrial	*self*-assured
pro-education	president-*elect*

Most prefixes are joined to the root word *without* hyphens (*unintelligent, antiterrorist, nonviolent, redo*). However, use hyphens with prefixes under the following conditions:

- There is ambiguity. For example:

  I had to *re-strain* the applesauce to get the lumps out. (Hyphen is used to avoid possible confusion with the word *restrain*)

- The root is capitalized. For example:

  I just found out that my best friend is *anti-American*.

- It would be awkward without the hyphen. For example:

  Sometimes you act *semi-intelligent*. (Without the hyphen, the double letter *i* would be confusing.)

4. Hyphens to Join Numbers. Use hyphens to write two-word numbers from twenty-one to ninety-nine. Also, use hyphens in compound adjectives containing a number. For example:

twenty-two	*five-year-old* child
thirty-five	*fifty-yard* dash
ninety-four	*one-dollar* bill

Hyphens are used to write fractions when they are adjectives. However, do not use hyphens when a fraction is used as a noun. For example:

That cake is *one-half* sugar and *one-half* butter. (Use hyphen because fractions are adjectives)
One half of my sandwich was rotten. (No hyphen because *one half* is a noun or subject of the sentence)

5. Hyphens to Indicate a Spelling or Hesitation. Use a hyphen to indicate a spelling or hesitation. For example:

"I brought c-a-n-d-y," I told my mother.
"I don't have a b-b-brother any more," I stammered nervously.

6. Hyphen to Divide a Word at the End of a Line. Use a hyphen to divide a word that will not fit at the end of a line. Be sure to divide the word between syllables. For example:

> Mr. Johnson had to move because he was not able to afford the mort-
> gage.

PRACTICE EXERCISE 70: USING THE HYPHEN

Place hyphens where needed in the following sentences. Some sentences may be correct.

1. My mother in law has become my good friend.

2. I ordered a well done hamburger for my lunch.

3. Self pity will not get you anywhere, so get rid of it.

4. Mr. Brooks, the senator elect, won the election by fifty nine percent.

5. The news show offered minute by minute coverage of the day's events.

6. Dr. Richards, an ex professor, wants to continue in private practice.

7. Phillip stammered when he said, "B but, I just c can't do it!"

8. The cup is four fifths full, but two thirds of it is water.

9. Do you like working a forty hour week?

[10h] The Dash [—]

The dash signals an abrupt shift in thought or break in the flow of a sentence. It is used in the following ways:

1. Dash to Set Off a Sharply Interrupting Element. Use the dash before and after a parenthetical element that breaks the thought of the sentence. Also, use the dash when any parenthetical element is long or has internal punctuation that would make it hard to distinguish. For example:

> The psychic told me—who believes psychics, anyway?—that I will have many
> children.
> The instructor finally convinced us—oh, the power of thought—to finish the
> course.
> The doctor told me to diet and—if only I had time, motivation, and the proper
> equipment—to exercise often.

2. Dash to Set Off an Appositive. Use the dash to emphasize an appositive (see Section 6d) or to set off one already punctuated with a comma. For example:

> I've never visited one special place—India.
> My friends—Jose, Mary, and Robin—will be arriving soon.

PRACTICE EXERCISE 71: USING THE DASH

Place a dash where appropriate in these sentences.

1. I heard that John has failed three tests yes, that is what I said this semester.
2. Mr. Jones my friend, my teacher, and my helper will always be there when I need help.
3. The blueberry pie oh, how good it is is in the oven.
4. Can you yes you come on the trip?
5. Reading, writing, and arithmetic all are necessary to get ahead in life.
6. We have been traveling for over a week there it is now.
7. You refused to help me you selfish person.
8. Bill, Beth, and I just left the building if only we knew you were coming.

[10i] Parentheses [( )]

Parentheses are used to enclose parenthetical elements of two types: (1) supplementary or explanatory material and (2) numbers or letters.

1. Parentheses to Set Off Supplementary Material. Similar to the comma and dash, parentheses are used to set off interrupting elements in a sentence. In most cases, there is no clear rule as to which punctuation mark to use. However, if the material is closely connected to the meaning of the sentence, it is best to use the comma (see Comma Rule 6). If you want to make a more complete break and emphasize the interrupting element, use the dash. Here are some examples of the use of parentheses:

> Your essay (the best I've ever read) will be published in the next issue of our magazine.
> Professor Jones (Harvard University) is coming to our college to teach.

If the parentheses are inside another sentence, do not capitalize the first word, and do not end what is inside the parentheses with a period.

2. Parentheses to Set Off Numbers or Letters. Use parentheses to enclose numbers or letters used in a list or as a reference. For example:

Tell me (1) your name, (2) your address, and (3) your phone number.
The lungs (see Figure A) are one of the important organs.
I am enclosing a check for twenty-five dollars ($25.00).
My book (500 pages) is now in the bookstore.

PRACTICE EXERCISE 72: USING PARENTHESES

Place parentheses in the appropriate places in these sentences.

1. The internal combustion engine see Plate 2 is a complicated device.

2. My mother I love her dearly is always calling and bothering me.

3. Before you leave, you should 1 make a list, 2 go shopping, and 3 pack your clothes.

4. You owe me thirty percent 30% of your profit.

5. John was the best student in the school he just graduated.

6. Jogging can give you problems see your doctor.

7. Please enclose your student fee of ten dollars $10.

8. I came to this country from China I really miss it.

[10j] Italics (Underlining)

Italics is *slanted* type. Italics can be indicated by underlining. Following are the ways to use italics.

1. Italics to Emphasize Certain Words. For example:

We *really* need more food and medical supplies.

2. Italics for Publications. Use italics to show titles of books, plays, movies, TV and radio programs, magazines, newspapers, and electronic publications (record, tape, compact disk, CD-ROM, and online publications). For example:

Diet for a Small Planet (Book)
Miss Saigon (Play)
The Godfather (Movie)
The Dating Game (TV show)
Time Magazine (Magazine)
Philadelphia Inquirer (Newspaper)
The Stranger (Record, tape, or compact disk)
NBC News Online (Online news program)

Use quotation marks, not italics, for names of smaller units of publication, such as chapters, short stories, essays, and poems (unless the title is the name of an entire book).

3. Italics for Names of Ships, Trains, and Aircraft. For example:

USS Nimitz (Ship)   the *Orient Express* (Train)   the *Challenger* (Spacecraft)

4. Italics for Titles of Paintings and Other Works of Art. For example:

the *Mona Lisa* (Painting)   Michelangelo's *Moses* (Sculpture)

5. Italics for a Word, Letter, Number, or Symbol Referred to as Itself. For example:

The word *but* indicates a contrast.
Always use a double *o* in the word *choose*.
I saw a *9* where you saw a *6*.
Use the exclamation point *!* sparingly.

6. Italics for Foreign Words. Use italics for foreign words that are not listed in the dictionary. For example:

It is *verboten* to go into that room. (German word meaning "forbidden")

PRACTICE EXERCISE 73: USING ITALICS

Underline any words in these sentences that should be in italics. Also, cross out any incorrect punctuation. Some sentences may be correct. For example:

Hector just read the book "Animal Farm" by George Orwell.

1. The Queen Elizabeth II has docked nearby.

2. How often do you read "Life Magazine"?

3. The missions of the Mercury and the Apollo laid the groundwork for the space shuttle Endeavour.

4. I always have trouble with the silent b in subtle.

5. I know that my sister says I'm crazy or, as we say in the old country, mishigas.

6. For my birthday I got the Best of the Beatles on compact disk.

7. City of Angels was my favorite TV program, so I'm sorry it went off the air.

8. My essay was entitled, "The Good Life."

[11] Capitalization

Capitalization emphasizes important words. It is a necessary aspect of correct writing. Following are the rules of capitalization.

[11a] Capitalize the First Word of Every Sentence

In addition to capitalizing the first word of every sentence, capitalize the first word of quoted sentences. For example:

Jim finally passed this course.
Mr. Smith said, "How can I help you?"
Why did you hit me?

[11b] Capitalize the Word *I*

For example:

My friend and **I** will arrive soon.

[11c] Capitalize All Proper Nouns

A proper noun (see Section 1a) is the name of a specific person, place, object, event, or idea. Furthermore, proper nouns can be used to describe (see Proper Adjectives, Section 1c). Capitalize the first letter of all proper nouns and proper adjectives. For example:

Proper Nouns	**Proper Adjectives**
John (person)	American
New York City (place)	Hispanic
Delaware River (place)	Caucasian
Bronx Community College (place)	Islamic
Civil War (historical event)	Buddhist
Pulitzer Prize (award)	Christian
Doctor of Philosophy (academic degree)	Indian
Democratic Party (organization)	Freudian
Titanic (ship)	Jewish
Mars (planet)	Elizabethan

Capitalize academic courses only if they are the specific names of the course. For example:

I am taking Chemistry 110, Sociology 100, and Art 160.
I need one more course in physics to graduate.

Cap

[11d] Capitalize Days of the Week, Months, and Holidays

For example:

Monday	October	Christmas
Saturday	June	Labor Day

Do *not* capitalize names of seasons (summer, fall, winter, spring). Also, do *not* capitalize directions (north, south, west, east) unless they refer to actual places. For example:

I live on the **West Coast**. However, I am moving to the **East**.

[11e] Capitalize the First and Last Word of Every Title

With just a few exceptions, capitalize every word in a title. Do *not* capitalize the following words unless they are the first word in the title:

- *a, an,* and *the*
- prepositions (*on, to, in, from, with*)
- the word *to* when used as an infinitive (*to* + verb; see Section 6c)
- coordinate conjunctions (*and, or, nor, but, yet, for, so*)

Here are some examples of proper capitalization of titles:

Of Mice and Men (Book)	*The Way to Diet* (Book)
The Scream (Movie)	*The Tonight Show* (TV show)
"Whole Lotta Love" (Song)	*Newsweek* (Magazine)
"The Lonely Bride" (Short story)	"My Family in America" (Essay)
Romeo and Juliet (Play)	*A Raisin in the Sun* (Play)

[11f] Capitalize Titles Preceding Names

For example:

Professor Johnson   **Sergeant Harris**   **Reverend Jackson**

Also, capitalize abbreviated titles before or after a person's name. For example:

Prof. Max   **Sam Waters, Ph.D.**   **Sen. John Glenn**

Do not capitalize titles after names unless the person has extremely high recognition. For example:

My brother is a professor of psychology.
Bill Clinton, the President, is in town.
(U.S. president has national distinction)

[11g] Capitalize Letters in Initials

For example:

  ABC   AIDS   WIBG   FBI   CIA   A.D.   L. M. Jones

PRACTICE EXERCISE 74: USING CAPITALIZATION RULES

In these sentences, circle any word that needs to be capitalized.

1. sometimes i need to rewrite my essay to correct errors.
2. my teacher, professor williams, is from yale university.
3. the irish settlers came here at the turn of the twentieth century.
4. let's go to the statue of liberty and ellis island for our fourth of july holiday.
5. on may 3 we will be able to see jupiter from the top of the empire state building.
6. the american playhouse will perform *death of a salesman* in the fall.
7. did you see "the david letterman show" on cbs last monday night?
8. david and i took sociology 100 at city university last year, but we failed the course in chemistry.
9. we are going south in the spring to see doctor king.
10. our favorite senator is sen. brown, whom we just saw on tv.

[12] Spelling

Sp

Sometimes students ask if spelling is really important. The answer depends on the type of writing. If you are freewriting or writing to discover ideas, it is best not to worry about spelling. However, if you are writing for an audience (your readers), it is best to pay careful attention to spelling. Poor spelling can affect your writing just like messy or dirty clothes can affect your physical appearance. Your instructors will expect your essays to be free of spelling errors.

Learning to spell correctly is not an easy task. Many English words are not spelled the way they sound. This is because the language is constantly changing and many words are borrowed from foreign languages. However, if you apply a few suggestions and follow some basic rules, you will be able to improve your spelling.

[12a] Spelling Habits

1. Use the Dictionary When Unsure about the Spelling of a Word. Although it is much easier to guess, it is better to be sure.

2.   Keep a List of All Words You Misspell. Try to figure out the spelling problem. The following list of common mistakes will help you categorize your errors:

- missing silent letters (*site* for *sight*)
- missing double consonants (*runing* for *running*) or vowels (*chose* for *choose*)
- confusing words that sound alike (*course* for *coarse*)
- confusing endings (*ladys* for *ladies*)
- missing letters (*curteous* for *courteous*)
- adding extra letters (*truely* for *truly*)
- missing syllables (*personly* for *personally*)
- confusing vowel combinations (*freind* for *friend*)

3.   Use Syllables When Spelling Words. Breaking longer words into syllables is particularly helpful. A syllable is each part of a word that can be pronounced. The word *understanding* has four syllables: *un-der-stand-ing.*

4.   Use Your Memory. Your memory for words will increase rapidly if you get in the habit of looking carefully at troublesome words and forming a mental image of them. Also, be sure to pronounce words correctly.

You can use some tricks to help you remember difficult words. Try to associate similar words, such as *dessert* and *desert.* Remembering the difference between these words can be easy. Simply think of how much you like to eat **two** *servings of dessert.* Now, you will be able to remember that *dessert* (the sweet things you eat at the end of a meal) is spelled with two *ss;* whereas *desert* (a dry, hot, sandy strip of land) is spelled with a single *s.* Sometimes it helps to use the root (main part) or another form of the same word. For example, if you remember that the root word *discuss* has a double *s,* then you will remember to double the *s* in *discussion.* If you think of *repeat,* it will help you remember that *repetition* has an *e* after the *p.* Spelling *dominant* will be easy if you think of the word *dominate.* Another way to remember spellings is to make up a little story. For example, the *princi**pal*** is my **pal***; a *princi**ple*** is a **rule.**

The words in the following list are frequently misspelled. Pronouncing each word or syllable carefully while you look at it will help you remember the correct spelling. Study this list a few words at a time and refer to it whenever you feel the need. Try to use creative memory techniques whenever possible.

Commonly Misspelled Words

absence	conceivable	fascinating	mourn
ache	conscience	financially	muscular
accident	conscientious	foreign	mystery
accommodate	conscious	forty	naturally
accompany	convenience	fulfill	ninety
achieve	cough	fundamental	nonsense
acknowledgment	courteous	governmental	noticeable
acquaintance	criticism	grammar	nuclear
acquire	curiosity	guarantee	nuisance
across	decision	guidance	occasion
actually	decreased	height	occurrence
adolescence	definitely	heroes	omission
advice	denied	hindrance	operate
advise	description	humorous	opinion
amateur	desert	hypocrisy	opportunity
among	desirable	ignorant	optimism
analysis	dessert	imagine	orchestra
answer	despair	independent	parallel
apologize	desperate	intelligence	particularly
apparent	develop	interest	patience
appearance	difference	interfere	peace
appreciation	disappoint	interrupt	perceive
approach	disastrous	irrelevant	performance
approximately	discipline	irresistible	permanent
arguing	discussion	judgment	permissible
arrangement	disease	knowledge	perseverance
athlete	dominant	laboratory	personally
autumn	doubt	laborer	personnel
auxiliary	efficient	leisure	persuade
beautifully	eighth	length	pleasant
business	embarrass	license	politician
caffeine	entertain	lieutenant	philosopher
calendar	environment	luxury	possession
capital	equipped	maintenance	precede
capitol	erroneous	management	prejudice
carefully	especially	maneuver	prevalent
category	exaggerate	marriage	privilege
challenge	excellent	mathematics	probably
chief	exercise	meant	procedure
cigarette	existence	miscellaneous	proceed
committee	experience	mischievous	professional

protein	restaurant	souvenir	unnecessary
psychology	rhythm	sponsor	unusual
pursue	ridiculous	straighten	using
qualified	sacrifice	strength	usually
quantity	saucers	studying	utilized
questionnaire	scenic	subtle	vacuum
quiet	schedule	synonym	variety
quite	scissors	technique	vegetable
realize	secretary	temperament	vein
really	seize	tendency	villain
receipt	sense	their	weather
recommend	separate	thorough	weird
referring	several	through	wholly
regularly	shining	tragedy	would
relieve	significance	transferred	xylophone
religion	similar	truly	your
reminisce	sincerely	twelfth	you're
repetition	sophomore	unanimously	
resistance	source	undoubtedly	

5. Proofread Your Writing Carefully to Avoid Spelling Errors. Try to identify difficult words like the ones on the list. Also, words that you know how to spell may be spelled improperly. The important point is to look carefully and avoid being hasty or careless.

[12b] Spelling Rules

Although there are exceptions to every rule, you can improve your spelling by learning five rules. The first rule will show you how to spell words containing the letter combinations *ie* and *ei*. The other rules point out spelling changes that may occur when suffixes are added to words. A suffix consists of one or more letters added to the end of a word. Suffixes may change the meanings of words, such as *thoughtful/thoughtless.* Even when meanings are not affected, suffixes allow words to be used as different parts of speech (such as when *read,* a verb, becomes *reader,* a noun).

Here are some more examples:

dark + er = darker   dark + est = darkest
entertain + ment = entertainment   entertain + ed = entertained
look + ing = looking   look + s = looks
play + er = player   play + ed = played
resist + ance = resistance   resist + ible = resistible

thought + ful = thoughtful   thought + less = thoughtless
tight + ness = tightness   tight + en = tighten

Rule 1: The Letters *ie* and *ei*. There are a few parts to this rule. However, most of it is captured by this popular rhyme:

Put an *i* before *e*
Except after *c*.

Following is a helpful addition to this saying:

Put an *i* before *e* when the sound is long *e* (as in *bee*).

Here are some examples:

ie (**Long *e***)	*ei* (**After *c***)
bel*ie*ve	c*ei*ling
br*ie*f	conc*ei*ve
f*ie*ld	conc*ei*ted
gr*ie*f	dec*ei*ve
p*ie*ce	perc*ei*ve
rel*ie*ve	rec*ei*ve
y*ie*ld	rec*ei*pt

Use *ei* when the sound is not long *e*. For example:

eight	heir
foreign	sleigh
freight	vein
height	weigh

Notice that most of these words have the long *a* sound (as in *ate*).

The following words are exceptions to the *ie* and *ei* rule.

Use *ie*	Use *ei*
ancient	caffeine
conscience	either
friend	leisure
science	neither
species	protein
	seize
	sheik
	weird

Copyright © 2000 Addison-Wesley Educational Publishers Inc.

Rule 2: The Final Letter *-e.* The rule that follows applies to words ending with a silent *-e.* For example:

> argue   date   extreme   fine   hope   nine   rose   tune

Although the final *-e* is not pronounced, it does have a purpose. In most cases the silent *-e* will cause the vowel that precedes it to be long (to say its own name). Compare *hop* (short *o*) to *hope* (long *o*) and *sit* (short *i*) to *site* (long *i*).

Drop the final *-e* in a word before adding a suffix (word ending) that begins with a vowel (*a, e, i, o, u,* and *y*). For example:

approve + al	approval
argue + ing	arguing
assure + ance	assurance
come + ing	coming
desire + able	desirable
dine + ing	dining
fame + ous	famous
love + er	lover
remove + able	removable
spine + y	spiny
take + er	taker
write + er	writer

Following are some exceptions to the final *-e* rule:

- Keep the final *-e* in words ending in *-ce* or *-ge* when adding a suffix beginning with *a* or *o.* For example:

advantage + ous	advantageous
courage + ous	courageous
notice + able	noticeable
outrage + ous	outrageous
replace + able	replaceable

- Keep the final *-e* in some words to avoid confusion with other words. For example: *dye + ing = dyeing*

- Double the final consonant in some words ending in silent *-e* only if the pronunciation changes. For example:

bite + en	bitten (short *i*)
write + en	written (short *i*)

- Keep the final *-e* when adding a suffix that begins with a consonant, not a vowel. For example:

care + less   careless
hope + ful   hopeful
love + ly   lovely
place + ment   placement
scarce + ness   scarceness

Rule 3: The Final Letter -y. Before adding a suffix to a word ending with -*y* preceded by a *consonant* (such as *baby* and *marry*), change the -*y* to *i*. For example:

baby + es   babies
beauty + ful   beautiful
body + ly   bodily
copy + er   copier
cry + ed   cried
deny + al   denial
happy + est   happiest
likely + hood   likelihood
lovely + est   loveliest
marry + age   marriage
ready + ness   readiness
rely + ance   reliance
thirty + eth   thirtieth

Here are a few exceptions: *dryer, flyer,* and *fryer.*

■ Do not change the -*y* to *i* when adding a suffix that begins with *i* (-*ing, -ish, -ist*). This would create an unwanted double *i*. For example:

baby + ish   babyish
copy + ing   copying

■ When adding a suffix to a word ending with -*y* preceded by a *vowel*, do not change the spelling. For example:

annoy + ance   annoyance
buy + er   buyer
love + ly   lovely
pay + ment   payment
play + ed   played
turkey + s   turkeys

Here are a few exceptions to this rule:

day/daily, lay/laid, say/said, pay/paid

Rule 4: Double Letters. All aspects of this rule apply only to suffixes beginning with a vowel (such as *-er, -ed, -ence, -ing, -ist*).

■ In one-syllable words that end with a single consonant preceded by a single vowel (such as *sit*), double the final consonant before adding a suffix beginning with a vowel. For example:

big + er	bigger
drop + ed	dropped
drug + ist	druggist
fat + est	fattest
swim + ing	swimming

■ In words with more than one syllable that end with a single consonant preceded by a single vowel, double the final consonant only if the accent is on the last syllable. For example:

admit + ance	admittance
begin + er	beginner
control + able	controllable
occur + ed	occurred
remit + ing	remitting

■ Do not double the final consonant when adding a suffix if the accent is not on the last syllable. For example:

cancel + ed	canceled
offer + ing	offering
travel + er	traveler

You may have the option of doubling the final consonant or not before adding a suffix to some words that are not accented on the last syllable. For example:

benefit + ed	benefited or benefitted
signal + ing	signaling or signalling

However, unless you are using British spellings, it is better not to double consonants in these words.

■ In some words the accent shifts to the first syllable when adding the suffix *-ence*. In these cases, do not double the final consonant. For example:

defer + ence	deference
confer + ence	conference
infer + ence	inference

prefer + ence	preference
refer + ence	reference

■ Do not double the final consonant before adding a suffix to words that do not end with a single consonant preceded by a single vowel. For example:

bend + ing	bending
cook + ed	cooked
deduct + ible	deductible
faint + ed	fainted
sail + or	sailor

Rule 5: The Suffixes *-cede, -ceed,* **and** *-sede.* All of these suffixes have the same sound (as in *seed*).

■ There are only three words in English that end with *-ceed*. They are the following:

exceed   proceed   succeed

■ There is only one word that is spelled with the suffix *-sede: supersede.*

■ All other words ending with this sound are spelled with *-cede.* For example:

concede	recede
intercede	precede

PRACTICE EXERCISE 75: USING THE *IE/EI* SPELLING RULE

Fill in the missing letters ie *or* ei *for each word. Use Rule 1 and remember to check for exceptions.*

1. rel_____ve

2. bel_____ve

3. conc_____t

4. rec_____pt

5. prot_____n

6. perc_____ve

7. v_____n

8. w_____gh

9. misch_____f

10. sc_____nce

11. w_____rd

12 l_____sure

13. fr_____nd

14. br_____f

15. dec_____ve

16. y_____ld

17. _____ght

18. p_____ce

19. _____ther

20. n_____ther

PRACTICE EXERCISE 76: USING SPELLING RULES FOR ADDING SUFFIXES

Add the suffix to each word, and write the proper spelling on the line.

1. desire + ing _____
2. love + er _____
3. approve + al _____
4. dine + ing _____
5. write + er _____
6. write + en _____
7. happy + ness _____
8. marry + age _____
9. fame + ous _____
10. notice + able _____
11. love + ly _____
12. mud + y _____
13. forty + eth _____
14. replace + ing _____
15. nine + teen _____
16. light + er _____
17. encourage + ing _____
18. courage + ous _____
19. fat + est _____
20. hop + ed _____
21. copy + er _____
22. fly + ing _____
23. fly + er _____
24. travel + ing _____
25. infer + ence _____
26. deduct + ible _____
27. exceed + ing _____
28. precede + ing _____
29. supersede + ed _____
30. day + ly _____

[13] Usage

Usage

Choosing the right words is not always easy. Some words are confusing because they have the same pronunciation as other words (called *homonyms*). Some words or expressions are appropriate only in everyday speech or informal writing (such as letters to friends or personal notes). This is called *colloquial usage*. Other words are to be avoided entirely (*nonstandard usage*). In *formal writing* (such as essays, reports, term papers), colloquial and nonstandard usage should be avoided. The following list should be helpful because it contains words that are frequently misused or confused with other words.

accept, except. *Accept* is a verb meaning "to approve" or "to receive"; *except* is usually a preposition meaning "not including." For example:

The talented actor *accepted* his Oscar.
Everyone was invited *except* you.

adapt, adopt. *Adapt* means "to accommodate" or "to adjust to conditions"; *adopt* means "to accept" or "to use as one's own." For example:

> The students had difficulty *adapting* to the five-hour class.
> We *adopted* a beautiful baby girl.

advice, advise. *Advice* is a noun meaning "helpful suggestion, recommendation or counsel"; *advise* is a verb meaning "to give advice." For example:

> The lawyer gave me good *advice*.
> The professor *advised* me to change the topic of my paper.

affect, effect. *Affect* is a verb meaning "to influence"; *effect* is usually a noun meaning "a result or consequence." For example:

> My writing teacher *affected* the way I write.
> The *effect* of the storm was widespread flooding.

aggravate, irritate. *Aggravate* means "to make worse"; *irritate* means "to provoke or annoy." *Aggravate* is sometimes used colloquially to mean "irritate." For example:

> The spicy food *aggravated* my stomach.
> Sally *irritates* me when she comes home late.
> I get so *aggravated* when I make a mistake. (Colloquial usage)

ain't. Nonstandard for *am not*. Try to avoid it in speaking; do not use it in writing.

all ready, already. *All ready* means that everyone is ready; *already* means "previously" or "by this time." For example:

> The students were *all ready* for the exam.
> Evan has *already* left the room.

all together, altogether. *All together* means "considered as a group"; *altogether* means "entirely" or "completely." For example:

> We sat *all together* at the dinner table.
> The student felt *altogether* foolish when he failed that easy test.

allusion, illusion. An *allusion* is an indirect reference to something; an *illusion* is a false perception or unreal impression of something. For example:

> In her speech she made an *allusion* to the Bill of Rights.
> The magician's trick was just an *illusion*.

a lot (of), lots (of), alot, allot. *A lot* or *lots* are colloquial for *many* or *much*. *Alot* is a misspelling of *a lot*. For example:

The teacher gave us *lots of* tests this semester. (Colloquial)
The teacher gave us *many* tests this semester. (Formal)
Fortunately, he gave us *a lot of* help. (Colloquial)
Fortunately, he gave us *much* help. (Formal)

Allot means "to appropriate, assign, or distribute according to a plan." For example:

The legislature *allotted* five million dollars for education.

alright. Nonstandard for *all right*. Do not use.

among, between. *Among* is used when there are more than two persons or objects; *between* is used when there are only two persons or objects. For example:

All three lawyers argued *among* themselves.
The fight was *between* my mother and father.

anyone, any one. *Anyone* is an indefinite pronoun meaning "any person"; *any one* means "a single person or thing." For example:

Anyone can come to my party.
Any one of the gifts will make me happy.

awful, awfully. *Awful* is an adjective meaning "filled with wonder, fright, or dread." For example:

Being lost in the snow was an *awful* experience.

In colloquial usage *awful* means "very bad." The adverb form *awfully* is used colloquially to mean "very" or "quite." It is nonstandard to use *awful* as an adverb meaning "very." For example:

The food tasted *awful*. (Colloquial)
The food tasted *very bad*. (Formal)
This essay is *awful* good. (Nonstandard)
This essay is *awfully* good. (Colloquial)
This essay is *very* good. (Formal)

awhile, a while. *Awhile* is an adverb. For example:

We studied *awhile* in the library.

Do not use *awhile* as the object of a preposition (*in, for, after*); instead, use *a while* (a noun). For example:

> The marathon lasted for *awhile*. (Nonstandard)
> The marathon lasted for *a while*. (Formal)

bad, badly. *Bad* (*not good*) is an adjective, and *badly* is an adverb. For example:

> You gave me a *bad* computer.
> The computer works *badly*.

Following a linking verb (*be, seem, feel*) use *bad*, not *badly*. For example:

> The man feels *bad* (not *badly*).

Colloquially, *badly* is used for "very much" or "greatly." For example:

> The student *badly* needed a passing grade. (Instead, use *much* or *greatly*.)

being as, being that. Colloquial for *as* or *because*. For example:

> *Being* that I am overweight, I need to go on a diet. (Colloquial)
> *Because* I am overweight, I need to go on a diet. (Formal)

beside, besides. *Beside* is a preposition meaning "by the side of." *Besides* is a preposition meaning "except" and an adverb (see Section 1e) meaning "in addition (to)." For example:

> My father sat *beside* me at my trial. (*by the side of*)
> He felt nothing *besides* pain. (*except*)
> *Besides*, he had brains. (*In addition*)

boyfriend, girlfriend. These compound words are colloquial. Write them as two words: *boy friend* and *girl friend*. For example:

> My *boy friend* (*girl friend*) will meet me at the airport.

brake, break. *Brake* means "to stop." *Break* means "to damage, exceed, or interrupt." For example:

> A car is coming head on, so put on the *brakes* now!
> The stone will *break* the window.
> I need a ten-minute *break*.

burst, busted, bust. *Burst* is a verb meaning "to break apart or explode." Its principal parts are *burst, burst,* and *burst.* The use of *busted* or *bust* is nonstandard and should be avoided. For example:

> With one squeeze I busted the balloon. (Nonstandard)
> With one squeeze I burst the balloon. (Standard)

can, may. *Can* means "to be able to"; may means "to have permission to" or "to have a possibility to." For example:

> You *can* hit the ball over the fence.
> You *may* come to my party if I invite you.
> It *may* rain today.

cannot. *Cannot,* the opposite of *can,* means "not to be able to." It is always written as a single word. For example:

> I *cannot* help you.

can't hardly, can't barely, haven't scarcely. See double negatives.

capital, capitol. *Capital* as a noun refers to the seat of government or to money. As an adjective, *capital* means "chief" or "excellent." A *capital* crime means "punishable by death." *Capitol* is always a building where a legislature meets. For example:

> Albany is the *capital* of New York.
> That was a *capital* suggestion.
> We will meet the congressman at the state *capitol* building.

cite, sight, site. *Cite* means "to name or mention"; *sight* means "to see"; *site* means "place" or "location." For example:

> The professor *cited* the source of the information.
> We *sighted* a UFO in the sky.
> The *site* of the new building is on my property.

coarse, course. *Coarse* means "rough in texture"; *course* refers to a unit of study or a path. For example:

> The surface of the wood was *coarse.*
> I had to study hard to pass the history *course.*
> The golf *course* was almost finished.

complement, compliment. *Complement* means "to complete or enhance." *Compliment* means "to express praise." Both words can be used as verbs or nouns. For example:

The fresh paint will *complement* the appearance of the house. (Verb)
Red trimming is a *complement* for the green background. (Noun)
The customers *complimented* the chef. (Verb)
A modest person will accept all *compliments*. (Noun)

continual, continuous. *Continual* means "repeated frequently." *Continuous* means "without interruption." For example:

The audience reacted to the show with *continual* laughter.
The roar of the waves was *continuous*.

council, counsel. *Council* is a noun that refers to an assembly of people. *Counsel* as a noun means "advice or guidance," or it refers to an attorney. *Counsel* as a verb means "to advise" or "to give a helpful recommendation." For example:

The *council* of ambassadors will meet on Sunday. (Noun)
The student needed the *counsel* of her minister. (Noun)
Mr. Jones *counseled* the distraught student. (Verb)

desert, dessert. *Desert* as a noun with the accent on the first syllable means "a dry, arid region of land." *Desert* as a noun with the accent on the second syllable means "a deserved reward or punishment." *Desert* as a verb (accent on the second syllable) means "to leave without any intention to return." *Dessert* is a noun meaning "sweets served as the final course of a meal."

We were trapped on the *desert* for a week.
Students who study hard will get their just *deserts*.
The scared soldiers *deserted* their companions by running away.
The ice cream made a great *dessert*.

device, devise. *Device* is a noun meaning "a form of equipment." *Devise* is a verb meaning "to invent." For example:

This *device* is not working properly.
Mark *devised* a plan to get higher grades.

different than, different from. *Different from* is more acceptable. However, use *different than* when the word *than* is used to introduce a dependent clause. For example:

The girls' clothing was *different from* the boys'.
The actual words he used were *different than* the words you told me.
(*Than* introduces dependent clause *than the words you told me*)

disinterested, uninterested. *Disinterested* means "impartial, not influenced by personal bias." *Uninterested* means "not interested." For example:

> To make a fair decision, a judge must be *disinterested.*
> The student did not listen because he was *uninterested* in the lecture.

double negatives. Two negatives together mean that you are affirming something. For example:

> He is *not unkind.* (Meaning "he is kind")

Hardly, scarcely, and *barely* mean "almost not at all." Therefore, they act as negatives in a sentence. For example:

> The victim was *barely* alive. (Meaning "almost dead")

Using any of these words with another negative creates a double negative, such as *can't hardly, can't scarcely, hasn't scarcely, won't barely,* and *can't barely.* For example:

> The pretty girl *hasn't scarcely noticed* me. (Double negative)
> The pretty girl *has scarcely noticed* me. (Correct)
> The pretty girl *hasn't noticed* me. (Correct)
> The old man *can't hardly* lift his head anymore. (Double negative)
> The old man *can hardly* lift his head anymore. (Correct)
> The old man *can't* lift his head anymore. (Correct)

dyeing, dying. *Dyeing* means "imparting color to a material." *Dying* means "to cease to be alive." For example:

> I am *dyeing* the coat blue.
> The old man is *dying* in the hospital.

each other, one another. *Each other* refers to two people. *One another* refers to more than two people. For example:

> Pete and Susan are so lucky to have *each other.*
> In that class all the students acted considerately to one another.

emigrate, immigrate. *Emigrate* means "to leave a country or region"; *immigrate* means "to enter a country or region." For example:

> The family *emigrated* from South America.
> The family *immigrated* to the United States.

eminent, imminent. *Eminent* means "prominent in rank." *Imminent* means "likely to occur." For example:

The Pope is an *eminent* person.
The flood is *imminent* because the dam broke.

etc. An abbreviation meaning "and other things." Avoid using it in formal writing. Instead, use *and others* or *so forth. Such as* is even better. For example:

On the picnic we brought all the necessary items: food, utensils, napkins, *etc.* (Colloquial)
On the picnic we brought all the necessary items, *such as* food, utensils, and napkins. (Formal)

farther, further. *Farther* means "to a more distant place"; *further* means "to a greater extent" or "in addition." For example:

This train cannot go any *farther* down the tracks.
I cannot help you any *further* to solve that problem.

fewer, less. *Fewer* refers to a number of things; *less* refers to an amount. For example:

There are *fewer* people in this class.
There is *less* liquid in this cup.

formally, formerly. *Formally* means "in a proper form." *Formerly* means "at a prior time." For example:

She was *formally* dressed for the wedding.
The musician *formerly* known as Prince has a new name.

forth, fourth. *Forth* means "forward." *Fourth* is a number. For example:

The wind blew the window shade back and *forth.*
That was the *fourth* meal you have eaten today.

good, well. Use *good* as an adjective meaning "excellent, worthy, moral, suited, or admirable." For example:

He is a very *good* tennis player.
I feel *good* about my decision. (*Feel* is a linking verb)

Use *well* as an adverb meaning "properly or efficiently". *Well* may also be used as an adjective meaning "healthy." For example:

The new machine worked *well.* (Adverb)
The doctor said that I was *well.* (Adjective)
I felt *well* after my headache went away. (Adjective because *felt* is a linking verb)

However, in formal speech and writing, do not use *good* as an adverb in place of *well.* For example:

My students write *well.* (Not *good*)
My horse ran *as well as* the favorite. (Not *as good as*)

hanged, hung. Use *hanged* as the past tense or past participle (see Section 1d) of *hang* only when it means "an execution." In all other cases, use *hung.* For example:

The villain was *hanged* by the neck until dead.
We *hung* the pictures on the wall.

have got. *Have got* is colloquial. In formal speech and writing, use *have.* For example:

We *have got* a big problem. (Colloquial)
We *have* a big problem. (Formal)

hear, here. *Hear* is a verb that refers to our ears. *Here* is an adjective that is the opposite of *there.* For example:

Did you *hear* that loud crash?
Come over *here* right away.

hisself, ourself, theirselves, themself. These are nonstandard forms of reflexive pronouns (see Section 1b). Instead, use *himself, ourselves,* and *themselves.*

if, whether. Use *whether* when there is an alternative or choice. For example:

My mom asked me *whether* I walked or took the bus.
The teacher wanted to know *if* you finished your homework.
(Do not use *or not* after *whether.*)

imply, infer. *Imply* means "to suggest." *Infer* means "to conclude based on a suggestion." Therefore, writers and speakers *imply* (make a suggestion), whereas readers and listeners *infer* (draw a conclusion). For example:

The writer *implies* that the humans will survive.
From that information we can *infer* that the bank will fail.

irregardless. Nonstandard usage; instead, use *regardless.* For example:

I don't care how much money you make. I will love you *regardless.*

its, it's. *Its* is the possessive form of the pronoun *it. It's* is a contraction for *it is.* For example:

Its length is twenty-one feet.
It's a very nice day today.

it's me. Colloquial for *it is I*. Although the expression has become acceptable in informal conversation, it is better to use the proper form in writing. For example:

It's me on the phone. (Colloquial)
It is I on the phone. (Formal)

kid, kids. Colloquial for *child* or *children*. Avoid in formal writing. For example:

Children in this country must attend school until they are sixteen years old.

kind of, sort of. Both expressions are colloquial. Better to use *somewhat* or *rather*. For example:

Babies are *kind of* helpless. (Colloquial)
Babies are *somewhat* (*rather*) helpless. (Formal)

later, latter. *Later,* a comparative form of *late,* means "after the due time" or "tardy." *Latter* is used to compare things; it refers to the last one mentioned.

Tom arrived *later* than Bill.
We took two tests in that class; unfortunately, I failed the *latter* one.

lay, lie. *Lay* always takes an object complement. *Lay* means "to set or to place." *Lie* never takes an object. *Lie* means "to rest." For example:

I will *lay* the book on the table. (Object is book)
I will *lie* down on the bed to rest. (No object)

Lay and *lie* are irregular verbs (see Section 1d for the principal parts).

lend, loan. *Lend* is a verb and *loan* is a noun. For example:

The bank will *lend* me the money. (Verb)
I thanked the bank manager for the *loan*. (Noun)

like, as. *Like* is a preposition (*like* me, *like* a miracle); *as* is a conjunction (*as* I said, *as* the snow melted, *as* in the movies). For example:

You look *like* me.
The character acted just *as* I had predicted.

loose, lose. *Loose* (rhymes with *moose*) is the opposite of *tight*. *Lose* (rhymes with *shoes*) means "to remove from one's possession." For example:

> The screw on the picture was *loose*.
> Did you *lose* your books again?

lot, lots, lots of. Colloquial for *many* or *much*. For example:

> We ate *lots of* popcorn at the movies. (Colloquial)
> We ate *much* popcorn at the movies. (Formal)

mad, angry. *Mad* means insane. In writing, do not use *mad* when the meaning is *angry*. For example:

> My mother was really *mad* at me. (Colloquial)
> My mother was really *angry* at me. (Formal)

may be, maybe. *May be* is a verb phrase similar to *might be*. *Maybe* is an adverb that means *perhaps*. For example:

> You *may be* late if you don't hurry. (Verb)
> *Maybe* I can help you. (Adverb)

media, phenomena. *Media* and *phenomena* are plural forms. *Media* usually refers to forms of mass communication (TV, radio, newspapers). *Phenomena* refers to remarkable things. The singular forms are *medium* and *phenomenon*. Do not use the plural forms when the context is singular. For example:

> The *media* are always trying to sell us something. (Plural)
> What *medium* did you use to record your song? (Singular)
> Rainbows are interesting *phenomena*. (Plural)
> The shooting star was quite a *phenomenon*. (Singular)

most, almost. *Almost* is an adverb meaning *nearly*. *Most* is the superlative form of *more* (see Section 1c). Do not use *most* when you mean *almost*. For example:

> *Most* all of the people have already left. (Colloquial)
> *Almost* all of the people have arrived. (Formal)

myself (herself, himself, ourselves, themselves, yourself). Do not use reflexive pronouns where a personal pronoun will fit. For example:

> The book was written by John and *myself*. (Nonstandard)
> The book was written by John and *me*. (Formal)

nauseated, nauseous. These words are frequently confused. *Nauseated* is a verb meaning "to become stricken with sickness or an impending feeling of vomiting." *Nauseous* is an adjective meaning "causing nausea; sickening; disgusting." For example:

> The odor of the onions *nauseated* me.
> The *nauseous* odor of the onions was filling the kitchen.

of. Nonstandard if used after *could* (*of*), *might* (*of*), *ought* (*of*), *should* (*of*), and *would* (*of*). Instead, use *could have, might have,* and so on. For example:

> I *should have* passed that test. (*Should've* is proper, but not *should of*)

Also, *of* is sometimes used unnecessarily after prepositions, such as *off, inside,* and *outside.* For example:

> Put the toys back *inside of* the box. (Nonstandard)
> Put the toys back *inside* the box. (Formal)

OK, okay. Colloquial usage; better to use *all right* or *correct.* For example:

> Although we were worried, everybody was *okay.* (Colloquial)
> Although we were worried, everybody was *all right.* (Formal)

orientate. Nonstandard form of the verb *orient* meaning "to cause to become adjusted to a situation." The noun form is *orientation.* For example:

> The students became *oriented* to college life very quickly.
> The counselor gave an *orientation* to the new students.

over with. *With* is unnecessary; omit it. For example:

> I was finally *over with* the flu. (Colloquial)
> I was finally *over* the flu. (Formal)

passed, past. *Passed* (past tense of the verb *pass*) refers to a movement or successful completion. *Past* refers to a former time. As a preposition, *past* means "beyond." For example:

> The successful student *passed* all the tests.
> The quarterback *passed* the football to another player.
> My dislike for you is all in the *past.*
> I walked right *past* you.

patience, patients. *Patience* means "calm behavior and a willingness to wait." *Patients* are people treated for health problems. For example:

Copyright © 2000 Addison-Wesley Educational Publishers Inc.

You need *patience* when waiting in a long line.
The doctor treated many *patients* today.

personal, personnel. *Personal* is an adjective meaning "private." *Personnel* is a noun meaning "workers" or "employees." For example:

My diary is *personal*.
Mr. Johnson sent a letter to all *personnel* in the company.

plenty. *Plenty* is colloquially used as an adverb. Instead, use *quite* or *very*. *Plenty* should be used as a noun meaning "abundance." For example:

The room was *plenty* big. (Colloquial)
The room was *quite* big. (Formal)
There was *plenty* for everyone. (Used as noun)

principal, principle. *Principal* can be a noun ("a leader, a chief part, or a sum of money") or an adjective ("highest in rank"). *Principle* is a noun meaning "a fundamental truth or law." For example:

Mr. Raines is our new school *principal*.
We earned twenty dollars in interest on our *principal*.
Many *principles* in physics are difficult to understand.

quiet, quite. *Quiet* (rhymes with *diet*) means "not noisy." *Quite* (rhymes with *right*) means "very." For example:

The students were *quiet* during the test.
I did *quite* well on the exam.

real, really. *Real* is an adjective meaning "genuine." For example:

That was a *real* diamond.

Do not use it as an adverb; instead, use *really* or *very*. For example:

The food is *real* good. (Colloquial)
The food is *really* good. (Formal)

reason is because, reason why. *The reason is because* is nonstandard usage. Instead, use *the reason is that* or just *because*. For example:

The *reason* I am late *is because* I was really sick. (Nonstandard)
The *reason* I am late is *that* I was really sick. (Formal)
I am late *because* I was really sick. (Formal)

The reason why is redundant. Instead, use either *why* or *the reason*, but not both. For example:

Do you want to know *the reason why* I was late? (Colloquial)
Do you want to know *why* I was late? (Formal)
Do you want to know *the reason* I was late? (Formal)

right. Colloquial when used for *directly* or *extremely.* For example:

Mom told us to go *right* to school. (Colloquial)
Mom told us to go *directly* to school. (Formal)
It was *right* kind of you to help. (Colloquial)
It was *extremely* kind of you to help. (Formal)

shape. Colloquial for *condition.* For example:

His broken leg was in very bad *shape.* (Colloquial)
His broken leg was in very bad *condition.* (Formal)

since, because. *Since* and *because* are used to denote cause. *Since* may also express time. For example:

Since the sun went down, we have been studying for the test.

However, it may not always be clear whether *since* is expressing cause or time. For example:

Since Mr. Jones left the school, the passing rate has declined.

To avoid the ambiguity, it is best to use *because* when expressing a cause-effect relationship. For example:

Because Mr. Jones left the school, the passing rate has declined.

sit, set. *Sit (sat)* is a verb meaning "to occupy a seat." *Set* is a verb meaning "to fix or put something in place." *Sit* never has an object complement (see Section 2c), whereas *set* almost always has one. For example:

I *sat* on the bed.
I *set* my books on the bed.

so. *So* is a conjunction used to mean "thus" or "therefore." Do not use *so* for *very* or *quite.* For example:

The meal was *so* good. (Colloquial)
The meal was *quite* good. (Formal)

stationary, stationery. *Stationary* means "fixed, not moving." *Stationery* is writing paper. For example:

> We once believed that the Earth was *stationary*.
> I just ordered a new set of personalized *stationery* for writing letters.

suppose to, supposed to. *Suppose to* is nonstandard. Always use *supposed to*. For example:

> You are *supposed to* complete this course.

sure, surely. *Sure* is an adjective; *surely* is an adverb. Colloquially, *sure* is sometimes used as an adverb. For example:

> My friends *sure* want to help me. (Colloquial)
> My friends *surely* want to help me. (Formal)
> I am *sure* that you will help. (Formal)

than, then. *Than* is a conjunction used to make comparisons. *Then* is an adverb meaning "at that time", or it can be an adverbial conjunction similar to *therefore*. For example:

> The teacher likes me better *than* you.
> The student *then* helped others to read.
> It rained for a while; *then* the river began to overflow its banks.

their, there, they're. *Their* is a possessive pronoun meaning "belonging to them." For example:

> Sean and Helen left *their* books in the classroom.

There is an adverb meaning the opposite of *here*. Also, *there* can be used as the introductory word of a sentence. For example:

> Put your books over *there*.
> *There* are already three books on that table.

They're is a contraction for *they are*. For example:

> *They're* here to collect for charity.

them, those. *Them* is a pronoun. *Those* is a pronoun that can be used as an adjective. Do not use *them* in place of *those*. For example:

> Don't drop *them* books on my foot! (Nonstandard)
> Don't drop *those* books on my foot! (Formal)

thorough, through, threw. *Thorough* means "complete." *Through* (pronounced like *threw*) means "from one end to the other" or "finished." *Threw* is the past tense of *throw*. For example:

The builders did a *thorough* job.
We came into the house *through* the window.
The man *threw* the ball to the child.

to, two, too. *To* is a preposition. For example:

He drove *to* Florida.

Two is a number. For example:

I gained *two* pounds today.

Too is an adverb meaning "also" or "excessively." For example:

I love you, *too*.
Hector was *too* sick to go to school.

Do not use *too* to mean *very*. For example:

I cannot write *too* neatly with this pencil. (Colloquial)
I cannot write *very* neatly with this pencil. (Formal)

toward, towards. *Toward* and *towards* are prepositions. Either is proper as long as you are consistent. For example:

Joe ran *towards* the north. Then, he turned and went *towards* the south.

try and. This expression is nonstandard; instead, use *try to*. For example:

Try and finish your homework. (Nonstandard)
Try to finish your homework. (Formal)

unique. *Unique* means "one of a kind" and "having no equal." For example:

San Francisco is a *unique* place to live.

There are no degrees of uniqueness; therefore, do not modify unique with *very*, *more*, or *most*. For example:

My mother is a very *unique* person. (Nonstandard)
My mother is even more *unique* than my father. (Nonstandard)
My mother is a *unique* person. (Formal)

weather, whether, if. *Weather* refers to outside conditions like temperature, rain, and wind. For example:

> The *weather* today was beautiful.

If refers to a condition. *Whether* refers to a condition involving a choice. Do not use *if* when presenting an alternative. For example:

> *If* you study, you will pass the test.
> I don't know *whether* you will pass or fail.
> (Not *if* because there is an alternative)

while, whereas. *While* is used as a conjunction meaning "during the time that." For example:

> The phone rang *while* I was in the bathtub.

Do not use *while* when an unspecified time period is involved. Instead, use *but, whereas,* or *though.* For example:

> Richard became my friend *while* Nellie is still my enemy. (Colloquial)
> Richard became my friend *whereas* Nellie is still my enemy. (Formal)

who, which, that. *Who* refers to persons; *which* refers to things; *that* refers to persons or things. For example:

> The lawyer *who (that)* took my case is very experienced.
> *The Wizard of Oz, which* is on TV tonight, is a great movie.

who, whom. See Section 4.

who's, whose. *Who's* is a contraction for *who is* or *who has. Whose* is the possessive form of *who* ("belonging to whom"). For example:

> *Who's* coming to dinner tonight? (Who is)
> *Who's* got the ball? (Who has)
> *Whose* book is this?

your, you're. *Your* is the possessive form of *you. You're* is a contraction for *you are.* For example:

> *Your* application has been accepted.
> *You're* the best student in the class.

PRACTICE EXERCISE 77: CORRECT USAGE

In the following sentences, underline colloquial expressions and nonstandard usage.
Write the correct or more proper forms on the line. For example:

all right, much   I did alright on the final exam because my teacher gave me
lots of practice.

1. _____ I passed everything accept Chemistry, an awfully difficult
course.

2. _____ Because you are so smart, I will adapt your advice.

3. _____ When we were finally altogether, Mr. Rogers said, "Let's
begin the rehearsal all ready."

4. _____ My friend felt badly for awhile.

5. _____ The lawyer set down besides her client.

6. _____ A war will brake the unity between six European countries.

7. _____ I can't hardly find the new building sight.

8. _____ I must complement the winner of the competition.

9. _____ Girls are definitely different from boys.

10. _____ How many students have emigrated to the United States?

11. _____ How is a frog different than a toad?

12. _____ The magician's trick was just an allusion.

13. _____ Everyone of us has a reason to be mad.

14. _____ I will apply for the job at the factory, irregardless of the
dangers.

15. _____ There are less students who I like in this class then in you're
class.

16. _____ I really get nauseous when I think that I formally lived here.

17. _____ Its such a beautiful day for you to walk my dog, but don't
pull on it's leash.

18. _____ Whose you're best friend?

19. _____ The reason I could not volunteer is because I could not raise my hand.

20. _____ You are a very unique teacher to let me lay here until the class is thorough.

[14] Proofreading Sentences

Proof

All formal writing (such as essays, reports, and term papers) should be free from errors. Therefore, it is important to proofread your papers before turning them in. It is during this final stage of writing that you look for and correct errors. Reading your paper out loud is a good way to get started because it can help you notice errors. Sometimes you will be asked to read other students' papers. In either case, you can use the following checklist to help you concentrate on the elements of a sentence. Section numbers are indicated next to each question so you can refer to a particular part of this handbook whenever necessary for help with a problem.

Checklist for Correctness of Sentence Elements

1. Does each sentence contain an *independent clause* with a subject and a verb? (Section 7a)
2. Are the *verbs* in the proper principal form and tense? Any irregular verbs? (Section 1d)
3. Are *helping verbs* included? (Section 1d)
4. Do *subjects* and *verbs* agree in number? Any words that come between the subject and verb? (Section 3a) Any indefinite pronouns *(each, anyone, some)*? (Section 3c)
5. Are the *pronouns* used properly? Agreement? Case? (Sections 1b and 4)
6. Are *adjectives* and *adverbs* used properly? Any comparative forms? (Sections 1c and 1e)
7. Any *compound sentences?* Are the independent clauses punctuated properly? (Section 7a)
8. Any *dependent clauses?* Are they punctuated properly? (Section 7b).
9. Check for errors in sentence structure: (1) *misplaced or dangling modifiers,* (2) *fragments,* and (3) *run-ons, comma splices,* and *shifts.* (Section 8)
10. Are all grammatical structures *parallel* in form? (Section 9)
11. Can you improve the quality of your writing by *expanding sentence parts* (Section 6c) or creating *compound* (Section 7a) or *complex sentences?* (Section 7b)
12. Are all sentences *punctuated* properly? (Section 10)
13. Are all words *capitalized* properly? (Section 11)
14. Are all words *spelled* properly? (Section 12)
15. Is there any colloquial or nonstandard *usage?* (Section 13)

PRACTICE EXERCISE 78: PROOFREADING SENTENCES

Underline any errors in the sentences in this paragraph. Use the checklist to help you find the errors. On the lines below, write a corrected version of each sentence that contains an error. You may put correct punctuation directly into the paragraph.

Self-actualization, as described by Abraham maslow is the need to fulfill our unique potential. Him considered it to be the highest level of human motivation. Also, he believed, that most people never reaches the state of self-actualization. However, we can look at it as a process rather than a goal. Its the process of searching for the highest expression of ourselves then it becomes like an inner light directing us toward fulfillment. For example, a person may enjoys playing the piano as a hobby. He do not have to become recognized artists to feel self-actualized.

_____

_____

_____

_____

_____

_____

_____

_____

_____

Credits

PHOTO CREDITS

1: © R. Lord/The Image Works; 23: The Stock Market; 24 TL: Corbis; 24 TR: Corbis; 24 CL: Corbis; 24 CR: Corbis; 24 BL: Corbis; 24 BR: Corbis; 62: Corbis; 113: Doug Menuez/PhotoDisc; 121: Corbis; 147: Scott Foresman; 153: David Young-Wolff/Tony Stone; 172: Joe Cornish/Tony Stone; 237: United Nations; 239: Sid Schuler/Anthro-Photo; 248: © Mike Kagan/Monkmeyer; 279: William Vandivert; 280: © 1965 by Stanley Milgram. From the film *Obedience*, distributed by the Pennsylvania State University, Audio Visual Services; 299: AP/Wide World; 306: Bob Fitch/Black Star; 313: AP/Wide World; 323: Paul Conklin/Monkmeyer.

TEXT CREDITS

Excerpt from www.ag.ohio-state.edu/~ohioline/lifetime/lt4-2d.htm. Reprinted by permission.

Anonymous, "A Man's Game" [student essay] from Barbara Fine Clouse, ed., *Cornerstones: Readings for Writers*. Copyright © 1996 by McGraw-Hill, Inc. Reprinted with the permission of the publishers.

Richard Applebaum and W. Chambliss, excerpts from *Sociology*. Copyright © 1995 by HarperCollins College Publishers. Reprinted with the permission of Addison Wesley Educational Publishers, Inc.

Curtis O. Byer and Louis W. Shainberg, excerpts from *Living Well: Health in Your Hands*, Second Edition. Copyright © 1995 by HarperCollins College Publishers. Reprinted with the permission of Addison Wesley Educational Publishers, Inc.

Gloria Cahill, excerpt from an interview with Rosie O'Donnell from *Radiance: The Magazine for Large Women* (Fall, 1997) [www.radiancemagazine.com\rosie.html]. Reprinted with the permission of Gloria Cahill and *Radiance: The Magazine for Large Women*.

Susan Cheever, excerpts from *Home Before Dark*. Copyright © 1984 by Susan Cheever. Reprinted with the permission of Houghton Mifflin Company. All rights reserved.

Sandra Cisneros, excerpts from *The House on Mango Street*. Copyright © 1989 by Sandra Cisneros. Reprinted with the permission of Susan Bergholz Literary Services, New York. All rights reserved.

Horace Coleman, "Poem for a Divorced Daughter" from *Between a Rock and a Hard Place*. Copyright © 1977 by Horace Coleman. Reprinted with permission.

George Edwards, Martin Wattenberg, and Robert Lineberry, excerpts from *Government in America*, Seventh Edition. Copyright © 1996 by HarperCollins College Publishers. Reprinted with the permission of Addison Wesley Educational Publishers, Inc.

Carol R. Ember and Melvin Ember, excerpt from *Anthropology: A Brief Introduction*. Copyright © 1998. Reprinted with the permission of Prentice-Hall, Inc., Upper Saddle River, NJ.

Josh R. Gerow, excerpts from *Essentials of Psychology*, Second Edition. Copyright © 1996 by HarperCollins College Publishers. Reprinted with the permission of Addison Wesley Educational Publishers, Inc.

Marvin Harris, excerpts from *Cultural Anthropology*, Fourth Edition. Copyright © 1995 by HarperCollins College Publishers. Reprinted with the permission of Addison Wesley Educational Publishers, Inc.

Robert L. Heilbroner, "Don't Let Stereotypes Warp Your Judgments" from *Think Magazine* (June 1961). Reprinted with the permission of the author.

Bob Herbert, "Presumed to Be Guilty" from *The New York Times* (February 2, 1996). Copyright © 1996 by The New York Times Company. Reprinted by permission.

Michael C. Howard, excerpts from *Contemporary Cultural Anthropology*, Fifth Edition. Copyright © 1996 by HarperCollins College Publishers. Reprinted with the permission of Addison Wesley Educational Publishers, Inc.

Susan Jacoby, "Unfair Game" from *The New York Times* (January 26, 1978). Copyright © 1978 by Susan Jacoby. Reprinted with the permission of Georges Borchardt, Inc. for the author.

Bel Kaufman, "Sunday in the Park" from *The Available Press/PEN Short Story Collection* (New York: Ballantine Books, 1985). Copyright © 1985 by Bel Kaufman. Reprinted with the permission of the author.

Raymond W. Kelly, "Handcuffing the Police" from *The New York Times* (February 1, 1996). Copyright © 1996 by The New York Times Company. Reprinted by permission.

Martin Luther King, Jr., excerpt from "Loving your Enemies" from *Strength to Love*. Copyright © 1963 by Martin Luther King, Jr.; copyright © renewed 1991 by Coretta Scott King. Reprinted with the permission of The Heirs to the Estate of Martin Luther King, Jr., c/o Writers House, Inc. as agents for the proprietor.

Index